BEST of the BEST
from
California
COOKBOOK

◆

Selected Recipes from California's
FAVORITE COOKBOOKS

D1046498

Adding a luxuriant tropical appearance, the stately silhouette of palms is an important and conspicuous element of the California landscape, especially notable in rows along boulevards.

BEST of the BEST
from
California
COOKBOOK

◆

Selected Recipes from California's
FAVORITE COOKBOOKS

EDITED BY
Gwen McKee
and
Barbara Moseley

Illustrated by Tupper England

QUAIL RIDGE PRESS
Preserving America's Food Heritage

Recipe Collection©2000 Quail Ridge Press, Inc.

Reprinted with permission and all rights reserved under the name of the cookbooks, organizations or individuals listed below.

An Apple a Day ©1996 Rea Douglas; *Apples Etc. Cookbook* ©1998 Santa Cruz, CA Chapter of Hadassah; *The Art Lover's Cookbook* ©1998 Fine Arts Museums of San Francisco; *The Artichoke Cookbook* ©1985 Patricia Rain; *Boutique Bean Pot* ©1992 Kathleen Mayes and Sandra Gottfried; *The California Cookbook* ©1994 Gulf Publishing Company; *California Country Cook Book* ©1996 Golden West Publishers; *California Gold* ©1992 California State Grange; *California Home Cooking* ©1997 Michele Anna Jordan; *California Kosher* ©1991 Women's League of Adat Ari El; *California Sizzles* ©1992 The Junior League of Pasadena, Inc.; *California Wine Country Cooking Secrets* ©1994 Kathleen DeVanna Fish; *The California Wine Country Herbs and Spices Cookbook* ©1998 Virginia and Robert Hoffman; *Celebrating California* ©1995 Children's Home Society of California; *Centennial Cookbook* ©1997 San Carlos School; *The Coastal Cook of West Marin* ©1991 Riley and Company; *The Complete Garlic Lovers' Cookbook* ©1987 Gilroy Garlic Festival Assn. Inc.; *Cooking Pure & Simple* ©1988 Kincaid House Publishing; *Cooking with Herbs* ©1997 Quail Botanical Gardens Foundation, Inc.; *Cooking with Mushrooms* ©1997 John Pisto; *Cooking with Wine* ©1997 Virginia and Robert Hoffman; *The Cuisine of California* ©1983 Diane Rossen Worthington; *The Cuisine of Hubert Keller* ©1996 Ten Speed Press; *Didyaeverhaveaday?* ©1988 Pamela Weis; *Dining by Design* ©1999 Junior League of Pasadena, Inc.; *Everybody's San Francisco Cookbook* ©1998 Good Life Publications; *The Expanding Light Cookbook* ©1999 Crystal Clarity Publishers; *"...Fire Burn & Cauldron Bubble"* ©1998 Julie Lugo Cerra; *The $5 Chef Family Cookbook* ©1997 Marcie Rothman; *The $5 Chef: How to Save Cash & Cook Fast* ©1991 Marcie Rothman: Five-Spot Press; *Fog City Diner Cookbook* ©1993 Ten Speed Press; *Food Festivals of Southern/Northern California: Traveler's Guide and Cookbook* ©1997 Bob Carter; *The Fork Ran Away with the Spoon* ©1996 Riley and Company; *Garlic Lovers' Greatest Hits* ©1993 Gilroy Garlic Festival Assn., Inc.; *The Golf Cookbook* ©1998 Sharon Gerardi and Nadine Nemechek; *The Great California Cookbook* ©1994 Kathleen DeVanna Fish; *The Great Vegetarian Cookbook* ©1994 Kathleen DeVanna Fish; *The Health Promoting Cookbook* ©1997 Alan Goldhamer; *Hot Wok* ©1995 Ten Speed Press; *The Carter House Cookbook* ©1991 Mark and Christi Carter; *International Garlic Festival®* *Cookbook* ©1994 Caryl L. Simpson/Garlic Festival®; *Jan Townsend Going Home* ©1996 Janice Lynn Townsend; *Jewish Cooking from Here & Far* ©1994 Congregation Beth Israel; *The Lafayette Collection* ©1995; *The Lazy Gourmet* ©1987 Valerie Bates; *A Little California Cookbook* ©1992 Chronicle Books; *Little Dave's Seafood Cookbook, Vol I* ©1998 David J. Harvey; *A Little San Francisco Cookbook* ©1990 Chronicle Books; *Marilyn Thomas the Homemaker Baker* ©1990 Marilyn Thomas; *Mendocino Mornings* ©1996 Arlene and Jim Moorehead; *Monterey's Cookin' Pisto Style* ©1994 John Pisto; *Monterey's Cooking Secrets* ©1994 Kathleen DeVanna Fish; *More Firehouse Favorites* ©1998 San Diego Fireman's Relief Association; *Muffin Magic...and More* ©1993 Kathleen Mayes; *Neptune's Table* ©1997 Don Hubbard; *The Oats, Peas, Beans & Barley Cookbook* ©1989,1980,1974 Edyth Young Cottrell; *Only in California* © Children's Home Society of California; *The Organic Gourmet* ©1995 Barbara L. Kahn; *Party Perfect and Pampered, the Ultimate Party Book* ©1995 Sally Holbrook; *Pea Soup Andersen's Scandinavian-American Cookbook* ©1988 Pea Soup Andersen's, Inc.; *The Potluck Cookbook* ©1997 The Bodega Land Trust; *Puddings from A-Z* ©1995 Fred Brengelman and Russ Levenworth; *Röckenwagner* ©1997 Ten Speed Press; *Roots: A Vegetarian Bounty* ©1995 Kathleen Mayes and Sandra Gottfried; *Salads from A-Z* ©1996 Frances Levine;

San Francisco à la Carte ©1979 The Junior League of San Francisco, Inc; *The San Francisco Chronicle Cookbook* ©1997 Michael Bauer and Fran Irwin; *San Francisco Flavors* ©1999 Junior League of San Francisco/Photographs, Jonelle Weaver/Illustrations Kelli Bailey; *San Francisco's Cooking Secrets* ©1994 Kathleen DeVanna Fish; *Sausalito–Cooking with a View* ©2000 Sausalito Woman's Club; *The 7 Day Cookbook* ©1997 Nadine Nemechek and Sharon Nemechek Gerardi; *Simply Vegetarian!* ©1989 DAWN Publications; *A Slice of Santa Barbara* ©1991 Juniõr League of Santa Barbara; *Sonoma County...its bounty* ©1997 E. D. Moorehead; *Soups from A-Z* ©1994 Frances Levine; *The Steinbeck House Cookbook* ©The Valley Guild; *Sterling Performances* ©1994 The Guilds of the Orange County Performing Arts Center; *Sun Sand and Sausage Pie...and Beach House Memories* ©1992 Sally Holbrook; *Taste California* ©1993 California Dietetic Association.

Library of Congress Cataloging-in-Publication Data

Best of the best from California : selected recipes from California's favorite cookbooks / edited by Gwen McKee and Barbara Moseley ; illustrated by Tupper England.
    p. cm.
    ISBN-10: 1-893062-54-6
    ISBN-13: 978-1-893062-54-2
    1. Cookery, American—California style. I. McKee, Gwen. II. Moseley, Barbara.
    TX715.2.C34 B47 2000
    641.59794—dc21   00-028160
                                                  CIP

Copyright ©2000 by Quail Ridge Press, Inc.
ISBN-10: 1-893062-54-6 • ISBN-13: 978-1-893062-54-2

First printing, June 2000 • Second, January 2004 • Third, October 2005

Photos courtesy of
California Division of Tourism • 1-800-862-2543 • www.gocalif.com
and San Francisco Convention & Visitors Bureau.
Cover photo: Pacific Grove at Monterey Bay by Robert Holmes/California Tourism.
Design by Cynthia Clark. Printed in South Korea.

QUAIL RIDGE PRESS
P. O. Box 123 • Brandon, MS 39043
e-mail: info@quailridge.com • www.quailridge.com

On a hilltop overlooking the Pacific Ocean, craftsmen labored nearly 28 years to create a magnificent estate of 165 rooms and 127 acres of gardens. Once the home of William Randolph Hearst, Hearst Castle™ is now a historical monument.

Contents

Preface

California cuisine almost defies description. It, like the state itself, is so deliciously full of an incredible variety of everything. It is the fruit plate, the salad bowl, the fish net, the wine glass . . . perhaps the dinner plate of the world.

After having read, reviewed and cooked from hundreds of incredible California cookbooks, we have come up with words that seem to describe California's cuisine best for us: *nouveau* is the key word, *fresh*, *light*, and certainly *creative*, then there's *wholesome*, and we'll throw in *zesty*, but overall, *unique* and *delicious!*

California is the envy of the world because of its vast amounts and varieties of fresh, locally grown ingredients. Indeed, California farms produce a cornucopia of vegetables, fruit, cheeses and meat products, some organically grown. And the year-round bounty of seafood from the Pacific Ocean certainly lends itself to exciting recipes befitting any taste. In addition, California's beautiful vineyards provide some of the best wines in the world.

With California cuisine you get not only abundant fresh fruits and vegetables, but wonderfully prepared seafoods, tangy-tasting breads . . . and then more specifically, Crab Louis, Cioppino, Cobb Salad, cracked Dungeness crab, barbecued tri-tip steak, date shakes, superb chocolates and desserts, etc. *Best of the Best from California Cookbook* brings a taste of California to your table with favorite recipes that Californians have created out of this incredible bounty. These recipes were selected from 123 choice California cookbooks from all over the state, whose authors and editors have selected their books' most popular favorites, and in so doing, are giving you a sample of their own special cookbook. (See page 335 for a complete catalog of contributing cookbooks.)

From sushi to souvlaki, the California kitchen serves dishes that come from all over the world—Mexico, China, Germany, Russia, Spain, France, England, Italy, Greece, etc.—each bringing their own spices and methods. Truly the flavors of the world meet in California. And because of its lush farmlands, orchards, ranches, vineyards, even game forests, California has all the ingredients for great cooking right in its own back yard.

Fortunately, California shares its wealth by making the ingredients readily available so that people everywhere can recreate this delightful cuisine. The chosen favorite recipes in this cookbook will take you to

California via your taste buds with the likes of Berry-Stuffed French Toast San Francisco Style or Hot Chile-Spinach Dip in a Bread Round. There are so many recipes in this book you'll want to try: Hazelnut Crusted Salmon with Spicy Peach Sauce, Fisherman's Wharf Garlic Prawns, Sun-Dried Tomatoes and Artichoke Pasta, Stardust Pesto Cheesecake, and then there's The Unburger, and yummy Espresso Pecan Fudge Pie, and how about Pebble Beach Pineapple Pizza?

Compiling this cookbook was a challenging undertaking requiring the teamwork of many individuals who love good food and appreciate a good recipe. The Californians we worked with were as sunny as their state, and we thank them for their cooperation and enthusiastic help. Each of the 123 contributing cookbooks is unique in its own way, perhaps highlighting a specific dish, a style of cooking, or simply the way people cook in their community. We have endeavored to reproduce these recipes as they appear in their own cookbooks, changing only style for uniformity. Though we literally searched high and low, we do beg forgiveness for any books that might have been included but were inadvertently overlooked.

We are grateful to the many newspaper food editors across the state who helped us with our research, and to book and gift store managers and personnel who answered our questions and shared their knowledge of area cookbooks. Thanks also to the very courteous people at chambers of commerce and tourist agencies around the state for proudly providing us with facts and photos. Tupper England has once again provided her special drawings that capture the feel of California . . . thanks, Tup. And thanks especially to staff members Annette Goode and Cyndi Clark for their extra effort.

The BEST OF THE BEST STATE COOKBOOK SERIES is all about "Preserving America's Food Heritage." We are proud to present this choice selection of recipes that we feel exemplifies the marvelous cuisine that is uniquely California . . . uniquely, the Best of the Best. No matter where you are, the recipes in this cookbook will enable you to experience the golden taste of The Golden State of California.

Gwen McKee and Barbara Moseley

Built in just over four years, the Golden Gate Bridge was completed in 1937 at a cost of $35 million. An all-time record of 162,414 vehicles crossed the bridge on October 27, 1989, due to an earthquake which closed other nearby routes.

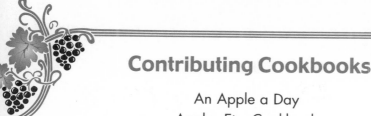

Contributing Cookbooks

An Apple a Day
Apples Etc. Cookbook
The Art Lover's Cookbook: A Feast for the Eye
The Artichoke Cookbook
Boutique Bean Pot
The California Cookbook
California Country Cook Book
California Gold
California Home Cooking
California Kosher
California Sizzles
California Wine Country Cooking Secrets
California Wine Country Herbs and Spices Cookbook
Calvary's Cuisine
Carter House Cookbook
Celebrating California
Centennial Cookbook
Cherished Recipes from the Valley
Children's Hospital Oakland Cookbook
The Coastal Cook of West Marin
The Complete Garlic Lovers' Cookbook
Cook Book
Cookin' with CASA
Cooking on the Fault Line—Corralitos Style
Cooking Pure & Simple
Cooking Treasures of the Central Coast
Cooking with Booze
Cooking with Herbs
Cooking with Mushrooms
Cooking with Wine
The Cuisine of California

Contributing Cookbooks

The Cuisine of Hubert Keller
Delicious Recipes from the Nimitz Community
Didyaeverhavaday?
Dining by Design
Dining Door to Door in Naglee Park
Diversity is Delta's Main Dish
Durham's Favorite Recipes
Everybody's San Francisco Cookbook
The Expanding Light Cookbook
Fabulous Favorites
Fair's Fare
Feeding the Flock
50th Anniversary Cookbook
"...Fire Burn & Cauldron Bubble"
The $5 Chef Family Cookbook
The $5 Chef: How to Save Cash & Cook Fast
Fog City Diner Cookbook
Food Festivals of Northern California
Food Festivals of Southern California
The Fork Ran Away with the Spoon
Friends of Cameron Airport Favorite Recipes
From a Sourdough's Pot
Garlic Lovers' Greatest Hits
The Golf Cookbook
Grandma's House Restaurant & Family Recipes
The Great California Cookbook
Great Chefs of Butte Valley
The Great Vegetarian Cookbook
The Health Promoting Cookbook
Heavenly Creations
Hot Wok

Contributing Cookbooks

Incredible Edibles
International Garlic Festival® Cookbook
Jan Townsend Going Home
Jewish Cooking From Here & Far
The Lafayette Collection
La Jolla Cooks Again
The Lazy Gourmet
A Little California Cookbook
Little Dave's Seafood Cookbook, Volume One
A Little San Francisco Cookbook
Mammoth Really Cooks Book II
Marilyn Thomas: The Homemaker Baker's Favorite Recipes
Mendocino Mornings
Monterey's Cookin' Pisto Style
Monterey's Cooking Secrets
More Firehouse Favorites
Muffin Magic...and More
Neptune's Table: Cooking the Seafood Exotics
New Covenant Kitchens
Nuggets, Nibbles and Nostalgia
The Oats, Peas, Beans & Barley Cookbook
The Old Yacht Club Inn Cookbook
Only in California
On the Road Again Cookbook
The Organic Gourmet
Our Favorite Recipes
Party Perfect and Pampered
Pea Soup Andersen's Scandinavian-American Cookbook
The Potluck Cookbook
Puddings from A-Z
Röckenwagner

Contributing Cookbooks

Roots: A Vegetarian Bounty
Salads from A-Z
San Francisco à la Carte
The San Francisco Chronicle Cookbook
San Francisco Flavors
San Francisco's Cooking Secrets
San Ramon's Secret Recipes
Sausalito: Cooking with a View
Seasons: Food for Thought and Celebration
The 7 Day Cookbook
Sharing Our Best
Simply Vegetarian!
A Slice of Santa Barbara
Sonoma County...its bounty
Sounds Tasty!
Soups from A-Z
The Steinbeck House Cookbook
Sterling Performances
Stirling City Hotel Afternoon Tea
The Stirling City Hotel Favorite Recipes
Sun, Sand and Sausage Pie...and Beach House Memories
Symphony of Flavors
Tahoe Parents Nursery School 40th Anniversary Alumni
Cookbook
Taste California
Taste of Fillmore
Tasty Temptations
Treasured Recipes
Tried and True Recipes
Watsonville Community Hospital Service League Favorite
Recipes 40th Anniversary Edition
We're Cookin' in Cucamonga

Beverages & Appetizers

More than 300,000 tons of grapes are grown annually in California vineyards such as this one in Napa Valley. From these grapes are produced more than seventeen million gallons of wine each year.

Guacamole
(Avocado Dip)

In making this traditional appetizer, the avocados may be smashed for the coarse texture that is traditionally Mexican, or puréed for a smooth texture. When covering guacamole, place plastic wrap directly on dip to keep color fresh. (Mix just before serving.)

2 avocados
2 tablespoons fresh lemon (or lime) juice

2 small green onions, chopped
½ teaspoon salt
Dash Worcestershire

Mash avocados and add seasonings, or combine all ingredients in blender. Makes about 1 cup.

WITH TOMATOES:
2 avocados, mashed or puréed
¼ cup sour cream
2 tablespoons minced onion
2 teaspoons salt
1 teaspoon chili powder

1 clove garlic, crushed
Dash Tabasco
4 teaspoons lemon juice
2 medium tomatoes, peeled and chopped

Combine all ingredients. Cover and chill. Makes about 3 cups.

WITH GREEN CHILE PEPPERS:
4 avocados, mashed or puréed
½ cup finely chopped canned green chile peppers

¼ cup onion, minced
1 teaspoon salt
¼ cup lemon juice

Combine all ingredients. Cover and chill. Makes about 3 cups.

California Country Cook Book

Patricia Rain's Fried Artichokes

18 small artichokes
Water
Juice of 1 lemon
2 cups flour
1/4 teaspoon salt

2 cups beer
1/4 cup oil
2 egg whites
1 quart oil

Clean and trim artichokes and prepare as for hearts. Cut in halves or quarters, depending on size, and immerse in a bowl of cold water into which the lemon juice has been squeezed.

Into a medium bowl, measure flour and salt and make a well in the center. Mix beer and 1/4 cup oil and pour into the well. Gently incorporate the flour into the liquid mixture with a whisk, stirring in one direction only, until batter is smooth. If possible, let the batter rest, covered and refrigerated, for 2 hours or overnight.

Beat egg whites to soft peaks and gently fold them into the batter. Once this step is done, the batter can stand at room temperature for about 15 minutes.

Heat 1 quart oil for deep frying in a wok, heavy saucepan or deep fryer to 350°. Drain artichoke hearts and dry well. Dip into batter and then gently drop them into hot oil. Let batter set about 30 seconds as they fry, then turn artichokes until golden brown. Fry in small batches to allow oil to return to 350° before frying next batch. Serves 6 - 8.

Note: Artichoke hearts are comprised of the pale green inner leaves and the firm-fleshed base of artichokes. Use the smallest artichokes available. Remove leaves until the light green ones appear. Cut off top and stem. Put hearts into acidulated water until ready for cooking. For salads and marinating, cook in boiling water until tender, drain and cover with vinaigrette or other sauce. For deep frying, keep in acidulated water (1 tablespoon vinegar or lemon juice per quart of water, or add lemon slices) until almost ready to cook. Wrap in a towel to dry before dipping in batter. Larger artichokes can be used if necessary; just cut hearts into quarters. Remove the furry center "choke" if artichoke hearts are cut, but leave pale green leaves intact.

The Artichoke Cookbook

Artichokes are rich in iodine, a nutrient not found in most foods. In fact, they rank 7th among fruits and vegetables in vitamin and mineral content, and are a good source of vitamins A, B, and C, as well as potassium. At the same time, artichokes are low in fat and sodium.

Artichoke Cheese Dip

1 (14-ounce) can artichoke hearts, packed in water
1 (6-ounce) jar marinated artichoke hearts
1 (4-ounce) can diced green chiles
6 tablespoons mayonnaise
1½–2 cups Cheddar cheese

Drain artichokes and chop. Mix them and place in greased 9x9-inch baking dish. Scatter chiles on top. Spread with mayonnaise. Sprinkle cheese on top. Bake at 350° for 15 minutes. Serve with tortilla chips.

...Fire Burn & Cauldron Bubble

Shrimp–Stuffed Artichokes

Whole steamed artichokes with the thistle-like choke removed from the center and a delicate shrimp salad filling the hollow, this is an elegant dish.

4 large artichokes, washed and trimmed
1 pound (about 2 cups) tiny cooked shrimp
2 tablespoons chopped parsley
1 tablespoon, or more, lemon juice
2 tablespoons olive oil
½ cup mayonnaise
Salt
Freshly ground pepper

Wash and trim artichokes. Steam them over boiling water in a covered kettle for 30–40 minutes, or until tender when pierced. Turn them bottoms up, place on paper towels, and chill thoroughly.

Carefully spread the center leaves of each artichoke open enough to expose the thistle-like choke. With a spoon, scoop and scrape the choke out, leaving the edible artichoke bottom intact. The artichoke should retain its shape, with a hole in the center for the filling.

Toss the shrimp with the parsley, dill or tarragon and 1 tablespoon lemon juice. Blend the oil and mayonnaise together, add to the shrimp mixture and toss to combine. Season with salt and pepper to taste, and additional lemon juice if necessary. Fill the artichokes with the mixture and serve.

A Little California Cookbook

Artichoke Dip

1 (8-ounce) can artichoke hearts
(water packed)
1 cup mayonnaise

1 (4-ounce) can diced chiles
1 cup grated Parmesan cheese

Dice drained artichokes. Mix all ingredients. Place in oven and bake 20 minutes at 350°. Serve with Wheat Thins or other crisp crackers.

Cooking Treasures of the Central Coast

Stuffed, Baked Eggplant Bundles

1 medium-size eggplant
Salt
1½ cups dry, unflavored bread
crumbs
½ cup freshly grated Parmesan
cheese

2 eggs, lightly beaten in a bowl
Frying oil
⅓ pound prosciutto, thinly sliced
⅓ pound fontina cheese, thinly
sliced
2 tablespoons olive oil

Peel eggplant and trim ends. Cut it lengthwise into ¼-inch-thick slices. Place slices in a large dish and sprinkle with salt. Let stand at room temperature for 30–40 minutes. The salt will draw out the eggplant's bitter juices. Pat slices dry with paper towels.

Combine bread crumbs and Parmesan cheese in a bowl. Dip eggplant slices into egg and coat them lightly with bread crumb mixture.

Heat ½ inch oil in a large skillet over medium-high heat. When the oil is hot, fry a few slices of eggplant at a time, until lightly golden on both sides. Drain on paper towels. (The dish can be prepared up to this point several hours ahead.)

Preheat oven to 375°. Place one slice of prosciutto and one of fontina cheese over each eggplant slice. Roll up loosely into a bundle. Secure each bundle with a toothpick.

Spread 2 tablespoons olive oil in a baking pan. Add bundles and bake 6–8 minutes or until the cheese is melted and bundles are nice and hot. Serve warm. Serves 4.

The Great California Cookbook

Eggplant Rolls with Roasted Peppers

Eggplant wrapped around cheese has become an extremely popular appetizer in California. It seems nearly everyone has a variation; some use feta instead of mozzarella, while others use fresh goat cheese mixed with herbs; some serve it with salsa; some bake the rolls until the cheese is melted. Be sure to cook the eggplant until it is soft and creamy; undercooked, it is tough and bitter. I serve these rolls on a bed of roasted peppers, but you can serve them solo, too.

Olive oil
5 or 6 Japanese eggplants, cut into ¼-inch-thick slices
4 ounces semi-soft cheese, such as fresh mozzarella, asiago, or Monterey Jack, chilled
2 large red bell peppers, roasted and cut into julienne

4 garlic cloves, thinly sliced
4 tablespoons balsamic vinegar
Kosher salt
Black pepper in a mill
2 tablespoons minced Italian parsley

Preheat oven to 350°. Pour thin layer of olive oil on baking sheet. Arrange eggplant slices on top, and drizzle each slice with a little more olive oil. Bake the eggplant until it is soft, creamy, and slightly golden, 20–25 minutes. Remove eggplant slices from the oven, transfer them to absorbent paper, and allow to cool.

Cut cheese into thin slices, and set a slice on each piece of eggplant. Roll the pieces lengthwise, and set rolls aside.

In a small bowl, toss together peppers, garlic, and 3 tablespoons of the vinegar. To serve, place pepper mixture on serving platter and arrange eggplant rolls on top. Season with salt and pepper, scatter parsley over all, drizzle with the remaining 1 tablespoon vinegar, and serve immediately. Makes 25–30 rolls.

California Home Cooking

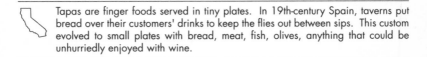

Tapas are finger foods served in tiny plates. In 19th-century Spain, taverns put bread over their customers' drinks to keep the flies out between sips. This custom evolved to small plates with bread, meat, fish, olives, anything that could be unhurriedly enjoyed with wine.

Eggplant Dip

This Middle Eastern dip can be served with raw vegetables, warm pita bread or crackers.

1 large eggplant	¼ teaspoon cayenne pepper,
¼ cup tahini	or 1 jalapeño, minced (optional)
Juice of 2 lemons	Olive oil for topping
3 green onions, finely chopped	2 tablespoons chopped fresh
1 garlic clove, minced	parsley
½ teaspoon ground cumin	

Preheat the oven to 450°. Puncture eggplant with a fork or knife in several places. Place in a pie pan or on a baking sheet and bake 30–45 minutes, or until soft. Cut the eggplant in half and remove the soft flesh, discarding skin. Mash the eggplant in a bowl. Mix in tahini and then lemon juice. Add green onions, garlic, cumin, and cayenne or jalapeño. Refrigerate for at least 1 hour. Serve the dip on a platter, drizzled with olive oil and sprinkled with fresh parsley. Serves 4–6.

The Art Lover's Cookbook: A Feast for the Eye

Bagna Cauda

The Bagna Cauda sits in the middle of the table in a pot (clay or iron) warmed by one candle. It must never boil. Our family makes a meal of this with a salad and red wine. Too good for mere mortals.

½ cup butter	½ cup cream reduced to ¼ cup
1 cup good olive oil	(optional)
½ ounce anchovy fillets, chopped	Coarse, crusty bread and
coarsely	vegetables for dipping
20 cloves garlic, peeled	

In a heavy-bottom saucepan, melt butter in olive oil over very low heat. Add anchovies and garlic and cook ½ to 1 hour gently, never allowing to boil. The next step is the source of much argument. It calls for whisking in the cream to make a smooth sauce. Some say, absolutely not! No cream! We like it both ways, so . . . judge for yourself. I like adding a ground dried porcini mushroom. Serve warm with crusty bread and/or vegetables.

International Garlic Festival® Cookbook

Red Pepper Pesto with Crostini

This pesto is a unique combination of ingredients that would also be nice with pasta.

1 (7-ounce) jar roasted red peppers,
  drained
1/2 cup fresh cilantro leaves
6 tablespoons olive oil
3 tablespoons balsamic vinegar
1 small clove garlic, chopped
1/2 teaspoon dry mustard

1/2 teaspoon ground coriander
Pinch of ground cinnamon
1/2 cup (about 2 1/2 ounces) whole
  toasted almonds
Salt and pepper to taste
1 French or sourdough baguette,
  cut into 1/4–1/3 inch slices, toasted

Combine the peppers, cilantro, oil, vinegar, garlic, mustard, coriander, and cinnamon in food processor bowl. Process until almost smooth. Add the almonds. Process until almonds are finely chopped but not ground. Season with salt and pepper. Serve with the crostini. Yields 10 servings.

Dining by Design

Roasted Red Pepper
and Herbed Goat Cheese Rolls

1 (12-ounce) jar whole roasted red
  bell peppers
8 ounces goat cheese
1 clove garlic, pressed

2 tablespoons fresh, minced herbs
  or 2 teaspoons dried (garlic
  chives, marjoram, oregano,
  parsley, rosemary, basil)

Cut peppers in 2-inch-wide strips. Mix goat cheese with garlic and herbs. Place 1 tablespoon cheese mixture at top of pepper strip and roll up. Chill and serve whole or slice crosswise and serve rounds on crackers. Serves 20.

Note: To roast your own peppers, blister them under broiler, turning when blackened so all surfaces have roasted. Place in plastic bag to steam. When cool, skin and remove seeds and inner membranes.

Cooking with Herbs

Hot Chile–Spinach Dip in a Bread Round

1 large round loaf unsliced Shepherd's bread or French bread
2–3 jalapeño chiles, minced
1 (7-ounce) can diced green chiles
1 small onion, chopped
2 tablespoons vegetable oil
2 tomatoes, chopped
1 (10-ounce) package frozen chopped spinach, thawed, drained and squeezed dry

1 tablespoon red wine vinegar
1 (8-ounce) package cream cheese, softened
2 cups grated Monterey Jack cheese
1 cup half-and-half
1 teaspoon cumin
Salt and pepper to taste
Tortilla chips

Preheat oven to 325°. Cut top off bread ¼ of the way down. Carefully scoop out inside, leaving a 1-inch shell. Reserve top.

In a medium skillet over medium heat, cook chiles and onions in oil, stirring, for 4 minutes, or until onions are softened. Add tomatoes and cook mixture, stirring, for 2 more minutes. Stir in spinach, vinegar, cream cheese, Monterey Jack cheese, half-and-half, cumin, salt and pepper, and heat gently.

Pour sauce into bread round, replace top and wrap in heavy foil. Place in a baking pan and bake for 1½ hours.

To serve, place the bread round on a platter and surround with tortilla chips for dipping. The dip may also be served in a chafing dish. Serves 8–10.

California Sizzles

Spinach/Cheese Frittata

1 tablespoon butter
1 tablespoon oil
2 cloves garlic, minced
2 tablespoons chopped onion
1/2 cup sliced mushrooms
3 eggs, beaten

1 (10-ounce) package frozen
  chopped spinach, drained
1 cup grated Jack or Longhorn
  cheese (or combination)
A pinch oregano leaves

In a 9- to 10-inch skillet, melt butter and oil. Sauté garlic, onion, and mushrooms. Add eggs and spinach. Mix all together and cook over low flame until eggs set and bottom is almost like a crust. Top with cheese and a pinch of oregano leaves. Slide onto a platter and cut in 6–8 slices.

Variation: Use other vegetables, like broccoli or zucchini; may be topped with salsa, or pass salsa at the table. Serves 6–8.

...Fire Burn & Cauldron Bubble

Florentine Spinach Tart

There are many Italian influences in our diverse California kitchens. Spinach grows abundantly in both Italy and California, and is the basis for many delicious recipes. This spinach tart is cut in small wedges and served as a tasty appetizer, or as additional dish for a picnic. If desired, it may be made ahead and kept refrigerated until needed. For full flavor, serve it at room temperature.

2 (10-ounce) packages of frozen
  chopped spinach (or 3 bunches
  fresh)
2 eggs, slightly beaten
1/4 cup grated Parmesan cheese
1 teaspoon nutmeg
1 teaspoon salt

1/2 teaspoon pepper
1 clove fresh garlic, peeled and
  minced
1 cup (8 ounces) ricotta or small
  curd cottage cheese
1 tablespoon olive oil
1/4 cup shelled pine nuts

Cook frozen spinach according to package directions. (If using fresh spinach, wash it, remove the stems, and cook with just as much water as will cling to the leaves.) Cool and drain well, then squeeze dry to remove excess juice. Combine the spinach with the eggs, Parmesan, nutmeg, salt, pepper, garlic, and cheese. Rub a 10-inch pie pan with olive oil. Spread the mixture evenly around the pan, and top with pine nuts. Bake at 350° for 20 minutes. Cool on a rack, and cut in wedges to serve. Serves 6–8.

Note: This tart can also be made in two 9-inch pans, but it will not be as high.

The California Cookbook

Caramelized Onion Tart

Vidalia, Walla Walla, and Maui onions are sweeter varieties of white onions and are well suited for an onion tart. Look for them in the early summer months. Bleu cheese adds a flavorful dimension to the onions but the tart can also be made without the cheese.

4 bacon slices, chopped
3 tablespoons butter
4 pounds sweet white onions
  suchas Vidalia, Walla Walla,
  or Maui, thinly sliced
1 teaspoon salt

1 teaspoon ground pepper
1 (17-ounce) box frozen puff
  pastry, thawed
¼ cup crumbled bleu cheese, such
  as Maytag bleu (optional)

In a large, heavy skillet over medium heat, cook bacon until golden, about 8 minutes. Reduce heat to low and add butter, onions, salt and pepper. Cook onions, stirring occasionally, for 45–55 minutes, or until deep golden brown and jam-like. Taste for seasoning. Use now or cover and refrigerate for up to one day.

Put 2 pastry sheets side by side on a lightly floured board. Press edges of sheets together and lightly crimp. To create a circular pastry, cut 2 inches dough from one long end of rectangle and attach to top, crimping edges together to seal them. Gently roll dough to smooth it out. Place in an 11-inch round tart pan with a removable bottom. Trim off excess dough. Freeze 20–30 minutes. Preheat oven to 425°. Fill crust with caramelized onions and bleu cheese, if desired. Bake until crust is golden, about 25 minutes. Let cool slightly and serve warm, or serve at room temperature. Makes 10–12 appetizer servings.

San Francisco Flavors

7 Layer Dip

2 small cans diced jalapeño
  peppers
2 cans chopped black olives
1 package taco mix
1 pint sour cream

1 (15 ounce) can chili with beans
1 (8 ounce) container guacamole
8 ounces grated sharp cheese
8 ounces grated Monterey cheese
2 or 3 medium-size tomatoes, diced

Put peppers and olives on bottom of a 9x13-inch baking dish, then taco mix. Make layers of sour cream, chili, guacamole, and cheeses. Then, on the top, put tomatoes and more olives, if desired. Dip with tortilla chips.

Diversity is Delta's Main Dish

Sweet-and-Sour Dipping Sauce

¼ cup cold water
¼ cup rice vinegar
3 tablespoons sugar
1 tablespoon soy sauce
1 (¼-inch) piece fresh ginger,
  peeled and minced

1 clove garlic, minced
2 tablespoons apricot jam
½ teaspoon cornstarch
¼ cup warm water

In a nonreactive bowl, combine cold water, vinegar, sugar, and soy sauce. Stir well to dissolve sugar, then stir in ginger and garlic. Transfer mixture to a small saucepan and bring to a simmer. Stir in apricot jam, mixing well; do not allow to boil.

In a small bowl, dissolve cornstarch in warm water; add to vinegar mixture and bring to a boil. As soon as it boils, remove from heat. Let cool before serving. Store any unused sauce in tightly capped container in refrigerator for up to 1 week. Makes about ⅔ cup.

Everybody's San Francisco Cookbook

Cucumber–Mint Salsa

1 medium cucumber
Salt and pepper to taste
1 cup plain yogurt

½ cup fresh mint leaves, finely
minced

Peel the cucumber, leaving a few slivers of green skin for color. Dice into small cubes. Place in a bowl, season with salt and pepper, and add remaining ingredients. Chill for 1 hour before serving. This will make about 2 cups.

The California Cookbook

Award Winning Crostini Di Paolo

1 ounce sun-dried tomatoes
1 cup Newman's Own Olive Oil
and Vinegar Dressing
2 medium cloves garlic, pressed
18 (½-inch) slices sweet
baguette*, toasted

1 large fresh Roma tomato, sliced
½ cup chopped black or kalamata
olives
½ cup crumbled mild feta cheese
½ cup capers (optional)
½ cup fresh basil, chiffonnade**

Soak the dried tomatoes in the Newman's Own Olive Oil and Vinegar Dressing overnight to soften the tomatoes and allow them to soak up the delicious flavor of the dressing.

Pour this mixture, adding the fresh garlic, into a blender, and blend to a paste. (This can be done ahead and kept in the refrigerator for a week.) Toast the baguette slices in a toaster oven until golden brown and crisp. Prepare tomato slices, olives, feta (fresh-grated Parmesan can substitute) and basil, keeping each in a separate bowl. Spread ½ teaspoon of tomato and dressing mixture on each slice of toast. Sprinkle in order with fresh tomatoes, olives, feta and capers. Garnish with fresh basil and serve. Place 3 prepared slices on a small plate and garnish with a sprig of basil or arrange all the slices on a serving platter. Fun to prepare the ingredients and let the guests create their own topping combinations. Serves 6.

*Like French bread rolls.
**Chiffonnade: Leaf vegetables sliced into very thin strips and sautéed in butter.

Sounds Tasty!

Valentine Reserve Stuffed Snow Peas

Served at the annual open house for the University of Santa Barbara.

50 crisp, unblemished snow peas
1 (8-ounce) package cream cheese, softened
4–5 green onions, minced
1 (8-ounce) can crab meat, drained

½ cup drained and chopped water chestnuts
1 teaspoon salt
½ teaspoon white pepper
Chopped pecans (½ cup)

Arrange snow peas in a large bowl and cover with boiling water. Let stand only about 1 minute. Drain peas well and immediately plunge into ice water; drain again and set aside. Trim a bare ¹⁄₁₆ inch from "string" side of peas and gently separate to make opening for filling.

Combine remaining ingredients except pecans, and blend well, adding 1 or 2 tablespoons heavy cream, if necessary, to thin mixture a little. Stuff peas, using a teaspoon or so of filling and roll filled edge in finely chopped pecans; chill. Save any leftover filling to use as a stuffing for won tons.

Mammoth Really Cooks Book II

Pico De Gallo

4 tomatoes, chopped
⅓ medium red onion, chopped
1 tablespoon lime juice
3 jalapeño peppers, finely chopped

½ teaspoon minced garlic
½ teaspoon black pepper
½ teaspoon cumin
1 cup chopped fresh cilantro

Combine all ingredients in a bowl. Let stand 1 hour in refrigerator. Serve with Fritos, tostadas, or any crisp bread for dipping.

We're Cookin' in Cucamonga

Chiles Rellenos

2 eggs, separated
⅔ cup milk
⅔ cup flour
½ teaspoon salt
1 tablespoon oil
Approximately 6 ounces Monterey
  Jack cheese

8–12 canned or fresh roasted
  poblano chiles
Oil (for frying)
Salsa

In processor, blend until smooth the egg yolks, milk, flour, salt, and 1 tablespoon oil. Beat egg whites stiff, but not dry. Fold into processor mixture. While the batter ripens, insert 1 or 2 slivers of cheese into chile pepper. If the chile breaks, just fold it around the cheese. Pat chiles dry, then dredge in some flour and drop softly into batter, coating both sides. Remove with a slotted spoon and into ½ inch or more of oil at 375°. Let batter puff and brown, about 1 minute. Serve immediately with salsa. (Leftover chiles turn soggy and cannot be rewarmed successfully.) Yields enough batter for 12 chiles.

We're Cookin' in Cucamonga

Brie and Mango Quesadillas

3 tablespoons butter
1 mango, thinly sliced
1 small red onion, thinly sliced
⅓ to ½ pound sliced Brie

4 flour tortillas
Cumin to taste
Avocado (garnish)
Cilantro (garnish)

Melt butter in large skillet. Layer mango, red onion, and Brie on one half of one side of each tortilla. Fold over tortilla. Sauté in pan until cheese is melted and tortilla is golden brown. Sprinkle outside of tortilla with cumin while browning. Garnish with avocado slices and cilantro. Cut tortilla into 4–6 slices. Serve warm. Yields 16–24 servings.

Celebrating California

The tallest tree in the world towers 368 feet over Redwood Creek National Park. The towering redwoods are awesome! A mature redwood tree releases 500 gallons of water into the atmosphere each day, and that is why it is said that redwoods create their own weather. Between Laytonville and Klamath along Highway 101, there are three redwood trees you can actually drive through.

Herbed Quesadillas

These are one of our favorite party hors d'oeuvres since they are so easy and fast to make.

½ red onion, peeled and cut in
  ¾-inch slices
2 tablespoons vegetable oil
8 (8-inch) flour tortillas
1 red bell pepper, roasted, peeled
  and cut into ½-inch strips
½ pound low-fat mozzarella
  cheese, grated

2 garlic cloves, peeled and minced
2 tablespoons fresh marjoram (or
  1 teaspoon dried)
2 tablespoons fresh oregano (or
  1 teaspoon dried)
Pinch of freshly ground black
  pepper

Preheat a grill or broiler. Brush the onion slices with 1 tablespoon of the oil. Grill or broil 6 inches from the heat for 4 minutes on each side.

Heat a skillet over high heat. Soften the tortillas by grilling for 30 seconds on each side.

Mix the onion, red pepper strips, mozzarella, garlic, marjoram, oregano and pepper. Divide evenly over 4 tortillas and top with remaining 4, pressing them down gently. Brush both sides lightly with oil.

Preheat oven to 400°. Bake the quesadillas for 3–5 minutes, or until lightly browned and the cheese is melted. Cut into quarters and serve immediately. Makes 16 pieces.

Wine note: One of the richer California Chardonnays or Sauvignon Blancs will balance the texture and flavors of this recipe.

California Wine Country Herbs and Spices Cookbook

Stardust Pesto Cheesecake

PESTO AND WINE SAUCE:

1 cup fresh basil leaves
1/3 cup grated Parmesan cheese
1/4 cup fresh parsley leaves
1/4 cup olive oil

2 tablespoons pine nuts
1/4 cup dry white wine
1/2 cup chopped roasted red bell
    peppers (from 7.25-ounce jar)

Combine first 5 ingredients in a food processor; purée until smooth. In small saucepan, heat wine just until warm. Remove from heat. Stir in pesto and bell peppers; set aside.

PESTO CHEESECAKE:

1/2 cup pasta stars, cooked
1 tablespoon butter, softened
1/4 cup bread crumbs, lightly toasted
1/2 cup plus 2 tablespoons freshly
    grated Parmesan cheese, divided
2 (8-ounce) packages light cream
    cheese, softened

1 cup ricotta cheese
1/4 teaspoon salt
1/8 teaspoon cayenne pepper
3 large eggs (room temperature)
1/4 cup pine nuts
Sprigs of fresh basil
2 fanned strawberries (garnish)

Cook pasta stars according to directions; drain; cool and set aside. Spread butter over bottom and side of 9-inch springform pan. In a small bowl, combine bread crumbs and 2 tablespoons Parmesan cheese. Coat the prepared pan; set aside.

In a large mixing bowl, beat cream cheese, ricotta cheese, 1/2 cup Parmesan cheese, salt, and cayenne pepper until light and fluffy. Add eggs, one at a time, beating well after each addition. Spoon 1/2 of the mixture into another bowl; stir in pasta stars. Add 1/2 cup pesto to remaining half and mix well. Spoon pesto mixture into prepared pan; smooth top. Spread cheese-star mixture evenly over the top; garnish with pine nuts.

Bake at 375° for 45 minutes. Cool on rack. Chill, tightly covered, for 8–10 minutes. Run knife around pan; remove side. Transfer to serving platter. Garnish with basil and fanned strawberries. Serve with wheat crackers. Makes 10–12 servings.

Fair's Fare

 No other state is host to a larger variety of plants than California (more than 5,000 native to California).

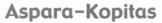

Aspara–Kopitas

Fashioned after spanikopeta, the Greek spinach and feta cheese pie, this appetizer is easy to make, has bold flavors, is elegant for parties and may be prepared ahead of time.

Olive oil
1½ pounds fresh asparagus,
   cleaned, trimmed, and cut into
   ½-inch diagonal pieces
¼ onion, minced
½ marinated red bell pepper, or
   pimento
3 cloves garlic, minced, or garlic
   powder

½ cup sliced mushrooms
Tarragon or Provençal herbs,
   to taste
Dash white wine or vermouth
1 package (2 sheets) frozen puff
   pastry dough (Pepperidge Farm)
8 ounces feta cheese, or favorite
   cheese
Egg white (optional)

Sauté in frying pan with oil, the asparagus, onion, bell pepper or pimento, garlic, and mushrooms until half cooked. Season with herbs and deglaze with wine or vermouth. Allow the mixture to cool for 10 minutes.

Unfold the pastry dough, then cut each sheet into 9 equal squares, yielding a total of 18 pieces. The defrosted dough can be easily rolled and should be rolled out a little thinner. Place a spoonful of the mixture onto a sheet of dough; sprinkle with cheese. Place another sheet on top and crimp the edges with a fork. Brushing the edges with egg white or water helps to seal them. Trim excess dough to square it. Brush each aspara-kopita with egg white before baking. Bake at 375° for about 15 minutes, or until puffed and lightly brown.

Food Festivals of Northern California

Listed as one of the "100 Best Events" in the nation, the Stockton Asparagus Festival draws over 80,000 visitors each year. The three-day event has contributed nearly $2 million to local charities since its inception 14 years ago.

Tiropetes

8 ounces phyllo dough	Four-Cheese Filling
1 cup butter, melted	

Let the wrapped phyllo stand at room temperature. Unwrap, cover with wax paper and a damp towel to prevent drying. Place 1 sheet of phyllo at a time on the work surface and brush with melted butter. Cut the phyllo horizontally into 5 strips. Place a small spoonful of Four-Cheese Filling at the end of a strip, fold the phyllo over the filling about ½ inch and roll up; the finished roll should resemble a cigar. Place on a baking sheet and brush with additional melted butter. Repeat with the remaining phyllo, filling and melted butter. Bake at 375° for 20 minutes or until golden brown. Tiropetes may be frozen before baking; use wax paper between layers to prevent sticking together.

FOUR-CHEESE FILLING:

4 eggs	¼ cup grated Parmesan or
8 ounces feta cheese, crumbled	Romano cheese
8 ounces dry curd cottage cheese	⅛ teaspoon pepper
4 ounces bleu cheese, crumbled	

Beat the eggs in a large mixer bowl. Add the cheeses and pepper and mix well. Note that there is no salt required; the cheeses provide enough. Yields 100.

La Jolla Cooks Again

Mushrooms and Olives in Filo

1/3 cup chopped onion	1/8 teaspoon garlic powder
2 tablespoons butter	1/4 cup black olives, chopped
3 cups chopped mushrooms, about 1 pound	1/4 cup sour cream
1/4 teaspoon black pepper	1 (1-pound) package filo pastry
	1 cup butter, melted

In a large skillet, sauté onions in 2 tablespoons butter until tender. Stir in mushrooms and spices; sauté for a few seconds. Remove from heat and add olives and sour cream. Preheat oven to 350°. Following package directions, place 2 sheets of filo pastry on cutting board; using pastry brush, brush with melted butter. Cut lengthwise into 2-inch-wide strips. Place 1 heaping teaspoon filling at end of strip. Fold over one corner to opposite side to form a triangle. Continue folding, keeping triangle shape. Brush triangles with melted butter. Place on ungreased cookie sheet. Repeat with remaining filo and filling. Bake approximately 20 minutes. Yields 64 appetizers.

Sterling Performances

2 Putt Pita Chips

Tasty chips for dips or plain with cocktails.

1/2 cup (1 stick) soft butter	1 tablespoon lemon juice
2 tablespoons chopped fresh parsley or 1 teaspoon dried	1/4 teaspoon garlic powder
1 tablespoon finely chopped chives or green onions	1 teaspoon lemon pepper seasoning
	6 pita breads, split in half horizontally

Preheat oven to 400°. Blend all the ingredients except pita into a paste. Spread each pita bread half with the butter paste and cut into wedge-shaped quarters. Place on 2 cookie sheets, not overlapping, and bake for 5–7 minutes until crispy and slightly brown. Yields 48 chips.

The Golf Cookbook

There are 963 golf holes in Palm Springs and the surrounding Coachella Valley.

Thai Minced Chicken in Lettuce Leaves

Lemongrass, cilantro, and fish sauce are staples of Thai cooking and are readily available in San Francisco's Chinatown and many supermarkets across the country. Traditionally, the minced chicken is served rolled up in lettuce leaves, but endive leaves or tartlet shells are better for passing.

MINCED CHICKEN FILLING:

3 boneless, skinless chicken breast halves

2 teaspoons olive oil

3 garlic cloves, crushed

1/4 cup minced fresh cilantro or basil

1 teaspoon ground pepper

1/4 cup soy sauce

1/4 cup fish sauce (nam pla or nuoc mam)

3 tablespoons fresh lime juice

2 tablespoons sugar

1/2–1 teaspoon cayenne pepper

2 stalks lemongrass, white part only, finely chopped

2 teaspoons grated fresh ginger

1/4 cup finely diced red onion

In food processor or using large chef's knife, finely chop chicken. In small skillet over medium-high heat, heat oil and sauté chicken for 5–8 minutes, or until opaque throughout. In medium bowl, combine cooked chicken and all remaining filling ingredients. Cover and refrigerate at least 30 minutes or overnight. Taste and adjust seasoning with lime juice, fish sauce, and/or cayenne.

30 small butter or red oak lettuce leaves, endive leaves, or tartlet shells

Fresh mint sprigs for garnish (optional)

Spoon 1 heaping tablespoon filling onto each lettuce or endive leaf or tartlet shell. Garnish with a mint sprig and serve. Makes 30 appetizers.

San Francisco Flavors

Country French Wrap

This recipe was created at the request of Chicken of the Sea for their gourmet tuna by The French Gourmet.

2 teaspoons whole grain mustard
2 tablespoons mayonnaise
1 teaspoon chopped fresh basil
1 teaspoon chopped fresh dill
1 teaspoon chopped fresh rosemary
1 teaspoon chopped fresh parsley
1 (6-ounce) can tuna in olive oil, drained
1 (6-inch) whole wheat tortilla

Blend mustard and mayonnaise in a medium bowl. Add herbs and mix well. Add tuna and toss lightly; the tuna should remain in chunks. Spread on the tortilla and roll up to enclose the filling. Cut into bite-size pieces and place on a serving plate. Garnish with avocado slices, spinach leaves, and chopped red tomato. Yields 2 servings.

La Jolla Cooks Again

Cheese Puffs Filled with Chipped Beef

CHEESE PUFFS:
2 tablespoons butter or margarine
¼ cup boiling water
¼ cup all-purpose flour, sifted
Dash salt
1 egg
¼ cup shredded Swiss cheese

In small saucepan, melt butter. Add water, flour, and salt. Stir vigorously until mixture pulls away from the sides of the pan and forms a ball. Cool slightly. Add egg and beat until mixture is smooth. Stir in cheese. Drop level teaspoons of dough on a greased cookie sheet. Bake in preheated 400° oven for 20 minutes. Remove from oven, split and cool. Fill puffs with Chipped Beef Filling.

CHIPPED BEEF FILLING:
1 (3½-ounce) package (about 1 cup) chipped beef, shredded
2 tablespoons green pepper, finely chopped
½ cup celery, finely chopped
½ teaspoon prepared horseradish
⅓ cup mayonnaise

Mix ingredients together thoroughly and fill each puff with the Chipped Beef Filling.

Party Perfect and Pampered

Prosciutto Pinwheels

1 ¼ cups shredded Gruyère cheese
5 teaspoons chopped fresh sage
   leaves

1 sheet frozen puff pastry, thawed
1 large egg, lightly beaten
1 ½ ounces thinly sliced prosciutto

Combine the Gruyère cheese and sage in a bowl. Arrange the pastry sheet, short side facing you, on a lightly floured surface; cut into halves crosswise. Place ½ sheet with long side facing you; brush the edge of the far side with the egg.

Layer with half the prosciutto and Gruyère cheese mix, avoiding the egg-moistened edge. Roll up jelly-roll fashion, shaping into a log. Wrap in wax paper. Repeat the process with the remaining pastry, prosciutto and cheese mixture. Chill, seam-side-down, in the refrigerator for 3 hours to 3 days or until firm.

Preheat oven to 400°. Grease 2 large baking sheets. Cut the logs crosswise into ½-inch slices. Arrange, cut-side-down, 1 inch apart on the baking sheets.

Bake in batches on the middle oven rack for 14–16 minutes or until golden. Remove to a wire rack to cool slightly. Serve warm. Yields 40 pinwheels.

Dining by Design

Grilled Portabello over Polenta

½ cup butter, unsalted, divided
1 tablespoon extra virgin olive oil
2 cloves garlic, chopped
½ pound portabello mushrooms, chopped fine
Salt and freshly ground pepper to taste

2 cups polenta (cornmeal)
6 cups beef stock
1 cup gorgonzola cheese, grated, divided
½ cup Reggiano Parmesan cheese, grated
1 cup heavy cream

In a medium-size skillet add 1 tablespoon butter, olive oil, chopped garlic, and mushrooms and sauté over medium heat for 4–6 minutes, or until done. Season lightly with salt and pepper.

Preheat oven to 350°.

Put cornmeal in a large pot; slowly whisk in beef stock. Add salt to taste and bring cornmeal to a boil. Lower heat to a simmer, and cook cornmeal for approximately 25 minutes, stirring often until mixture thickens. Slowly add 3 tablespoons butter, ⅔ cup gorgonzola, and Reggiano Parmesan to polenta, stirring briskly to melt and combine ingredients. Add cream and stir briskly with a wooden spoon. Continue cooking for another 10 minutes or so until cornmeal has thickened. Stir in a couple of tablespoons of water if mixture becomes difficult to stir.

Pour cooked polenta into a well-buttered baking dish, spreading polenta with a plastic spatula to form a layer of uniform thickness. Place polenta in fridge for 20–30 minutes, until cooled. Using a cookie cutter or sturdy glass, cut firm polenta into 3- to 4-inch circles.

Place polenta circles on greased baking dish. Place some sautéed mushrooms on each circle and add a bit of grated gorgonzola cheese. Place baking dish in preheated oven and bake for 15 minutes. Remove from oven and allow to cool for several minutes before serving. Serves 6.

Cooking with Mushrooms

SAN DIEGO ZOO

Cocktail Meatballs

These meatballs have been popular at every event in town, from the Christmas Ball to the Valentine Reserve tour.

1 pound ground beef	2 tablespoons oil
1 egg, slightly beaten	1 (10-ounce) jar chili sauce
¼ cup fine, dry bread crumbs	1 (12-ounce) jar grape jelly
½ onion, finely chopped	1 teaspoon lemon juice
1 teaspoon salt	2 teaspoons brown sugar
¼ teaspoon pepper	

Combine beef, egg, crumbs, onion, salt and pepper. Form into balls the size of a walnut. Heat oil in skillet; add meatballs and brown all sides. In a saucepan, stir together chili sauce, grape jelly, lemon juice, and brown sugar. Add browned meatballs to the sauce. Cover and simmer for 30 minutes. Serve warm from chafing dish.

Okay to double the meatball ingredients, but do not double the sauce.

Mammoth Really Cooks Book II

Linda's Salmon Party Log

2 cups cooked salmon	¼ teaspoon salt
1 (8-ounce) package cream cheese, softened	¼ teaspoon liquid smoke
2 tablespoons lemon juice	½ cup chopped pecans
2 tablespoons very finely chopped onion	3 tablespoons coarsely snipped parsley
1 large teaspoon prepared horseradish	

Drain and flake salmon, removing any skin or bones. Combine salmon with cream cheese, lemon juice, onion, horseradish, salt, and liquid smoke; mix thoroughly. Chill several hours or overnight.

Shape salmon mixture into an 8x2-inch log, chill well. Mix pecans and parsley (may be kept in refrigerator prior to rolling on log). Roll salmon log in mixture and chill for another 2 hours. Serve with Triscuits or crackers of your choice.

Food Festivals of Northern California

Ceviche

3 pounds halibut, fresh or frozen
(if boneless, use about 1½ to
2 pounds)
1 cup lime juice, fresh or bottled
1 pound canned tomatoes, broken
into pieces, with juice
1 (3-ounce) jar pimiento-stuffed
olives, drained

1 medium onion, chopped
½ cup ketchup
½ cup olive oil
1 teaspoon leaf oregano, crumbled
1 scant teaspoon bottled red
pepper seasoning
1 teaspoon salt
Avocado (optional)

The night before: Trim skin and bones from halibut. Cut into ½-inch cubes. Place in a deep bowl (glass or china). Pour lime juice over top to cover fish. Cover and chill overnight.

The next day: Drain fish, rinse under cold water; place in a large bowl. Add all other ingredients and toss lightly.

May be topped with avocado. Serve with tortilla chips. Serves 10–12.

Variation: Fresh tomato may be added, if desired. Red snapper, salmon or tuna may be substituted for halibut.

California Kosher

La Jolla Salmon with Capers and Green Onions

6 ounces fresh salmon, poached
(may substitute 1 (6½-ounce) can
salmon plus 2 tablespoons liquid)
1 tablespoon capers
4 green onions, diced, with tops
discarded

1 tablespoon mayonnaise
1 tablespoon Dijon mustard
1 teaspoon lemon juice

Flake salmon into pieces in a medium mixing bowl. Gently add remaining ingredients and stir until just blended. Serve with crackers.

California Sizzles

St. Helena is the western home of the Culinary Institute of America.
Pasadena is the birthplace of famous chef Julia Child.

Fresh Baked Oysters with Spinach and Fresh Herbs

12 very fresh oysters in shells
1 yellow onion, chopped
3 cloves garlic, minced
1 cube (2 tablespoons) unsalted
   butter
1/2 cup fresh basil, chopped
1 tablespoon fresh thyme,
   chopped

1/4 cup fresh parsley, chopped
2 bunches of spinach, cleaned,
   chopped, and drained
1 cup bread crumbs
Salt and pepper, to taste
2 cups rock salt
1 cup Parmesan cheese, grated

Place oysters on a baking sheet in a 350° oven until they just begin to open. Shuck the oysters, leaving them in the half shell. Sauté the onion and garlic in butter until translucent. Add basil, thyme, and parsley. Sauté lightly. Squeeze all excess moisture from the spinach and add to the sauté mixture briefly. Remove from the heat and place mixture into a food processor. Process until evenly minced. Do not purée. Empty the mixture into a bowl. Stir in the bread crumbs and add salt and pepper. Spread rock salt on a baking sheet and place oysters on top. Cover each oyster with a dollop of spinach mixture and a sprinkle of grated Parmesan. Bake at 350° for 15–20 minutes. Serve.

Carter House Cookbook

Chili Cheese Shrimp

16 ounces cream cheese, softened
2 tablespoons Worcestershire sauce
1/4 teaspoon grated lemon peel
1 tablespoon lemon juice
1/2 cup sliced green onions

1/8 teaspoon Tabasco sauce
12 ounces bottled chili sauce
1 tablespoon horseradish
12 ounces small cooked shrimp

In a bowl, beat the first 6 ingredients together until smooth. Spread into the bottom of a shallow one-quart dish. Mix the chili sauce and horseradish. Spread this over the cream cheese mixture. Top with shrimp. Serve cold with crackers.

The Lafayette Collection

Crabmeat Stuffed Mushrooms

16 large mushrooms
⅓ cup butter or margarine
1½ cups flaked crabmeat
2 large eggs
2 tablespoons mayonnaise

¼ cup chopped green onions
2 teaspoons lemon juice
½ cup seasoned bread crumbs,
   divided

Dip washed mushroom caps into melted butter. Place them, cap-side-down in a buttered baking dish. Combine crabmeat, eggs, mayonnaise, green onions, lemon juice, and half of the bread crumbs. Fill each mushroom cap with mixture. Sprinkle remaining bread crumbs over the mushrooms and dot with butter. Bake in a preheated oven at 375° for 15 minutes. Makes 4 servings as a main dish or 8 servings for appetizer.

Little Dave's Seafood Cookbook

Sticky Chicken

1 cup soy sauce
1 cup white wine vinegar
¾ cup sugar
4 cloves garlic, minced

4 green onions, chopped
2 tablespoons grated fresh ginger
30 chicken drummettes

In a large bowl, combine the soy sauce, vinegar, and sugar, stirring until the sugar dissolves. Add the garlic, green onions, and ginger; mix well. Arrange the chicken in a glass dish and cover with the marinade to coat. Refrigerate overnight, stirring occasionally.

Pour the chicken and marinade into a large skillet or wok. Cook over medium heat until the liquid evaporates and forms a sticky coating on the chicken, approximately 45 minutes. Do not over-cook or the chicken will fall off the bones. Serve hot or at room temperature.

The Lafayette Collection

Mahogany Chicken Wings

In this version of spicy chicken wings, the wings are cloaked in a syrupy sauce similar but not identical to classic teriyaki; orange juice, orange zest, and hot pepper flakes create a more complex flavor.

1½ cups fresh orange juice
1½ cups soy sauce
1½ cups packed brown sugar
6–8 garlic cloves, minced
1 (1½-inch) piece fresh ginger, peeled and minced
Zest of 2 oranges, minced fine

½ teaspoon crushed red chile flakes
40 chicken drummettes, rinsed and dried
4–5 scallions, trimmed and cut into small rounds
1 orange, sliced thin

Combine orange juice, soy sauce, sugar, garlic, ginger, orange zest, and chile flakes in a heavy saucepan over medium heat. Heat the mixture through and stir to dissolve sugar. Remove sauce from heat and let it cool. Place chicken drummettes in a glass or crockery bowl or baking dish and pour cooled marinade over them, turning them so they are well coated. Cover dish and refrigerate it for several hours or overnight.

Preheat oven to 375°. Remove wings from marinade (do not discard marinade) and arrange on oiled baking sheets. Bake, turning once and basting with marinade 2 or 3 times, about 45 minutes, or until glossy.

Place wings on a serving platter, scatter scallions over the top, and garnish with orange slices. Serve immediately, with plenty of napkins.

Variation: Use a whole chicken, cut up, in place of chicken drummettes, and serve as a main course with steamed rice. Bring remaining marinade to a boil, reduce by half, and spoon it over the rice. Garnish with scallions and orange slices.

California Home Cooking

The High Sierra is waves of bare granite exquisitely sculpted by sun, snow, and rain under the tutelage of time. On its slopes resides the world's largest living thing, the magnificent sequoia—some weigh up to 2.7 million pounds! Not far away, the world's oldest living thing, the bristlecone pine, perseveres in the White Mountains.

Pacific Rim Rumaki

½ chicken liver
Sprinkling soy sauce
½ water chestnut

½ strip bacon
1 (1-inch) square of pineapple or
   papaya (optional)

Sprinkle the liver with soy sauce. Wrap the liver and water chestnut in the bacon strip. Securely hold in place with small bamboo skewer (leaving room on top for fruit, if used). Place on a metal rack or baking sheet (to catch the drippings) in a 400° oven, until bacon is crisp, about 15–20 minutes. If you cook rumaki over charcoal, turn skewer while cooking so each side is cooked evenly. Serves 1.

The California Cookbook

Beer Cheese Spread

A marvelous spread on crackers, it keeps for weeks in a crock in the refrigerator . . . a lovely hostess gift.

½ onion, cut into pieces
1 clove garlic, minced
2 tablespoons Dijon-style mustard
2 tablespoons catsup
1 tablespoon horseradish
1 (3-ounce) package cream cheese,
   room temperature

¾ pound sharp Cheddar cheese,
   cut into ½-inch cubes, room
   temperature
½ cup flat beer

In a food processor place onion, garlic, mustard, catsup, horseradish, cream cheese, ⅓ of the Cheddar, and ½ of the beer. Process for 40 seconds. Scrape down sides of bowl. Add remaining beer and another ⅓ of Cheddar. Process another 60 seconds. Scrape down sides again and add remaining cheese. Process another 60 seconds. Let ripen in the refrigerator in a covered bowl for several hours at least. Let stand at room temperature until it reaches spreading consistency. Makes 2 cups. Serves 8–10.

The Lazy Gourmet

Caponata

Caponata is a most requested recipe. Even people who hate eggplant love it, as long as you tell them it has eggplant in it after they have tasted it.

2 small eggplants, peeled and cut into 1-inch cubes	½ teaspoon basil
Olive oil	½ teaspoon oregano
2 onions, coarsely chopped	½ teaspoon Italian seasoning
1 cup celery, cut into ½-inch pieces	½ teaspoon seasoned salt
3 cloves garlic, chopped	1 tablespoon sugar
1 large can whole pear-shaped tomatoes	1 tablespoon wine vinegar
1 (8-ounce) can tomato sauce or purée	1 cup ripe green olives, coarsely chopped
½ teaspoon caper juice	1 cup ripe black olives, coarsely chopped
	½ cup seedless raisins
	2 tablespoons capers

Salt eggplant and let sit about 1 hour for bitter liquid to drain. Rinse eggplant to remove extra salt. Pat dry.

In a large nonstick pan, sauté eggplant in olive oil until browned. Do eggplant in batches to prevent crowding. You only need about 2 tablespoons oil per batch. Remove to casserole dish. Sauté onions in oil for a short while, until soft. Add to casserole dish. Add to sauté pan the celery, garlic, tomatoes, tomato sauce, caper juice, basil, oregano, Italian seasoning and seasoned salt. Cook sauce for 20 minutes, dissolve sugar in wine vinegar and add to sauce. Meanwhile, add olives, raisins and capers to eggplant. Pour sauce over the mix. Bake at 375° for about 1 hour or more, or until thick and everything looks soft. Chill and serve. Makes about 2 quarts.

Note: Serve with assorted specialty crackers such as Water Crackers or Euphrates or as an antipasto. Caponata also makes a wonderful pizza topping, or if you add more tomatoes and sauce, and don't cook it down too much, it is wonderful on pasta.

Caponata is better after it sits for a few days. It keeps well in the refrigerator and freezes beautifully. You can substitute fresh herbs for the dry, but in much larger quantities. If you cannot find green olives, use all black. (Cosentino's market carries the green ones). Recipe can be doubled easily. Cook for a little longer.

Dining Door to Door in Naglee Park

Tapenade

This is a delicious spread for crackers and thinly sliced bread. Also good mixed with steamed or water sautéed vegetables and as a spread for sandwiches. Tapenade is so good, you'll wonder why you never made it before.

1 can pitted black olives, 6 ounces
   dry weight
5 anchovy fillets
1/2 cup plumped sun-dried
   tomatoes, finely chopped
1 tablespoon finely chopped
   parsley
1 tablespoon finely chopped basil
1 tablespoon minced garlic
2 tablespoons lemon juice

2 tablespoons virgin olive oil
2 tablespoons capers
1/2 teaspoon Canned Fire, or
   1/4 teaspoon cayenne
1 teaspoon Bouquet Garni, or
   1/4 teaspoon each of the
   following dried herbs: oregano,
   marjoram, basil, and tarragon
3 tablespoons mayonnaise

Chop olives, anchovies, tomatoes, parsley, and basil in processor using pulsing technique so that ingredients are chopped and not puréed, or mince by hand. Press garlic into olive mixture. Add rest of ingredients and mix well.

Serve with assorted crackers, thinly sliced sourdough bread, crostini, or sliced carrots and celery. Makes 1 1/2 cups.

The Organic Gourmet

Hummus

This delicious Middle Eastern garbanzo spread is often used as a dip with vegetables or on pita bread . . . an excellent source of protein.

2 cups garbanzo beans (cooked or canned)
⅔ cup water
3 tablespoons raw tahini
2 cloves garlic, peeled (optional)
1 teaspoon salt

2 tablespoons olive oil
2 tablespoons fresh lemon juice
2 tablespoons fresh parsley leaves
1 pinch cayenne
2 pinches paprika

Blend beans with water, tahini, garlic, salt, olive oil and lemon juice in food processor until smooth. Add parsley, cayenne, and paprika; blend for an additional minute.

Place hummus in a bowl and sprinkle olive oil on top of dish to prevent drying. You can decorate with paprika, sprigs of parsley or mint, and sliced or whole olives.

The Expanding Light Cookbook

Cucumber Sandwiches

Cucumber, sliced in ¼-inch rounds
Salt
Dark rye bread, sliced and frozen

Butter, soft spreadable
Mayonnaise
Dill weed, chopped

Sprinkle cucumber with salt and set aside until needed. Trim crusts from frozen bread. Butter bread slices, covering the entire slice. (This will keep the bread from becoming soggy when adding cucumber.) Cover bread slices with mayonnaise, layer on cucumber slices and sprinkle with dill weed. Cover with plastic wrap and refrigerate till serving time. These sandwiches can be held in refrigerator 2–3 hours.

Stirling City Hotel Afternoon Tea

Cranberry Chutney Spread

1 (16-ounce) can whole cranberry sauce
½ cup wine vinegar
½ cup golden raisins or currants
1 tablespoon Worcestershire sauce

1 cup sugar
2 tablespoons molasses
1 (8-ounce) package cream cheese, softened
Chopped walnuts (optional)

In a saucepan, combine cranberry sauce, vinegar, raisins, Worcestershire sauce, sugar, and molasses and simmer for 30 minutes. Cool before storing in refrigerator. Spoon over cream cheese and top with chopped walnuts or pecans. Serve surrounded with crackers on a decorative tray. Serves 10.

Sterling Performances

Shrimp Mousse

1½ cups small shrimp
½ cup finely chopped celery
3 tablespoons fresh lemon juice
2 tablespoons white wine vinegar
1 teaspoon prepared horseradish
½ teaspoon freshly ground pepper
½ teaspoon salt

1 envelope unflavored gelatin
¼ cup cold water
½ cup heavy cream
1 cup mayonnaise
Cucumber slices
Avocado slices
8 large cooked shrimp

Combine small shrimp, celery, lemon juice, vinegar, horseradish, pepper and salt. Marinate 30 minutes. Soften gelatin in cold water and carefully dissolve over low heat. In a large bowl whip cream until stiff. Add mayonnaise, gelatin, small shrimp and their marinade, and adjust seasonings. Pour mixture into an 8-inch ring mold or fish mold that has been oiled or has been rinsed in cold water. Stirring occasionally until it starts to set, chill mousse 4–5 hours or overnight.

Unmold onto a chilled serving platter; garnish with cucumber and avocado slices and large shrimp. Serve with crackers. Serves 12.

Note: This may also be served as a luncheon dish, for 4–6 people, or as a first course in individual molds, for 8.

San Francisco à la Carte

Mini Quichettes

These are so versatile and easy they should be in everyone's repertoire.

PASTRY:

½ cup butter   1 cup flour
1 (3-ounce) package cream cheese,
   softened

Beat together butter and cream cheese till smooth; add flour and form into a ball. Wrap in wax paper and chill for 30 minutes or longer. The pastry can be made a day ahead. Make miniature pie shells by shaping dough into 1-inch balls and pressing into bottom and sides of small muffin cups about 1½–2 inches in diameter.

FILLING:

4 ounces small shrimp   ½ cup milk
1 medium onion, chopped   ⅛ teaspoon nutmeg
  and lightly sautéed   Freshly ground pepper
½ cup grated Swiss cheese   to taste
2 eggs, lightly beaten

Preheat oven to 450°. In each miniature pie shell, place a few small shrimp, then a little sautéed onion, then a little grated cheese. Combine eggs with milk, nutmeg, and ground pepper, and pour into cups. Bake for 10 minutes. Reduce heat to 350° and continue baking 15 minutes more. Serve immediately.

These can be frozen after baking and reheated at 450° for 10 minutes directly from the freezer. The Filling in this recipe may be prepared by substituting one of the following for the shrimp: crab, canned clams, chopped cooked ham, or sautéed chopped bacon Serves 6–8.

San Francisco à la Carte

Bleu Cheese Soufflé

This is a glorious dip that is so very attractive. The cheese taste is quite sharp, and it goes well with drinks. Who would ever expect a soufflé with cocktails? Well worth the time and effort.

1 envelope unflavored gelatin	4 ounces bleu cheese, softened
2 tablespoons cool water	1 egg, separated
4 tablespoons sweet butter, softened	1 teaspoon Dijon mustard
4 ounces cream cheese, softened	½ cup heavy cream, whipped

Soften gelatin in cool water, then gently stir over low heat to dissolve. Using a food processor or electric mixer, beat together butter and cheeses, adding egg yolk, mustard, and gelatin. Beat egg white until stiff but not dry, and gently fold into mixture. Then fold in whipped cream.

Prepare a 1-cup soufflé dish with a collar of oiled wax paper or foil. Tie to dish with string. Spoon mixture into dish so that it comes up over sides and up to top of collar. Chill for several hours or overnight. Remove collar and serve with crackers or raw vegetables. Serves 12.

San Francisco à la Carte

Curry Mayonnaise

1 cup mayonnaise	2 tablespoons brown sugar
1 tablespoon curry powder	½ cup dried cranberries

Mix first 3 ingredients well. Add dried cranberries. Use as spread for turkey or ham sandwiches.

Stirling City Hotel Afternoon Tea

Piñons, Pecans, Pumpkin Seeds

1 cup shelled piñon nuts	1 teaspoon butter
1 cup pecan halves	Generous dashes cayenne and
1 cup shelled green pumpkin seeds	cumin

Toast seeds and nuts lightly in large ungreased skillet over low heat with butter. Add spices as mixture starts to brown. As you smell the roasting cumin, transfer the mix to a paper bag, salt lightly and shake to distribute the seasonings. Serve warm or room temperature. (Green pumpkin seeds can be found in natural foods stores.)

We're Cookin' in Cucamonga

Café Mocha

1 (14-ounce) can sweetened
condensed milk
1 (4-ounce) Baker's German sweet
chocolate bar

1 cup whipping cream
Hot brewed coffee

Melt chocolate and sweetened condensed milk in top of double boiler over low heat. Stir occasionally. Cool.

Whip cream until soft peaks form. Fold into cooled chocolate mixture. Cover tightly and refrigerate for up to one week. For each serving, place ¼ cup chocolate mixture in a large coffee cup or mug. Fill with hot brewed coffee. Stir and serve immediately. Serves 10.

Symphony of Flavors

Date Shake

You'd be apt to find creamy, sweet, fruity milkshakes at roadside diners. In the Southern California desert, which produces the entire United States' supply of dates, you'll find them made from dates.

**The flesh from any desired fruit or
10 large pitted dates**
¾ cup milk

1 teaspoon vanilla extract
2 scoops vanilla ice cream

Chop fruit finely by hand and place in a blender. Add 2–3 tablespoons of milk and blend until smooth. Add remaining milk, vanilla, and ice cream and whirl briefly just until blended. Serve immediately in a tall glass. Serves 1.

A Little California Cookbook

The arrival of the first date palm from the Middle East in the 1890s spurred large-scale date farming in California. Some 26,000 tons of dates are harvested annually in Riverside and Imperial counties. Today several varieties thrive in the desert. The Date Festival developed the date shake, a combination of ice cream or frozen yogurt, milk, and chopped dates, whipped into a foamy delight.

Vodka Slush Summer Drink

What a great treat for a warm day.

7 cups water
¾ cup sugar
2 green tea bags (use regular if
  no other)
1 (12-ounce) can frozen lemonade,
  undiluted

1 (12-ounce) can frozen orange
  juice, undiluted
2 cups vodka
2 liters 7-Up, Sprite, or Slice

Bring water and sugar to a boil. Dissolve sugar and remove from heat. Steep tea bags in this mixture for 10 minutes. Cool. Add frozen lemonade, orange juice, and vodka to the above mixture. Blend and freeze in a couple of plastic tubs. When ready to serve, fill glass with ¾ cup of slush and add ½ cup of 7-Up or such. Enjoy. Serves 25–30.

Cooking with Booze

Spicy Bloody Marys

2 quarts spicy V-8 juice
1½ teaspoons prepared
  horseradish
½ teaspoon celery salt
¼ teaspoon cayenne pepper

½ teaspoon black pepper
2 teaspoons Worcestershire sauce
¼ teaspoon Tabasco sauce
Vodka
Celery stalks

Combine V-8 juice, horseradish, celery salt, cayenne and black peppers, Worcestershire and Tabasco sauce. Chill well. Mix individual Bloody Marys to desired strength. Garnish with celery stalks.

Children's Hospital Oakland Cookbook

Bread & Breakfast

The California Citrus State Historic Park at Riverside is located on land considered to be the finest navel orange growing region in the world.

Breakfast Scones

2 cups flour	1 stick butter (1/2 cup)
1/2 teaspoon baking soda	1 egg yolk
2 teaspoons baking powder	3/4 cup buttermilk
3/4 teaspoon nutmeg	2 tablespoons sugar
1/2 teaspoon salt	1 cup raisins

Preheat oven to 375°. In a food processor, combine flour, baking soda, baking powder, nutmeg, and salt. Add butter in small pieces, mixing until it's a grainy cornmeal consistency. Remove and put in a bowl.

Whip together egg yolk and buttermilk. Add sugar and raisins. Add this to flour mixture. Knead 10–12 times. It will be very sticky, so flour hands well. Flatten into a mound 6 inches in diameter. Cut into wedges. It will yield 6 nice-size scones. Scoop onto cookie sheet. Bake 20–25 minutes or until golden brown.

The Coastal Cook of West Marin
Recipe from Tomales Country Inn

Biscuits Supreme

2 cups flour	4 teaspoons baking powder
1/2 teaspoon salt	1/2 cup butter
1/2 teaspoon cream of tartar	2/3 cup milk
3 teaspoons sugar	

Sift flour, salt, cream of tartar, sugar, and baking powder. Cut in butter until mixture resembles coarse crumbs. Add milk all at once and stir just until dough follows fork around bowl. Pat on lightly floured wax paper, or roll 1/2 inch thick. Cut with cutter or knife. Bake at 450° for 10–12 minutes. Makes about 16 medium biscuits.

Note: Add more sugar to dough to use as shortcakes for berries.

We're Cookin' in Cucamonga

 California ranks first among U.S. states in population with more than 30 million people.

Garlic Potato Bread

Thin, light, and crispy—it looks a bit like pizza crust, and it has a Middle Eastern flavor. Great with Hummus (page 47) and green salad.

1 large russet potato, peeled and cubed	1 clove garlic, peeled and minced
1 cup lukewarm potato water	1 cup whole wheat flour
1 tablespoon active dry yeast	1½ cups unbleached white flour
1 teaspoon honey	1 teaspoon salt

Preheat oven to 350°. Boil potato in water until soft, but not mushy. Strain and save water. Let cool to room temperature. Set aside. In a small bowl, mix potato water, yeast, and honey, and let foam for 10 minutes. In a large bowl, combine the remaining ingredients with mashed potato.

Add active dry yeast mixture to flour mixture and combine thoroughly. Knead for 10 minutes. Put in a well-buttered bowl, and brush top with generous amount of soft butter or ghee.* Cover and let rise until size is doubled (approximately 30 minutes). Punch down the dough and roll to about ½-inch thickness (should be round and flat, like a pizza).

Brush the top of the dough with soft butter or ghee again and let rise for about 20 minutes. Before baking, you can sprinkle the top with rosemary. Bake at 350° for 15–25 minutes, or until golden brown. It should be light and fluffy.

*Cooked slowly and longer than clarified butter, ghee has a nutty flavor.

The Expanding Light Cookbook

Linda's Cornbread

1 egg	1 cup flour
½ cup sour cream	¾ cup brown sugar
½ cup buttermilk	½ teaspoon baking soda
1 cup cornmeal	½ teaspoon salt

Preheat oven to 450°. Grease a 9-inch pie pan. Place pie pan in the oven and as it is heating, prepare the batter. Combine egg, sour cream, and buttermilk in a bowl. In a separate bowl, mix cornmeal, flour, brown sugar, baking soda, and salt. Add dry ingredients to wet ones and mix thoroughly. Carefully pour batter into hot pie pan and bake for 15–18 minutes. Serve warm. Serves 6–8.

Sounds Tasty!

Tom's Original Sourdough Bread

2 cups milk (or sour milk)
⅓ cup sugar (or honey)
⅓ cup shortening
1 teaspoon salt
1 package active dry yeast with
    2 tablespoons warm water
    (optional)

5+ cups flour
1½ cups Sourdough Starter

Scald milk; add sugar, shortening, and salt; cook to dissolve and mix. Cool to warm (80°) and add yeast-water mixture and/or Starter, and ½ the flour; mix and let sit until active. (If no yeast is added, increase resting and raising times). Add remainder of the flour 1 cup at a time, mixing until dough stiffens. Knead, adding flour until dough is just not sticky. Grease hands and form dough into a ball for rising.

Let rise covered with a cotton cloth for 1½ to 2½ hours until doubled. Punch down and let rise again. Divide into 2 balls, cover and let rest 10 minutes, shape into loaf pans (9x5x3) and let rise about 1 hour. Bake 40 minutes at 400°. Turn out to cool.

SOURDOUGH STARTER:
This method gives a quick and sure starter, if a first batch is needed quickly.

2 cups unsifted flour
1½ cups water
2 tablespoons sugar

1 teaspoon yeast
1 teaspoon salt
1 tablespoon vinegar

Mix dry ingredients in a crock or bowl. Add water, beat well and add the vinegar; beat again. Cover starter with light cloth and let sit in a warm place until well soured or fermented (12–24 hours). After using part of this mixture, replace it with 1-to-1 flour and water, and refrigerate.

From a Sourdough's Pot

Sourdough bread has long been a symbol of San Francisco since Isadore Boudin opened his North Beach bakery in 1849. The bread's tangy taste comes from a special yeast starter, though some claim that San Francisco's air gives the yeast a characteristic flavor that cannot be exported. The Acme Bread Company in Berkeley produces 30,000 sourdough baguettes a week.

Sourdough Pancakes

These pancakes, which are lighter than air, were the mainstay of the forty-niners' diet.

1 cup all-purpose flour, unsifted	½ teaspoon baking soda
2 tablespoons sugar	1 egg, beaten
1½ teaspoons baking powder	1 cup Sourdough Starter (see page 56)
½ teaspoon salt	½ cup milk
	2 tablespoons cooking oil

In a bowl combine flour, sugar, baking powder, salt, and baking soda. Combine egg, Sourdough Starter, milk, and oil. Stir into the flour mixture until well combined. Using 2 tablespoonfuls of batter for each pancake, bake on a hot, lightly greased griddle until golden brown, turning once. Makes about 28 pancakes.

San Francisco à la Carte

Crusty Water Rolls

5 tablespoons yeast	16 cups flour, divided
5 tablespoons sugar	⅔ cup oil
2 tablespoons salt	10 egg whites, beaten until
5 cups hot water (120°)	fairly stiff

Mix first 4 ingredients and let set for 5–10 minutes. Add 8 cups flour, oil, and egg whites; stir. Add about 8 more cups flour and mix on dough hook of mixer until dough comes away from sides of bowl. Turn into greased bowl and refrigerate 6 hours or overnight (or allow to rise and make rolls right away). Punch down. Break into smallish balls. Place on greased cookie sheet. Let rise again. Bake about 10–12 minutes in 350° oven. Makes 100 rolls.

Note: Can be divided. After baking, brush with garlic and dill-flavored melted butter.

The Steinbeck House Cookbook

Seed Bread

This bread has been shared at the Easter sunrise gathering at Bodega Pastures since 1981.

3 cups whole-wheat flour
3 cups all-purpose flour
1/2 cup brown sugar
4 teaspoons baking powder
1 teaspoon salt
1 teaspoon baking soda

1 cup poppy seeds
1 cup sesame seeds
1 cup shelled sunflower seeds
1/4 cup butter
2 eggs
2 2/3 cups milk

Stir flours, brown sugar, baking powder, salt, baking soda, and seeds together in a large bowl. Cut the butter in with two knives or a fork until the mixture resembles coarse meal. Stir in the eggs and milk and mix just until the mixture is absorbed. Turn the dough onto a floured surface and knead gently 10 times until smooth. Divide in two and shape each half into a ball. Place each in separate greased 8-inch round cake pans and brush with milk. With a sharp knife, cut a cross in the dough. Bake in 375° oven for 1 hour and 10 minutes. Cool before serving. Makes two 8-inch round loaves.

The Potluck Cookbook

Garlic Clove Bread

2 loaves frozen white bread dough, thawed
1/3 cup butter, melted and cooled to lukewarm

1/4 teaspoon basil
2 tablespoons chopped parsley
1 small onion, chopped
5 cloves fresh garlic, minced

Cut or snip off pieces of dough about the size of an English walnut. Place into a greased 10-inch Bundt pan. Combine the melted butter, basil, chopped parsley, onion, and minced garlic. Pour over dough. Cover and let rise until double in size (about 1 1/2 hours). Bake in 375° oven until golden brown (about 30–35 minutes). Cool in pan for 10 minutes and then remove from pan and serve.

The Complete Garlic Lovers' Cookbook

Skillet Sun-Dried Tomato & Cheddar Bread

2 cups yellow cornmeal
2 cups all-purpose flour
1/4 cup granulated sugar
2 tablespoons baking powder
1 jalapeño, seeded, finely diced
1 cup Cheddar cheese, grated

1/2 cup sun-dried tomatoes, chopped, drained of oil
2 eggs
2 cups milk
2/3 cup peanut oil

Combine all dry ingredients in a medium mixing bowl. Stir in jalapeño, Cheddar, and chopped tomato.

In a separate bowl, whisk together eggs and milk in the peanut oil. Lightly oil and heat an 8-inch cast-iron skillet until very hot. Pour in batter and bake at 400° for approximately 40 minutes. If using an 8-inch baking pan, add additional 20 minutes to the cooking time. Yields 8–10 servings.

The Great Vegetarian Cookbook

Breakfast Bundt Cake

1/4 cup chopped nuts
1 package yellow cake mix
1 package instant vanilla pudding
3/4 cup oil
3/4 cup water

4 eggs
1 teaspoon vanilla
1 teaspoon butter extract
2 teaspoons cinnamon
1/4 cup sugar

GLAZE:
1 cup confectioners' sugar
1/2 teaspoon vanilla
1/2 teaspoon butter extract

1 tablespoon plus 1/2 teaspoon milk

Grease and flour Bundt pan; sprinkle nuts in bottom. Combine cake mix, pudding, oil, and water, and mix well. Add eggs, one at a time, and mix well. Add vanilla and butter extract. Beat at high speed for 8 minutes. Pour 1/3 of batter into pan; sprinkle with half mixture of cinnamon and sugar. Add another 1/3 batter and sprinkle again. Add rest of batter. Bake 40–45 minutes at 350°. Cool and remove from pan. Mix Glaze ingredients till smooth. Drizzle with Glaze while still warm.

Watsonville Community Hospital 40th Anniversary Edition

Aunt Pam's Monkey Bread

4 tubes Pillsbury Buttermilk
   Biscuits
1⅓ cups sugar, divided

2 teaspoons cinnamon, divided
1 stick butter
1 teaspoon vanilla

Quarter biscuits. Mix ⅔ cup sugar and 1 teaspoon cinnamon. Shake 4–6 pieces of dough at a time in mix. Remove and drop into buttered tube pan until all used up. Melt butter; add ⅔ cup sugar, 1 teaspoon cinnamon, and vanilla. Boil. Pour syrup over biscuits. Bake at 350° for 40 minutes. Invert immediately.

Nuggets, Nibbles and Nostalgia

Pumpkin Bread

1 cup oil
¾ cup water
4 eggs
1 teaspoon vanilla
2 cups pumpkin
3 cups flour
3 cups sugar

2 teaspoons baking soda
1 teaspoon salt
1½ teaspoons nutmeg
1½ cups raisins (preferably
   white)
1 cup chopped nuts

Grease and flour 3 (1-pound) coffee cans well. Mix liquids, eggs, vanilla, and pumpkin. Add dry ingredients, raisins, and nuts. Mix just until well blended. Fill cans a little over ½ full. Bake at 350° for 60 minutes, or until pick comes out clean.

Cooking Treasures of the Central Coast

Mendocino Streusel Coffeecake

If you're looking for a light coffeecake with, as professional bakers would say, just the right "crumb," this is it. From Margaret Fox of Mendocino's Café Beaujolais, named more than once the best place to eat breakfast in California.

STREUSEL:

¾ cup packed brown sugar
1 tablespoon ground cinnamon
2 tablespoons fine instant coffee
  powder

3 tablespoons cocoa powder
1 cup finely chopped walnuts

Stir brown sugar with cinnamon, coffee powder, cocoa, and walnuts; set aside.

COFFEECAKE:

2¾ cups all-purpose flour
1½ teaspoons baking powder
1½ teaspoons baking soda
½ teaspoon salt
12 tablespoons (1½ sticks) butter,
  room temperature

2 teaspoons vanilla extract
1½ cups granulated sugar
3 eggs
1 pint sour cream
Confectioners' sugar

Heat oven to 375°. Have ready a buttered and floured 10-inch Bundt pan, or coat it with a nonstick cooking spray. Stir flour with baking powder, baking soda, and salt; set aside. Beat butter with an electric mixer until light and fluffy. Add vanilla and sugar; beat mixture 3 minutes. Add eggs and beat at high speed 5 minutes, until mixture is light and creamy. Alternately add flour mixture in 3 additions, using lowest speed of mixer, and sour cream in 2 additions, beating only until smooth after each addition.

Spread a thin layer of batter in bottom of prepared pan. Sprinkle with ⅓ of Streusel mixture. Continue making these layers until there are 4 of batter and 3 of Streusel. The top layer should be batter and it should be thin. Bake coffeecake until a toothpick inserted in center comes out clean, about 1 hour. Take it out of oven to a rack and let cool 5 minutes in pan. Turn cake out of pan and sprinkle with sifted confectioners' sugar before serving. Yields 12–16 servings.

Jan Townsend Going Home

Pineapple-Zucchini Bread

3 eggs
1 cup oil
1¾ cups sugar
2 teaspoons vanilla extract
2 cups grated zucchini
3 cups flour
1 teaspoon baking powder

2 teaspoons baking soda
2 teaspoons cinnamon
¾ teaspoon nutmeg
1 teaspoon salt
1 cup chopped walnuts
1 cup drained crushed pineapple

Beat eggs in mixer bowl until light and foamy. Add oil, sugar, and vanilla; mix well. Mix in zucchini. Add flour, baking powder, baking soda, cinnamon, nutmeg, and salt; mix well. Stir in walnuts and pineapple. Spoon into 2 greased 9x5-inch loaf pans. Bake at 350° for 1 hour. Remove to wire rack to cool. Yields 24 servings.

California Gold

Cranberry Banana Bread

2 cups sifted flour
1 teaspoon baking soda
1 teaspoon salt
1¼ cups sugar
1 egg, beaten
⅓ cup orange juice
1 teaspoon grated orange rind

2 tablespoons white vinegar
¼ cup salad oil
⅔ cup mashed ripe bananas
1¼ cups fresh cranberries, cut in
  halves
1 cup chopped walnuts

Into mixing bowl, sift together dry ingredients. Combine egg, orange juice, rind, vinegar, and salad oil. Add all at once to flour mixture, stirring just until all flour is moistened. Fold in mashed bananas, cranberries, and nuts. Pour into greased loaf pan. Bake in 350° oven for 60–70 minutes.

Durham's Favorite Recipes

Banana Nut Mini-Chocolate Chip Bread

1/2 cup butter, softened
1 cup sugar
2 eggs
2 tablespoons milk
2 cups flour
1 teaspoon baking soda, dissolved in
   1/4 cup hot water
2 cups ripe bananas
1/2 cup mini-chocolate chips
1/2 cup chopped walnuts or
   pecans
1/4 cup ground nuts

Cream butter in a large bowl; add sugar and cream well. Add eggs and milk; mix well. Alternately add flour and soda water; mix well. Mash bananas and fold into mixture with wooden spoon. Fold in mini-chocolate chips and 1/2 cup chopped nuts. Pour batter into greased and floured 9x5x3-inch pan. Sprinkle top of loaf with 1/4 cup ground nuts. Bake in 350° oven about 1 hour, testing for doneness after 50 minutes. Cool in pan for 10 minutes; remove to rack.

For muffins, pour batter into muffin tins (about 2/3 full) that have been greased and floured. Sprinkle with ground nuts. Bake for 25–30 minutes or until muffins test done.

Fair's Fare

Peanut Butter Bread

2 cups all-purpose flour
2 teaspoons baking powder
3/4 teaspoon salt
2/3 cup smooth peanut butter
2/3 cup packed brown sugar
1 teaspoon vanilla
1 1/2 cups milk

Combine flour, baking powder, and salt. Beat together peanut butter, brown sugar, and vanilla. Gradually add milk, beating until smooth; add to flour mixture, blending until dry ingredients are moistened. Pour into greased 8 1/2 x4 1/2 x2 1/2-inch loaf pan. Bake at 350° for 60–65 minutes or until tests done. Cool on wire rack 10 minutes. Remove from pan. Cool thoroughly. Wrap loosely and refrigerate or store in bread keeper one day before slicing. For sandwiches, spread with softened cream cheese and/or jelly.

The Stirling City Hotel Favorite Recipes

Carmen Kozlowski's Raspberry Bread

This was made in Carmen's Kitchen with Julia Child during a segment of "Good Morning America."

1 cup butter, softened	1 teaspoon cream of tartar
1 cup sugar	1 teaspoon baking soda
1 teaspoon vanilla	½ cup buttermilk
4 eggs	1 cup Kozlowski Farms Red
3 cups flour	Raspberry Jam
½ teaspoon salt	

Cream butter, sugar, and vanilla together. Add eggs, one at a time, beating well after each addition. Mix the dry ingredients and add alternately with the buttermilk. Marble in the raspberry jam. Pour into 2 greased and floured loaf pans. Bake at 325° for 40 minutes or until done. (Bread should spring back when touched lightly in the center.)

Sonoma County...its bounty
Recipe from Kozlowski Farms

Cran-Apple Spice Muffins

2 cups all-purpose flour	⅓ cup oil
½ cup sugar	1 egg
1 teaspoon baking soda	1 cup coarsely chopped fresh or
1 teaspoon cinnamon	frozen cranberries (do not thaw if
½ teaspoon salt	frozen)
1 cup unsweetened applesauce	½ cup chopped pecans

Preheat oven to 350°. Grease bottoms only of 12 muffin cups, or line with paper baking cups. In a large bowl, combine flour, sugar, soda, cinnamon, and salt. In a small bowl combine applesauce, oil, and egg; blend well. Add to dry ingredients; stir just until dry ingredients are moistened. Stir in cranberries and pecans.

Divide batter evenly in greased muffin cups. Bake at 350° for 25–30 minutes, or until a toothpick inserted in center comes out clean. Cool 2 minutes and remove from pan. Makes 12 muffins.

An Apple a Day

Raspberry Muffins

"The room, the fire, the town... everything was great! But could we have a dozen muffins to go, please?"

2½ cups flour
¼ cup sugar
¼ cup packed brown sugar
1 tablespoon plus 1 teaspoon
   baking powder
½ teaspoon cinnamon

2 eggs, slightly beaten
1 cup milk
½ cup butter or margarine, melted
1 tablespoon flour
6 ounces raspberries, fresh or
   frozen

TOPPING:
½ cup walnuts, chopped
1 cup packed brown sugar
½ cup flour

1 tablespoon grated orange peel
1 tablespoon cinnamon

In a large bowl, mix together flour, sugar, brown sugar, baking powder, and cinnamon. In another bowl, combine eggs, milk, and margarine or butter. Add to dry ingredients and stir until just blended, being careful not to over-mix. Coat raspberries with a small amount of flour and fold into batter. Spoon into muffin tins. Combine Topping ingredients and top each muffin with 1 teaspoon of the mixture. Bake for 20–25 minutes, until tester comes clean.

Mendocino Mornings

Cherry Pink Affairs

These romantic pink-tinged muffins are more meaningful than a box of candy, and express love in the tenderest way possible; your sweetheart can't fail to get the right message. Delicious romance!

1¾ cups bleached all-purpose flour
2 teaspoons baking powder
½ teaspoon salt
⅓ cup granulated sugar
1 (9-ounce) jar maraschino
  cherries (reserve juice)

1 large egg
¼ cup nonfat skim milk
¼ cup (½ stick) melted butter or
  soy margarine
Frosting (optional), see below

Line muffin wells with pink and white paper cases (or for a charming touch, use heart-shaped muffin pans).

Sift together the dry ingredients in a 2½-quart mixing bowl; stir to blend and make a well in center.

Drain cherries, reserving juice. Finely chop and measure cherries (should be ¾ cup).

In a 1½-quart bowl, whisk egg, ½ cup reserved cherry juice, milk and melted butter. Pour egg mixture into dry ingredients and stir until just moistened. Gently fold in chopped cherries. Spoon batter into prepared muffin wells.

Bake in a preheated oven at 400° for 15–20 minutes until muffins are delicately brown, and a test toothpick comes out clean. Serve warm with love. Makes about 12 (2½-inch) muffins.

FROSTING:

For the lover with a sweet tooth, cool muffins for a few minutes, then coat tops with a simple frosting as follows: ½ cup confectioners' sugar blended with remaining maraschino cherry juice and a drop or two of almond extract. Beat until smooth.

Muffin Magic...and More

Banana Pumpkin Muffins

2 ripe, medium bananas
1/2 cup canned pumpkin
1/2 cup sugar
1/4 cup low-fat milk
1/4 cup oil

1 egg
1¾ cups all-purpose flour
2 teaspoons baking powder
1 teaspoon pumpkin pie spice
1/2 teaspoon salt

Preheat oven 375°. Prepare 12-muffin pan by lining with paper or coating with nonstick cooking spray. Mash bananas, then mix with pumpkin, sugar, milk, oil, and egg until well blended. In a separate mixing bowl, combine flour, baking powder, pumpkin pie spice, and salt. Stir banana mixture into flour mixture until evenly moistened. Spoon evenly into muffin cups. Bake in oven for 20 minutes. Cool before serving.

Nutritional Analysis Per Serving: Cal 169; Fat 5.39gm; Chol 16mg; Sod 156mg.

Taste California

Alegra's Six Week Muffins

These are the best bran muffins I have ever tasted.

1 (15-ounce) box Raisin Bran
3 cups sugar
5 cups flour
5 teaspoons baking soda

2 teaspoons salt
4 eggs, beaten
1 cup oil
1 quart buttermilk

In a very large bowl, mix Raisin Bran, sugar, flour, baking soda, and salt. Add eggs, oil, and buttermilk. This batter will keep up to six weeks in the refrigerator. As you are ready to use it, fill muffin tins 2/3 full and bake at 400° for 15–20 minutes depending on tin size. Yields 4–5 dozen.

The Lazy Gourmet

Bran Muffins

1 ½ cups sugar
½ cup oil
2 eggs, beaten
2 cups buttermilk
2 ½ cups flour, sifted
2 ½ teaspoons baking soda
½ teaspoon salt
2 cups All-Bran
1 cup boiling water
1 cup raisins
¼ cup chopped dates
1 cup chopped pecans

Combine sugar, oil, eggs, and buttermilk in bowl; mix well. Sift in flour, baking soda, and salt; mix well. Mix in cereal. Stir in boiling water, raisins, dates, and pecans. Chill, covered, overnight. Stir batter; spoon into greased muffin cups. Bake at 400° for 20–25 minutes or until golden brown. Yields 18 servings.

California Gold

Grebbles
(German Donuts)

1 cup sour cream
1 cup buttermilk
3 eggs
1 teaspoon salt
1 teaspoon baking soda
¼ cup granulated sugar
2 teaspoons baking powder
4 ½ cups flour
Powdered sugar

Mix all ingredients except powdered sugar into a soft dough and refrigerate. Roll dough as you would donuts. Cut in squares, cutting 2 slits in center. Twist and fry in hot oil at 350° until browned. Roll in powdered sugar and serve, preferably warm. Makes about 30–40 donuts.

Heavenly Creations

Apple Nut Hot Cakes

Vegetable oil
1 cup all-purpose flour
2 tablespoons sugar
2 teaspoons baking powder
½ teaspoon salt
½ teaspoon cinnamon
¾ cup milk

3 tablespoons margarine or butter, melted
2 teaspoons vanilla
2 egg whites
½ cup shredded apple
½ cup chopped walnuts

Heat skillet or griddle to 375°. Grease lightly with oil. Lightly spoon flour into measuring cup; level off. In large bowl, combine flour, sugar, baking powder, salt, and cinnamon; blend well. Stir in milk, margarine, and vanilla. In small bowl, beat egg whites until stiff peaks form. Fold into flour mixture with apple and walnuts.

To form pancakes, pour about ¼ cup batter onto hot skillet. Cook 1½–2 minutes or until golden brown. Serve with margarine and warm syrup. Makes 10–12 (4-inch) pancakes.

An Apple a Day

Cottage Pancakes

These pancakes are very light.

3 eggs, separated
1 whole egg
1 cup cottage cheese, small curd (or ricotta cheese)

¼ cup flour
¼ teaspoon salt
1 apple, grated
Margarine or butter for frying

Beat 3 egg whites until stiff; set aside. Place whole egg and egg yolks in bowl with cottage cheese, flour, salt, and apple. Blend well. Fold in egg whites. Heat butter or margarine in skillet. Drop batter by tablespoonfuls into skillet and fry until golden brown. Turn only once.

Apples Etc. Cookbook

There are seven mountain peaks in California above 14,000 feet. They are called "fourteeners," the highest of which is Mt. Whitney.

Sweet Potato and Pecan Waffles with Cranberry Butter

CRANBERRY BUTTER:

½ cup fresh or frozen cranberries (thawed)

¼ cup maple syrup

1 cup unsalted butter, at room temperature

In a small saucepan, combine cranberries and maple syrup. Over low heat, cook mixture, stirring frequently, 5 minutes, or until cranberries have popped and softened. Allow cranberries to cool, then transfer to bowl of electric mixer; add butter. Mix at low speed until well combined, but not so long that butter becomes uniformly pink. You should still be able to see little bits of the cranberry skin in butter. Transfer to an attractive serving bowl, cover with plastic wrap, and refrigerate until needed.

WAFFLES:

1 small red yam or sweet potato

1 tablespoon vegetable oil

1 cup all-purpose flour

1 tablespoon firmly packed brown sugar

1 teaspoon baking powder

¼ teaspoon salt

1¼ cups milk

1 large egg

1½ tablespoons unsalted butter, melted

⅓ cup coarsely chopped pecans

Preheat oven to 350°. Rub outside of yam with vegetable oil, prick with fork, and place on baking sheet in oven. Bake until very tender, about 1 hour, then cool on a rack. When yam is cool enough to handle, scoop out flesh and discard skin. Set aside ⅔ cup of flesh and reserve rest for another use. Mash sweet potato with a fork until very smooth. Lower oven temperature to warm (200°).

In large mixing bowl, combine flour, brown sugar, baking powder and salt; blend well. In separate mixing bowl, whisk together milk, egg and butter. Stir milk mixture and sweet potato purée into dry ingredients (don't worry if there are a few lumps; it's better not to over-blend). Fold in chopped pecans.

Heat a waffle iron until very hot, then pour in amount of waffle batter recommended by manufacturer. Immediately close cover and cook until done, according to manufacturer's instructions. Keep warm in low oven as you cook remaining waffles. Using large end of fruit baller, scoop out ball of cranberry butter and place on top of each waffle. Serve immediately. Yields about 8 waffles.

Röckenwagner

Berry Stuffed French Toast— San Francisco Style

Is this French toast or a bread pudding? This dish is so rich, yet light, we think it may even be an improvement on bread pudding. Note that like a bread pudding, the longer it is allowed to soak before baking, the fuller the flavor.

12 slices San Francisco sourdough bread	**10 eggs**
8 ounces low-fat cream cheese	**1/3 cup maple syrup**
1 cup berries, your choice, fresh or frozen	**2 cups low-fat milk**

Remove crusts from bread and cut into cubes. Oil a 9x13-inch baking dish. Spread half of bread cubes over bottom of pan. Cut cream cheese into cubes and distribute over bread layer. Spread berries over cream cheese. Place remaining bread cubes over top.

Beat eggs, maple syrup and milk together well. Pour over bread. Cover with foil and refrigerate overnight. Press down on foil to make sure all bread is soaked.

In the morning, preheat oven to 350°. Bake, covered with foil, 30 minutes, then remove foil and bake an additional 30 minutes until center is set and top is lightly browned. Let stand 10 minutes before slicing. Serve with Berry Sauce.

BERRY SAUCE:

1 cup water	**1 cup berries, fresh or frozen**
1 cup sugar	**1 tablespoon butter**
2 tablespoons cornstarch	

Stir water, sugar, cornstarch, and berries over medium heat until thickened. Add butter and stir until melted. Pour over individual pieces of French toast with a twist of lemon for decoration. Serves 6.

Mendocino Mornings

San Francisco had a population of fewer than 1,000 residents when James Marshall discovered gold at Sutter's Mill in January 1848. By the decade's end, it had burgeoned to 50,000; by comparison, it took New York City 190 years to reach that size. Though the gold rush ended in 1864, today California is second only to Nevada in gold production. Gold is the official state mineral of California.

French Toast Soufflé

16 slices French bread, pre-sliced
16 ounces cream cheese, cubed
12 eggs

2 cups milk
½ cup pure maple syrup
Warm maple syrup for serving

Remove crust and cube bread. In a 9x13-inch pan, layer ½ bread, cream cheese, then the remaining bread. In a bowl, beat eggs. Add milk, pure maple syrup, and mix well. Pour over all layered ingredients. Cover with plastic wrap and refrigerate overnight.

Preheat oven to 375°. Bake uncovered for 45 minutes. Cut into squares and serve with warm maple syrup. Serves 8.

The Lafayette Collection

Breakfast Casserole

12 slices bread, cubed
1 pound pork sausage, cooked,
   drained
¼ pound sharp Cheddar cheese,
   grated
6 eggs
Salt and pepper to taste

1 teaspoon mustard
2½ cups milk
1 can golden mushroom soup
1 small can condensed milk
1 (4-ounce) can mushrooms,
   drained

Butter a 9x13-inch casserole. Put bread in casserole; cover with sausage, then with cheese. Beat eggs with salt, pepper, mustard, and milk. Pour over all. Cover and refrigerate overnight. In the morning or before serving, mix soup, condensed milk, and mushrooms. Pour over all. Bake 1 hour at 350°. Serves 6–8.

New Covenant Kitchens

English Muffin Breakfast Casserole

1 pound hot pork sausage	2 teaspoons prepared mustard
3 English muffins, cut in halves	1/2 teaspoon salt
8 eggs	1/4 teaspoon black pepper
2 1/2 cups milk	2 cups grated sharp Cheddar
2 tablespoons chopped onions	cheese, divided
2 tablespoons chopped green pepper	

Brown, drain, cool, and crumble pork sausage. Place muffins, split-side-down, in a 9x13-inch buttered glass baking dish. In another bowl, whisk together eggs, milk, onions, green pepper, mustard, salt, and pepper until well mixed. Fold into the egg mixture the crumbled sausage and 1/2 cup of the grated cheese. Pour the egg mixture over the muffins. (The muffins will be floating.) Cover and refrigerate overnight (at least 12 hours).

To bake, preheat oven to 325°. Remove the casserole from the refrigerator, top with the remaining cheese, and bake for 55–65 minutes. The casserole will be set when done. Serve hot. Serves 6–8.

San Ramon's Secret Recipes

Festive Egg Squares

This is our favorite Christmas morning meal. I serve it with muffins and juice. Enjoy!

1 pound bulk pork sausage, cooked and drained (or diced ham)	1 1/4 cups buttermilk baking mix
4 ounces sliced mushrooms	12 eggs
1/2 cup sliced green onions, with tops	1 cup milk
2 medium chopped tomatoes	1 1/2 teaspoons salt
2 cups shredded mozzarella cheese (about 8 ounces)	1/2 teaspoon pepper
	1/2 teaspoon dried oregano

Layer sausage (or ham), mushrooms, green onions, tomatoes, and cheese in greased 9x13x2-inch baking dish. Beat remaining ingredients; pour over sausage mixture. Cook, uncovered, in 350° oven until golden brown and set, about 30 minutes. Cut into 12 (3-inch) squares.

50th Anniversary Cookbook

San Francisco–Style Eggs Benedict

In this rendition of Eggs Benedict, poached eggs top fresh asparagus and a pancetta waffle. However, tradition isn't totally abandoned. Lemon hollandaise smothers it all. (Look for Meyer lemons to enhance the sauce further.)

PANCETTA WAFFLES:

4 slices pancetta or bacon, cut into 1-inch pieces
1 cup cake flour
1 teaspoon baking powder
1/2 teaspoon salt
1 cup heavy cream
2 eggs at room temperature

In small skillet, cook pancetta or bacon over medium-high heat until lightly browned. Using a slotted spoon, transfer to paper towels to drain. Preheat waffle iron. In blender or food processor, combine flour, baking powder, and salt. Pulse quickly to blend. Add pancetta or bacon, cream, and eggs and process 6 seconds. Scrape sides of container. Pulse 3 seconds to fully mix. Pour 1/2 cup of batter onto hot waffle iron and cook about 5 minutes, or until golden brown. Keep warm in low oven. Repeat to cook remaining batter. (To make ahead, let waffles cool, then wrap in plastic wrap, place in a freezer bag, and freeze. To thaw, place in toaster or 350° oven and cook until heated through.)

HOLLANDAISE SAUCE:

3 egg yolks at room temperature*
Salt and ground white pepper to taste
1 1/2 cups (3 sticks) unsalted butter
2 teaspoons grated lemon zest
2 tablespoons fresh lemon juice
1 tablespoon snipped fresh chives

In blender or food processor, combine egg yolks, salt and pepper, and process 10 seconds. In small saucepan, melt butter until it foams. With the machine running, pour melted butter in a thin stream into blender or processor. Add zest and lemon juice and pulse to incorporate. Pour sauce into a bowl and place over pan filled with 2 inches of hot water to keep sauce warm. Stir in chives just before serving. (You can also keep the hollandaise warm in a Thermos.)

12 asparagus stalks, trimmed
1 tablespoon Chardonnay or white wine vinegar
8 eggs

Cook the asparagus in skillet of salted boiling water 3 minutes, or until easily pierced with a knife. Drain and reserve. Bring a large skillet of water to boil. Add vinegar and reduce heat to a simmer. Break eggs, one at a time, into a saucer and slice into water. With

(continued)

(continued)

a spoon, gently bring egg white over center of each yolk to keep whites intact. Cook 4 minutes for soft-centered yolks. With slotted spoon, transfer eggs to a clean dish towel. (To make eggs ahead of time: Cook eggs for 3 minutes. Place in bowl of ice water to stop cooking. Before serving, cook poached eggs in simmering water 1 minute to reheat.)

To serve, place a hot waffle on each of 4 warm plates and top with 3 asparagus stalks, 1 poached egg, and some hollandaise. Serves 4.

Hint: Chef Thomas Keller, The French Laundry Restaurant, says add a few tablespoons of white vinegar to the poaching water. The vinegar will keep the egg whites from falling apart in the water and keep the egg whole. You won't be able to taste the vinegar.

San Francisco Flavors

*For those people concerned about raw eggs, pasteurized liquid eggs or pasteurized liquid egg whites can usually be successfully substituted.

Mexican Breakfast Bake

1 pound ground beef or turkey
¼ cup diced green bell peppers
¼ cup diced red bell peppers
1 cup canned chili (no beans)
½ cup grated Monterey Jack
 cheese
½ cup grated Swiss cheese

2 tablespoons plain yogurt
4 tablespoons sour cream (low-fat
 or non-fat)
2 cups biscuit baking mix
2 eggs, beaten
¾ cup milk
Parmesan cheese

Brown ground meat. Add bell peppers, chili, grated cheeses, yogurt, and sour cream. Mix thoroughly. In bowl, mix together the biscuit mix, eggs, and milk. Spread half on bottom of greased 9x13-inch pan. Spread meat mixture over, then top with rest of batter. Sprinkle with Parmesan cheese, and bake at 400° about 25 minutes. Serves 6–8.

On the Road Again Cookbook

Mark Twain once wrote, "The coldest winter I ever spent was a summer in San Francisco."

Frittata with Dijon–Hollandaise Sauce

This delicious frittata will ruin you for "regular" omelets forever!

FRITTATA:

1 (8-ounce) package cream cheese, softened
½ cup flour
1 dozen eggs
1 red onion
5 cloves garlic
3 zucchini
4 chanterelle mushrooms
1 yellow sweet pepper
¼ cup fresh basil leaves, chopped and loosely packed
¼ pound Swiss cheese, grated
¾ teaspoon salt
¼ teaspoon white pepper

Grease a 12-inch tart pan with removable bottom. Preheat the oven to 300°. Whip together cream cheese, flour, and 4 eggs. Set aside. Chop finely, process, or grate: red onion, garlic, zucchini, chanterelle mushrooms, yellow sweet pepper, and fresh basil leaves. Place mixture into a cloth napkin and squeeze out all excess moisture. Then place mixture into large mixing bowl. To the cream cheese mixture, add 8 more eggs, the grated Swiss cheese, salt, and white pepper. Whip together well. Add cheese-and-eggs mixture to mixing bowl of chopped vegetables. Blend well. Pour batter into the prepared pan. Bake at 300° for 1 hour. Just before the Frittata comes out of the oven, prepare the sauce.

DIJON-HOLLANDAISE SAUCE:

3 egg yolks
Juice of ½ lemon
¼ teaspoon salt
2 dashes white pepper
1 dash cayenne pepper
½ stick unsalted butter, softened
2 tablespoons coarse-grain Dijon mustard

In a double boiler, whip egg yolks and lemon juice until mixture has a custard-like consistency. Add salt, white pepper, and cayenne pepper. In a separate pan, melt butter, then add it very slowly, a few drops at a time, to the egg yolk mixture, whipping constantly. Add mustard and blend well. Top Frittata with Dijon Hollansaise Sauce. Serves 6.

Carter House Cookbook

Kitchen Garden Bread

Prepare at least 8 hours before baking.

1 round loaf bake-and-serve
   sourdough bread
2 medium yellow onions, sliced
   very thin
1/2 pound mushrooms, sliced
   very thin
1 tablespoon brown sugar
Salt to taste

1 1/2 cups fresh herbs and
   vegetables (green onions, broccoli)
1 (8-ounce) package cream cheese
1/2 cup grated Cheddar cheese
1/2 pound hot Pepper Jack cheese,
   grated
6 eggs, beaten
1 cup milk

Slice bread in half so that you have two rounds and scoop out most of soft center. Place rounds on greased cookie sheet.

Sauté onions and mushrooms (in small amount of oil or butter) until tender, adding the brown sugar and a little salt about halfway through. Set aside. Sauté herb and vegetable mix. Set aside.

Cut cream cheese into 1-inch cubes and distribute evenly over both bread halves and top with the onion/mushroom mixture. Sprinkle Cheddar cheese over the onion/mushroom mixture. Layer 1/2 of the herb/vegetable mix over the top, sprinkle on pepper Jack cheese, then top with remaining herb/vegetable mix.

Mix eggs and milk together with any extra herbs you like and pour evenly over bread. Cover and refrigerate overnight if possible, or for at least 8 hours.

The next day, bake uncovered at 375° for 35–45 minutes until nicely browned on top and center is set. Slice into wedges with a pizza cutter or large knife. Serve hot. Serves 16–20.

Mendocino Mornings

Lasagna Bread

½ pound sausage
½ pound hamburger
½ clove garlic, minced
1 tablespoon parsley flakes
½ teaspoon basil
½ teaspoon oregano
½ teaspoon salt
Dash pepper
¾ cup chopped onion

1 can tomato paste
1 cup creamed cottage cheese
1 egg
¼ cup grated Parmesan cheese
2 cans crescent rolls
2 (7 x 4-inch) mozzarella slices
1 tablespoon milk
1 tablespoon sesame seeds

Brown meats; add all seasonings, onion, and tomato paste. Simmer for 6 minutes. Mix cottage cheese, egg, and Parmesan cheese. On a large cookie sheet, press the crescent rolls into 15x13-inch rectangle. Spoon half of the meat mixture onto the middle of the dough, leaving a border on the sides and enough dough at the top and the bottom to enclose ingredients like an envelope. Follow meat mixture with cheese mixture, then the other half of the meat mixture, placing slices of mozzarella cheese last. Enclose ingredients, pressing dough together. Brush with milk and sprinkle sesame seeds. Bake at 375° for about 25 minutes or until crust is golden brown. Serves 6.

Feeding the Flock

Bruschetta
"The original garlic bread"

2 cloves garlic (1 minced, 1 cut)
3 Roma tomatoes, diced
Extra virgin olive oil (about ¾ cup)
Salt and pepper to taste

10 fresh basil leaves, finely
chopped
4 slices Tuscan country bread

Mix together minced garlic, tomatoes, olive oil, salt, pepper, and basil. Set aside. Grill both sides of the bread. Rub one side of the bread with a garlic clove. Then add tomato mixture. Grill again for 30 seconds. Garnish with basil leaf. Buon Appetito!

International Garlic Festival® Cookbook

Mahony's Bruschetta

An outstanding dish. Keep a bottle of olive oil in the refrigerator to which have been added four to five heads of peeled garlic. That way you'll have it ready for bruschetta; or add lemon juice for a salad dressing, to prepare oysters and linguine, or to add to pasta water for flavor and to prevent boilover.

1 loaf French or Italian bread without seeds (day-old bread works fine)
10 large cloves fresh garlic, peeled
¾ cup olive oil, preferably extra virgin
1½ cups whipping cream

½ cup grated Locatelli cheese (hard Romano cheese)
½ cup grated Parmesan cheese, preferably imported Italian
3 tablespoons butter
1 tablespoon chopped parsley
Paprika

Cut bread diagonally in 1-inch slices, without cutting through bottom crust.

In food processor or blender, chop garlic fine with steel blade and add olive oil with processor running to make a thin paste. Slather garlic paste on cut surfaces and on top and side crusts of bread.

Place in 350° oven, directly on rack (with pan on shelf below to catch drippings), and bake for 10–12 minutes, until top is crispy looking.

While bread is in oven, heat whipping cream in heavy saucepan. Do not boil. Stir in cheeses slowly so that sauce is absolutely smooth (a wire whip works well for this). Stir in butter and keep sauce warm until bread is ready.

Wait until everyone is seated at the table. Then place crispy bread in a warmed, shallow serving dish with sides. Finish cutting through bottom crust and pour sauce over. Sprinkle with parsley and paprika and serve immediately. This dish cools very quickly. Makes 6 servings.

Note: Each guest should be provided with a small saucer for the bruschetta, as it is best eaten with a knife and fork.

Garlic Lovers' Greatest Hits

Annie's House Sandwich

2 slices sourdough bread
Garlic Spread
Thousand Island Salad Dressing
½ avocado, mashed

4 ounces lean roast beef or turkey
  breast, sliced thin and warmed
2 ounces Jack cheese, grated
2 ounces Cheddar cheese, grated

Heat large skillet on medium heat. Cover outside of each piece of sourdough with Garlic Spread. Spread Thousand Island Dressing on inside of one slice and mashed avocado on the other. Place roast beef or turkey on the avocado side and top with cheeses. Place Thousand Island side of the bread on top of meat, and grill on both sides until cheese is melted and bread is lightly browned. Serves 1.

GARLIC SPREAD:

4 tablespoons margarine, room
  temperature

¼ teaspoon garlic powder
⅛ teaspoon dried parsley

THOUSAND ISLAND SALAD DRESSING:

4 tablespoons low-fat mayonnaise
½ teaspoon pickle relish

½ teaspoon ketchup

Incredible Edibles

Apricot Pepper Jelly

¼ cup jalapeño peppers, with
   stems and seeds removed
3 cups assorted bell peppers, cut
   into thin slices
2 cups apple cider vinegar

1½ cups dried apricots, cut into
   thin strips
6 cups sugar
1 teaspoon vegetable oil
1 pouch liquid pectin

Process jalapeño peppers in blender until fine. Combine bell peppers, vinegar, jalapeño peppers, dried apricots, and sugar in a large saucepan. Bring to a boil. Add oil to prevent foam from forming. Boil for 10 minutes. Remove from heat. Stir in pectin. Place in sterilized canning jars and process in boiling water bath for 10 minutes. Yields 6 half-pints.

Sounds Tasty!

Arlene's Spicy Baked Pears with Yogurt

This award-winning recipe makes a great breakfast starter, but is also a tasty dessert when served warm with a little vanilla ice cream or Crème Fraîche (page 332).

½ cup dark brown sugar
Cinnamon
Mace
Pinch of ground cloves
5 large ripe pears

¾ cup orange juice
¼ cup butter
Vanilla yogurt
Grated nutmeg

Preheat oven to 350°. Line bottom of 10x15-inch baking dish with the brown sugar. Sprinkle sugar layer generously with cinnamon, mace and pinch of cloves. Slice pears in half; remove cores and stems. Lay pears cut-side-down on sugar mixture. Pour orange juice over pears and top with butter. Bake for 15–20 minutes, or until pears are tender.

To serve, place each pear cut-side-down on a serving dish and pour some of the juice mixture over. Place a dollop of yogurt along side and top with freshly grated nutmeg. Serves 10.

Note: This recipe can be prepared in advance by combining all the ingredients except the orange juice. Pour over just before baking.

Mendocino Mornings

Apple Butter

6 pounds tart cooking apples, cored,
  quartered (18 cups)
5 cups apple cider or apple juice
1 cup cider vinegar

4 cups sugar
2 teaspoons ground cinnamon
1/2 teaspoon ground cloves
1/2 teaspoon ground allspice

In a large kettle, combine apples, apple cider or juice, and vinegar. Bring to a boil. Cover; simmer for 30 minutes, stirring occasionally. Press through a food mill or sieve. Return pulp to kettle. Stir in remaining ingredients. Bring to a boil. Simmer, uncovered, for 1 1/2 hours or until very thick, stirring often.

Spoon hot butter into clean jars, leaving 1/2 inch headspace. Wipe rims; adjust lids. Process in boiling water bath for 10 minutes for 1/2 pints or pints (start timing when water boils). Makes 8–10 half-pints.

An Apple a Day

Soups

Shown above at a souvenir shop in Los Angeles are some of the most famous street signs and city markers in the nation.

Chilled Avocado Soup

There are many versions of avocado soup in California, some served chilled, some hot. Some include cream, which I find eclipses the flavor of the avocado. To my palate, this creamy but creamless version, bright, tangy, and mildly spicy, with the edge of sweetness that avocados have, is the best.

2 tablespoons olive oil	3½ cups chicken stock
1 small yellow or white onion, minced	2 tablespoons fresh lime juice
3 serrano chiles, minced	3 tablespoons minced cilantro leaves
2 garlic cloves, minced	Kosher salt
3 ripe Haas avocados	Black pepper in a mill

Heat olive oil in a small skillet over medium heat; add onions and sauté until limp and fragrant, about 10 minutes. Add serranos, sauté 5 minutes, then add garlic and sauté 2 minutes more. Remove from heat and let cool slightly. Cut avocados in half and remove pits. Scoop out flesh and place in blender or food processor. Add half the stock and onion mixture, and purée. Transfer to a large container, stir in remaining stock, and refrigerate until soup is well chilled, at least 3 hours.

To serve, stir in lime juice and half the cilantro, season with salt and pepper, and ladle into chilled soup bowls. Sprinkle remaining cilantro over each portion and serve immediately. Serves 4–6.

Variations:

With Cherry Tomato Salsa: Cut 1 cup cherry tomatoes into quarters, and toss with 2 tablespoons minced onion, 1 minced serrano chile, juice of half of lime, and kosher salt and black pepper to taste. Spoon a little salsa over each portion of soup.

With Bay Shrimp: Toss 8 ounces cooked bay shrimp with juice of 1 lime and 1 tablespoon minced onion. Divide among chilled soup bowls and ladle soup on top.

With Bacon and Bleu Cheese: Fry 4 strips bacon until crisp, drain on absorbent paper, then crumble and scatter some over each serving of soup. Crumble 2 ounces of bleu cheese and scatter it over the soup.

California Home Cooking

 Avocados that make up so many Southwestern recipes were scarce until the 1920s when a mailman in southern California named Rudolph Haas figured out how to best grow them. Today, the most popular avocados in the U.S. are the "Haas" variety and come from California.

Chilled Zucchini Bisque

2 (10½-ounce) cans chicken broth,
  condensed or homemade
1 cup water
2 cups thinly sliced zucchini
¼ cup chopped onion
3 tablespoons rice
1 tablespoon curry powder

½ teaspoon ground ginger
½ teaspoon dry mustard
Salt and pepper to taste
1½ cups milk
Yogurt (optional)
Green onion, chopped

In 3-quart saucepan, combine broth, water, zucchini, onion, rice, curry powder, ginger, and mustard. Cover and simmer 20 minutes. Pour small amounts into blender and whirl until smooth. Season to taste. Allow to stand 6 hours or overnight.

Just before serving, add milk. May add a dollop of yogurt, if desired. Add a few green onions for color. Serve cold. Makes 6 servings.

Cook Book

Strawberry Soup

First-prize winner—Watsonville Strawberry Festival 1999.

4 cups strawberries
1 cup sugar
1 cup sour cream
4 cups cold water

1 cup Rosé wine
Oyster crackers
Whole strawberries for garnish

Put ¼ of each ingredient (except crackers) in blender. Blend. Repeat 3 times. Serve in soup bowl; garnish with whole strawberries. Serve with oyster crackers. May be served in glasses for appetizer or dessert. Serves 8.

Apples Etc. Cookbook

Cucumber Soup

This is one of my favorite summertime soups. It has a delicate flavor and works nicely as a first course.

3 large cucumbers
1 medium-size onion
3 tablespoons butter or
  margarine
3 tablespoons flour
3½ cups chicken broth

1 cup scalded milk
1–2 sprigs fresh mint
½ teaspoon dill weed
Salt to taste
½ cup sour cream

Peel cucumbers and slice in half lengthwise. Scrape seeds out of each half with a spoon, then cut cucumber halves into pieces. Peel onion and cut in half, also lengthwise. Lay each cut half flat on a board and slice thinly crosswise. Melt butter or margarine over low flame in a heavy pot. Sauté onion and cucumber until softened. Sprinkle on flour, stirring into cucumber-onion mixture, then pour in chicken broth. Scald milk and add along with a sprig or two of fresh mint, a sprinkling of dill weed, and salt. Cook over a low flame until cucumber is soft. Remove mint before putting mixture through a food mill, a sieve, or into a food processor. Chill in refrigerator several hours. Before serving, stir in sour cream. Serve with croutons and sprinkle with chopped chives. Serves 6.

Soups from A–Z

French Onion Soup

¼ cup butter
2 pounds yellow onions, thinly
  sliced
1½ quarts beef stock
Salt and papper

1 baguette French bread, sliced
  ¼ inch thick
Parmesan cheese
2 tablespoons butter to finish

In a large saucepan, melt butter and sauté onions until golden brown. In a medium stock pot, add onions to beef stock. Salt and pepper to taste. Bring to boil, reduce heat and simmer 10–15 minutes. To serve, put soup in preheated bowls, add slices of French bread, top with freshly grated Parmesan cheese and dot of butter. Place under broiler until bread is slightly brown and cheese is starting to melt. Serve immediately.

Great Chefs of Butte Valley

Cream of Broccoli Soup

Serve as a main dish on a winter's day, or as a side dish any time. Goes great with ham or game.

2 vegetable bouillon cubes
½ cup hot water
6 tablespoons melted butter
6 tablespoons flour
1 pint milk
1 pint half-and-half

1 bay leaf
1½ teaspoons herb salt
1 small jar Cheez Whiz
2 (10-ounce) packages frozen
    chopped broccoli, cooked

Dissolve bouillon cubes in water. Blend butter and flour in saucepan until smooth. Add milk and half-and-half gradually, stirring constantly. Cook over low heat until thickened; continue stirring. Add bouillon solution and remaining ingredients except broccoli, and cook, stirring constantly, until smooth. Stir in broccoli and heat through. Serves 4–6.

From a Sourdough's Pot

Butternut Squash Soup

1 tablespoon butter
1 medium onion, finely chopped
1 small clove garlic, minced
½ teaspoon curry powder
⅙ to ⅛ teaspoon dried red pepper
    or seeds (crushed)
2½ pounds butternut squash

3¾ cups chicken broth
1 cup water
¼ teaspoon nutmeg
1 tablespoon creamy peanut butter
1 teaspoon Worcestershire sauce
½ cup heavy cream

In a small skillet, melt butter and gently cook onion, garlic, curry powder, and red pepper until wilted (not brown). Peel and seed squash and cut into 1-inch cubes (for even cooking).

In a large pot, mix squash, broth, water and nutmeg. Bring to a boil. Add onion mixture and boil gently, covered, until squash is very tender. Remove from heat and stir in peanut butter and Worcestershire sauce.

Purée mixture in a blender, then add cream. Stir thoroughly. Reheat on low, if necessary. Serves 6–8.

Dining Door to Door in Naglee Park

Carrot Soup with Sorrel Sauce

It is a showy soup with contrasting orange and green colors.

4 large carrots
1 small potato
1 onion, chopped
1 chunk ginger, diced

1 tablespoon olive oil
1–2 tablespoons white miso (bean paste)

Cut carrots and potato into chunks; cover with water in a saucepan. Boil until tender. Meanwhile, sauté onion and ginger in olive oil. Put carrots, potatoes, onion mix, and miso into blender or Cuisinart with cooking water and purée. Serves 2.

SORREL SAUCE:
3 cloves garlic, chopped
Few drops olive oil
1–2 sprigs parsley

Scant tablespoon white miso
2 sorrel leaves

Put all ingredients into a blender, or mortar and pestle, and mix until smooth, adding a little water if needed. Spoon this green mixture onto the bright orange soup and serve.

The Fork Ran Away with the Spoon

Pumpkin Soup
with Bleu Cheese Cream and Chives

2 cups pumpkin, fresh or canned
1 yellow onion, sliced
2 tablespoons butter
3 cups chicken stock
Salt and pepper to taste

Nutmeg to taste
Sugar to taste (optional)
Bleu cheese, garnish
Chives, garnish

If using fresh pumpkin, cut pumpkin in half width-wise and remove seeds. Place on cookie sheet cut-side-down and bake at 325° for 30 minutes or until soft. Cool and spoon out pumpkin meat.

In a 2-quart pot, sauté onion in butter until soft and lightly browned. Add pumpkin and chicken stock to onion and bring to a boil, stirring constantly for 5 minutes. Purée in a blender until smooth. Adjust seasonings by adding stock if needed. Season to taste with salt, pepper, nutmeg and sugar. Serve warm, garnished with crumbled bleu cheese and snipped chives.

California Wine Country Cooking Secrets

Lentil Soup

2 cups dried lentils
2 quarts water
1 large yellow onion, chopped
2 carrots, sliced or coarsely grated
3 stalks celery, sliced
½ green pepper, diced
1 teaspoon minced garlic (or granulated garlic, not garlic salt)
¼ cup burgundy wine or sherry

2 large fresh tomatoes, diced, or 1 can tomato sauce or V-8 juice
1 tablespoon chopped parsley
2 tablespoons cooking oil or butter
1 teaspoon Italian seasoning (or poultry seasoning)
1 tablespoon tamari or soy sauce
1 teaspoon seasoned salt
2 teaspoons miso (soybean paste)

Rinse lentils; place in large kettle and add water. Add onion, carrots, celery, green pepper, garlic and wine. Bring to boil; cover and simmer until lentils are done (about 30 minutes to 1 hour).

Add all other ingredients except miso and simmer an additional 20–30 minutes. Just before serving, mix miso with a little soup broth; stir into soup. Serves 8.

Optional vegetables: Zucchini, crookneck squash, chopped cabbage or 1 to 2 small potatoes. Add more water, if needed. This soup will get quite thick.

Cooking Pure & Simple

Easy Split Pea Soup

1 tablespoon olive oil
1 large onion, chopped
3 cloves garlic, chopped
2 large carrots, chopped
1 stalk celery, chopped
2 cups dried split peas, picked
 over and rinsed
1 bay leaf

Large pinch dried thyme
1 meaty ham hock, or other
 smoked meat such as turkey, or
 1 smoked sausage, whole
8 cups water
Salt and pepper to taste, depending
 on meat used

In a large pot, heat olive oil and add onion, garlic, carrots, and celery. Sauté until vegetables begin to soften or sweat. Add remaining ingredients. Bring to a boil for 1 or 2 minutes, then turn to simmer, cover, and cook about 45 minutes to 1 hour or until peas are soft.

Remove ham hock, if using, or meat, and cut into small pieces. Remove bay leaf. Purée in a food processor or food mill, if desired, or leave soup chunky. Serve with croutons or a loaf of crusty bread and a salad. Makes about 8 cups.

The $5 Chef Family Cookbook

Split Pea and Yam Soup

9 cups soup stock or water
2 cups dry split peas
3 large yams, peeled and diced
2 potatoes, peeled and diced
3 ribs celery, diced
1 yellow onion, chopped, or 1
 tablespoon dried flakes

1 tablespoon garlic powder
1 teaspoon dill weed
1/2 teaspoon oregano
1/2 teaspoon thyme
2 bay leaves

Bring soup stock or water and split peas to a boil while preparing other ingredients. Add yams and potatoes, and simmer 30 minutes, stirring occasionally. Add celery, onion, and spices, and simmer until peas are tender (about 30 minutes). Remove bay leaves. (If a smooth texture is desired, blend in a food processor until smooth.) Serves 7.

Per serving: Cal 294; Prot 16gm; Fat 8gm; Linoleic Acid 3gm; Fiber 5.1gm; Calcium 71mg; Sod 40.1mg; Iron 3.3mg; Carotene 1068ug; Vit C 20mg; Vit E 2.5mg; Selenium .002mg; Zinc 2.1mg.

The Health Promoting Cookbook

Creamy Garlic Spinach Soup with Garlic Croutons

This soup has fabulous flavor, but be sure to serve it with the homemade garlic croutons.

1 large bunch spinach, stalks removed	½ cup butter (1 stick)
4 cups chicken broth (preferably homemade)	¼ cup flour
	½ cup light cream
2 large carrots, grated	½ cup whipping cream
1 large onion, chopped	Salt and freshly ground pepper to taste
8 cloves fresh garlic, finely chopped	Sour cream (optional)
	Garlic Croutons

Chop spinach coarsely. Combine with chicken broth and carrots in 2- to 3-quart pot. Cook 5–10 minutes until carrots are tender and spinach wilted. Remove from heat. Meanwhile, sauté onion and garlic very gently over low to medium heat in butter, about 20–30 minutes. Onion should be very tender and translucent, but garlic should not be browned! Add flour and cook, stirring constantly 5–10 minutes.

Combine spinach-broth and onion-garlic mixtures in food processor or blender in small batches. Purée until smooth. Clean pot and return soup to pot. Add cream, whipping cream, salt and freshly ground pepper to taste. Heat until hot, but not boiling. Garnish with a dollop of sour cream and Garlic Croutons. Makes 4 servings.

GARLIC CROUTONS:

¼ cup olive oil	Salt and pepper to taste
1 teaspoon garlic powder	1 loaf day-old sourdough French bread
1 teaspoon crushed dry parsley	
¾ teaspoon Hungarian paprika	

Combine olive oil, garlic powder, parsley, paprika, salt and pepper to taste. Cut bread into ½-inch cubes and work garlic-oil mixture into bread. Spread cubes in shallow baking pan and bake at 325° for about 25 minutes. Store in tightly covered container.

The Complete Garlic Lovers' Cookbook

 Ninety percent of the nation's garlic is processed in Gilroy.

Bean, Barley and Mushroom Soup

This hearty soup is a great favorite of ours. It's ethnic (Jewish) cooking from the Midwest—keeping the cold out and tummy-satisfying. Served with French or sourdough bread and a fresh salad, it makes a complete dinner.

1 cup dried lima beans, soaked
   overnight, rinsed and drained
4 tablespoons pearl barley,
   soaked and drained
2 large onions, chopped
2 ribs celery, chopped
1 medium carrot, chopped

2 tablespoons chopped fresh
   parsley
8 cups water
1/2 pound fresh mushrooms, sliced
1 1/2 teaspoons salt, or to taste
1/2 teaspoon freshly ground black
   pepper, or to taste

In a large soup pot, combine beans, barley, onions, celery, carrot, parsley, and water. Cover and cook over low heat about 2 1/2 hours or until beans are tender. Add mushrooms, salt and pepper. Cook for 10 minutes. Correct seasoning. Makes 5–6 servings.

Boutique Bean Pot

Garlic Soup

14 large cloves garlic, minced
2 tablespoons butter
2 tablespoons minced parsley
1 tablespoon flour

8 cups beef broth
1/4 teaspoon freshly ground
   pepper
6 egg yolks, beaten

In a heavy saucepan over low heat, brown garlic lightly in butter with minced parsley, stirring constantly so as not to burn. Add flour and stir until slightly browned. Add broth and pepper. Simmer at least 30 minutes to 1 hour. Just before serving, turn off heat and slowly add egg yolks, stirring constantly. Serve at once. Serves 6.

Sausalito: Cooking with a View

Garlic Mushroom Soup

20 cloves fresh garlic, peeled
1½ pounds fresh mushrooms, divided
4 tablespoons olive oil, divided
2 cups toasted bread crumbs
1 bunch fresh parsley, stems removed, finely chopped

10 cups chicken broth
Salt and pepper to taste
Dash hot pepper sauce
Dry sherry wine to taste (optional)

Finely chop garlic and 1 pound of the mushrooms. Cut remaining mushrooms into thin slices. In a 4-quart saucepan, heat 2 tablespoons of the olive oil and sauté garlic and mushrooms for 3 minutes. Remove from pan and set aside. Sauté bread crumbs in remaining oil. Add garlic and mushroom mixture to crumbs, stir in parsley and sauté for 5 minutes. Add broth and simmer, stirring frequently for 15 minutes. Season to taste with salt, pepper, hot pepper sauce, and dry sherry, if desired. Yields 8–10 servings.

Note: If a thicker soup is desired, stir in a few teaspoons of cornstarch dissolved in a little cold water and simmer for a few minutes until soup clears and thickens.

Celebrating California

Peanut Butter Carrot Soup

½ cup margarine
2 cups chopped carrots
½ cup chopped onion
½ cup chopped celery
3 tablespoons flour

2 quarts chicken stock
¼ teaspoon celery salt
1 cup creamy peanut butter
1 cup half-and-half

Melt margarine in large soup kettle. Add carrots, onion, and celery. Sauté until veggies are soft, but not brown. Stir in flour, mixing thoroughly. Add chicken stock and stir until soup comes to a boil and thickens slightly. Add celery salt and continue to cook on low heat for 20–30 minutes. Remove from heat. Add peanut butter and half-and-half to kettle, then pour contents into a blender and purée until all ingredients are well mixed. Return soup to kettle and heat thoroughly. Serves 4.

Incredible Edibles

Hangover Soup

I've been told that Hungarians say this soup will help cure a hangover. I can't vouch for that claim, but I think the soup is wonderful whether it has restorative powers or not. And who knows? Maybe it does.

4–5 pieces of thickly sliced bacon	1 clove garlic, crushed
1 large onion, peeled and chopped	1/2 pound smoked sausage,
1/2 cup orzo	sliced
2 teaspoons sweet Hungarian	Salt and pepper to taste
paprika	1 tablespoon flour
3 cups sauerkraut, drained, rinsed	3 tablespoons fresh chopped dill
and finely chopped	weed or 1 teaspoon dried
6 cups water	1/2 cup sour cream

Cut bacon into pieces, sauté until crisp, drain and reserve.

Discard all but 3 tablespoons bacon fat remaining in pan. Sauté onion in it until it has begun to soften and add the orzo, browning it with onion as you would rice for pilaf. When onion is tender, remove pan from heat and add sweet Hungarian paprika. Drain and rinse sauerkraut in a colander. Squeeze moisture out and chop rather finely. Add to onion mixture and stir until blended. Pour in 6 cups water, crushed garlic, sausage and salt and pepper to taste. Bring to boil, turn down heat, and cook slowly, covered, for half an hour. Stir flour and dill weed into sour cream. Add a little hot soup to equalize temperatures before stirring into soup pot. Cook slowly, stirring until thick and smooth. Add bacon, correct seasoning and serve. Serves 6.

Soups from A–Z

Crab and Rice Chowder

1 small onion, chopped	2 cups chicken broth
1/2 pound mushrooms, thinly sliced	2 cups milk
2 tablespoons salad oil	1 (17-ounce) can cream-style corn
2 cups coarsely chopped broccoli	1/3 pound crabmeat
1 small red pepper, chopped	3 cups cooked rice
1/2 teaspoon thyme leaves	Salt and pepper

Sauté onion and mushrooms in oil till limp. Add broccoli, bell pepper, and thyme. Simmer till broccoli is tender, about 4 minutes. Stir in chicken broth, milk, and corn. Cook, uncovered, about 10 minutes or until hot. Stir in crabmeat and rice. Simmer, uncovered, until hot, about 2 minutes. Ladle soup into bowls. Add salt and pepper to taste. Serves 5–6.

Cooking Treasures of the Central Coast

Cioppino

Traditionally served on Friday nights in North Beach's Italian restaurants, this fish soup is loaded with the catch of the day in a rich tomato stock. Crusty sourdough bread is essential for soaking up all the delicious broth.

¼ cup olive oil
1 large red onion, thinly sliced
1 large leek, white part only, washed and chopped
1 shallot, minced
3 garlic cloves, minced
1 fennel bulb, trimmed and thinly sliced
1 bay leaf
⅛ teaspoon saffron threads
3 tablespoons minced flat-leaf parsley
Salt and freshly ground pepper to taste

6 tomatoes, peeled, seeded, and chopped
1 cup fish stock or clam broth
1 cup dry white wine
2 pounds fresh white fish, such as sea bass or monkfish
8 ounces shrimp
1 live Dungeness crab, cleaned and sectioned*
8 ounces bay scallops
8 ounces mussels, scrubbed and debearded, or cherrystone clams

In a soup pot over medium heat, heat olive oil and sauté onion, leek, shallot, garlic, fennel, bay leaf, saffron, and parsley for 8–10 minutes, or until vegetables are tender. Add salt and pepper. Add tomatoes and cook for 3 minutes. Add fish stock or clam broth and wine. Simmer for 15 minutes. Add fish and shellfish and simmer 5–10 minutes, or until shrimp is pink, the fish is firm, and mussels or clams have opened. Do not overcook, or fish will be tough. Discard any clams or mussels that do not open. Serves 6.

*To clean and section Dungeness crabs, keep the crabs in a paper bag in the refrigerator until cooking. To stun the crabs, approach one from behind, grasp the legs and the claw on each side with each hand, and crack the center of the underside of the shell with a sharp blow against the hard edge of a table or counter. Pull the top shell off the crab and remove the gray gills and green tomalley (crab liver). To make serving easier, use a large cleaver to cut the crabs in half, then cut the body into portions, each with a leg. Crack the shells with a nutcracker or hammer.

San Francisco Flavors

Camping Chowder

A can of this, a can of that. Just too easy to be so good.

Polish sausage, thinly sliced, or
  1 can minced clams
2 medium onions, minced (or
  dried onion flakes)
1 (16-ounce) can cream-style corn
1 (13-ounce) can evaporated milk
1 (14-ounce) can cream of potato
  soup (or canned potatoes)

3 cups water
1 teaspoon salt
⅛ teaspoon pepper
4 tablespoons butter (optional)
2 cloves garlic, minced (optional)

Brown sausage and drain on paper towels. If you use fresh onions, brown with sausage. Dump remaining ingredients in a pot and heat slowly. Serves 5–6.

On the Road Again Cookbook

Winter's Day Clam Chowder

1 cup minced onion
1 cup chopped celery
1 carrot, diced

2 cups diced potatoes
4 tablespoons chopped parsley
2 (6½-ounce) cans chopped clams

Cover vegetables with water in kettle and add juice from clams. Set clams aside. Cook vegetables 20 minutes or until partially tender.

¾ cup butter
¾ cup flour
1 quart half-and-half

½ teaspoon salt
Pinch of pepper
½ teaspoon sugar

While vegetables are cooking, melt butter in a separate pan. Blend in flour and half-and-half, and stir constantly over low heat. Stir in salt, pepper, and sugar.

When vegetables are cooked, drain off about half the water and mash vegetables slightly with potato masher to add consistency to soup. Add half-and-half mixture to vegetables and cook over low heat 5–10 minutes. Add clams and serve. Do not overcook after adding clams.

Marilyn Thomas: The Homemaker Baker's Favorite Recipes

Baked Ripe Olive Minestrone

A popular favorite at our house. It makes a lot and freezes well for future use. This recipe is from the old Palo Alto Times.

1½ pounds lean beef stewing meat
1 cup coarsely chopped onion
1 teaspoon minced garlic
1 teaspoon salt
¼ teaspoon pepper
2 tablespoons olive oil
3 (10½-ounce) cans beef broth
2 cans water
1½ teaspoons Italian herb
   seasoning

1 (1-pound) can tomatoes
   (undrained)
1 (15¼-ounce) can kidney beans
   (undrained)
1¾ cups pitted canned ripe olives
1 cup liquor from ripe olives
1½ cups thinly sliced carrots
1 cup small seashell macaroni
2 cups sliced zucchini
Grated Parmesan cheese

Preheat oven to 400°. Cut beef into 1¼-inch cubes. Mix together beef, onion, garlic, salt and pepper in a Dutch oven. Add olive oil and stir to coat meat evenly. Brown, uncovered, in preheated oven about 40 minutes, stirring once or twice.

Reduce heat to 350°. Add broth, water and Italian seasoning. Cover and cook 1 hour until meat is almost tender. Remove from oven and stir in tomatoes, kidney beans, ripe olives, canned ripe olive liquor, carrots, and macaroni. Sprinkle zucchini on top. Cover and return to oven to bake 40–45 minutes longer, until macaroni is tender. Serve with grated Parmesan cheese. Makes about 3½ quarts.

Seasons: Food for Thought and Celebration

Super Taco Soup

8 ounces ground beef
½ cup chopped onion
1½ tablespoons flour
2 cups water
1 (17-ounce) can whole kernel corn, drained
1 (16-ounce) can kidney beans

1 (16-ounce) can tomatoes
2 tablespoons taco seasoning
1 tablespoon mild taco sauce
1 teaspoon seasoned salt
¼ teaspoon garlic powder
Salt to taste

Brown ground beef and onion in skillet, stirring frequently; drain. Add flour, stirring until dissolved. Add water. Pour into large saucepan. Add corn, beans, tomatoes, taco seasoning, taco sauce, seasoned salt, garlic powder, and salt. Bring to a boil; reduce heat. Simmer for 20 minutes, stirring occasionally. Ladle into serving bowls. Garnish with shredded Cheddar cheese, sliced green onions, crushed tortilla chips, and sour cream. Yields 8 servings.

California Gold

Tortilla Soup

2 tablespoons vegetable oil
4 corn tortillas, cut into strips
1 cup chopped onion
2 teaspoons minced garlic
2–4 tablespoons canned diced green chiles
7–8 cups chicken broth

2 cups chopped cooked chicken
1 cup whole kernel corn
½ cup chopped red bell pepper
1 tablespoon fresh lime juice
1–2 teaspoons cumin
¼ cup chopped cilantro for garnish

In a heavy soup pot, heat oil over medium-high heat. Add tortilla strips and cook until crisp, 2–3 minutes. Remove with slotted spoon and drain on paper towels. Add onion, garlic, and chile peppers to pot and cook 3 minutes. Add remaining ingredients and simmer 10 minutes. Spoon into bowls and garnish with tortilla strips and cilantro. Yields 9 cups.

California Kosher

Pizza Soup

1 pound hamburger
¼ pound pepperoni
1 pound sausage or ½ pound
 Italian sausage
1 onion, chopped
1 (28-ounce) can tomatoes,
 blended
2 (8-ounce) cans tomato sauce

1 small can chopped black olives
2 cups water
3 chicken bouillon cubes
¾ teaspoon garlic powder
½ teaspoon oregano
1 cup (uncooked) small shell
 macaroni, cooked
Shredded mozzarella cheese

Brown hamburger, pepperoni, and sausage with onion until all is tender. Add everything except macaroni and cheese. Simmer 15 minutes. Add cooked macaroni and cheese and simmer another 15 minutes. Top each bowl with shredded mozzarella cheese and serve.

Nuggets, Nibbles and Nostalgia

Vegetable Chili

1 medium onion, sliced thin
1 sweet yellow pepper, seeded and
 chopped
1 tablespoon vegetable oil
1 tablespoon ground cumin
1 tablespoon chili powder
1 (28-ounce) can chopped
 tomatoes
1 (15-ounce) can white beans,
 drained and rinsed

2 small zucchini, sliced in ¼-inch
 rounds
1 (4-ounce) can chopped mild chiles
2 cloves garlic, minced
½ teaspoon sugar
¼ teaspoon salt
Dash hot red-pepper sauce

Cook onion and yellow pepper in oil. Add cumin and chili powder. Add tomatoes with liquid, beans, zucchini, chiles, garlic, sugar, and salt. Cook 30 minutes, stirring occasionally. Add pepper sauce to taste. Cover and refrigerate overnight. Reheat before serving. Makes 4 servings.

Heavenly Creations

Garden Chili

A crusty cornbread makes an ideal accompaniment.

3 cloves garlic, minced
2 cups chopped onions
2 cups sliced fresh mushrooms
2 cups sliced fresh sweet peppers
  (red, yellow or green or a
  combination)
2 tablespoons olive oil
4 cups peeled and chopped fresh
  tomatoes
3 tablespoons chili powder

1 teaspoon ground cumin
1 tablespoon crushed dried
  oregano
1/2 teaspoon salt
4 cups sliced raw zucchini
4 cups unsalted cooked black beans
  (well-rinsed canned beans may
  be used)
2 cups water

In heavy skillet or Dutch oven, sauté garlic, onions, mushrooms, and peppers in olive oil about 10 minutes or until tender. Add tomatoes, chili powder, cumin, oregano, and salt. Bring to gentle boil. Reduce heat and simmer about 25 minutes. Add zucchini and continue simmering 5 minutes longer. Stir in cooked beans and water; heat through. Adjust seasonings to taste. Yields 11 (1-cup) servings.

Note: To peel tomatoes easily, cover with boiling water and allow to stand about 2–5 minutes. Drain and rinse under cold water. Core and peel. Skins should slip off easily.

Nutritional Analysis Per Serving: Cal 278; Fat 10.1gm; Chol 61mg; Sod 630mg.

Taste California

Red, White, and Black Chili

No one will miss the meat or the fat in this unusual spicy chili.

1 medium onion, chopped
1 bell pepper, chopped
2 cloves garlic, chopped
2–3 jalapeño chiles, seeded and
  chopped
1 1/2 teaspoons ground cumin
1 1/2 tablespoons chili powder
1/2 teaspoon ground cinnamon
2 teaspoons oil

1 (15-ounce) can red beans,
  undrained
1 (15-ounce) can white beans
  (cannellini or lima), undrained
1 (15-ounce) can black beans,
  undrained
1 (14-ounce) can diced tomatoes
  with juice
1/2 teaspoon salt

In a large nonstick saucepot over medium low heat, sauté onion, pepper, garlic, jalapeño, cumin, chili powder, and cinnamon in oil until onions are soft. Add the beans and tomatoes. Bring to a boil, lower heat, cover and simmer 15 minutes. Taste for salt. Yields 4–6 servings.

The 7 Day Cookbook

White Chili

1 pound dried Great Northern
  white beans, rinsed, picked over
2 pounds boneless chicken breasts
1 tablespoon olive oil
2 medium onions, chopped
4 garlic cloves, minced
2 (4-ounce) cans chopped green
  chiles
2 teaspoons ground cumin
1½ teaspoons dried oregano,
  crumbled

¼ teaspoon ground cloves
¼ teaspoon cayenne pepper
6 cups chicken stock or canned
  broth
3 cups grated Monterey Jack
  cheese (about 12 ounces)
Sour cream
Salsa
Chopped fresh cilantro

Place beans in large heavy pot. Add enough cold water to cover by at least 3 inches, and soak overnight.

Place chicken in large heavy saucepan. Add cold water to cover and bring to simmer. Cook until just tender, about 15 minutes. Drain (reserve broth) and cool. Remove skin. Cut chicken in cubes. Drain beans.

Heat oil in chicken pot over medium-high heat. Add onions and sauté until translucent, about 10 minutes. Stir in garlic, then chiles, cumin, oregano, cloves, and cayenne, and sauté 2 minutes. Add beans and stock and bring to boil. Reduce heat and simmer until beans are very tender, stirring occasionally, about 2 hours. (Can be prepared 1 day ahead. Cover and refrigerate. Bring to simmer before continuing.)

Add chicken and 1 cup cheese to chili and stir until cheese melts. Season to taste with salt and pepper. Ladle chili into bowls. Serve with remaining cheese, sour cream, salsa and cilantro. Serves 8.

Cooking on the Fault Line—Corralitos Style

Bud's Famous
Three-Bean Chili Con Carne

½ cup dried black beans
1 cup dried pinto beans
½ cup dried kidney beans or red beans
2 bay leaves
5 cups peeled canned tomato bits
2 tablespoons salt
4 cloves garlic, finely chopped, divided
1 tablespoon oregano
1 tablespoon crushed hot chiles
2 pinches dried sage
¼ cup red wine vinegar

1½ cups onions, chopped
½ stick butter
1 cup bell pepper (red and green) chopped
1 cup chopped celery
½ cup finely chopped parsley
1 pound coarse-ground lean pork
1½ pounds coarse-ground lean beef
⅓ cup chili powder
⅛ cup cumin
3 tablespoons dark brown sugar
1 cake Ibarra Mexican chocolate

Wash dried beans thoroughly. Cover with water and soak at least 1 hour. Bring to rapid boil with bay leaves, then simmer until tender; add water, if needed. Add tomatoes, salt, ½ garlic, oregano, crushed hot chiles, sage, and red wine vinegar while simmering beans.

In a large frying pan, sauté onions in butter. Stir in bell peppers, celery, parsley, and rest of garlic.

In small frying pan, sauté pork and beef together until all rawness is gone. Pour juice from meat into a skillet. Add chili powder, cumin and dark brown sugar. Bring to boil and cook for several minutes.

Add these spices to meat and now add meat to the simmering beans. Next, add all vegetables to large pot of beans; simmer on low heat uncovered, stirring every so often. Add Mexican chocolate. If beans become dry, add tomato juice or V-8. Garnish with red and white chopped onions and grated Jack and sharp Cheddar cheeses. Serves 6–8.

The Coastal Cook of West Marin
From The Shop in Blonias

 Death Valley has the lowest elevation in the continental United States. There's a 135-foot tall thermometer in Baker near Death Valley to let you know how hot you are!

Thai Spicy Prawn Soup

This fragrant soup is easy to prepare. The spiciness comes from cayenne pepper, which is balanced by the lightly sweet coconut milk. Try to locate fresh kaffir lime leaves in an Asian market. They impart wonderfully perfumed flavor to the soup.

2 tablespoons grated fresh ginger
1 teaspoon cayenne pepper
2 tablespoons peanut oil
6 cups chicken stock or canned low-salt chicken broth
½ cup jasmine rice
1 cup unsweetened coconut milk
6 tablespoons Thai fish sauce (nam pla, found in the Asian section of most supermarkets)
8 ounces crimini or white mushrooms, sliced
1 small red bell pepper seeded, deveined, and cut into ¼-inch strips
1 small onion, chopped
2 tablespoons chopped fresh cilantro
1 stalk lemon grass, white part only, cut into 1-inch pieces
5 fresh or dried kaffir lime leaves (optional)
1 pound medium shrimp, shelled and deveined
2–3 tablespoons fresh lime juice
Chopped green onions, including green portion, and cilantro for garnish

In large heavy saucepan, combine ginger, cayenne, and peanut oil. Cook over medium-high heat for 1–2 minutes. Add stock or broth, and bring mixture to a boil. Add rice, reduce heat, and simmer for 15–20 minutes, or until rice is tender. Add coconut milk, fish sauce, mushrooms, pepper, onion, cilantro, lemon grass, and lime leaves to rice. Simmer for 5 minutes, stirring once or twice. Add the shrimp and cook 3–5 minutes, or until they have turned pink. Stir in lime juice. Serve hot, garnished with green onions and cilantro. Serves 6.

San Francisco Flavors

Cauliflower Soup

Cauliflower is probably the most subtle member of the cabbage family. Be sure the cauliflower you use is young and rather small. The older and larger the cauliflower, the more it will taste like cabbage. You can make this soup substituting broccoli for cauliflower with good results.

2 small cauliflower	**½ cup milk**
3 tablespoons butter or margarine	**½ cup heavy cream**
3 tablespoons flour	**Salt and pepper to taste**
5–6 cups chicken stock	**2 teaspoons lemon juice**

Peel away all leaves and most of stalk of cauliflower and slice thinly. It's easy enough to do if you cut it in half, lay cut-half flat on your work surface, and slice crosswise. Set aside.

Melt butter or margarine in soup kettle. Add flour to make a roux*, but don't let it color. Add the chicken stock and stir with a wire whisk until smooth. Reduce heat and simmer about 15 minutes before you add sliced cauliflower. Simmer until cauliflower is soft. Purée soup and add milk and cream. Mix in salt and pepper to taste and add the lemon juice. Serve with croutons. Serves 6–8.

*A roux is a mixture of melted butter and flour cooked together until bubbly, and used as a thickener for liquids. The proportions of flour/butter to liquid vary, depending on how thick you want the liquid to become.

Soups from A–Z

Salads

San Francisco's cable cars are the city's only moving historic landmarks, originating in the late 1800s by wire-rope inventor Andrew Smith Hallidie. The cars still run seven days a week.

Classic Avocado Salad

½ head Boston lettuce
½ head romaine
½ head chicory
½ pint cherry tomatoes, halved
2 avocados, peeled and sliced

3 slices bacon, cooked and
  crumbled
3 ounces Roquefort or Bleu
  cheese, crumbled

Into large salad bowl, tear greens in bite-sized pieces. Add tomatoes and avocados. Sprinkle with bacon and cheese. Toss lightly with Herb Dressing.

HERB DRESSING:
1 cup vegetable oil
6 tablespoons wine vinegar
¼ cup lemon juice
1 teaspoon salt

1 teaspoon sugar
½ teaspoon basil leaves
2 cloves garlic, crushed
Dash pepper

Combine all ingredients and chill, covered. Makes 1½ cups.

California Country Cook Book

Guacamole Salad

Nice for a summer supper with grilled cheese sandwiches and fresh fruit.

SALAD:
½ head lettuce
2 tomatoes
1 (4½-ounce) can sliced black
  olives
¼ cup green onions

1 cup tuna
1 cup Fritos
½ cup sharp Cheddar cheese,
  grated

In a large salad bowl, tear lettuce into pieces. Dice tomatoes and add. Add olives, green onions, and tuna. Toss with the Dressing. Break Fritos into pieces. Top salad with Fritos and cheese. Toss and serve immediately. Serves 4–6.

DRESSING:
½ cup mashed avocados
1 tablespoon lemon juice
½ cup sour cream
⅓ cup olive oil
1 clove garlic, minced

½ teaspoon chili powder
½ teaspoon sugar
¼ teaspoon salt
¼ teaspoon Tabasco sauce

Make Dressing by combining above ingredients.

The Lazy Gourmet

Marinated Artichokes

Fresh California artichokes are available in most markets throughout the year. These marinated artichokes are better on the second day. They'll keep several weeks in the refrigerator if stirred occasionally.

3 quarts water
2 cups white vinegar
3 cloves garlic
1 teaspoon salt
24 baby artichokes, whole, but
   trimmed to edible stage

1 cup wine vinegar
1 cup salad or olive oil
½ teaspoon garlic powder
3 tablespoons minced parsley

Bring water, white vinegar, garlic, and salt to a rolling boil. Stir in artichokes. Continue stirring for 1 minute. Cover and boil for 12–15 minutes or until tender. Drain and let cool. Cut artichokes into halves or quarters, depending on size. (If there are any purple leaves, snip off.) Mix together wine vinegar, oil, garlic powder, and parsley. Add artichokes. Stir, cover, and refrigerate.

Food Festivals of Southern California

 The 1947 Artichoke Queen was Marilyn Monroe, then a struggling young starlet on a publicity tour. Castroville is known as the "Artichoke Capital of the World," producing some 80 percent of the nation's artichoke crop.

Artichoke Salad

1 package chicken Rice-A-Roni	2 (6-ounce) jars marinated
1/2 cup mayonnaise	artichoke hearts, drained
1 tablespoon Worcestershire sauce	(reserve marinade)
1 tablespoon lemon juice	6–8 green onions
1 teaspoon curry powder	1 cup chopped celery
Dash hot sauce	1/2–1 green pepper

Prepare chicken Rice-A-Roni according to package directions, omitting butter. Cool mixture in refrigerator. Meanwhile, combine mayonnaise, Worcestershire sauce, lemon juice, curry powder, hot sauce, and reserved artichoke marinade; mix well. Finely chop onions, including tops, celery, green pepper, and artichokes in large, covered bowl. Pour mayonnaise mixture over all ingredients and stir well. Chill overnight for best flavor. Serves 6–8.

More Firehouse Favorites

Imam Bayeldi

This recipe for a first course salad came from Stanley's, an Armenian restaurant in Fresno, California.

2 large eggplants	1/4 cup chopped parsley
1 green pepper	1 clove garlic
2 medium onions	Salt and pepper to taste
1/4 cup olive oil, divided	1/4 teaspoon basil
1 tomato, diced	1 (8-ounce) can tomato sauce

Cut unpeeled eggplants in quarters lengthwise and salt them liberally. Let stand for 1/2–1 hour. Turn oven to 450°.

Dice green pepper and onions and sauté in 2 or 3 tablespoons of olive oil. When soft, add diced tomato and chopped parsley, garlic, salt and pepper and basil. Cook 4 or 5 minutes and set aside.

Wash salt off eggplants and pat dry. Put quarters on large shallow pan (like a cookie sheet) that will hold them all side by side. Brush with olive oil and put in 450° oven until light brown. Remove from oven and slit each quarter from end to end without piercing skin. Open each quarter like a boat and fill with onion mixture. Pour tomato sauce over and bake at 375° a half hour. Chill and serve cold on lettuce leaves. Serves 8.

Salads from A–Z

Spring Asparagus Salad

12 spears asparagus
½ cup salad oil
3 tablespoons red wine vinegar
1 clove garlic, minced

½ onion, sliced
Salt and pepper to taste
2 cups fresh sliced mushrooms
1 firm ripe tomato, diced

Cut asparagus diagonally to 1½–2 inches long; place in boiling water for 2–3 minutes. Drain; rinse with COLD water. Combine salad oil, vinegar, garlic, onion, and seasonings. Combine vegetables and pour dressing over all. Let stand for 30 minutes to combine flavors before serving. Serves 4.

Cooking on the Fault Line—Corralitos Style

Broccoli Salad

Flowerets of 2 bunches broccoli
1 cup raisins
½ cup chopped onion
⅓ cup walnuts
10–12 slices crisp-fried bacon,
   crumbled

2 tablespoons vinegar
2 tablespoons honey
⅔ cup mayonnaise

Combine broccoli, raisins, onion, walnuts, and bacon in large bowl; mix well. Mix vinegar, honey, and mayonnaise in small bowl. Pour over broccoli salad; toss well. Spoon into serving dish. Chill, covered, overnight. Yields 8 servings.

Variation: May add cauliflower and bell pepper or may substitute 2 tablespoons sugar for 2 tablespoons honey.

California Gold

Paula's Broccoli Salad

1 large bunch fresh broccoli (about
   1½ pounds; don't use much of
   the stems unless you peel them)
3 green onions, chopped
½ cup chopped Bermuda onion
½ pound fresh mushrooms (about
   8 medium), washed well, sliced
½ cup Wishbone Italian Dressing

1 cup grated Cheddar cheese
½ cup grated Swiss cheese
½ cup coarsely chopped walnuts
   (optional)
1 avocado, diced in large chunks
Salt and pepper to taste
½ cup mayonnaise

Wash and chop first three ingredients. Add sliced mushrooms and Italian dressing and let sit for ½ hour or longer. Just before serving, add cheeses, walnuts, avocado, and seasonings; stir in mayonnaise and blend well. Serves 8–10.

Cooking Pure & Simple

Pea Salad

2 boxes frozen peas (place in
   colander and run cold water to
   separate)
1 cup chopped celery
¾ cup chopped green onions
½ pound lean bacon, fried crisp
2 hard-boiled eggs, chopped

Juice from 1 lemon
Salt and pepper to taste
¼ pint sour cream
¼ cup mayonnaise
1 small can water chestnuts,
   drained, chopped

Mix all above ingredients and garnish with tomato wedges.

Children's Hospital Oakland Cookbook

24 Hour Salad

1 head lettuce	1 (10-ounce) package frozen peas
5 hard-boiled eggs, sliced	½ medium onion
Salt and pepper	1½ cups mayonnaise
½ teaspoon sugar	½ pound Swiss cheese, grated
1 pound bacon, fried crisp	

Cover bottom of 9x13-inch dish with 1 inch chopped lettuce; then cover with egg slices. Sprinkle with salt and pepper and a little sugar. Break up fried bacon and spread over eggs. Next, spread frozen peas (not cooked) over bacon. Thinly slice onion over peas. Stir mayonnaise and spread over onions. Spread grated Swiss cheese over all. Cover and let stand in refrigerator 24 hours.

Taste of Fillmore

Fresh Cucumber Salad

Will keep up to 2 months.

7 cups thinly sliced unpeeled cucumbers	1 cup vinegar
	2 cups sugar
1 cup sliced onions	1 teaspoon celery seed
1 cup sliced green peppers	1 teaspoon mustard seed
1 tablespoon salt	

Mix first 4 ingredients and let stand for 1 hour. Mix next 4 ingredients in saucepan and bring to a boil. Cool liquid mixture; pour over cucumber mixture. Store in refrigerator. Yields approximately 3 pints.

Durham's Favorite Recipes

The Rose Bowl Parade is Pasadena's most colorful attraction. It began in 1890 when the Valley Hunt Club hosted a sort of picnic on New Year's Day. One wealthy family on Orange Grove Boulevard opted to weave ivy and garden roses through their buggy spokes for the ride, over to the festivities. Not to be outdone, neighbors braided geraniums into their horses' manes and tails and tied satin ribbons on bridles and reins. The colorful group "paraded" from Orange Grove to Sportsman Park along the rutted dirt road strewn with rose petals. Voilà!

Gorgonzola Salad

8 whole Belgian endives
2 tablespoons lemon juice
1 tablespoon chopped Italian parsley
1/3 cup extra virgin olive oil

1 tablespoon walnut oil
Salt and freshly ground pepper
1 cup walnuts, toasted
8 ounces Gorgonzola, cut into 8 thin slices

Separate endive spears into large bowl. Set aside. In small mixing bowl, whisk together lemon juice, parsley, oils, salt and pepper to taste. Pour over endive and add walnuts. Toss gently to avoid bruising endive.

Divide among 4 chilled salad plates. Top each salad with 2 slices of Gorgonzola. Serves 4.

Monterey's Cooking Secrets

Curried Spinach Salad

2 pounds spinach leaves
2 unpeeled apples, chopped
2/3 cup dry roasted Spanish peanuts
1/2 cup raisins

1/3 cup green onions, sliced thin
2 tablespoons toasted sesame seeds
1 cup cooked, diced chicken (optional)
1/2 cup sliced mushrooms (optional)

DRESSING:
1/2 cup white vinegar
2/3 cup oil
1–4 tablespoons finely chopped chutney

1 tablespoon curry powder
1 teaspoon dry mustard
1/4 teaspoon Tabasco sauce

Mix salad ingredients. Combine Dressing ingredients and pour over salad. Toss and serve. Serves 6.

The Potluck Cookbook

 The Franciscan missionaries were responsible for planting the first grapevines in California two-hundred years ago. They also planted olive trees. California olive oil is now experiencing a renaissance.

Spinach Salad

BALSAMIC VINAIGRETTE:

1 large shallot, finely chopped
⅓ cup balsamic vinegar
1 cup olive oil

1 teaspoon Dijon Mustard
½ teaspoon salt
½ teaspoon freshly ground pepper

Mix ingredients in a large cup or jar. Stir to blend well. Chill 2–3 hours before using.

1 bunch spinach, washed,
  stems removed
¼ pound bean sprouts
¼ pound pine nuts

1 tablespoon butter
1 clove garlic
¼ pound bay scallops

Mix spinach, sprouts, and pine nuts in large salad bowl. Melt butter in frying pan. Add garlic and scallops. Over high heat, cook 3–5 minutes until scallops are opaque and firm. Remove to plate to cool. Add cooled scallops to spinach mixture. Pour vinaigrette over and mix well. Serve on individual plates. Serves 4–6.

The Old Yacht Club Inn Cookbook

Spinach Salad with Oranges and Black Olives

A colorful salad that complements Mexican and Spanish entrées.

1 (6-ounce) bag pre-washed baby
  spinach
1 large orange, peeled, cut into
  bite-size pieces

¼ cup sliced black olives
¼ cup thinly sliced sweet red
  onion

DRESSING:

½ cup oil
¼ cup orange juice
2 tablespoons lemon juice
1 tablespoon honey

½ tablespoon Dijon mustard
¼ teaspoon ground cumin
1 teaspoon salt
¼ teaspoon freshly ground pepper

Whisk together dressing ingredients. Toss salad ingredients with dressing, saving a few pieces of orange and olives to put on top. Sprinkle reserved orange pieces and olives on top for presentation. Yields 4 servings.

The 7 Day Cookbook

Vicious Garlic Salad

¼ teaspoon dry mustard
⅛ teaspoon black pepper
1¼ teaspoons salt
2 large cloves garlic, crushed
2 tablespoons fresh lemon juice
¼ cup olive or salad oil
¼ cup grated Parmesan cheese
¼ pound fresh mushrooms, sliced
1 head romaine lettuce, cleaned and chilled

Blend first 7 ingredients in wooden salad bowl. Add fresh mushrooms and toss lightly. Let mixture stand at room temperature 2–3 hours to marinate well. When ready to serve, add romaine lettuce torn into bite-sized pieces. Toss gently. Yields 4–6 servings.

Variation: Avocado or drained artichoke hearts may be used in addition to mushrooms for variety.

Celebrating California

Taco Tabbouleh

This can be made spicier or milder, according to individual tastes. The name refers to the fact that Mexican ingredients are added to the salad.

1½ cups boiling water
1 cup bulgur wheat
1 (15-ounce) can kidney beans, drained
1 bunch green onions, sliced
2–3 celery stalks, sliced
½ cup chopped green or red bell pepper
½ cup minced fresh parsley
1 or 2 tomatoes, chopped

DRESSING:
⅓ cup white wine vinegar
⅔ cup vegetable oil
2 garlic cloves, minced
1 teaspoon chili powder
1½ teaspoons minced fresh oregano, or ½ teaspoon dried oregano
½ teaspoon ground cumin
2 or 3 tablespoons bottled salsa or canned diced green chilies

Pour boiling water over bulgur. Cover and let stand for about 1 hour. Drain, if necessary. Add vegetables. Combine all Dressing ingredients and mix with salad. Serves 8–10.

The Art Lover's Cookbook: A Feast for the Eye

Baja Salad

Great for a festive luncheon on the patio.

1 (16-ounce) package dried black beans, picked over, soaked overnight in cold water to cover, and drained
1 red bell pepper, diced
1 green bell pepper, diced
⅓ cup chopped green onions
1 (10-ounce) package frozen corn, thawed
⅓ cup chopped cilantro
8 chicken breast halves, skinned and grilled
1–2 avocados, sliced, garnish
1 cup salsa, garnish
½ cup sour cream, garnish
Chopped cilantro, garnish

In large saucepan, combine black beans and enough cold water to cover by 2 inches. Bring water to boil and simmer 45 minutes to 1 hour, or until tender, but not too soft. Drain black beans and mix with vegetables in large mixing bowl. Toss with Cumin-Lime Dressing. Place vegetables with dressing on large round platter. Cut chicken into strips and arrange on top with sliced avocado. Drizzle salsa on top. Put extra salsa, sour cream, and cilantro in bowls.

CUMIN-LIME DRESSING:
½ cup lime or lemon juice
1 tablespoon Dijon mustard
2 tablespoons ground cumin
1 teaspoon minced garlic
1 teaspoon pepper
½ teaspoon salt
¾ cup olive oil
¾ cup vegetable oil

Mix together dressing ingredients and let stand for 1 hour or more.

Note: This can also be made with grilled shrimp instead of chicken.

California Sizzles

California Caesar Salad

Sun-dried tomatoes marinated in olive oil give a contemporary twist to the classic Caesar salad.

GARLIC CROUTONS:

**3 teaspoons of oil from sun-dried
 tomatoes**

2 garlic cloves, chopped
3 cups (½-inch) bread cubes

In a skillet over medium heat, warm 3 tablespoons of oil from tomatoes, and garlic. Add bread cubes; toss to coat. Transfer in a single layer to a baking sheet. Bake in a preheated 325° oven, tossing occasionally, until crisp and golden, about 12–15 minutes. Cool.

DRESSING:

2 garlic cloves
1 (2-ounce) can anchovies, drained
½ cup olive oil
¼ cup freshly squeezed lemon juice
½ teaspoon Dijon-style mustard
½ teaspoon Worcestershire sauce
Coarsely ground black pepper to taste

**1 head romaine lettuce, washed
 and dried**
Garlic Croutons
**½ cup drained marinated
 sun-dried tomatoes, oil reserved**
¼ freshly grated Parmesan cheese

Purée garlic and anchovies in a blender or food processor. Add oil, lemon juice, mustard, and Worcestershire sauce; blend thoroughly. Season with pepper. Gently tear lettuce into a salad bowl. Top with Garlic Croutons, tomatoes, and cheese. Drizzle with Dressing. Toss and serve immediately. Makes 4–6 servings.

A Little San Francisco Cookbook

Southwestern Rice and Bean Salad

2 cups cold, cooked long-grain rice
1 (16-ounce) can kidney beans,
  rinsed and drained
1 (8¾-ounce) can whole kernel
  corn, drained
½ cup sliced green onions with
  tops
½ cup picante sauce
¼ cup Italian dressing
1 teaspoon ground cumin

Combine all ingredients in a large salad bowl. Cover and refrigerate for 2–3 hours. Makes 8–10 servings.

The Steinbeck House Cookbook

Appaloosa Wagon Wheels

Imagine sitting around a campfire in the Old West, with the beans and corn cooking in the pot. This salad goes well with any grilled foods at summertime outdoor barbecues.

1 cup cooked Appaloosa beans,
  drained
1 cup cooked wagon-wheel pasta
  (or small elbow macaroni),
  drained
1 cup canned whole kernel corn,
  drained
¼ cup chopped fresh parsley
⅓ cup olive oil
¼ cup cider vinegar
2 tablespoons Dijon mustard
2 garlic cloves, minced
1 teaspoon ground cumin
1 teaspoon chili powder
1 teaspoon cayenne pepper
  (optional)

Mix beans, pasta, corn, and parsley in a medium bowl. In a smaller bowl, blend oil, vinegar, mustard, garlic, cumin, chili powder, and cayenne pepper. Toss together with bean and pasta mixture. Serve at room temperature. Makes 4–6 servings.

Boutique Bean Pot

No expense was spared as craftsmen labored for 28 years to create the hilltop estate of William Randolph Hearst at San Simeon. The imposing 115-room Casa Grande and its 127 acres of gardens have magnificent mountain and ocean views surrounding it in all directions. Priceless antiques, hand-carved ceilings, marble sculptures, even full-grown cypress trees were imported to grace this magnificent mansion. Today Hearst Castle's palatial opulence is a major tourist attraction not to be missed.

Cobb Salad

The best Cobb Salad is made with freshly prepared ingredients, carefully seasoned. This wonderful combination of flavors and textures was invented by Bob Cobb at Hollywood's Brown Derby Restaurant in 1936.

DRESSING:
¾ cup olive oil
3 tablespoons red wine vinegar
½ teaspoon salt
¼ teaspoon freshly ground black pepper

To make Dressing, combine oil, vinegar, salt and pepper in tightly capped jar and shake vigorously until blended; set aside.

SALAD:
2 hard-boiled eggs, peeled and chopped
2 tablespoons chopped fresh parsley or chives
Salt and pepper
2 large red, ripe tomatoes, peeled, seeded and diced
2 cups finely diced cooked chicken breast
4 cups finely chopped iceberg lettuce
2 cups chopped chicory or curly endive
1 cup watercress sprigs
½ cup crumbled bleu cheese
1 avocado, peeled and diced
6 slices bacon, cooked crisp and crumbled

In small bowl, toss eggs with parsley or chives, a sprinkling of salt and pepper, and 2 tablespoons Dressing. In another bowl, toss tomatoes with 2 tablespoons Dressing, and season with salt and pepper. In another bowl, season chicken with salt and pepper and toss with 2 tablespoons Dressing. In large bowl, toss together lettuce, chicory, and watercress sprigs. Pour on remaining Dressing and toss to combine; season with salt and pepper to taste.

Spread greens in a shallow mound on large platter or salad bowl. Arrange eggs, tomato, chicken, cheese, avocado, and bacon nicely on top. Take to the table and toss just before serving. Serves 6–8.

A Little California Cookbook

Picnic Salad

DRESSING:

2 tablespoons salad oil
2 tablespoons white wine vinegar
¾ teaspoon dry mustard

½ teaspoon dried oregano
½ teaspoon dried basil
1 clove garlic, chopped

Whisk together ingredients in a small bowl.

SALAD:

4 ounces spaghetti, cooked
1 (6-ounce) jar marinated
  artichoke hearts, drained
½ small zucchini, thinly sliced
1 carrot, shredded

2 ounces sliced salami, cut into
  strips
1 cup shredded mozzarella cheese
2 tablespoons grated Parmesan
  cheese

Place spaghetti, artichokes, zucchini, carrots, salami, and moz-zarella and Parmesan cheeses in a large salad bowl. Add Dressing to Salad and toss to cover. Serves 4.

Centennial Cookbook

Double Noodle Salad

1 pound boneless chicken breast
4 ounces of Soba noodles (Japanese
  buckwheat noodles)
3 ounces fresh snow peas

3 ounces fresh bean sprouts
1 stalk celery, chopped
1 (3-ounce) can chow mein noodles
Chopped iceberg lettuce

DRESSING AND MARINADE:

2 tablespoons rice vinegar
2 tablespoons soy sauce

2 tablespoons sesame oil
Dash or 2 Tabasco sauce

Poach chicken breast and when cool enough to handle, cut in bite-size pieces. Marinate in 3 tablespoons Dressing.

Cook Soba according to directions on package; drain and cool in a colander under running water. When cool, drain well of excess water and add to chicken. Steam snow peas until crisp-tender; cool in ice water and drain. Blanch bean sprouts for a minute in boiling water; drain and cool in ice water. Drain again. Chop celery and mix with drained snow peas and bean sprouts. Combine with chicken and Soba and toss with remaining Dressing. Garnish with crisp noodles and serve on a bed of chopped iceberg lettuce. Serves 4.

Salads from A–Z

Chinese Chicken Salad

SESAME DRESSING:

2 tablespoons sesame seeds
1 tablespoon sugar
1 teaspoon salt

2 teaspoons oriental sesame oil
1/3 cup rice vinegar
1/4 cup salad oil

Brown sesame seeds in a small dry (no oil) nonstick pan; combine with remaining ingredients in covered jar. Shake well until sugar is dissolved. Set aside.

SALAD:

1 head Napa cabbage, shredded
1 each red and green bell pepper,
   cut in strips
1/2 cup thinly sliced radishes
1/2 cup chopped green onions
1/2 cup cilantro, chopped

Snow peas (optional)
2 to 3 chicken breasts, cut in strips
2 tablespoons sesame oil
2 tablespoons soy sauce
1/2 cup peanuts or cashews

In a large bowl, combine Napa cabbage, bell peppers, radishes, onions, cilantro, and snow peas. Brown chicken strips in sesame oil, and soy sauce until done.

Just before serving, add chicken and peanuts to salad; mix. Add Sesame Dressing and mix well. Good without chicken too!

Tasty Temptations

Springtime Chicken or Shrimp Salad

10 ounces corkscrew macaroni
2 chicken breasts, cooked and
   cubed, or 2 cups shrimp
4 eggs, hard-boiled and chopped
1 bunch green onions, thinly sliced
1 cup thinly sliced celery
1 cup frozen petite peas, uncooked
2 teaspoons dried dill weed

Salt, white pepper and paprika to
   taste
4 ounces pimiento, chopped and
   drained
1/2 cup ranch dressing
1/2 cup mayonnaise
1 or 2 teaspoons Schilling Salad
   Supreme Seasoning

Cook macaroni per directions on package; drain and rinse with cold water, draining well. Combine chicken and pasta with remaining ingredients. Prepare a day before and if it needs more dressing, add a little ranch dressing. Serves 8–10.

Calvary's Cuisine

Paul and Phil's Chicken Salad

Instead of making a salad, put this mixture between slices of bread. (Best thing about cooking is that it isn't a rigid science like algebra or physics.)

2 cups thinly sliced cooked chicken
¾ cup mandarin oranges, drained
¾ cup roasted whole cashews
¼ cup finely chopped cilantro
2 small green onions (including tops), thinly sliced

1 red bell pepper, diced
¾ cup mayonnaise
1 tablespoon lemon juice
2 teaspoons sesame oil
4 cups Italian salad mix (includes radicchio)

Toss chicken with mandarin oranges, cashews, cilantro, onion, and bell pepper. Whisk mayonnaise with lemon juice and sesame oil. Stir dressing with chicken mixture. Heap chicken salad onto salad mix on a platter. Yields 8 servings.

Jan Townsend Going Home

"Please Make That for the Bowl" Salad

½ pound penne pasta, cooked and cooled
1 cup frozen green peas, thawed
4 cooked chicken breast halves, diced
1 (4-ounce) package crumbled bleu cheese

½ red onion, diced
½ cup mayonnaise
1 tablespoon curry powder
Juice of 1 lemon
Salt and pepper to taste

In a large bowl, mix together pasta, peas, chicken, bleu cheese, and onion. Combine remaining ingredients in a small bowl and mix well. Toss salad with dressing until coated. Chill. Serve on a bed of lettuce. Serves 6.

Symphony of Flavors

Salinas Valley, known as the Salad Bowl of the World, produces numerous fruits and vegetables including lettuce, broccoli, artichokes, strawberries and carrots. Agriculture is the number one industry in all of Monterey County, grossing $2 billion per year. Since the 1880s when refrigerated boxcars were invented, people all over the country—and now the world—have been enjoying California fruits and vegetables.

Seared Salmon Medallions with Orange–Ginger Salsa

1 shallot, finely diced
2 ounces red wine vinegar
1 tablespoon Dijon mustard
4 ounces extra virgin olive oil
Salt and pepper
8 Roma tomatoes, peeled and
　seeded
1 tablespoon diced fresh ginger

1 orange, juice and zest
1 tablespoon diced cilantro
Rice vinegar
Sesame oil
12 ounces baby greens
8 (3-ounce) salmon medallions
4 red cherry tomatoes, halved
4 yellow cherry tomatoes, halved

To prepare vinaigrette, place diced shallot in large salad bowl. Add red wine vinegar, mustard, and olive oil. Mix and season with salt and pepper. Set aside.

To prepare salsa, dice Roma tomatoes and place in mixing bowl. Add ginger, juice and zest of orange and cilantro. Season with rice vinegar and sesame oil. Add salt and pepper to taste. Set aside. Clean, wash and dry baby greens. Toss with vinaigrette and divide evenly on four plates. Sear salmon in frying pan until done. Place 2 medallions on top of greens on each plate. Top salmon with orange-ginger salsa and garnish with cherry tomatoes. Serves 4.

Sounds Tasty!

Marti's Seafood Salad

Serve as a light lunch on a hot day, or as a main part of dinner.

DRESSING:
1 cup mayonnaise
1 1/2 teaspoons Madras curry
Juice of 1 lemon

1 tablespoon soy sauce
Ground black pepper to taste

Mix together and let sit 1 hour.

SALAD:
1/2 pound fresh cooked crab,
　sprinkled with lime juice
1/2 pound small shrimp
1 1/2 pounds fresh bean sprouts

1 (20-ounce) package frozen peas
　and pearl onions
1 cup chopped celery
1 chopped green bell pepper

Toss all together in large salad bowl. Mix with Dressing. Let sit until peas and onions are thawed.

From a Sourdough's Pot

Crab Louis

This classic salad originated in San Francisco, and every wharfside restaurant features its own version. Tiny shelled shrimp, called bay shrimp in San Francisco, can be substituted for crab.

LOUIS DRESSING:

½ cup mayonnaise
½ cup sour cream
3–4 tablespoons tomato-based
  chili sauce
1 tablespoon fresh lemon juice

Few drops hot pepper sauce
¼ cup finely diced green bell
  pepper
¼ cup finely sliced green onions

Combine ingredients in a small bowl; blend well. Cover and refrigerate at least 1 hour to let flavors blend.

1 head iceberg lettuce
¾ to 1 pound cooked crabmeat,
  shredded
Louis Dressing

2 medium tomatoes, cut in wedges
2 hard-cooked eggs, cut in wedges
Capers
Black olives

Rinse, core, and drain lettuce. Place 1 large lettuce leaf on each of 4 plates. Shred remaining lettuce to make 6 cups. (Refrigerate any remaining lettuce for another use.) Place shredded lettuce on lettuce leaves. Arrange crabmeat evenly over it. Spoon about half of dressing over crabmeat. Garnish each plate with tomato wedges, egg wedges, capers, and olives. Serve remaining dressing separately. Makes 4 servings.

A Little San Francisco Cookbook

Shrimp Mold

1 can tomato soup
3 (3-ounce) packages cream cheese
1 package unflavored gelatin
¼ cup warm water
1 cup mayonnaise

¾ cup finely chopped celery
¾ cup finely chopped green onions
1 cup (small can) shrimp, crumbled
  fine

Heat tomato soup. Dissolve cream cheese in soup. Soak unflavored gelatin in warm water. Cool soup and add gelatin mixture. Blend remaining ingredients well and turn into desired mold (lightly greased) and chill until set. Serve with crackers or on lettuce.

San Ramon's Secret Recipes

Shrimp Potato Salad

Here is a good way to vary the flavor of your potato salad using shrimp, sour cream, and different herbs. This dish is both filling and delicious.

**5 medium red potatoes, cut into
  ¾-inch cubes
2 tablespoons butter
1 clove garlic, pressed
½ pound shrimp, shelled,
  deveined and chopped
½ cup sour cream**

**½ cup Pimientoed Sweet Red
  Pepper
2 teaspoons dried dill
1 teaspoon paprika
½ cup chopped fresh parsley
Salt and coarse ground pepper**

Boil potatoes until cooked but still firm. Meanwhile, melt butter in saucepan and sauté garlic and chopped shrimp until shrimp is uniformly pink. Drain and cool potatoes, then mix in shrimp, garlic, and remaining ingredients. Chill before serving. Serves 2.

PIMIENTOED SWEET RED PEPPER:
1 or 2 sweet red peppers

Cook red pepper(s) under broiler or on grill until skin begins to blister and turn black. Turn often during process for even cooking. Remove pepper(s) to bowl and cover with plastic wrap to steam. After pepper(s) cool, peel off easily removed skin and remove seeds. Meat can then be cut into smaller pieces for use and stored in a jar of olive oil with cut-up garlic cloves. Lasts about a week in refrigerator.

Neptune's Table

Bacon and Chive Potato Salad

6 cups quartered, unpeeled small
    red potatoes
¾ cup mayonnaise
2 tablespoons stone ground mustard

8 slices bacon, crisply cooked,
    crumbled
¼ cup chopped chives, or sliced
    green onions

Add potatoes to boiling water; cook 14 minutes or until tender. Drain. Mix mayonnaise and mustard in large bowl. Add potatoes, bacon, and chives; mix lightly. Refrigerate. Makes 6 servings.

Tasty Temptations

Fruited Wild Rice Salad

DRESSING:
¼ cup oil
⅓ cup orange juice

1 tablespoon honey

Combine Dressing ingredients and set aside.

SALAD:
1 cup uncooked wild rice
2 Delicious apples, chopped
Juice of 1 lemon
1 cup golden raisins
1 cup seedless red grapes, halved

2 tablespoons minced fresh mint
2 tablespoons parsley
2 tablespoons chives
Salt and pepper to taste
1 cup pecan halves

Cook rice according to package directions; drain, if needed, and allow to cool. In a large bowl, toss apples with lemon juice. Add raisins, grapes, mint, parsley, chives, and rice. Add Dressing and toss. Season with salt and pepper. Cover and chill several hours or overnight. Just before serving, add pecans and toss. Serves 8–10.

Cherished Recipes from the Valley

Spinach Apple Salad

2 tablespoons cider vinegar
2 tablespoons vegetable oil
¼ teaspoon salt
¼ teaspoon sugar
1 cup diced unpeeled apple

¼ cup chopped sweet onion
¼ cup raisins
2 cups torn fresh spinach
2 cups torn romaine

In a small bowl, combine vinegar, oil, salt, and sugar; mix well. Add apple, onion, and raisins; toss lightly to coat. Cover and let stand for 10 minutes. Just before serving, combine spinach and romaine in a large salad bowl; add dressing and toss. Yields 4–6 servings.

An Apple a Day

Pecan and Roquefort Salad

⅓ cup sugar
¼ cup unsalted butter
¼ cup orange juice
1½ teaspoons salt
1¼ teaspoons cinnamon
¼ to ½ teaspoon cayenne pepper
¼ teaspoon ground mace

2 cups pecan halves
2 heads Boston lettuce
2 (6-ounce) packages Roquefort
   cheese, crumbled
1 medium red onion, thinly sliced
3 green onions, thinly sliced
Raspberry Vinaigrette

Preheat oven to 250°. Line 10x15-inch jellyroll pan with foil. In a heavy saucepan over low heat, combine and heat sugar, butter, orange juice, salt, cinnamon, cayenne pepper, and mace until butter melts and sugar is dissolved. Increase heat to medium. Add nuts and toss until well coated. Spread nuts in a single layer on the foil-lined pan. Bake 1 hour, stirring every 15 minutes. Transfer nuts to another large sheet of foil. Separate nuts with a fork. Cool completely. Place lettuce, cheese, and onions in a salad bowl and chill. At serving time, toss all ingredients together. Serves 8.

Note: The cayenne-flavored nuts in this recipe may be stored in the refrigerator in an airtight container approximately one month. Bring to room temperature before serving. If nuts are sticky, bake on foil-lined pan at 250° until crisp, approximately 20 minutes. These nuts are good appetizers, too.

RASPBERRY VINAIGRETTE:
½ cup olive oil
3 tablespoons raspberry vinegar
1 tablespoon minced shallots

¼ teaspoon salt
⅛ teaspoon white pepper

Combine oil, vinegar, shallots, salt and pepper, stirring until well blended. Yields ¾ cup.

Sterling Performances

Orange, Kiwi, and Jicama Salad with Lime Dressing

This is a particularly pleasing accompaniment to Sunday brunch. Mexican jicama, navel oranges, and kiwi provide an exotic flavor combination, typical of California cooking. Today almost all of the world's kiwi fruits are grown in either California or New Zealand, and California supplies the majority for the American market.

1 head salad bowl lettuce, separated into leaves
1 head romaine lettuce, torn into small pieces
2 stalks celery, thinly sliced
1/2 pound jicama, peeled and diced

2 green onions, thinly sliced
3 kiwi, peeled, sliced 1/4 inch thick
3 navel oranges, peel and pits removed, sliced 1/4 inch thick
1 small red onion, thinly sliced into rings

Line a serving bowl with salad bowl lettuce leaves. In a medium bowl, combine romaine, celery, jicama, and green onions. Toss well, then mound in center of lettuce leaves in serving bowl. Top with circle of overlapping kiwi and orange slices. Arrange onion rings on top.

DRESSING:
Juice of 2 limes
Juice of 1 orange
1/2 teaspoon salt

Finely ground pepper to taste
1/4 cup walnut oil

In a small bowl, combine lime juice, orange juice, salt and pepper. Whisk in walnut oil. Pour dressing over salad and serve. Salad may be prepared up to 4 hours ahead and kept in refrigerator; top with Dressing just before serving. Serves 6–8.

Note: Water chestnuts or Jerusalem artichokes can be substituted for the jicama.

The Cuisine of California

Curried Banana Salad

4 bananas, chopped
Lemon juice
3 stalks celery, chopped
1/4 cup raisins, plumped in water

1/4 cup slivered almonds
Iceberg lettuce, chopped
Unsweetened coconut*
Chutney

DRESSING:
1 cup mayonnaise
3 teaspoons curry powder
1 teaspoon dry mustard

Juice of 1/2 lemon
Tabasco sauce to taste

Chop bananas and sprinkle with lemon juice so they won't discolor. Mix together with celery, raisins, and almonds. Blend dressing ingredients and fold in banana mixture.

Serve on a bed of chopped iceberg lettuce, sprinkle with grated coconut and top with chutney. I use Major Grey's Chutney, but there are many other wonderful chutneys available that would be excellent substitutes. Serves 6–8.

*If you are unable to locate unsweetened coconut, fresh or canned, use sweetened.

Salads from A–Z

Heavenly Orange Fluff

2 (3-ounce) packages orange
   Jell-O
1 (13 1/2-ounce) can crushed
   pineapple
1 (6-ounce) can frozen orange juice
   concentrate, thawed

2 (11-ounce) cans mandarin
   oranges, drained
1 (3 3/4-ounce) package instant
   vanilla pudding mix
1 cup cold milk
1 cup whipping cream, whipped

Dissolve Jell-O in 2 1/2 cups boiling water; add undrained pineapple, and orange juice concentrate. Chill until partially set. Fold in oranges; pour into 9x13-inch pan. Chill until firm.

Beat pudding and milk with rotary beater until smooth. Fold in whipped cream; spread over gelatin. Chill. Makes 12–15 servings.

Calvary's Cuisine

Ruby Red Salad

2 cups lite cranapple juice
1 (6-ounce) package sugar-free
   raspberry Jell-O
1/3 cup raspberry wine
2/3 cup cold water

1 cup crushed pineapple in juice
1 cup diced red apple
1 cup pine nuts
1/2 cup finely chopped celery
   (optional)

Heat cranapple juice to boil; add raspberry Jell-O, and stir until dissolved. Add wine and water, and stir to mix. In a 9-inch square pan, spread pineapple with juice evenly over bottom of pan; add apples, pine nuts, and celery. Pour cranapple juice mixture in pan. Put clear plastic wrap on top of cranapple juice so it touches total surface of juice. Refrigerate until set. Serves 6–8.

Tasty Temptations

Cottage Cheese and Jell–O Salad

1 (3-ounce) package orange or
   raspberry Jell-O
1 small container cottage cheese
1 small container Cool Whip

1 small can crushed pineapple,
   drained
1 can mandarin oranges, drained

Beat dry Jell-O into cottage cheese until well mixed. Beat in Cool Whip, then add pineapple and oranges.

Feeding the Flock

Grandma's House Emerald Salad

2 cups crushed pineapple
1 small package lemon Jell-O
1 small package lime Jell-O

3½ cups boiling water
2 cups miniature marshmallows
4 bananas, sliced

TOPPING:
5 tablespoons flour
1 cup sugar
Juice from pineapple
2 eggs

4 teaspoons margarine
½ pint sour cream
Grated Cheddar cheese

Drain pineapple well and save juice for topping. Mix Jell-Os with boiling water and pour into 9x13-inch pan. Cool slightly and add pineapple, marshmallows, and bananas. Refrigerate to set Jell-O.

In a saucepan combine flour, sugar, juice from pineapple with enough water to make 2 cups, eggs and margarine. Cook until thick. Remove from heat and fold in sour cream. Spread on set Jell-O. Sprinkle grated Cheddar cheese over top. Serves 10–12.

Grandma's House Restaurant & Family Recipes

Cranberry Pineapple Salad

1 (3-ounce) package orange gelatin
1 cup boiling water
½ cup cold water
½ cup crushed pineapple, drained

1 (16-ounce) can whole cranberry
    sauce
¼ cup chopped nuts
½ cup chopped celery

Dissolve gelatin in hot water. Add cold water and chill until partially thickened. Fold into gelatin the pineapple, cranberry sauce, nuts, and celery. Pour into 1-quart molds and chill until firm. Makes 6–8 servings.

Durham's Favorite Recipes

Glen Ellen Fire and Ice Salad

FRESH FRUIT SALSA:

2 apples, diced
2 pears, diced
1/2 jalapeño, diced very fine
1/4 cup diced red onions
Salt and pepper

1/8 cup lemon juice
1/8 cup red wine vinegar
1/4 cup fresh mint, chopped
1/2 bunch fresh cilantro, chopped

Toss together all ingredients; let marinate for 6 hours.

SALAD:

3/4 cup sugar
1 1/2 cups sweet pecans

1 pound mixed greens
2 ounces goat cheese, grated

Heat sugar over low heat until it turns to a caramel-colored liquid; spread pecans on cookie sheet and drizzle caramel over top. Let cool. Chop pecans in fourths. Place mixed greens on chilled salad plate; top with fruit salsa, a healthy sprinkling of goat cheese and a handful of sweet pecans. Serves 10.

Sonoma County...its bounty
Recipe by Christian Bertrand, Glen Ellen Inn Restaurant

Arugula, Prosciutto and Pear Salad

1/4 pound prosciutto, thinly sliced
1 1/2 cups arugula

1 pear, thinly sliced

Arrange prosciutto around outside edges of plate. Dress arugula and pear slices in center with Vinaigrette Dressing. Serves 4.

VINAIGRETTE DRESSING:

1/2 cup sherry vinegar
1/4 cup honey
2 tablespoons chopped rosemary

4 tablespoons minced shallots
3 cups olive oil
Salt and pepper to taste

In a medium-sized saucepan, combine vinegar, honey, rosemary, and shallots until warm. Remove from heat and let cool. Whisk in olive oil and season with salt and pepper.

San Francisco's Cooking Secrets

Northwest Roquefort Apple Slaw

½ head green cabbage, shredded fine
½ head red cabbage, shredded fine
1 cup Savoy cabbage, shredded fine
2 large unpeeled Delicious apples, ¼-inch dice
1 celery stalk, ¼-inch dice
½ cup diced red onion
1 tablespoon plus 2 teaspoons sugar, divided
½ cup dry white wine (preferably Sonoma County)
⅓ cup fresh lemon juice
¼ cup salad or walnut oil
2 hard-boiled egg yolks, mashed
1 tablespoon German-style mustard
1 teaspoon salt
Freshly ground black pepper
½ cup heavy cream (lightly whipped to hold soft peaks)
4 ounces (about 1 cup) Roquefort cheese
Walnuts to garnish

In a large bowl, combine cabbages, apples, celery, onion, and 2 teaspoons sugar.

In a separate bowl, whisk together wine, lemon juice, oil, egg yolks, mustard, remaining 1 tablespoon sugar; salt and pepper to taste. Fold in cream. Pour dressing over vegetables and toss. Add Roquefort and toss again. Garnish with walnuts. Chill well before serving. Serves 8–10.

The Potluck Cookbook

Pancetta–Wrapped Onions with Greens

1/4 cup balsamic vinegar
3 tablespoons red wine vinegar
1 tablespoon Dijon mustard
1 tablespoon each fresh basil and thyme, chopped
1 garlic clove
3/4 cup olive oil
1/4 cup bacon fat, melted
2 red onions, unpeeled

1/3 cup water
8 paper-thin pancetta slices or regular bacon slices
4 cups bite-size mixed greens
1/4 cup chopped roasted red bell pepper, drained (available in jars)
16 paper-thin slices Parmesan cheese

In a medium bowl, whisk together balsamic and red wine vinegars, Dijon mustard, herbs, and garlic until blended. Slowly whisk in the oil and bacon fat. Set vinaigrette aside.

Place onions in baking pan; drizzle with 5 tablespoons vinaigrette, stirring to coat onions. Add water to pan and bake at 325° until onions are tender, basting occasionally with pan juices, about 45 minutes. Cool and peel onions. Cut into 4 pieces, leaving core intact.

Increase oven to 400°. Wrap each onion quarter in pancetta. Place onions on baking sheet and bake until pancetta is cooked through, about 15 minutes. Toss greens and red bell pepper in a large bowl with remaining vinaigrette to taste. Divide greens among individual plates and top with cheese. Arrange onions around greens and serve. Serves 4.

Trade Secret: Serve with a wedge of grilled bread rubbed with garlic.

The Great California Cookbook
Recipe from Cory Schreiber, Cypress Club, San Francisco

Marinated Tomatoes

This has become a summer treat and tradition for picnics. It's great for buffets.

4 cups tomato chunks
1 cup sliced fresh mushrooms
1/2 chopped fresh onion (or to taste)
1/4 cup olive oil

1/4 cup vinegar (rice, Balsamic, cider)
1 teaspoon chopped basil leaves
Pinch dried oregano leaves
Garlic salt to taste

In a large bowl place tomato chunks, mushrooms, and onions. Mix oil, vinegar, basil, oregano, and garlic salt. Marinate overnight in a covered bowl.

...Fire Burn & Cauldron Bubble

Lemon Ginger Dressing

A robust, crowd-pleasing dressing that can accent any dish.

1 cup canola oil
2/3 cup fresh lemon juice
6 tablespoons tamari or Bragg
    Liquid Aminos
1/3 cup water

2 tablespoons peeled and sliced
    fresh ginger
3 tablespoons sunflower seeds
2 teaspoons dry mustard
2 cloves garlic, peeled (optional)

Blend in blender until smooth. Keep refrigerated. Makes 2 1/2 cups.

The Expanding Light Cookbook

Balsamic Mustard Dressing

3 cloves garlic, pressed
1/3 cup balsamic vinegar
1/3 cup maple syrup

2 teaspoons prepared mustard
1 teaspoon toasted sesame oil
Salt and pepper to taste

Whisk ingredients together. There will be enough dressing for 2 salads. Pour remainder into jar and refrigerate. Makes about 2/3 cup.

The Organic Gourmet

Vegetables

In 1890, a large tract of land became the country's first national park. Containing 1,082 square miles, Yosemite boasts the heaviest stands of timber, the choicest meadows, and some of the world's largest waterfalls.

Steamed Artichokes
with Garlic Mayonnaise

4 large artichokes	**1 bay leaf**
½ lemon (juice only)	**2 garlic cloves**

Cut artichokes ½ inch from top cone and clip leaf tips. Squeeze juice from lemon over artichokes. Steam in 1 inch of boiling water, with bay leaf and garlic cloves, for 30 minutes. Remove and drain by holding artichoke upside down and squeezing. Place on serving dish and fan leaves out around the plate. Serve hot or cold with Pisto's Garlic Mayonnaise. Serves 4.

PISTO'S GARLIC MAYONNAISE:

2 eggs*	**2 garlic cloves**
Salt and pepper to taste	**½ teaspoon tomato paste**
1 teaspoon lemon juice	**Pinch of saffron**
1 teaspoon red wine vinegar	**½ cup light olive oil**
½ teaspoon dry mustard	

Place all ingredients except oil in a food processor. Process for 8 seconds. With machine running, slowly drizzle oil into mixture. Blend until thick. Chill for 1 hour. Spoon mayonnaise into center of each artichoke. Makes 1 cup.

*See note page 75.

Monterey's Cookin' Pisto Style

Spinach Frittata

This basic frittata recipe lends itself to endless variations.

2 (10-ounce) packages frozen chopped spinach	**3 tablespoons oil**
3 eggs	**3 tablespoons matzo meal or bread crumbs**
3 ounces (¾ cup) grated Parmesan cheese	**8 ounces small curd cottage cheese (optional)**

Place spinach in large mixing bowl and let stand until thawed. *Do not drain.* Blend in all other ingredients. Pour into a greased 9-inch square pan. Bake at 350° about 1 hour or until golden brown. Allow to cool 10 minutes and cut into serving portions. Serves 8.

California Kosher

Krasnopolski

You can split this recipe between 2 casserole dishes and freeze one.

1 (10-ounce) package frozen
  chopped spinach
6 eggs, beaten
1 (1-quart) carton farmer-style
  cottage cheese

½ pound sharp Cheddar cheese,
  grated
4–6 tablespoons flour
¼ pound margarine, melted

Thaw spinach. Combine with remaining ingredients. Bake in a 2-quart greased casserole dish at 350° for 1 hour. Serves 8–10.

The Lazy Gourmet

Grandma Doyne's Spinach Parmesan

A real goodie!

2 (10-ounce) packages frozen
  chopped spinach
Salt to taste
½ cup Parmesan cheese
6 tablespoons minced onion

6 tablespoons cream
5 tablespoons melted butter,
  divided
½ cup cracker crumbs

Cook salted spinach until tender. Drain thoroughly. Add cheese, onion, cream, and 4 tablespoons of the butter. Pour into a greased shallow baking dish. Mix cracker crumbs with remaining butter and sprinkle over top. Bake at 350° for 10–15 minutes. Serves 6.

Grandma's House Restaurant & Family Recipes

Fried Cabbage

Great with pork or anything else.

1 or 2 large carrots, peeled, sliced in thin rounds
1 large onion, peeled and diced
½ stick butter
1 or 2 heads cabbage, coarsely chopped

Salt and pepper to taste
1–3 tablespoons vinegar
2 tablespoons water

In large pan cook carrots and onion in butter till al dente, stirring so it doesn't burn. Add cabbage, stirring it down as you add. When all cabbage is added, season with salt, pepper, and vinegar to taste, then add water and cover. Lower heat to simmer, about 20 minutes. Stir now and then to test for doneness, making sure pan is not dry. Serves 6–10.

New Covenant Kitchens

Green Beans with Garlic

4 teaspoons soy sauce
1 teaspoon sugar
1 tablespoon dry sherry or water
1 tablespoon sesame seeds
1½ tablespoons vegetable oil

3 cloves garlic, minced
1 tablespoon freshly minced ginger
1 pound green beans, ends trimmed, cut diagonally into 2-inch lengths

In a small bowl, combine soy sauce, sugar, and sherry. Set aside.

Using a wok or frying pan over low heat, cook sesame seeds, stirring constantly until lightly browned, approximately 3 minutes. Remove from pan and set aside.

Increase heat to medium-high and add oil to wok. When hot, stir in garlic, ginger and beans. Cook, stirring, approximately 90 seconds. Add soy mixture. Cover pan and reduce heat to medium. Cook, stirring occasionally, until beans are tender but crisp, approximately 7 minutes. Uncover, increase heat to high and boil, stirring, until liquid has almost evaporated, approximately 1–3 minutes. Pour beans onto a platter and sprinkle with toasted sesame seeds. Serves 4–6.

Variation: For a spicy version, add red pepper flakes.

The Lafayette Collection

Onion Pie

PIE CRUST:

2/3 stick butter   **1 1/2 cups flour**

Melt butter in saucepan; remove from fire. Stir in flour. Press this mixture into a pie pan and prick with a fork.

FILLING:

1 tablespoon olive oil
5 tablespoons butter, divided
7 cups thinly sliced yellow or white onions
2 tablespoons flour

2 eggs or 3 yolks
2/3 cup heavy cream
Pinch nutmeg
1 teaspoon dry mustard
2 cups grated Swiss cheese, divided

Preheat oven to 375°. In a skillet, melt oil and 3 tablespoons butter. Add onions and cook over medium heat until transparent (20–30 minutes). Add flour; stir around. Let cool in a bowl. In another bowl, whisk eggs and cream, adding spices. Add onions to egg mixture. Stir in half or a third of the cheese; save rest for top. Pour in pie shell. Sprinkle on cheese. Dot with pea-sized butter pieces (about 2 tablespoons). Bake at 375° for 1 hour. Serves 6.

The Fork Ran Away with the Spoon

Roasted Onions in Balsamic Vinegar

2 pounds small yellow onions
2 tablespoons olive oil
2 tablespoons balsamic vinegar
Salt and freshly ground black pepper to taste

1 tablespoon chopped fresh herbs (thyme, oregano, or rosemary)

Set oven to 400°. Do not peel onions. Make a small X in the root ends. Bring a large saucepan of water to a boil; drop in onions and simmer steadily for 5 minutes. Drain onions and rinse them with cold water. When cool enough to handle, peel, leaving roots intact. Cut into quarters. (Small onions can be left whole.) Toss them in a bowl with oil, vinegar, salt, pepper, and thyme, oregano, or rosemary. Transfer onions to 9-inch baking dish and bake, uncovered, for 60–70 minutes until onions are very tender and beginning to caramelize on the edges. Serve hot or at room temperature. Especially good with grilled meats or fish.

Treasured Recipes

Cheese–Stuffed Eggplant

2 small eggplants (about 1 pound each)
1 medium onion, chopped
2 cloves garlic, finely chopped
1/4 cup vegetable oil
8 ounces mushrooms, thinly sliced
2 tomatoes, cut into wedges
1 cup salted peanuts
1 1/2 cups soft bread crumbs
2 tablespoons snipped parsley
1/2 teaspoon salt
1/2 teaspoon ground marjoram
1/2 teaspoon ground oregano
2/3 cup grated Parmesan cheese

Cut eggplants lengthwise into halves. Cut and cube enough eggplant from shells to measure about 4 cups, leaving a 1/2-inch wall on side and bottom of each shell; reserve shells. Cook and stir eggplant cubes, onion, and garlic in oil in 10-inch skillet over medium heat, 5 minutes. Add remaining ingredients, except cheese. Cover and cook over low heat, 10 minutes. Place eggplant shell in ungreased shallow pan; spoon peanut mixture into shells. Sprinkle cheese over filled shells. Cook, uncovered, in a 350° oven until eggplant is tender, 30–40 minutes. Serves 4.

Treasured Recipes

Mexican Eggplant

1 pound ground beef, turkey, or chicken
1 large eggplant, peeled
1/4 cup salad oil
1 (20-ounce) can tomatoes, well drained
1 (8-ounce) can tomato sauce
1 small onion, chopped
1/2 teaspoon cumin
1/2 teaspoon garlic salt
1 (4-ounce) can green chiles
1 1/2 cups grated Cheddar cheese

Brown beef quickly. Cube eggplant and cook 5 minutes in rapidly boiling water. Drain well. Mix remaining ingredients, except cheese, and set aside. Layer beef, eggplant, and remaining mixture in 1 1/2-quart casserole. Cover and bake 1/2 hour at 375°. Uncover. Top with grated cheese. Reduce temperature to 350° and bake for an additional 15 minutes. Serves 4 as main entrée.

Heavenly Creations

Garlic Swiss Chard

Fresh red or green leaf chard makes a very satisfying and quick-cooking vegetable dish. Serve it with broiled, grilled, or roasted foods or with heartier dishes. A splash of vinegar may be added just before serving, or serve vinegar at the table for guests to add if desired.

1 large bunch chard, red or green,
or spinach, stems removed, rinsed
with water still clinging to leaves,
and coarsely chopped
1 large clove garlic, pressed or
minced

Drizzle of olive oil, less than
1 tablespoon
¼ cup water
Salt and pepper to taste

Put all ingredients in a large skillet. Cover and cook on high heat 2 or 3 minutes or until chard begins to wilt. Stir and turn heat to medium. Continue cooking a few more minutes or until chard is soft. Serve warm or at room temperature either alone or on top of rice, beans, couscous, or bulgur. Serves 2–4.

The $5 Chef Family Cookbook

Turnip Puff Casserole

White turnips are available all year, so this lovely casserole can be made often, whatever the season.

2 tablespoons butter or margarine
¼ cup minced onion
2 tablespoons unbleached
all-purpose flour
3 cups mashed, cooked turnips

1 teaspoon salt
2 teaspoons granulated sugar
⅛ teaspoon freshly ground black
pepper
2 large eggs, separated

Melt butter in a large pan; add onion and sauté until tender. Add flour and stir well to blend. Add turnips, salt, sugar, pepper, and beaten egg yolks. In a small bowl, whisk egg whites until stiff and fold into turnip mixture. Pour into a buttered 2-quart casserole dish. Bake at 350° for 40 minutes. Makes 4 servings.

Serving contains about: 135 cal; 5g prot; 12g carb; 3g fiber; 8g fat; 121mg chol; 682mg sod.

Roots: A Vegetarian Bounty

Baked Cheese Tomatoes

6 tomatoes, scalded and skinned
4 tablespoons butter
½ cup finely minced onion
3 tablespoons flour
¾ cup light cream or milk
1 teaspoon salt
¼ teaspoon pepper
⅛ teaspoon dry mustard
⅛ teaspoon nutmeg
Dash Worcestershire sauce
¼ teaspoon basil
1 cup grated Cheddar cheese
¾ cup soft bread crumbs
1 cup soft, buttered bread crumbs
   (for topping)
Salt and pepper

Cut a slice off tops of tomatoes and scoop out center pulp. Turn upside down and drain. Meanwhile, melt butter and add onion. Sauté onion until it is transparent, not brown. Blend in flour. Gradually add cream or milk, salt, pepper, mustard, nutmeg, Worcestershire, and basil. Cook until thickened. Add cheese and ¾ cup bread crumbs. Arrange tomatoes in shallow baking dish, cut-side-up. Sprinkle inside with salt and pepper. Fill with cheese mixture. Sprinkle top with 1 cup buttered bread crumbs. Bake in 375° oven 15–20 minutes. Serves 4–6.

Sun, Sand and Sausage Pie

Cauliflower & Leek Sauté

1½ cups sliced leeks (use just
   white and light green part)
2 teaspoons clarified butter
2 cloves garlic
¼ cup water
2 cups cauliflower, tops cut into
   ½-inch flowers
½ teaspoon dried thyme
¼ cup lemon juice
¼ cup lemon zest
Salt and pepper to taste
½ cup bread crumbs
2 teaspoons Zesty Seasoning or
   other non-salt seasoning
3 tablespoons grated Pecorino,
   Romano, Asiago or Parmesan
   cheese
2 tablespoons Tapenade (page 46,
   optional)

Slice leeks in half lengthwise, then into ¼-inch slices.
   Heat a heavy skillet to medium. Add clarified butter and then leeks. Sauté leeks for about 5 minutes or until slightly browned on edges. Press garlic directly into skillet and stir about 30 seconds. Add water, then cauliflower. Stir often about 5 minutes or until stems are tender, and water has mostly evaporated. Add rest of ingredients, stir and serve. Makes 4 servings.

The Organic Gourmet

Saki Sesame Broccoli

2 cups water
1 large bunch broccoli (stems cut away)
½ teaspoon garlic granules
½ teaspoon sesame seeds
3 tablespoons saki

2 tablespoons soy sauce
1 tablespoon vinegar (preferably apple cider)
1 tablespoon olive oil
3 tablespoons sugar
½ teaspoon sesame seeds

In large saucepan, boil water. Discard stem shoots from broccoli, leaving a small spear. Place speared flowerets in boiling water for 2–3 minutes. Sprinkle garlic granules and salt and pepper over cooking broccoli. Remove broccoli from saucepan with slotted spoon to medium-size bowl, and set aside.

In a small pan, combine saki, soy sauce, vinegar, olive oil, sugar, and sesame seeds. Heat over medium to low heat while blending all ingredients. Stir constantly about 5–10 minutes until liquids are clear and glazed. Pour over broccoli and serve. Serves 4–6.

Cooking with Booze

Broccoli Cheese Pie

CHEESE CRUST:
2 cups grated Cheddar cheese
1¼ cups flour
1 teaspoon salt

1 teaspoon dry mustard
¾ cup butter, melted

Using pastry blender, combine cheese with flour, seasonings and melted butter. Press on bottom and sides of a 10-inch pie pan.

FILLING:
1 medium onion, chopped
1 tablespoon butter
¼ pound sliced fresh mushrooms, sautéed until all water has evaporated
2 tablespoons flour
1 cup light cream

1 teaspoon salt
¼ teaspoon nutmeg
Dash pepper
3 eggs, slightly beaten
2 cups chopped, cooked fresh broccoli

Sauté onion in butter. Add sautéed mushrooms. Stir in flour. Add light cream, salt, nutmeg, and pepper. Simmer 1 minute. Whisk in beaten eggs. Blend well. Add broccoli. Pour into 10-inch unbaked Cheese Crust. Bake at 350° for 40–45 minutes or until knife inserted in center of pie comes out clean. Serves 6–8.

The Steinbeck House Cookbook

Soy–Oat Patties with Tomato Sauce

1 cup soaked soybeans (½ cup dry)
½ cup water
2 tablespoons flake yeast or 1
    tablespoon powdered yeast
1 tablespoon soy sauce
1 tablespoon oil
¼ teaspoon onion powder
Dash garlic powder
1 teaspoon Italian seasoning
½ teaspoon salt (or to taste)
⅝ cup regular rolled oats

Combine all ingredients except rolled oats in blender and chop fine; or soaked beans may be ground in a food chopper and combined with other ingredients. Place in bowl. Add rolled oats and let stand 10 minutes to absorb moisture.

Drop from tablespoon or half-cup scoop in electric skillet or oiled baking pan. Cover.

Bake at 350° (medium-high) for 10 minutes until nicely browned. Turn. Cover and bake additional 10 minutes. Reduce heat and cook 10 minutes more. Serve with Tomato Sauce. Yields 4 (2-patty) servings.

TOMATO SAUCE:
½ cup chopped onions
½ cup chopped green pepper
1 tablespoon oil
2 cups cooked tomatoes (save juice)
1 tablespoon sugar
½ teaspoon salt
1 teaspoon sweet basil

In saucepan, sauté onions and pepper in oil. Add juice from tomatoes and bring to a boil. Let simmer until reduced about half in volume. Cut tomatoes in small pieces, or mash and add with sugar and seasonings to juice. Let simmer briefly. (Should be quite thick.) Serve over patties.

The Oats, Peas, Beans & Barley Cookbook

Yosemite National Park offers many breathtaking views. El Capitan is the largest single granite rock in the world, standing nearly 4,000 feet from base to summit. Bridalveil Falls is the height of a 62-story building. Yosemite Falls drops 2,425 feet, making it the highest in all North America.

Paprika Oven-Roasted Potatoes

2 pounds new potatoes, quartered
Salt to taste
½ cup olive oil
6 tablespoons butter
1 onion, chopped
6 cloves garlic, minced
2 teaspoons fresh oregano leaves

2 teaspoons fresh thyme leaves
2 tablespoons paprika
½ teaspoon white pepper
2 tablespoons all-purpose flour
½ cup hot chicken broth or
   water

Preheat oven at 400°. Bring water in large saucepan to boil. Add potatoes and salt and return to a rolling boil. Boil for 10 minutes. Remove from heat, drain, and set aside.

In a large sauté pan or wide saucepan, combine olive oil and butter and melt over medium-low heat. Do not allow butter to brown. Once butter is melted, add onion and garlic. Raise heat to medium-high and cook until onions are soft and golden, about 7 minutes. Add oregano, thyme, paprika, and white pepper. Mix well and add potatoes. Mix well to coat potatoes with mixture. Cook over medium-high heat 2 minutes, stirring often to prevent sticking and burning.

Meanwhile, stir flour into hot chicken broth until well dissolved. Add to potatoes and cook until sauce thickens, about 3 minutes longer. Remove from heat.

Transfer potatoes to an ovenproof earthenware dish (cazuela) or glass or ceramic baking dish. Bake 15 minutes. Serve hot. Makes 8 servings as a tapa.

Everybody's San Francisco Cookbook

Patate Al Forno

Potatoes baked in the oven with cheese and herbs.

1 egg
2 cups cream
Salt, pepper, and nutmeg to taste
¼ pound Gruyère cheese, grated, divided
4 medium potatoes, peeled and sliced very thin

1 garlic clove
4 tablespoons soft butter, divided
1 tablespoon mixed fresh herbs (rosemary, thyme, oregano), finely chopped

In a bowl, beat egg with cream and add seasonings to taste. Stir in two-thirds of cheese, reserving rest. Mix potatoes gently into cream mixture. Select a baking dish that is big enough so that the potato mixture will fill it no more than 2 inches deep. Rub baking dish thoroughly with garlic clove and then butter pan well with 1 tablespoon butter. Pour potato-cream mixture into prepared pan. Sprinkle top of potatoes with remaining ⅓ of cheese and herbs and then dot with remaining butter. Bake at 325° for 1 hour, or until tender. Keep warm until ready to serve. Serves 4–6.

Sonoma County...its bounty
Recipe by Chef Michael Ghilarducci, The Depot Hotel Restaurant & Italian Garden

Wild Mushroom Potato Lasagna

A wildly flavorful lasagna made with potato layers filled with a variety of mushrooms. Look for golden and black chanterelles when they come to the market in the fall; both will lend wonderful flavor and color to this dish. Use your food processor to slice the potatoes—the thinner the better. This also makes a great first course.

1 pound wild mushrooms, such as
    chanterelles, oysters, stemmed
    shiitakes, or crimini
3 tablespoons butter
1 tablespoon minced fresh thyme
2 garlic cloves, minced
Salt and freshly ground pepper to
    taste

4 russet potatoes, peeled and cut
    into ⅛-inch slices
½ cup chicken stock or canned
    low-salt chicken broth
1 cup heavy cream

Preheat the oven to 375°. Slice or break mushrooms into ⅛-inch thick pieces. In a large saucepan, melt the butter over medium-high heat. Add mushrooms and cook until lightly browned, about 5 minutes. Stir in thyme and garlic and cook 2 minutes. Season with salt and pepper.

Lightly butter a gratin dish or square Pyrex dish. Add a layer of half the potatoes and season with salt and pepper to taste. Spread mushrooms over potatoes. Layer remaining potatoes on top. Season with salt and pepper to taste.

In a small bowl, mix the stock or chicken broth and cream together. Pour over potatoes and bake 40–45 minutes, or until liquid is absorbed and potatoes have a golden crust. Cut into wedges or squares and serve warm. Serves 6.

San Francisco Flavors

California's coastline from Oregon to Mexico measures about 840 miles, but if you count all the nooks and crannies, it's more than 1,264 miles. There are 9,970 acres of coastal waters designated as state parks, and 420 public beaches.

Roasted Red Potatoes with Garlic and Thyme

An easy, flavorful way to roast potatoes.

8–10 small red potatoes
10 cloves garlic
¼ cup olive oil

1 tablespoon dried thyme (or
  2 tablespoons fresh)
Salt and pepper

Wash potatoes and pat dry with paper towel. Cut in half and place in glass baking dish. Peel garlic cloves, leaving whole, and sprinkle among potatoes in pan. Pour olive oil over potatoes and garlic, then sprinkle with thyme.

Bake in a 375° oven about an hour or until potatoes are soft when tested with a fork. Season with salt and pepper to taste. Serves 4.

California Wine Country Herbs and Spices Cookbook

Cheesed Potatoes in Foil

3 large baking potatoes, pared
Salt
Cracked or coarsely ground pepper
4 or 5 slices bacon, crisp-cooked

1 large onion, sliced
8 ounces sharp processed American
  cheese, cubed
½ cup butter or margarine

Slice potatoes into a big piece of heavy aluminum foil and sprinkle with salt and pepper. Crumble bacon over. Add onion and cheese. Slice butter over all. Mix on foil; bring edges up—leaving space for expansion of steam—and seal well with double fold. Place package on grill and cook over coals about 1 hour or till done; turn several times. (Or cook on grill with barbecue hood down, about 45 minutes, or cook in 350° oven 1 hour.) Makes 4–6 servings.

Tasty Temptations

The highest point in the contiguous 48 states—Mt. Whitney at 14,495 feet—is in the Sequoia National Park. The lowest point—Badwater at 282 feet below sea level—is in Death Valley National Park. These two points are less than 100 miles apart.

Potato Latkes

4 large potatoes (or 6 medium)
1 small onion
2 eggs
1 tablespoon flour

$^1\!/_8$ teaspoon baking powder
$^1\!/_2$ teaspoon salt
Dash pepper

Grate potatoes with onion, by hand or blender. Drain excess water. Add eggs, flour, baking powder, salt and pepper. Mix well. Fry in hot oil, turning when golden brown. Drain on paper towels before serving. Serve with applesauce, sugar, cinnamon or sour cream. Serves 6.

Jewish Cooking from Here & Far

Pisto's Mushroom Potatoes

3 ounces morels, sliced
6 baby artichokes
2 lemons
$^1\!/_2$ cup extra virgin olive oil
3 tablespoons unsalted butter, divided
3 baking potatoes, peeled and cut into bite-size pieces

$^1\!/_2$ onion, chopped
2 shallots, chopped
2 Roma tomatoes, seeded and quartered
2 cloves garlic, chopped
1 teaspoon freshly cracked black pepper
3 sprigs Italian flat-leaf parsley

Reconstitute mushrooms in warm water for 20 minutes.

Prepare baby artichokes by cutting off stalks and top 15% of leaves. Remove outer leaves until you get down to soft yellow leaves. Quarter artichokes and place in bowl with juice of one lemon and water to cover. (With baby artichokes it is not necessary to remove core.)

In a large skillet, add $^1\!/_3$ cup olive oil, 2 tablespoons butter, potatoes, $^3\!/_4$ of the chopped onion, 4 artichokes, and 1 shallot, and sauté over high heat for 10–15 minutes, turning occasionally. To tell if done, check thickest part of potatoes, which should be easily pierced with a fork or knife tip. When almost done, add tomatoes. Remove from heat.

Heat a small skillet coated with olive oil over medium heat. Add garlic, black pepper, mushrooms, remaining shallots, onions, artichokes, and remaining butter. Sauté for 6–8 minutes. Serve on large platter, with mushrooms poured over potatoes. Garnish with sprigs of parsley and quartered lemon. Serves 4.

Cooking with Mushrooms

Creamy Beet and Potato Gratin

3 pounds beets
1½ pounds potatoes
4 tablespoons butter
½ cup grated Parmesan cheese
¼ cup grated Gruyère or Swiss
  cheese
1 teaspoon salt
1 teaspoon freshly ground black
  pepper
1 tablespoon minced fresh
  rosemary
1 cup heavy cream
¾ cup milk
⅓ cup fresh bread crumbs

Preheat oven to 350°. Place beets and potatoes in separate pots; cover with water and bring to a boil. Reduce heat, partially cover and simmer 20–30 minutes, or until both beets and potatoes are tender when pierced with the tip of a knife. Drain and peel. Cut beets and potatoes into ¼-inch slices, still keeping them separated.

Butter a shallow gratin dish with 1 tablespoon butter. Arrange a layer of beets in the dish, sprinkle with ⅓ of the cheeses, salt, pepper and rosemary; dot with 1 tablespoon butter. Cover with a layer of potatoes (using all the potatoes). Sprinkle with another ⅓ of cheeses, salt, pepper and rosemary. Dot with another tablespoon butter. Add a final layer of beets, and top with remaining cheeses, salt, pepper and rosemary. Pour cream and milk over all, top with bread crumbs and dot with remaining tablespoon butter. Bake 30–40 minutes, or until sauce is bubbling and topping is golden brown.

The San Francisco Chronicle Cookbook

Potato and Asparagus Frittata

Potatoes and asparagus blend together superbly, although the frittata can be made with almost any vegetable and potato.

1 small onion, peeled and thinly sliced
1 small carrot, scraped and cut into 1-inch-long thin julienne strips
2 garlic cloves, minced
1 teaspoon chopped fresh basil
2 medium tomatoes, seeded and chopped
2 tablespoons cooking oil, divided

3 small cooked Yellow Finnish or Yukon Gold potatoes
6–8 asparagus spears, cooked and cut into 2-inch pieces
1/2 teaspoon freshly ground black pepper (or to taste)
4 large whole eggs
4 egg whites
1/3 cup grated Parmesan cheese

Sauté onion, carrot, garlic, basil, and tomatoes in 1 tablespoon oil, until onions are translucent, about 6–8 minutes. Add potatoes. Cook and stir until browned. Add asparagus and cook until heated through. Remove vegetables from heat, add pepper and set aside. Wipe out sauté pan and add remaining tablespoon of oil. In a medium bowl, whisk together all the eggs and Parmesan cheese. Add vegetables to egg mixture and return to pan. Cook over low heat until bottom of mixture is golden brown, about 5–8 minutes. Place pan under broiler and broil about 2 minutes, until frittata is puffy and golden brown. Serve immediately. Makes 4 servings.

Each serving contains about: 313 cal; 17g prot; 30g carb; 4g fiber; 15g fat; 219mg chol; 291 mg sod.

Roots: A Vegetarian Bounty

Golden Potatoes

8 red potatoes
1/4 cup butter
1 cup shredded sharp cheese
1 can cream of chicken soup

2 cups sour cream
1/3 cup chopped onion
1 teaspoon salt

Boil potatoes in jackets; chill unpeeled. Peel and shred potatoes. In saucepan, melt butter and cheese, using low heat. Add soup, sour cream, onion, and salt; stir. Pour mixture over potatoes and gently stir to blend. Pour into greased baking dish. Bake 45 minutes at 350°. Serves 6–8.

Durham's Favorite Recipes

Sweet Potato Soufflé

3 cups mashed sweet potatoes (can use canned)
2 eggs
1/3 stick margarine, melted
1/2 teaspoon salt
1/2 cup milk
1 cup sugar
1 teaspoon vanilla

Mix above ingredients together; put in greased 10x7-inch pan.

TOPPING:
1 cup brown sugar
1/3 cup flour
1/3 stick margarine, melted
1 cup chopped pecans or walnuts

Mix Topping well and sprinkle over potatoes. Bake in 350° oven for 35 minutes. Makes 8–10 servings. (All can be made ahead and frozen).

Fabulous Favorites

Sweet Potatoes and Apples

4 large sweet potatoes
2 cups water
1 teaspoon salt
3 large Granny Smith apples
4 tablespoons butter or margarine, melted
1/2 cup sugar
1 cup milk

In a covered medium saucepan, boil whole potatoes in 2 cups salted water for 30–35 minutes or until tender. Drain and slip off skins. Cut into 1/2-inch slices.

Quarter, peel and core apples. Cut into thin slices. Grease medium-size baking dish and alternate layers of apples and sweet potatoes. Mix sugar in melted butter and pour over layers.

Pour milk over the top. Cover and bake for 1 hour in a 325°oven. Uncover after 30 minutes of cooking time to brown. Serves 4–6.

Cook Book

Legend has it that Walt Disney looked all over Southern California before deciding on 75 acres of orange trees in the quiet farming community of Anaheim for the site of his first amusement park. Almost unheard of prior to 1955, Orange County soon became as familiar to the world as Hollywood and Beverly Hills, and just as big a lure. Less well-known, but worth exploring, are the many slow-paced communities—Old Town Orange, downtown Seal Beach, and the rural enclaves in the foothills of the Santa Ana Mountains—that reflect California's life before Disneyland.

Fresh Corn Pudding

Fresh corn is the key to this simple pudding.

12 medium-size ears fresh corn, shucked
About ⅔ cup milk or cream as needed for curdled cream consistency

Salt and freshly ground pepper to taste
1–2 tablespoons sugar (optional)
3–5 tablespoons butter

Preheat oven to 375°. Using a corn scraper (available in some supermarkets and kitchenware stores) or a grater, scrape juice from kernels into a buttered baking dish. Add enough milk or cream to make the corn look like thick curdled cream (more is needed for old corn and winter corn). Add salt, pepper, and optional sugar (if corn is not fresh from the garden). Dot with butter. Bake 45 minutes to 1 hour, or until pudding is firm. Serves 4.

The Art Lover's Cookbook: A Feast for the Eye

Divine Corn Casserole

Very easy. Everyone raves about it.

1 egg
½ cup butter, melted (may use less)
1 can creamed corn
1 can plain corn

1 (8-ounce) carton sour cream
1 package Jiffy Cornbread Mix
1 cup grated Cheddar cheese (optional)

Mix all ingredients, except cheese and Jiffy mix, together. Add Jiffy mix. Pour ½ into 2-quart casserole. Add ½ of cheese on top. Add rest of mix. Top with remaining cheese. Bake at 350° for 45 minutes.

50th Anniversary Cookbook

Sweet 'n' Sour Baked Beans

2 (16-ounce) cans pork and beans
4–5 wieners, cut into bite-size
  pieces
1 (8-ounce) can pineapple chunks,
  drained
¼ cup catsup

¼ cup chopped green pepper
2 tablespoons brown sugar
2 tablespoons soy sauce
1 tablespoon instant minced onion
1 tablespoon cider vinegar

Heat oven to 375°. Combine all ingredients in 2-quart casserole.
Bake 40 minutes or until bubbly around edges. Serves 4.

Cooking Treasures of the Central Coast

Baked Beans Extraordinaire

½ pound bacon, cut in pieces
1 medium onion, chopped
1 can kidney beans, drained
1 can butter beans, drained
1 (28-ounce) can pork and beans,
  undrained

¾ cup Mrs. Butterworth's maple
  syrup
½ cup catsup
2 teaspoons dry mustard

Fry bacon and pour off fat. Add onion and brown. Add to mixture of beans. Mix syrup, catsup, and mustard together. Add to
beans. Bake for 2 hours at 325°. Wonderful! Serves 6–8.

...Fire Burn & Cauldron Bubble

Bonanza Baked Beans

½ pound bacon, diced
2 onions, diced
¾ cup brown sugar
½ cup ketchup
¼ cup vinegar
¼ teaspoon garlic salt
¼ teaspoon dry mustard

1 can pork and beans
1 can butter beans and ham
1 can green lima beans, drained
1 can kidney beans, drained
1 can jalapeño navy beans
  (optional)

Preheat oven to 350°. Brown bacon, drain well, reserving 3 tablespoons of drippings, and set aside. To reserved bacon drippings, add next 6 ingredients. Simmer 20 minutes. Add remaining ingredients and diced bacon. Pour into a casserole and bake covered for 1 hour. Serves 10–12.

The Lafayette Collection

Zucchini Pie

1 cup chopped onions
4 cups sliced zucchini
½ cup butter or margarine
2 tablespoons parsley flakes
½ teaspoon salt
½ teaspoon pepper
¼ teaspoon garlic powder

¼ teaspoon basil leaves
¼ teaspoon oregano
2 eggs, well beaten
8 ounces mozzarella
1 (8-ounce) can refrigerated
  crescent rolls
2 tablespoons mustard

Preheat oven to 375°. Cook onions and unpeeled zucchini in butter until tender, about 10 minutes. Stir in parsley and seasonings. In large bowl, combine eggs and cheese. Stir in vegetable mixture. Separate rolls into 8 triangles. Place in ungreased 11-inch quiche pan or 10-inch pie plate. Press over bottom and up sides to form crust. Spread crust with mustard and pour vegetable mixture into crust. Bake 10–20 minutes, or until knife comes out clean. Cover crust with foil last 10 minutes if it begins to get too brown. Let stand 10 minutes before cutting.

Taste of Fillmore

Crisp Zucchini Pancakes

3 medium-size zucchini, trimmed
  and shredded (about 1 pound)
¾ teaspoon salt, divided
½ cup chopped onion
1 tablespoon unsalted butter

2 eggs, slightly beaten
¼ cup unsifted all-purpose
  flour
⅛ teaspoon pepper
Vegetable oil (for frying)

Place zucchini in colander after shredding. Sprinkle with ½ teaspoon salt. Set aside for 30 minutes. Squeeze as much liquid as possible from zucchini with your hands. Reserve.

Sauté onions in hot butter in a medium-size skillet over medium-high heat until softened, 3 minutes. Transfer reserved zucchini and onion to a large bowl. Stir in eggs, flour, remaining ¼ teaspoon salt and pepper. Pour oil into clean skillet to a depth of ⅛ inch, and heat. Drop slightly rounded tablespoonfuls of batter into hot oil. Flatten to 3-inch diameter with back of spoon. Cook, turning once, 1 minute on each side, or until golden. Remove pancakes with a slotted spoon. Drain on paper towel. Keep hot until all pancakes are cooked. Serve immediately. Makes 14 pancakes.

...Fire Burn & Cauldron Bubble

Savory Split Pea Pancakes

1 cup split peas, rinsed and
  drained
2 cups water
2 cups finely chopped onion
2 garlic cloves, minced

1 egg, well beaten
¼ cup all-purpose flour
1 teaspoon salt
½ teaspoon pepper
Yogurt or sour cream

In a saucepan, combine split peas and water. Cover; bring to boil. Reduce heat and simmer 30–35 minutes or until peas are tender. Cool slightly. Stir in onion, garlic, egg, flour, salt and pepper.

Heat a skillet or griddle over high heat. Coat lightly with oil or shortening. Drop batter by large spoonfuls onto hot skillet; spread batter evenly. Cook until surface bubbles burst; edges will look slightly dry. Turn pancakes and cook until underside is golden. Garnish with yogurt or sour cream. Makes about 12 pancakes or 4 servings.

Pea Soup Andersen's Cookbook

Tofu Stroganoff

1½ blocks (18 ounces) firm tofu
5 tablespoons butter, divided
1 medium onion, chopped
10 mushrooms, thickly sliced
2 tablespoons dried chives
½ to 1 teaspoon garlic powder
¼ teaspoon salt
¼ teaspoon black pepper
1 tablespoon vegetable oil
2 cups sour cream
2–4 tablespoons tamari
1–2 tablespoons cooking sherry

Rinse tofu, then drain on paper towels to remove excess water. In a large skillet sauté 2 tablespoons butter, onion, mushrooms, chives, garlic powder, salt and black pepper until onion is soft and transparent. Remove mixture from skillet and set aside. Add remaining butter and oil to skillet. Brown tofu, sliced in strips, in 2 batches, using more butter and oil as needed. Add mushroom mixture to tofu. Just before serving add sour cream, tamari, and sherry. Cook over low heat. Do not boil. To thin sauce, add more sour cream. Adjust sherry, to taste. Serve over noodles. Serves 4.

Simply Vegetarian!

Cheesy Garden Casserole

1 (7¼-ounce) package long-grain and wild rice combo
3 cups sliced zucchini or yellow squash
1 green pepper, sliced
1 medium onion, sliced
1 can sliced mushrooms
2 cups shredded Cheddar cheese
2 cups spaghetti sauce
1 cup shredded Swiss cheese

Cook rice according to package directions. Simmer sliced vegetables together in water to cover until tender and then drain. Place half of the cooked rice in a greased 9x12-inch casserole pan. Spoon half of the vegetables over rice. Top with Cheddar cheese and half the spaghetti sauce. Layer remaining rice, vegetables and sauce, and sprinkle with Swiss cheese. Bake uncovered at 375° for 35 minutes.

Dining Door to Door in Naglee Park

The Mess

2 cups small red potatoes, cooked
  and chopped to 1/4-inch cubes
Seasoned salt
Chives to taste
1/2 cup chopped tomatoes
1/4 cup chopped green bell pepper
1/2 cup chopped zucchini

1/4 cup chopped green onions
1/2 cup sliced mushrooms
1/2 cup grated Cheddar cheese
1/2 cup grated Jack cheese
1 tablespoon sour cream
3 slices of avocado
Paprika

Place seasoned potatoes and next five ingredients in omelette pan, layering everything. Mix Cheddar and Jack cheeses together and place on top of veggies. Place another omelette pan upside-down on first pan, using it as a domed lid (or use domed lid). Heat through until cheeses are completely melted, about 5 minutes.

Slide Mess onto a dinner plate, loosening edges by scraping around sides with a rubber spatula. Top with three slices of avocado fanned out, a dollop of sour cream and a pinch of paprika. Serves 1.

Incredible Edibles

Chile Sauce

This is a wonderful recipe for canning.

4 quarts, or 8 pounds, tomatoes,
  peeled and diced
1/2 large bunch celery, chopped fine
1 pound white onions, peeled and
  chopped fine
1 green pepper, chopped fine
3 cups white vinegar

2 tablespoons salt
1 pound brown sugar
1/2 teaspoon cinnamon
1 small bottle prepared
  horseradish
1/2 teaspoon pepper
1/2 teaspoon powdered cloves

Combine first six ingredients and simmer over low heat uncovered until reduced by half (about 2 hours), then add brown sugar, cinnamon, horseradish, pepper, and cloves. Continue to simmer over low heat, uncovered. Cook until thick, about 1 hour. Allow mixture to cool slightly and transfer to airtight containers and refrigerate, or can in sterilized jars according to conventional methods. Makes about 4 quarts.

Sun, Sand and Sausage Pie

Salsa Brava

2 medium carrots, julienned
1/2 white cabbage, shredded
1/2 medium onion, diced
1/2 green pepper, diced
1/2 red pepper, diced

4 serrano chiles
1 teaspoon salt, divided
3/8 teaspoon black pepper
1 cup white vinegar
1/2 tablespoon sugar

Combine carrots, cabbage, onion, green and red peppers, chiles, and 1/4 teaspoon salt in large bowl. Mix black pepper, vinegar, sugar, and 3/4 teaspoon salt together and pour over vegetables. Put in lidded jar for 8 hours in refrigerator before serving. Will last 1 week. Goes well with fish or steak.

Centennial Cookbook

Apple Cranberry Relish

1 can whole cranberry sauce
1 can frozen orange juice
1 large apple, chopped
1/2 cup chopped walnuts

1 tablespoon cinnamon
1 tablespoon ground cloves
1 cup grape wine

Combine all ingredients. Chill. Eat and enjoy. Serves 8–12.

Apples Etc. Cookbook

Baked Pineapple

This is a long-time family favorite to go with ham, especially at Easter.

1 (14½-ounce) can crushed
   pineapple
1/2 cup sugar
2 tablespoons cornstarch

2 eggs
1/2 teaspoon cinnamon
1–2 tablespoons butter

Mix first four ingredients well. Place in greased casserole. Sprinkle with cinnamon; dot with butter. Bake until firm, 30 minutes at 350°. Easy to make and delicious.

Fabulous Favorites

Marinated Beets

2 tablespoons red wine vinegar or
  rice vinegar
¼ teaspoon thyme
⅛ teaspoon mace or nutmeg
⅓ cup salad oil

1 (15-ounce) can sliced beets,
  drained
2 tablespoons minced shallots
Salt and pepper to taste

Mix vinegar and herbs; let stand 20 minutes. Slowly whisk in oil until mixture thickens. Pour over drained beets. Stir in minced shallots. Add salt and pepper to taste. Chill several hours or overnight, but best served at room temperature. Makes about 2 cups.

Nuggets, Nibbles and Nostalgia

Corn-Raisin Chutney

Here's a zesty raisin relish that includes fresh summer corn, although frozen can be used. Make it ahead; it won't spoil on a picnic. Use the relish as a delicious side dish with grilled chicken, or as a dressing for cold salad such as greens or plain boiled potatoes.

1 ear fresh corn, kernels removed,
  or approximately 1 cup frozen
  corn
1 cup raisins
½ cup cider vinegar
½ small onion, finely chopped
1 small slice fresh ginger, finely
  chopped

¼ small green or red pepper,
  chopped (optional)
2 tablespoons sugar
1 teaspoon mustard seeds
1 teaspoon dry mustard
Dash salt
Dash red pepper flakes

Put all ingredients in a saucepan. Bring to a boil. Cover and simmer for 10–15 minutes. Cool and serve. Serves 4.

The $5 Chef: How to Save Cash & Cook Fast

Pasta, Rice, etc.

The 1000 block of Lombard Street in San Francisco is nicknamed "the crookedest street in the world," with eight switchbacks in its one-block descent. It was installed in 1922 to make the street accessible to automobiles.

California Rice

A delicious rice dish, equally good with poultry or pork.

1 cup short-grain brown rice
2 cups chicken stock
1 cup Riesling or Chenin Blanc,
 divided
1 teaspoon salt
3 tablespoons butter, divided
¾ cup slivered dried apricots
¾ cup quartered pitted prunes

1 cup chopped celery
1 cup chopped onions
2 teaspoons crumbled dried sweet
 basil
½ teaspoon crumbled thyme
¾ cup coarsely chopped walnuts,
 lightly toasted
¼ cup chopped parsley

In a 3-quart saucepan with a tight-fitting lid, combine rice, chicken stock, ½ cup of the wine, salt, and 1 tablespoon butter. Bring to a boil. Lower heat until liquid is just simmering. Cover and simmer about 1 hour without removing lid. When liquid has evaporated, remove from heat and allow to steam, covered, for 10–15 minutes. Fluff rice with fork.

Meanwhile, place apricots in small pot. Top with prunes and remaining ½ cup of wine, and bring to a boil. Remove from heat and set aside to cool. Melt remaining 2 tablespoons butter in skillet. Add celery, onions, basil and thyme. Sauté over medium heat for 5 minutes. Add to rice, along with cooled fruits, walnuts and parsley. Toss well to combine. Spoon into buttered baking dish, cover, and heat in 325° oven for 30 minutes before serving. Serves 8.

California Wine Country Herbs and Spices Cookbook

Spinach–Wild Rice Casserole

1 package mixed white and wild rice
1 (10-ounce) can beef stock
2 (10-ounce) packages frozen
  chopped spinach
8 ounces cream cheese, softened
Salt to taste
1 pound mushrooms, thinly sliced
2 tablespoons butter

Preheat oven to 350°. Butter a 2-quart casserole. Set aside. Cook rice as directed on package, substituting beef stock for an equivalent amount water. Cook spinach, covered, until tender; drain well and combine with cream cheese. Add salt. Sauté mushrooms in butter until just golden. In prepared casserole, layer half rice, half spinach, and half mushrooms. Repeat layers. Cover and bake 40 minutes. Serves 6.

San Francisco à la Carte

Mexican Rice

A colorful, flavorful rice dish.

5 cups water
2½ cups white basmati rice or
  jasmine rice (rinsed 3 times)
¼ cup olive oil
1 red bell pepper, thinly sliced
  ¾ inch long
4 green onions, thinly sliced
1 tablespoon dried oregano
1 tablespoon chili powder
3 cloves garlic, peeled and
  minced
1 serrano chile, seeded and finely
  minced (optional)
2 tablespoons tomato paste
¼ cup water
1 cup frozen corn, thawed
  (optional)

Place water in a pot and bring to a boil. Add rice and simmer until water is absorbed and rice is cooked, approximately 10–15 minutes. Meanwhile, sauté in olive oil in pan, pepper and green onions. Add oregano, chili powder, garlic, and chile.

Sauté for 3–5 minutes. Add tomato paste, water and corn. Mix and cook for 3 minutes. Add cooked rice and sauté an additional 5 minutes. Add salt to taste. Serves 6–8.

The Expanding Light Cookbook

Green Rice
(Arroz Verde)

2 poblano chile peppers, seeded and chopped
1/2 green pepper, seeded and chopped
3 garlic cloves, chopped
1/2 cup coarsely chopped fresh cilantro
1/2 cup coarsely chopped parsley
1/4 cup safflower oil
1/2 cup finely chopped yellow onion
1 cup long-grain white rice
1 1/3 cups chicken stock or water
1/2 teaspoon salt

Combine chiles, sweet pepper, garlic, cilantro, and parsley in a food processor and purée. Reserve. In a deep-sided frypan, sauté onion and rice until grains are coated with oil. Add puréed chile mixture and cook 2 more minutes. Add stock and salt; bring to boil. Stir once, reduce heat, cover and simmer for 17 minutes. Remove from heat and let stand covered, 5 minutes. Fluff with a fork, garnish with cilantro and parsley and serve. Serves 4.

The Fork Ran Away with the Spoon

Sausage–Rice Casserole

1 pound hot pork sausage
1/4 teaspoon pepper
1 cup chopped celery
1 cup chopped green pepper
1 cup chopped onion
2 (11-ounce) cans chicken rice soup
1 1/4 cups uncooked rice
1 (8-ounce) can mushrooms and liquid
1 soup can water

Cook sausage until crumbly. Add pepper and chopped celery, green pepper and onion. Cover and steam until tender. Add remaining ingredients and bake in a large casserole dish for 45–60 minutes at 350°. Stir once while baking so top will not dry out. Serves 8 large portions.

Cook Book

Pine Nut and Orange Wild Rice

5 cups water, divided
1 cup wild rice
1 cup brown rice
1 cup dried currants
½ cup pine nuts, toasted
4 tablespoons chopped cilantro
2 tablespoons grated orange zest

¼ cup olive oil
2 tablespoons freshly squeezed
   orange juice
Freshly ground black pepper
   to taste
Parmesan cheese, freshly grated

Pour 3 cups of water in a saucepan. Bring to a boil and add wild rice. Stir, reduce heat, cover, and simmer for 25 minutes. Drain, if necessary, and place in a large bowl. Pour remaining 2 cups water in a separate saucepan. Bring to a boil and add brown rice. Stir, reduce heat, cover pan, and simmer for 15 minutes. Place in the bowl with wild rice.

Gently toss remaining ingredients, except grated cheese, with the two rices. (Rice can be prepared 3 hours ahead to this point. Cover, but do not refrigerate.) An hour before serving, preheat oven to 350°.

Place rice in an ovenproof casserole and cover with aluminum foil. Before serving, heat through for 20 minutes. After heating, sprinkle with freshly grated Parmesan cheese. Serves 6–8.

A Slice of Santa Barbara

Rice Pancakes

4 tablespoons melted margarine
3 eggs, beaten
2 cups cooked rice
2 teaspoons baking powder
1 teaspoon salt
¼ cup cream or milk
Shortening for frying

Mix ingredients in order given, adding milk last. Fry in small amount of shortening, turning when browned. Serves 4.

Cherished Recipes from the Valley

Mexicorn Casserole

1½ pounds ground beef
2 onions, chopped
12 ounces wide noodles
2 cups grated sharp Cheddar cheese
2 (28-ounce) cans diced tomatoes
2 cans Green Giant Mexicorn
(including liquid)
½ cup sliced ripe olives
Salt and pepper to taste

Thoroughly cook meat, breaking into small pieces with added onions. Cook and drain noodles. In large mixing bowl, mix all ingredients. Divide into two large casseroles—freeze one, have one for dinner. Cook 20–25 minutes in 350° oven. Serve with tossed salad and garlic bread.

We're Cookin' in Cucamonga

Overnight Macaroni Bake

1 cup uncooked macaroni
1 cup milk
1 can cream of mushroom soup
1 cup (or more) cubed Cheddar cheese
1 teaspoon minced onion
1 cup (or more) cubed ham

Mix everything together in a buttered, medium-sized casserole dish. This must stand in the refrigerator overnight.
    The next day, bake at 350° about 40 minutes. Serves 2–4.

On the Road Again Cookbook

Risotto in Puff Pastry
with Fresh Porcini Mushrooms

½ ounce dry porcini mushrooms
6 tablespoons butter, unsalted
1 small onion, chopped fine
2 garlic cloves, chopped
2 cups Arborio rice
1 cup dry white wine
6 cups hot chicken broth

½ cup freshly grated Parmesan
  cheese
Salt and freshly ground pepper
1 pound fresh porcini mushrooms
3 tablespoons extra virgin olive oil
6 rounds of pizza dough, 7 inches
  each

Place dry mushrooms in warm water for 10 minutes; remove and drain, chop fine and set aside.

Melt half the butter in a deep pan over moderate heat. Add dry mushrooms, onion and garlic. Sauté until soft. Add rice and stir for 2 minutes. Pour in wine and cook until liquid evaporates. Add boiling chicken broth ½ cup at a time, stirring constantly until each addition is absorbed before adding the next. The rice should always be covered by a veil of broth. When rice is cooked, about 15 minutes, add Parmesan cheese, remaining butter, salt and pepper to taste.

Preheat oven to 450°. Sauté fresh mushrooms in olive oil. Spoon rice into a 6x2-inch deep soufflé container; cover with sautéed porcini mushrooms. Cover with pizza dough and bake until golden brown, about 4 minutes. Serve immediately. Serves 6.

The Great California Cookbook

Sun–Dried Tomatoes
& Artichoke Pasta

1 (12- to 16-ounce) package
  mostacolli pasta
2 tablespoons olive oil
1 medium onion, chopped
2–4 cloves garlic, chopped
1 can artichoke hearts in water,
  drained

1 (8-ounce) jar sun-dried tomatoes
  in oil
½ cup bread crumbs
½ cup fresh parsley, chopped or
  ¼ cup dried
1 cup pasta water
Parmesan cheese

Cook pasta. While pasta is cooking, heat oil in large skillet; add onion and garlic. Cook until onion is soft; add artichokes, sun-dried tomatoes, bread crumbs, and parsley; heat through. Add 2 ladles of water pasta is cooking in, to artichoke mixture. Drain pasta and add to artichoke mixture. Transfer to serving dish; sprinkle with Parmesan cheese. Serves 10.

Tasty Temptations

Pasta with Artichokes

12 tiny fresh artichokes (or
  1 package frozen artichoke hearts)
1 onion, chopped
3 tablespoons butter
2 cloves garlic, pressed or finely
  chopped
½ cup white wine
Juice of ½ lemon

1 cup heavy cream
8 ounces fresh fettuccine (white,
  green or mixed), cooked
⅓ cup toasted cashews, pine nuts,
  or almonds, chopped
½ cup freshly grated Parmesan
  cheese
Salt and pepper to taste

Trim artichokes and prepare as for hearts, cutting in halves or quarters. (If using frozen artichokes, thaw package and use as they come from package.)

Sauté onion in butter until translucent. Add garlic, wine, lemon juice and artichokes. Cover and cook over medium heat 1–2 minutes. Add heavy cream and cook, uncovered, 2–3 minutes longer until mixture thickens slightly. Add fresh fettuccine, chopped nuts and Parmesan cheese. Toss, then add salt and freshly ground pepper to taste.

The Artichoke Cookbook

Pappardelle with Caramelized Onions, Pancetta and Arugula

Try to find the sweet Vidalia, Walla Walla, and Maui onions for this casual dinner dish of pasta ribbons tossed in a broth of sweet onions, smoky pancetta, and tart arugula.

2 tablespoons extra virgin olive oil
6 ounces pancetta or bacon, chopped
2 tablespoons butter
2 sweet white onions, sliced
1 teaspoon sugar
4 cups chicken stock or canned low-salt chicken broth
Salt and freshly ground pepper to taste
1 pound dried pappardelle pasta
2 cups arugula
⅓ cup grated Romano cheese

In large cast-iron skillet over medium high, heat 1 tablespoon oil. Add pancetta or bacon and cook until crisp, stirring occasionally. Transfer to paper towels to drain. Pour off all but 1 tablespoon fat from skillet. In same skillet, melt 1 tablespoon butter with remaining 1 tablespoon oil over medium-high heat. Add onions and sugar and cook, stirring frequently, until well browned, about 10 minutes. Reduce heat to low and continue cooking, stirring occasionally, for 20 minutes, or until very soft and caramel-colored. Remove half the onions and reserve them. Turn heat to high, and gradually add stock or broth to onions in the pan, stirring to scrape up browned bits from bottom of pan. Cook 10 minutes. Add salt and pepper.

In large pot of salted boiling water, cook pasta until not quite al dente, about 9 minutes. Drain and add to mixture in skillet. Add arugula, cover, and cook 1 minute, or until pasta is al dente. Stir in remaining 1 tablespoon butter and pancetta or bacon. Serve immediately in shallow bowls; garnish with reserved onion and cheese. Serves 4.

San Francisco Flavors

 Seventy-five percent of California's water comes from Northern California via the California Aqueduct.

Tricolor Fusilli with Wild Mushrooms

HOT WOK SEASONINGS:

4 cloves garlic, finely minced

2 large shallots, finely minced

HOT WOK SAUCE:

1/2 cup chicken stock

1/4 cup rice wine or dry sherry

2 tablespoons oyster sauce

1 tablespoon dark sesame oil

1 tablespoon cornstarch

2 teaspoons fresh thyme leaves

1 teaspoon tomato paste

1 teaspoon Asian chile sauce

In a small bowl, combine the Hot Wok Seasonings. In another small bowl, combine the Hot Wok Sauce ingredients; set both aside.

HOT WOK INGREDIENTS:

1/2 pound mixed fresh mushrooms (chanterelles, shiitakes, portabellos, morels, buttons)

1 cup small snow peas

3 whole green onions

1/2 cup pine nuts

6 ounces dried tricolor fusilli

2 tablespoons cooking oil

2 tablespoons unsalted butter

1/4 cup rice wine or dry sherry

Preheat oven to 325°. Trim tough stems from mushrooms. Cut mushrooms into 1/4-inch-thick slices, then set aside. Snap stem end off each snow pea, pulling away fiber that runs along top ridge. Cut green onions on a sharp diagonal into 1/2-inch lengths. Combine with snow peas and green onions and refrigerate. Toast pine nuts in preheated oven until golden, about 8–12 minutes. Set aside fusilli pasta. In a small container, combine cooking oil and butter; set aside. Set aside 1/4 cup rice wine.

Bring water to a vigorous boil. Lightly salt water and add pasta. Cook until just cooked and slightly firm to the bite, about 8 minutes. Immediately transfer pasta to a colander to drain. Meanwhile, place a wok over the highest heat. When very hot, add oil and butter to center. Roll oil around wok and when it gives off just a wisp of smoke, add Hot Wok Seasoning. Stir-fry seasonings, and as soon as they turn white, about 5 seconds, add mushrooms. Stir and toss mushrooms until they soften slightly, about 3 minutes. As you stir-fry mushrooms, add 1/4 cup rice wine, so that mushrooms soften more quickly and develop a fuller flavor.

Stir in snow peas and green onions. Continue cooking until snow peas turn bright green, about 1 minute. Add cooked pasta. Stir Hot Wok Sauce, and then pour it into the wok. Stir and toss until all the ingredients are glazed with sauce. Taste and adjust seasonings. Immediately transfer pasta to a heated platter or dinner plates, sprinkle on the toasted pine nuts, and serve. Serves 6–8 as a side dish or 4 as the main entrée.

Hot Wok

Penne Pasta with Roasted Asparagus

2 pounds asparagus
3 teaspoons olive oil, divided
Salt and pepper
8 ounces penne pasta
¾ cup low-sodium chicken stock

2 tablespoons fresh lemon juice
1 ounce fresh Parmesan, grated
2 tablespoons fresh parsley,
  chopped
Coarse-grind pepper

Snap off woody bottoms of asparagus; discard. Cut into diagonal pieces (approximately 3 per stalk). Toss asparagus with 1½ teaspoons oil; add salt and pepper to taste. Place on baking sheet in single layer. Roast in oven (400°), tossing asparagus several times, until browned, about 15 minutes (less if pencil-thin stalks). Remove from pan and set aside.

Meanwhile, cook penne in large pot of salted boiling water until al dente. Drain. Transfer pasta to large sauté pan. Add chicken stock and lemon juice; cook over high heat until liquid is almost completely absorbed, about 5 minutes. Add remaining olive oil, cheese, asparagus, and salt to taste. Cook and toss until mixed. Stir in parsley. Serve immediately sprinkled with coarse-grind pepper. Serves 4–6.

Option: Sprinkle with toasted pine nuts or almonds.

Treasured Recipes

Penne Pasta with Sun–Dried Tomatoes and Mushrooms

Zesty sun-dried tomatoes are complemented by the earthy flavors of shiitake mushrooms, garlic and the lush flavors of the wine.

1 (11-ounce) package penne pasta
2 tablespoons olive oil
1 medium yellow onion, sliced
   ¼ inch thick
1 tablespoon chopped garlic
1 (½-ounce) package dried
   shiitake mushrooms (reconstituted
   according to package directions
   and sliced in ¼-inch strips)

½ cup Chardonnay wine
1 (3-ounce) package sun-dried
   tomatoes (softened according to
   package directions; cut in half)
½ teaspoon crushed red pepper
Salt and pepper
2 tablespoons butter
2 tablespoons chopped fresh basil
1 cup grated basil Jack cheese

Cook pasta following package directions. In large nonstick frying pan, heat olive oil until it starts to smoke. Add the onion and sauté until golden brown (about 5 minutes). Add garlic and mushrooms and sauté 2 minutes longer. Add wine and tomatoes; reduce liquid until almost dry. Add crushed red pepper. Salt and pepper to taste. Remove from heat and stir in butter.

Toss mixture thoroughly with pasta and basil. Top with grated cheese. Goes great with a Caesar salad and garlic bread. Serves 6 as a first course; 4 as an entrée. Serve with a Chardonnay.

Cooking with Wine

Toasted Pasta

To let the flavors meld, make this dish a day ahead and reheat before serving. Serve it alone or with almost any chicken dish and a salad.

1–2 tablespoons olive oil
1 (12-ounce) package small shaped
  pasta (shells, butterflies, etc.)
1 (15-ounce) can stewed tomatoes

3 cups water
Salt and pepper to taste
Pinch of sugar, if desired,
  depending on acidity of tomatoes

Put oil in a large saucepan and heat on medium. Add pasta and pan-fry until golden brown, stirring so pieces don't over-brown. Add tomatoes, water, salt and pepper. Bring to a boil, turn to simmer, and cook semi-covered, for about 10 minutes. Stir occasionally to keep pasta from sticking. Taste, correct seasoning, and add sugar, if desired. Cook until pasta is tender and liquid is absorbed.

Remove from heat and let sit, covered, about 10 minutes. Before serving, stir again. If reheating, be sure to cover and use low heat. Serve with Parmesan cheese on the side. Serves 6.

Variation: Further embellishments include a pinch of dried herbs or some chopped fresh basil, oregano, or parsley.

The $5 Chef Family Cookbook

Pasta with Lemon Chicken

1 tablespoon extra virgin olive oil
2 cloves garlic, minced
1 pound boneless, skinless chicken
  breasts, cut into ½-inch strips
½ pound fresh mushrooms, sliced
Juice of 1 lemon
1 teaspoon butter-flavored sprinkles
½ teaspoon oregano

¼ teaspoon black pepper
1 (10½-ounce) can chicken broth,
  defatted
2 tablespoons cornstarch
2 tablespoons finely chopped fresh
  parsley
1 pound spiral pasta, cooked

In a large nonstick skillet, heat oil over medium heat. Add garlic and stir for about 30 seconds until lightly browned; do not burn. Add chicken strips and cook, stirring, until no longer pink, about 5 minutes. Remove chicken and set aside. In same skillet over medium heat, place mushrooms. Cook and stir for 5 minutes until lightly browned. Add lemon juice, butter sprinkles, oregano, and pepper.

In a separate bowl, combine broth and cornstarch, stirring until cornstarch is completely dissolved. Add to mushroom mixture along with chicken strips. Simmer until sauce thickens, stirring gently. Serve over hot spiral pasta (sauce sticks to it) and sprinkle with parsley. Serves 4.

More Firehouse Favorites

California Prunes and Mustard

3 tablespoons chopped sun-dried tomatoes
4 large California pitted prunes, chopped
2 tablespoons mustard
2 tablespoons butter, divided
1 tablespoon olive oil
1/3 cup chopped leeks (1 leek)
1 cup chopped fresh zucchini
1 tablespoon minced garlic
1/2 cup chopped fresh basil
3/4 cup chopped wild mushrooms
4–5 ounces fettuccine pasta
2 tablespoons Zinfandel
1/2 cup chopped fresh parsley
1/2 cup chopped pecans

In a large pot, bring salted water to boil in preparation for cooking pasta. Mix together sun-dried tomatoes, chopped prunes, and mustard. Set aside.

In sauté pan over medium heat, melt 1 tablespoon butter and oil together, and sauté leeks and zucchini for 3–4 minutes. Add minced garlic and sauté for 30 seconds, then add basil and mushrooms; sauté for 1 minute before adding the tomato/prune mixture. Sauté for 1–2 minutes more. The pan will start to brown on bottom. Remove vegetables and keep warm.

Begin cooking pasta. While pasta is cooking, add remaining 1 tablespoon of butter to sauté pan to loosen pan drippings; then splash pan with wine and deglaze. Return vegetables to pan to reheat and coat for several seconds; turn off heat. Quickly drain pasta and rinse under hot water; shake to remove all water, then toss with light coat of olive oil. Put pasta on hot plates and add freshly cracked black pepper and spoon vegetables on top. Sprinkle with fresh parsley and chopped pecans. Serve immediately. Serves 2.

California Wine Country Herbs and Spices Cookbook

On 80,200 acres, California produces 100% of the prunes in the U.S.— about 220,000 tons annually. In 1905, a California prune grower, Martin Seely, finding himself short of labor, imported monkeys from Panama to pick the fruit. The monkeys proved to be very efficient, but unfortunately ate all the prunes!

Chicken Fettuccine

This dish was created in our home by our friend, Chef Dan Richard. Delicious!

SAUCE:

½ stick butter
¼ cup flour

2 cans chicken broth, chilled
1 cup dry white wine

Melt butter in 2-quart saucepan over low heat. Add flour and blend well. Cook over low heat approximately 3 minutes, stirring whole time. Add cold broth, white wine, and chicken scraps from Stir Fry (optional). Stirring constantly, bring to a gradual boil. Then reduce heat to simmer and cook 45 minutes.

PASTA:

12 ounces Creamette fettuccine noodles

Canola oil for pasta (1 teaspoon)

Start water for pasta 25 minutes before sauce is done. Add canola oil to water. When pasta is done, pour in colander. (If not using right away, rinse in hot water and oil.)

STIR FRY:

1½ whole chicken breasts, deboned and cut into little strips about 2 inches long, ¼ inch wide (save scraps for sauce)
1 red bell pepper, cut into strips
1 teaspoon olive oil for frying
2 small zucchini, split and sliced at angle
1 jar artichoke crowns (hearts), well rinsed, sliced (optional)

½ bunch scallions or green onions, chopped
½ pound mushrooms, cut in half or sliced
2 tablespoons fresh chopped basil
1 tablespoon garlic powder
Salt to taste
½ pint cream
½ cup sour cream

Ten minutes before sauce is done, stir-fry chicken and peppers in olive oil until chicken is done; remove to plate. Stir-fry zucchini, artichokes, scallions, and mushrooms in olive oil. Add chicken and peppers back in. Add basil, garlic powder, and salt to taste. Stir. Remove from heat. To sauce add cream and sour cream. Do not let boil, just simmer 3–5 minutes. Mix everything together and serve. Feeds a lot!

Taste of Fillmore

Fettuccine Gloriosa

This fabulous seafood fettuccine is worth every minute it takes! It helps to have two cooks in the kitchen, one who prepares the moules and the second who prepares the calamari.

MOULES: (MUSSELS)

¾ stick butter	8 sprigs parsley, chopped fine
3–4 cloves fresh garlic, minced	18–24 fresh mussels or clams (or
1 medium-size onion or 5–6	combination), scrubbed clean
shallots, diced	1 cup dry white wine

In pan with lid, melt butter and add garlic, onions, and parsley. When onions are translucent, add mussels. Cover, and when mussels start to open, add the wine. Stir and remove from stove when mussels have opened. If any do not open, they should be removed and discarded.

CALAMARI: (SQUID)

⅓ cup olive oil	2 tablespoons oregano
6–12 cloves fresh garlic, peeled	1 cup dry white wine
and crushed	1 lemon, halved
2 pounds calamari, cleaned and cut	1 (8-ounce) can tomato sauce
into 2-inch strips	2 shakes Tabasco sauce, or to taste

Heat olive oil in skillet; add garlic and cook until garlic is golden brown. Add calamari, cook for about 1 minute, add oregano, and then wine. Cook about ½ minute longer, squeeze juice of both lemon halves over mixture and, for good measure, throw in the lemon halves. Add tomato sauce and Tabasco, and simmer for about 1 minute.

Combine mussels and calamari to create sauce.

FETTUCCINE:

2 teaspoons salt	1 pound white or green fettuccine
Water	(preferably homemade)
2 tablespoons olive oil	Parmesan cheese

In large pot, bring salted water to a rapid boil. Add olive oil and then fettuccine. When cooked al dente, strain and place on large pasta platter. Mix with combined sauce. Arrange mussels around platter, decorate with sprigs of parsley, sprinkle liberally with freshly grated Parmesan cheese and serve. Serves 4–6.

Garlic Lovers' Greatest Hits

Pasta Capri—A Domenico's Original

Perhaps the most copied dish in Monterey!

½ pound linguini pasta
1 ounce olive oil
6 green onions
2 medium shallots
1 ripe tomato
6 ounces butter
12 ounces bay shrimp, cooked and peeled

½ cup black and green olives, pitted and chopped
½ cup sliced black olives
Freshly cracked black pepper
¼ cup dry white wine
Lemon and parsley for garnish

Cook pasta according to package instructions, in lightly salted, boiling water. Drain and toss lightly with olive oil. Chop onions and shallots coarsely. Dice tomato. Preheat a large, oiled sauté pan over high heat. Add butter, shrimp, tomato, and onions and sauté for 1 minute. Add shallots, olives, and black pepper and sauté for 1 minute. Add wine, reduce heat and simmer until creamy. Add more wine or pasta water if it becomes too dry. Place drained pasta in bowl and pour sauce on top of pasta. Garnish with sliced lemon and parsley. Serves 2.

Monterey's Cookin' Pisto Style

Clam Sauce with Pasta

Clams combine nicely with other ingredients to make wonderful sauces for spaghetti or other pasta.

1 tablespoon butter
1 tablespoon olive oil
2 large, finely chopped cloves garlic
½ medium tomato, chopped
½ bottle clam juice
2 (6.5-ounce) cans chopped clams
3 sliced mushrooms

¼ cup dry white wine
1 dash Tabasco sauce or pinch cayenne pepper
Salt and pepper to taste
½ cup chopped Italian parsley (regular parsley can substitute)
Freshly grated Romano cheese
Pasta of choice

Melt butter and oil to blend, add garlic and lightly sauté. Add tomato and clam juice and cook down until tomato is soft. Mix in clams and their juice, mushrooms, wine, and spices. Cook down until liquid is reduced by half. Use additional clam juice to adjust flavor or consistency, if necessary. Serve over pasta with parsley and grated Romano cheese, crusty Italian garlic bread, green salad and a dry red wine. Serves 2.

Neptune's Table

Fettuccine with Chicken and Mushrooms

1 pound boneless, skinless chicken breasts, cubed
4 tablespoons butter
1/2 pound mushrooms, sliced
2 cloves garlic, minced
1 large shallot, finely chopped
1/4 cup white wine
1 cup chicken stock

1 pound fresh fettuccine
2 tablespoons olive oil
1 tablespoon fresh tarragon leaves, minced
3 green onions
2 tablespoons pine nuts
Dash lemon juice
Salt and pepper

Bring 1 1/2 quarts of water to a boil. Sauté chicken in butter. Add mushrooms, garlic, and shallot. Stir a little bit. Add wine to deglaze the pan. Pour in chicken stock. At the same time put pasta into boiling water to cook for about 3 minutes. Add olive oil to pan with chicken and mushrooms. Add fresh tarragon, green onions, pine nuts, lemon juice, and salt and pepper to taste. Drain pasta and mix with chicken and mushroom mixture. Serve immediately. Serves 4–5.

Sausalito: Cooking with a View

Fettuccine with Walnuts and California Avocado

Prize winner at the California Avocado Festival.

2 tablespoons olive oil
1/2 cup diced sun-dried tomatoes
1/4 cup sherry wine vinegar
1/2 cup chopped fresh basil
2 tablespoons chopped green onions
1/4 cup diced green bell pepper

2 tablespoons chopped walnuts
1 California avocado, diced, divided
1 1/4 pounds dried fettuccine noodles (if not available, substitute any dried pasta)
Salt and pepper to taste

In a large bowl combine olive oil, sun-dried tomatoes, vinegar, basil, green onions, bell pepper, walnuts, and 1/2 the avocado. Toss ingredients well so they are evenly coated with oil and vinegar.

Cook pasta in boiling water for 3 minutes or until al dente. Drain pasta and pour into salad bowl with other ingredients while pasta is still hot. Toss all ingredients and serve immediately using remaining California avocado as garnish on top of pasta. Yields 6 servings.

Celebrating California

Shrimp and Scallop Fettuccine

¼ pound (1 stick) butter
5 finely chopped cloves garlic
½ pint half-and-half
¼ pound medium shrimp, peeled, chopped in half
¼ pound bay or quartered sea scallops

1 (16-ounce) package fettuccine or flat egg noodles
Freshly grated Parmesan cheese
Salt and pepper to taste
1 teaspoon nutmeg

Bring to boil water sufficient to cook noodles when needed.

To make the seafood sauce: melt butter and sauté garlic for 1 minute over medium heat. Add half-and-half. Heat and stir continuously in frying pan until large bubbles form. Add shrimp and scallops and continue stirring until shrimp has turned pink. Remove from stove and keep warm.

Cook pasta as directed on package; drain and place in large bowl. Pour on sauce and sprinkle with Parmesan cheese, salt, pepper and nutmeg. Toss to mix and serve with cold, crisp salad (Caesar dressing is a good choice) and a dry white wine. Serves 2.

Neptune's Table

Chile Relleno Casserole

1 (7-ounce) can diced green chiles
1 (7-ounce) can green chile salsa
½ pound Monterey Jack cheese, grated
¾ pound Cheddar cheese, grated

2 eggs
½ teaspoon salt
1 tablespoon flour
1 teaspoon ground cumin
1 cup evaporated milk

Preheat oven to 375°. Combine diced chilies and chile salsa. Pour ½ of this mixture into 8x8-inch baking dish. Top with both cheeses and cover with remaining chile mixture. Beat eggs with salt, flour, cumin, and milk. Pour egg mixture over cheese-covered chiles. Bake, uncovered, for 35–40 minutes. Watch that casserole does not burn. Serves 6.

Sterling Performances

California's state motto is *Eureka!*, a Greek word meaning "I have found it!" The motto was adopted in 1849 and alludes to the discovery of gold in the Sierra Nevada.

Enchilada Casserole

Surprising use of spinach, yogurt and turkey in a favorite Mexican-inspired casserole.

1 pound ground turkey
1 onion, chopped
1 package taco seasoning or other packaged Mexican seasoning
2 (10-ounce) packages frozen, chopped spinach

1 cup plain yogurt
1 1/2 cups salsa (mild or medium), divided
8 corn tortillas
1 1/2 cups shredded mozzarella cheese or other lowfat cheese

Preheat oven to 350°. Combine turkey and onion in a skillet and brown. Add taco mix, thawed undrained spinach, and yogurt, and mix well. In 3-quart casserole dish, pour 1/2 salsa. Turn 4 tortillas in salsa to coat lightly, then spread them overlapping on bottom of dish. Spoon 1/2 turkey/spinach mixture over tortillas. Cover with 4 more tortillas, rest of the salsa, then remaining meat. Top with shredded cheese. Bake, covered, for 30 minutes. Yields 8 (1-cup) servings.

Nutritional Analysis Per Serving: Cal 278; Fat 10.1gm; Chol 61mg; Sod 630mg.

Taste California

Green and White Lasagna Bundles

2 eggs, beaten
1 (15-ounce) container ricotta cheese
1/4 cup grated Parmesan cheese
1/2 teaspoon salt
1 (10-ounce) package chopped broccoli, thawed and drained

1/4 cup snipped chives
1 1/2 cups spaghetti sauce, divided
8 lasagna noodles, cooked
1/2 cup (2 ounces) shredded mozzarella cheese

Stir together eggs, ricotta cheese, Parmesan cheese, and salt; set aside. In large skillet, lightly spray with nonstick spray. Add broccoli and chives. Cook and stir over medium heat for 5 minutes. Add broccoli mixture to cheese mixture. Stir well.

Preheat oven to 350°. Spread a thin layer of spaghetti sauce in bottom of 12x7 1/2x2-inch baking dish. To assemble, place 1 noodle on a piece of wax paper, then place 1/2 cup of the broccoli mixture in a mound 1/4 inch from end. Roll noodle around mixture. Place seam down in baking dish. Repeat with remaining noodles. Pour spaghetti sauce over rolls. Sprinkle with mozzarella. Cover with foil. Bake 35–45 minutes.

Cooking Treasures of the Central Coast

Chicken Lasagna

1 package lasagna, uncooked
½ pound fresh mushrooms,
   washed and sliced
7 tablespoons butter
1½ cups dry vermouth, divided
4 tablespoons flour
4 cups whole milk

1 teaspoon chopped fresh
   tarragon
Salt and pepper to taste
5 cups cooked, boned, and
   shredded chicken
2 cups shredded mozzarella
   cheese

Cook lasagna as specified on package until just tender; drain well and set aside. Sauté mushrooms in 3 tablespoons butter for about 3 minutes. Add 1¼ cups vermouth and allow to simmer until vermouth has almost completely evaporated. Set aside. Melt remaining 4 tablespoons butter in saucepan. Stir in flour and cook until bubbly. Gradually stir in milk and cook over low heat, stirring constantly, until thick and creamy. Stir in mushrooms, remaining ¼ cup vermouth, and tarragon. Add salt and pepper to taste. Simmer about 3 minutes and set aside.

Grease 9x13-inch baking dish. Place a layer of cooked lasagna on bottom of dish, then a layer of chicken. Pour some of vermouth sauce over top, and sprinkle with cheese. Repeat these layers several times, ending with cheese layer. Bake in preheated 350° oven about 40–45 minutes, or until bubbly and crusty on top. Makes about 8 servings.

Party Perfect and Pampered

Vegetarian Lasagna

10 lasagna noodles
1 tablespoon vegetable oil
1 tablespoon salt
2 tablespoons olive oil
1 medium yellow onion, chopped
1½ teaspoons minced garlic
½ pound fresh mushrooms,
   washed and sliced
2 medium carrots, grated
2 bunches fresh spinach, washed,
   stemmed and chopped, or
   1 (10-ounce) package frozen
   chopped spinach

1 (15-ounce) can tomato sauce
1 (6-ounce) can tomato paste
½ teaspoon salt
½ teaspoon seasoned salt
1 teaspoon dried oregano
1 teaspoon basil (or mixed Italian
   seasoning)
1 pound ricotta cheese
1 pound Jack cheese, shredded
½ cup Parmesan cheese

Cook lasagna noodles in large pot with vegetable oil and salt added just as water begins to boil. Cook 8–10 minutes; drain and rinse in cold water.

Heat olive oil in large pan. Add onion and garlic; sauté for 2 minutes. Add mushrooms and carrots; cook for 10 minutes. Add spinach and cook for 1 minute more. Add tomato sauce, tomato paste, and seasonings.

Oil 9x13x3-inch baking dish; line bottom with 3 lasagna noodles. Layer with ⅓ ricotta cheese, ⅓ vegetable filling and ¼ Jack cheese; repeat 2 more times; top with remaining Jack cheese and Parmesan cheese. Bake at 350° for 45 minutes. Serves 8–12.

Cooking Pure & Simple

Napa is not the only California valley that produces fine wines. Edna Valley and Arroyo Grande Valley wine regions have just the right mix of cool coastal air and warm dry days to produce some of California's best wines (especially Chardonnay and Pinot Noirs). According to *Wine Spectator*'s California wine guide, there are over 560 wineries in California...and counting.

Mexican Lasagna

This dish is colorful as well as tasty. A great potluck dish.

1½ pounds ground beef
1½ teaspoons cumin
1 tablespoon chili powder
1 teaspoon garlic powder
1 small onion, chopped
1 (14½-ounce) can stewed tomatoes
1 (2-ounce) can chopped green chiles

1 (8-ounce) can tomato sauce
10–12 small corn or flour tortillas
2 cups small curd cottage cheese
1 cup each Monterey Jack cheese
   and spicy Velveeta cheese
1 egg

TOPPINGS:
1½ cups grated Cheddar cheese
1 cup chopped tomatoes
2½ cups shredded lettuce
4 green onions, chopped

1 (4-ounce) can black olives,
   chopped (or more)
Sour cream
Salsa

Brown ground beef with seasonings and chopped onion. Add stewed tomatoes, chopped green chiles, and tomato sauce. Cover and let simmer 15–20 minutes. Cover bottom of 9x13-inch pan with small tortillas torn into pieces. Place beef mixture over tortillas. Add a second layer of tortillas. In a small bowl, blend cottage cheese, Jack cheese, spicy Velveeta cheese, and 1 egg with wire whip. Pour over top layer of tortillas. Place in 325° oven and bake for 20 minutes. Remove from oven and add Toppings as desired. Cut in squares and serve with sour cream and salsa. Serves 8–12.

Fabulous Favorites

California Pizza

California is a land of fantastic pizzas. They are everywhere—in the finest restaurants, fast-food chains, supermarket aisles, and California kitchens. Pizza is a food nearly everyone adores with a passion. The famous chef Wolfgang Puck tops his pizzas with lamb and duck sausage, smoked salmon with caviar, chanterelles, eggplant and leeks, or spicy chicken strips. With every season there is some new pizza topping trend. Pizza is fun and easy to make in your own kitchen. It is a good beginning cooking procedure for young cooks.

1 package dry yeast	**1 teaspoon salt**
1 cup warm water	**2 tablespoons olive oil**
1 teaspoon sugar	**3½ cups flour sifted, divided**

Dissolve yeast in warm water. Remember, water should be just warm, not hot. Stir until the yeast is dissolved. Add sugar, salt, and olive oil. Stir in 2 cups of sifted flour. When that is blended in, add remaining flour. Knead for a few minutes to blend all ingredients. Form dough into a ball and place in a lightly greased bowl. Cover with a dampened towel and set in a warm place to rise.

When dough has doubled in size (this will take about 45 minutes), punch it back down. Remove from bowl and roll out in desired pizza shapes. This will make 5 or 6 nine-inch pizzas.

Preheat oven to 425°. Prepare pizza top by lightly brushing olive oil over surface. Top with a thin spreading of tomato sauce; fresh tomatoes peeled and sliced; or crushed canned tomatoes. Next comes your choice of the following, or any other, desired toppings.

Italian sausage, cooked and crumbled. Sardine pieces. Grated mozzarella cheese. Cubes or thin slices of precooked eggplant. Sliced olives, capers, sliced mushrooms, prosciutto, sliced red or white onions, minced garlic, tiny shrimp, minced clams, anchovies, artichoke hearts, etc. A little salt, pepper, oregano, or basil may be sprinkled on top. Bake for 10–15 minutes.

The California Cookbook

Margarita Pizza

¼ cup frozen orange juice
  concentrate, thawed
¼ cup tequila
¼ cup fresh lime juice
2 cloves garlic, crushed
1 teaspoon dried oregano
⅛ teaspoon ground red pepper
Salt and black pepper to taste

2 cups cubed chicken breasts
1 tablespoon olive oil
1 unbaked homemade or
  commercial pizza crust
1 cup shredded mozzarella
  cheese
Extra virgin olive oil
Orange Salsa

Combine orange juice concentrate, tequila, lime juice, garlic, oregano, red pepper, salt and black pepper in a bowl and mix well. Add chicken and mix to coat. Marinate, covered, in refrigerator for 4 hours to overnight. Drain chicken and discard marinade. Sauté chicken in 1 tablespoon olive oil on medium heat until cooked through. Spread over pizza crust and sprinkle with cheese. Drizzle desired amount of extra virgin olive oil over top. Bake according to pizza crust requirements. Garnish with chopped fresh cilantro and lime wedges. Serve with Orange Salsa.

ORANGE SALSA:

1 whole orange
6 tablespoons finely chopped red
  onion
4 tablespoons chopped fresh
  cilantro

2 tablespoons fresh lime juice
2 tablespoons olive oil
½ teaspoon dried oregano
Salt to taste

Peel and seed orange and chop into ½-inch pieces. Combine orange, red onion, cilantro, lime juice, olive oil, oregano, and salt in a small bowl and mix well. Refrigerate, covered, 2 hours or longer. Use as additional garnish or topping for pizza. Yields 6 servings.

La Jolla Cooks Again

Pebble Beach Pineapple Pizza

½ cup sweet and sour sauce
1 (12-inch) Italian bread shell
1 small bell pepper, cut into thin
  strips

2 ounces cooked ham, cut into thin
  strips
1 cup pineapple tidbits, drained
1 cup shredded mozzarella cheese

Preheat oven to 450°. Spread sweet and sour sauce evenly over bread shell. Arrange bell pepper, ham, and pineapple over sauce. Sprinkle with cheese. Bake for 8–10 minutes. Serve immediately. Yields 4 servings.

The Golf Cookbook

Garlic Spring Rolls
with Garlicky-Lime Sauce

The traditional Chinese egg roll sparkles anew with the pungent power of garlic and the plucky pucker of lime.

35 cloves fresh garlic, peeled, divided
⅔ cup fresh lime juice
½ cup fish sauce (nuoc man)*
¼ cup bottled diced jalapeños
2 teaspoons sugar
½ cup chopped water chestnuts
2 cups ground pork
5 green onions, chopped
½ cup grated carrot
2 teaspoons sugar
1 teaspoon salt

1 teaspoon coarsely ground black pepper
4 cups thinly sliced Napa cabbage (Chinese cabbage)
18 spring roll wrappers (thawed, if frozen)*
⅓ cup canola oil, or as needed
Boston lettuce for garnish (optional)
Pickled carrot for garnish (optional)
Green onion brushes for garnish (optional)

To make sauce, in a food processor, finely chop 20 cloves garlic. Mix garlic with lime juice, fish sauce, jalapeños, and sugar; reserve.

To make spring rolls, in a food processor, chop remaining garlic. In a bowl, thoroughly mix garlic with water chestnuts and next 6 ingredients. Gently fold in Napa cabbage.

On a work surface lightly dusted with cornstarch, wet edge of 1 wrapper; put 2 tablespoons filling in center. Fold 1 corner over filling. Fold sides; roll tightly. Repeat with remaining wrappers. Heat half the oil (or more as needed) in a large nonstick frying pan; fry 9 rolls, turning frequently, until golden brown. Drain on paper towels; keep warm. Repeat with remaining rolls.

Arrange spring rolls on a serving platter with a bowl of sauce in the middle. Garnish with lettuce, carrot and green onion. Makes 6 servings.

*Sold in Asian grocery stores

Garlic Lovers' Greatest Hits

Spinach Mushroom Pesto Quiche

Also known as the "pizza quiche," this rich and flavorful dish also makes a tasty dinner entrée served with a fresh green salad.

1½ cups water	¼ cup chopped sun-dried tomatoes
½ cup polenta	3 eggs, beaten
¼ cup Parmesan cheese	1¼ cups milk
½ teaspoon salt	½ cup cottage cheese
1 large tablespoon pesto	5 ounces frozen spinach, thawed
1 cup shredded mozzarella	with liquid squeezed out
1 cup thinly sliced mushrooms	¼ cup grated Parmesan cheese
3 cloves garlic, minced	1 Roma tomato, thinly sliced

Preheat oven to 350°. Lightly oil bottom of one pie plate. In small saucepan, mix water and polenta and bring to a boil. Reduce heat and stir until thickened. Add Parmesan and salt and mix well. Pour into pie plate, covering bottom. Let cool until solidified, about 5–10 minutes. Spread pesto over polenta and sprinkle with mozzarella.

Sauté mushrooms, garlic and sun-dried tomatoes. Beat together eggs, milk and cottage cheese. Add sautéed mushroom mixture and spinach. Mix well. Pour into pie plate. Top with Parmesan and decorate with tomato slices. Bake for 45 minutes until center is set. Serves 10–12.

Mendocino Mornings

Marie's Famous Crab Quiche

1 cup shredded Swiss cheese	1 cup light cream
1 unbaked (9-inch) pie shell	Salt to taste
1 (7½-ounce) can crabmeat,	½ teaspoon grated lemon peel
drained and flaked	(optional)
2 green onions (including tops),	¼ teaspoon dry mustard
sliced thinly	Dash mace (optional)
3 eggs, beaten	¼ cup sliced almonds

Sprinkle cheese over bottom of pie shell. Top with crab; sprinkle with onions. Combine eggs, cream, salt, lemon peel, dry mustard, and mace. Pour over crab. Top with almonds. Bake at 325° for 45 minutes or until set. Remove from oven and let stand 10 minutes before serving. Serves 6.

Nuggets, Nibbles and Nostalgia

Polenta De Moya

3 cups water
2 tablespoons vegetarian broth
1 cup polenta (coarse cornmeal)
½ pound spinach leaves, washed, chopped
3 tablespoons olive oil
3 cloves garlic, minced

1 pound assorted mushrooms, sliced
¼ cup dry white wine
Pinch of thyme and marjoram
Salt and ground pepper to taste
4 ounces Gorgonzola cheese
Fresh chives

Bring water to a boil; add broth and slowly stir in polenta. Reduce heat to simmer for about 20 minutes, stirring to keep from lumping. Add chopped spinach and combine. Spread into greased baking pan.

Heat olive oil in skillet, add garlic, and sauté for 1–2 minutes. Add sliced mushrooms and cook for 3–5 minutes. Stir in wine, herbs, pepper and salt to taste. Simmer 2 minutes. Pour over polenta; crumble Gorgonzola on top and sprinkle fresh snipped chives. Broil until bubbly.

Note: If mushrooms are too juicy, lift out with slotted spoon and put over polenta. Put liquid on high heat and reduce to ¼ cup (1–2 minutes.) Pour over mushrooms and continue.

The Potluck Cookbook

The Unburger

This humble little creation I formulated for The Greenery, in keeping with the policy of no red meat. I had no idea how popular it would become! Many strict vegetarians were thrilled by its existence, and many people who just like new and delicious taste treats became downright "hooked."

5 cups cooked brown rice
2½ cups ground almonds
2 cups sunflower seeds, hulled and ground
1½ tablespoons cumin
1 tablespoon minced garlic (or garlic powder)

2 tablespoons soy sauce
2 teaspoons seasoned salt
2 teaspoons curry powder
1 egg
Flour for dredging

Combine all ingredients in a large mixing bowl; mix well with very clean hands. Shape into patties, lightly flour on both sides and either microwave for approximately 1 minute, or pan-fry in small amount of vegetable oil. Serve on whole-grain buns, with Unburger Spread, tomato slice and lettuce or sprouts; top with a slice of cheese, if desired. Makes about 20 patties.

UNBURGER SPREAD:

2 cups mayonnaise
1 teaspoon chili powder or cayenne pepper

2 tablespoons soy sauce

Combine all ingredients; whisk until smooth and well blended. Store in airtight container in refrigerator.

Note: This "Unburger" mixture also makes a delicious burrito. Crumble a portion of unburger mixture, add pinto beans, chile salsa, cheese and onions; warm in microwave or lightly oiled frying pan. Place serving portion on flour tortilla, sprinkle with grated cheese and roll "burrito-style."

Cooking Pure & Simple

Often shrouded in a thick fog, the Golden Gate Bridge sways 27 feet to withstand winds of up to 100 miles per hour. Its two great cables contain enough strands of steel wire (about 80,000 miles) to encircle the equator three times, and the concrete poured into its piers and anchorages would pave a five-foot sidewalk from New York to San Francisco.

Noodle Pudding Soufflé

This tasty buffet casserole will become a frequent favorite—company or not.

1 (8-ounce) package medium noodles
Salted water
¼ pound butter or margarine,
  softened
½ cup sugar
½ pint cottage cheese (1 cup)
1 pint dairy sour cream (2 cups)
½ teaspoon salt
2 teaspoons vanilla extract
5 eggs
Cinnamon

Preheat oven to 350°. Grease a 9x13-inch baking dish; set aside. In a large saucepan, cook noodles in boiling salted water to cover until tender, 8–10 minutes. Drain and set aside.

In a large bowl, beat butter or margarine and sugar. Add cottage cheese, sour cream, salt and vanilla. Mix in eggs, 1 at a time, beating after each addition. Stir in cooked noodles. Pour into prepared baking dish. Sprinkle top with cinnamon. Bake 50–55 minutes, until golden brown. Let stand 5 minutes before cutting into squares. May be frozen and reheated. Serves 12.

Apples Etc. Cookbook

Meats

Once a chilling destination for maximum-security convicts, Alcatraz now sees hundreds of thousands more tourists per year than the total number of prisoners in its entire 29-year life as a federal penitentiary.

Filet Mignon in Mushroom Sauce

1 ounce olive oil	Salt and pepper to taste
1 small shallot	2 (¾-inch) filet mignon medallions
¼ bunch flat-leaf parsley	¼ cup beef stock or bouillon
4 garlic cloves	¼ cup cognac or brandy
2 cups assorted wild mushrooms	¼ cup heavy cream
1 tablespoon sherry	2 tablespoons Dijon mustard

Heat olive oil in saucepan and over medium flame. Chop shallots, parsley and garlic coarsely. Add sliced mushrooms and sauté for 8–10 minutes. Add to saucepan and stir.

Add sherry and salt and pepper. Simmer for 15 minutes or until liquid has evaporated. Preheat a cast-iron skillet for 10 minutes on medium heat. It should be very hot. Salt and pepper meat. Place medallions in the hot skillet and cook for approximately 2–3 minutes on each side for rare to medium-rare meat. Remove medallions and deglaze skillet with beef stock or bouillon.

Slowly add mushrooms and cognac, being aware that it might ignite. Reduce heat slightly before adding the cream and mustard. Stir until mixture thickens. Place medallions on a bed of mushrooms. Pour the remaining sauce over medallions and serve. Serves 2.

Monterey's Cookin' Pisto Style

Grilled Filet Mignon
with Cognac Cream Sauce

COGNAC CREAM SAUCE:

8 large egg yolks	2 tablespoons water
1 cup heavy cream	4 tablespoons sugar
1 cup cognac	1 tablespoon sweet butter

Combine egg yolks, cream, cognac, water, and sugar in top of double boiler set over simmering water. Stirring constantly, heat mixture about 9 minutes or until sauce thickens slightly. Do not boil. Add butter; melt thoroughly. Keep sauce warm until ready to use.

STEAKS:

Filet mignon, 1 per person	2 cloves garlic, crushed
Extra virgin olive oil	Salt and pepper to taste

Rub each steak with garlic and olive oil. Season with salt and pepper. Grill steaks over a medium-hot fire. Drizzle steaks with Cognac Cream Sauce before serving.

Carter House Cookbook

Beef Filets in Flaky Pastry

2 tablespoons butter
6 (6-ounce) beef filets, trimmed
6 tablespoons Madeira or sherry
   wine, divided
¾ pound fresh mushrooms,
   minced

1 package frozen puff pastry
   sheets
Salt
Fresh ground pepper

Melt butter in a heavy skillet. Sear steaks on both sides until browned. Pour in 2 tablespoons of wine and evaporate off. Transfer steaks to a platter and chill. To pan, add remaining wine and mushrooms. Cook over medium heat, stirring until all liquid evaporates. Chill mixture.

Roll out pastry on a lightly floured board to make a circle 8 inches in diameter. Place some of mushroom mixture in center of each circle. Place filet on top. Salt and pepper lightly. Fold pastry over steak and enclose tightly. Place on a baking tray, seam-side-down. Cover and refrigerate at least 15 minutes or as long as overnight.

Preheat oven to 425°. Bake for 18–20 minutes or until pastry is nicely browned. For first 10 minutes, place baking sheet on lowest oven rack. After 10 minutes, move to highest rack. Serve with bearnaise sauce.

Tahoe Parents Nursery School 40th Anniversary Alumni Cookbook

Bohemian Tri-Tip

2 jalapeño peppers, divided
1 head garlic, divided
3 pounds tri-tip (bottom sirloin)

2 cups soy sauce
2 teaspoons pepper

Dice ¾ of a jalapeño and 3 cloves of garlic. Stuff the jalapeño and garlic into the tri-tip. Dice remaining jalapeños and garlic and combine with the soy sauce and pepper. Mix well. Marinate the tri-tip in the soy sauce mix for 2–4 hours. Barbecue at a low temperature for ½ hour per side. Feeds 4.

More Firehouse Favorites

Silicon Valley is considered to be the home to the computer revolution that has changed the lives of virtually everyone in the world.

California Tri-Tip

Tri-tip is California's own cut of beef and it's become a popular one. Tri-tip is the popular name for the triangle tip, part of the bottom sirloin. Barbecued whole is a popular way to serve tri-tip, which is smaller than most roasts we're accustomed to seeing in markets.

2 (2-pound) whole beef tri-tips
1¼ cups beef broth
⅔ cup lime juice
½ cup olive oil
2 tablespoons dried cumin

2 tablespoons dried coriander
5 garlic cloves, minced
Vegetable oil
Salt and freshly ground pepper

Remove all fat from tri-tips. Make marinade by whisking broth with lime juice, olive oil, cumin, coriander and garlic until well blended. Place tri-tips in glass baking dish. Pour marinade over beef and cover. Refrigerate at least 6 hours, no longer than 24.

Remove tri-tips from marinade. Barbecue over medium-hot coals, turning occasionally, about 1 hour for medium-rare or until desired doneness. Use a meat thermometer or instant-read thermometer to be certain meat is cooked the way you want it. Brush meat with oil frequently while barbecuing. To serve, cut across the grain into thin slices; season with salt and pepper. Yields 12 servings.

Jan Townsend Going Home

Western Beef Sauté

3 tablespoons oil
1 pound top sirloin, thinly sliced
1 large onion, sliced
1 (6-ounce) can sliced mushrooms

⅛ teaspoon ground ginger
⅛ teaspoon dry mustard
1 tablespoon soy sauce
1 tablespoon sake (optional)

Heat oil in skillet. Sauté meat. Add onions and mushrooms. Add remaining ingredients. Quickly cook and stir until onions are tender. Serves 4.

Our Favorite Recipes

Vietnamese Marinade

Great marinade for chicken or pork.

¾ cup soy sauce
1 clove garlic, finely minced
1 small onion, finely minced

1 tablespoon granulated sugar
¼ cup water
1 tablespoon lemon juice (optional)

Mix together and marinate for 2 or more hours.

50th Anniversary Cookbook

Marinated Beef on a Stick

1 finger fresh ginger root, about
   3 inches
1 whole garlic bulb, separated and
   peeled
1 cup sugar

½ cup salad oil
¼ cup soy sauce
¼ cup sherry wine
1–1½ pounds beef sirloin or beef
   tenderloin

Chop ginger root and garlic very fine, and place in a mixing bowl. Add sugar and mix well. Stir in salad oil, soy sauce and wine. Cut beef into very thin strips, cutting on the bias. Place in marinade. Beef sirloin needs to be marinated for at least 2 hours; beef tenderloin needs only 1 hour.

Remove from marinade and skewer on bamboo sticks using 3–4 pieces of beef on each skewer. Place on barbecue grill and quickly turn from one side to the other, basting as they cook. Or you may broil them in the oven 3–4 inches from the flame for about 3 minutes on a side, basting as you turn them over. You will need about 18–20 skewers.

Party Perfect and Pampered

Souvlaki

MARINADE:

1 cup olive oil
2 cloves garlic, mashed
Salt and pepper to taste
Juice of 2 lemons

1 cup red wine
2 pounds lamb or lean beef, cubed
    or cut into strips
Wooden skewers

Make Marinade with oil, garlic, salt, pepper, lemon juice, and red wine. Pour over meat and marinate overnight.

Soak wooden skewers in water for at least 1 hour to prevent them from burning. Skewer meat and cook over charcoal until just pink inside. Baste frequently with Marinade.

PILAF:

1 cup rice
½ stick butter
1 lemon, more if desired

2 cups hot chicken broth
½ teaspoon salt

For Pilaf, brown rice in butter; add lemon juice. When color changes, add chicken broth and salt. Cover and cook over low heat for about 30 minutes. Serves 6.

Food Festivals of Northern California

Sandbagger Steak

For the man in your life.

3 beef bouillon cubes, crushed
1 teaspoon crushed garlic
2 tablespoons red wine
1 tablespoon Dijon mustard

4 beef loin or rib-eye steaks, cut
    ¾ inch thick
1 tablespoon butter
⅓ cup water

Mix bouillon, garlic, wine, and mustard and spread on both sides of each steak. Fry steaks in a large nonstick skillet in butter over medium-high heat 8–10 minutes for rare or until desired doneness. Remove steaks to serving platter; add water to hot pan, scraping up any brown bits of flavoring, and pour this pan gravy over steaks before serving. Yields 4 steaks.

The Golf Cookbook

Beef and Chicken Brochette

½ cup soy sauce
½ cup oil
3 green onions, sliced
1 tablespoon brown sugar
1 teaspoon powdered ginger
1 clove garlic, minced
2 teaspoons lemon juice
1 teaspoon vinegar

1½ pounds boneless sirloin, cut in cubes
2 boneless chicken breasts, cut in cubes
1 green pepper, cut in 1-inch squares
1 onion, cut in 1-inch pieces

Make a marinade of soy sauce, oil, green onions, brown sugar, ginger, clove garlic, lemon juice and vinegar. Marinate meat, chicken and vegetables for several hours. Drain.

Alternate meat, chicken, green peppers and onions on skewers. Place skewers on rack with drip pan. Broil, turning once, to desired doneness. Serves 6–8.

The Lazy Gourmet

Santa Barbara Shish Kabobs

There is such an abundant variety of good things on these skewers that this recipe calls for a party. The marinade is sensational.

MARINADE:

½ cup vegetable oil
¼ cup soy sauce
½ cup red wine
1 teaspoon ground ginger
3 small garlic cloves, crushed

1½ teaspoons curry powder
2 tablespoons catsup
¼ teaspoon pepper
¼ teaspoon hot pepper sauce

Blend all ingredients in a blender or food processor. Set aside.

KABOBS:

1 pound sirloin steak, cut into 1-inch-thick squares
1 pound boneless leg of lamb, cut into 1-inch-thick squares
1 pound pork tenderloin, cut into ½-inch-thick squares
1 eggplant, sliced in ½-inch squares

2 apples, peeled and cut into 6 wedges
1 green bell pepper, seeded and cut into pieces
1 cup cut pineapple
10 mushrooms
½ pound bacon, sliced

Place meat in a shallow dish, keeping each type of meat separate. Divide ¾ of the Marinade over the 3 meats. Cover and refrigerate 24 hours, stirring once or twice.

A few hours before serving, place eggplant, apples, green pepper, pineapple and mushrooms in a medium bowl. Add remaining Marinade. Marinate 2–3 hours at room temperature, stirring occasionally. To cook Kabobs, wrap a half slice of bacon around each piece of lamb. On large skewers, alternate beef, mushrooms, lamb, eggplant, pineapple, pork, green peppers and apple. Barbecue or broil for 5–10 minutes on each side. Serves 8.

California Sizzles

The legend of Bigfoot lives on. Earliest reports of this man-animal near Willow Creek were made in 1886; but as recently as 1960, at least 50 sightings by reliable people keep the mystery ever present. The latest "hearing" was on September 10, 1998, when a camper reported "the most scariest howl!" he had ever heard.

Beef Stew Burgundy

This stew has a very rich and robust flavor.

5 medium onions, sliced thin
2 tablespoons bacon drippings
3 pounds·lean beef stew meat,
   cut in 1-inch cubes
1 1/2 tablespoons flour
Salt and pepper

1 tablespoon chopped thyme
1 tablespoon chopped marjoram
2 cups beef broth
1 cup Merlot wine
1/2 pound fresh mushrooms, sliced

In heavy skillet, sauté onions in bacon drippings until brown. Remove onions from pan and set aside. Add meat and brown in same pan. When browned, sprinkle with flour, salt, pepper, thyme and marjoram; toss well. Add broth and wine; mix well. Simmer for 3 1/2 hours. (Add additional broth and wine as needed to keep meat barely covered.)

Return onions to skillet and add the mushrooms to simmer during the last hour of cooking or until meat is tender. Serve with rice, noodles or polenta. Serves 8. Serve with a Merlot or a Carignan.

Cooking with Wine

Flank Steak, California Style

The marinated steak can also be grilled. The leftovers are great for fajitas.

2 tablespoons soy sauce
1/4 cup fresh lime juice
1/4 cup beer
2 tablespoons olive oil
2 garlic cloves, pressed

2 jalapeño chiles, seeded, minced
1/2 teaspoon freshly ground pepper
1/2 teaspoon salt
2 pounds flank steak

In blender, combine and purée all ingredients except flank steak. Cut 4 shallow slashes across the grain on each side of flank steak. Place in a glass dish and pour in marinade, rubbing garlic into slashes. Cover and refrigerate for at least 2 hours, but preferably overnight.

Remove steak from refrigerator 30 minutes before cooking. Preheat broiler. Place steak on a broiler pan (reserve marinade) about 4 inches from heat and cook about 6 minutes per side for rare, 8 minutes for medium and 10 minutes for well done. The length of time depends on thickness of steak. Don't overcook meat. Meanwhile, boil marinade in a small saucepan to reduce it. Slice steak on diagonal and serve reduced marinade alongside. Serves 6.

The Art Lover's Cookbook: A Feast for the Eye

Steak Sandwich with Avocado Salsa and Roasted Peppers

¼ cup plus 1 tablespoon olive oil
2 large garlic cloves, minced
2 teaspoons dried oregano
2 teaspoons ground cumin
1 (2-pound) flank steak
Salt and pepper
2 firm but ripe avocados, pitted, peeled and chopped

1 (16-ounce) container thick chunky salsa, well drained
1 (10- to 12-inch) round loaf sourdough bread
1 (7-ounce jar) roasted red bell peppers, drained, thinly sliced
7 ounces thinly sliced Monterey Jack or provolone cheese

Prepare barbecue (medium-high heat) or preheat broiler. Combine ¼ cup olive oil, garlic, oregano and cumin in a small bowl. Rub mixture over both sides of steak. Sprinkle steak with salt and pepper. Grill or broil to desired doneness, about 5 minutes per side for medium-rare. Transfer steak to work surface. Cool. Cut steak across grain into thin strips.

Toss chopped avocados with salsa in medium bowl. Season salsa with salt and pepper.

Using a serrated knife, split bread loaf in half lengthwise. Scoop out bread from center of each half, leaving 1-inch thick layer of bread and crust intact. Brush cut surface with remaining 1 tablespoon olive oil. Arrange steak slices in hollow of bottom half of bread. Arrange bell peppers over steak. Arrange cheese over peppers. Spoon avocado salsa over cheese. Top with second half of bread. Wrap sandwich in foil and refrigerate at least 4 hours and up to 8 hours. Cut sandwiches into wedges and serve. Serves 6–8.

Symphony of Flavors

Holiday Brisket

1 cup dark brown sugar
½ cup cider vinegar
½ cup wine or water

1 package dry onion soup mix
1 (5-pound) brisket

Mix first 4 ingredients together. Pour over brisket in roasting pan. Cover tightly with foil. Bake at 350° for 3 hours. (Check pan periodically to make sure there's enough liquid; add more water or wine as necessary.) You may slice brisket after 3 hours of baking and return it to pan for 1 more hour. Serves 8–10.

Jewish Cooking from Here & Far

Bar-B-Que Brisket

A definite holiday favorite that leaves your mouth watering for more!

1½ teaspoons salt
1 teaspoon garlic salt
2 teaspoons Worcestershire sauce
1 teaspoon onion salt

2 teaspoons pepper
2 teaspoons celery salt or seed
4–5 pound brisket (or chuck roast)

Mix all ingredients together and rub into both sides of brisket. Bake in a heavy closed foil container on a baking sheet or pan. Bake at 225° for 8 hours or overnight. Pour off most of the liquid, except about ¼ cup or less. Refrigerate to cool.

Slice thin (about ½-inch slices) and return to pan. Add Brisket Sauce and bake at 325° for 45–60 minutes.

BRISKET SAUCE:

1 cup sugar
1 cup favorite barbecue sauce

1 cup bottled Russian dressing

Mix together.

Sharing Our Best

Barbeque Sauce

Good basic barbecue sauce used at the Christ Church celebration.

½ cup chopped onions
½ cup chopped celery
1 clove garlic, minced
¼ pound butter
3 tablespoons olive oil
½ cup bouillon
¼ cup vinegar
1 cup chunky salsa (mild or hot)
1 tablespoon Worcestershire sauce

¼ cup brown sugar
2 tablespoons dry mustard
1 cup catsup
¼ teaspoon salt and pepper
3 (or more) drops of Tabasco sauce
⅛ teaspoon cinnamon
⅛ teaspoon cloves
1 teaspoon curry powder

Sauté onions, celery and garlic in butter and oil until transparent. Add remaining ingredients and simmer for no more than 15 minutes. (Cooking too long will make spices bitter!)

Seasons: Food for Thought and Celebration

Lemon Grass Beef

3 tablespoons crushed lemon grass
2 tablespoons soy sauce
2 tablespoons dry sherry
1 teaspoon sugar
1/2 cup water
2 pounds beef, cut into 1 3/4-inch
  strips
3/4 teaspoon salt
1/4 teaspoon pepper

2 cloves garlic, minced
1 teaspoon fresh minced ginger
1 tablespoon cornstarch
3 tablespoons cooking oil, divided
1 medium onion, thinly sliced
1/4 pound mushrooms, cut in
  quarters
Chopped green onion for garnish

Combine lemon grass, soy sauce, sherry, sugar and water. Simmer covered for 15 minutes. Strain and set aside. Mix together beef, salt, pepper, garlic, ginger and cornstarch. Brown beef mixture in 2 tablespoons of oil over high heat in two batches. Set aside.

Add 1 tablespoon oil to pan and brown onions and mushrooms. Return meat to pan. Add lemon grass mixture. Heat thoroughly. Serve over rice or noodles. Garnish with green onions. Serves 6–8.

Note: Lemon grass, also known as sorrel, is easy to grow in the backyard and gives a refreshing taste to many dishes.

Cooking with Herbs

Beef in Walnut Sauce

A crockpot recipe.

4 pounds rump roast, cubed
Seasoned flour
Olive oil (about 3 tablespoons)
1/2 cup water
1 (8-ounce) can tomato sauce
4–6 cloves garlic, minced
1/3 cup cider vinegar

1 whole cinnamon stick
8 whole cloves
8 whole allspice
1 cup ground walnuts
1 tablespoon lemon juice
Sliced sourdough French bread,
  toasted

Dredge meat in seasoned flour. Shake off excess. Heat oil in large frying pan. Brown meat well. Transfer to crockpot. Pour water into frying pan to loosen drippings. Add to crockpot with tomato sauce, garlic and vinegar. Place cinnamon stick, cloves and allspice in a tea ball of cheesecloth. Add to pot. Cover. Cook on LOW (200°) for 8–10 hours. Add walnuts and lemon juice. Serve over toasted French bread slices. Serves 8–10.

Treasured Recipes

Boneless Stuffed Veal Breast

5 pounds boneless veal breast
1–1½ teaspoons each: pepper,
  salt, paprika, garlic powder,
  onion powder
Ground ginger, to taste
6 potatoes, thickly sliced
3–4 cloves garlic, chopped

3 carrots, sliced
2 onions, sliced
3–4 whole allspice
2 bay leaves
½ cup chicken broth
½ cup white wine

STUFFING:
1 cup cooked white rice
1 cup cooked wild rice
1 large egg, beaten
1 large onion, chopped

3–4 ribs celery, chopped
1 tablespoon dried or fresh parsley
Salt and pepper to taste

Have butcher remove all bones and make pocket in veal breast. Mix seasonings; rub inside and outside of veal with mixture. Mix together Stuffing ingredients and fill pocket with mixture.

Preheat oven to 300°. Line bottom of roasting pan with potatoes, garlic, carrots, onions, allspice and bay leaves. Place stuffed roast on top and add chicken broth and wine to baste top of roast.

Bake, partially covered, at 300° to 325° for 1 hour, and uncovered for another 1½ hours or until done and brown. Baste occasionally and add more liquid if necessary.

Remove roast to a serving platter; slice across the grain and cover to keep warm. Serves 5–6.

California Kosher

Veal Marsala

6 veal cutlets, medium-thick slices
   of range-fed veal
2 cups seasoned bread crumbs
2 tablespoons extra virgin olive oil

2 tablespoons unsalted butter
Salt and pepper to taste
1 lemon, cut in wedges
4 sprigs Italian flat-leaf parsley

Prepare veal by sprinkling with water. Then cover each cutlet with plastic wrap and pound lightly. Unwrap and rub each cutlet with a drop or two of olive oil. Dredge cutlets in bread crumbs, pressing hard so they adhere to the meat.

Heat a skillet, and add olive oil, butter, salt and pepper. Place coated veal chops three at a time in skillet. Cook veal chops for 4–6 minutes on each side over medium-high heat. Clean skillet after each batch to avoid charred bread crumbs.

Serve veal chops on plate with Mushroom Marsala Sauce drizzled over top and along sides. Garnish with lemon and sprigs of flat-leaf parsley or fresh basil.

MUSHROOM MARSALA SAUCE:

1 cup wild mushrooms (2 or 3
   varieties if possible), sliced
¼ cup water
3 cloves garlic, chopped
6 green onions, sliced (white part
   only)

2 tablespoons extra virgin olive oil
2 tablespoons chopped Italian
   flat-leaf parsley
½ cup Marsala wine

In a large skillet, heat water, mushrooms, garlic, and onions over low heat and sauté a few minutes. Add olive oil and stir. Add parsley and wine; then stir until slightly reduced (approximately 4–5 minutes). Serves 6.

Cooking with Mushrooms

Italian Pot Roast

½ cup fat
2 large onions, chopped
4 cloves garlic, minced
3–4 pounds beef rump roast
¼ to ½ teaspoon salt and pepper

1 teaspoon powdered ginger, to taste
2 cups sliced mushrooms
1 cup pitted ripe olives (slice half)
1 (8-ounce) can tomato sauce

Heat fat in Dutch oven. Add onions and garlic; cook until golden. Sprinkle meat with salt, pepper and ginger; rub into meat. Brown on all sides; cover and cook gently for 2 hours.

Add mushrooms, olives, and tomato sauce. Cook about 1 hour longer or until meat is tender. Skim gravy before serving. Thin or thicken as necessary with water or flour-water. Good served with noodles. Serves 6–8.

Cooking on the Fault Line—Corralitos Style

Russian Hill Beef Stroganoff

1 pound filet mignon or top sirloin steak
¼ cup butter, divided
1 medium-size white onion, thinly sliced

⅓ pound fresh mushrooms, thinly sliced
½ cup sour cream
Salt and pepper to taste
Parsley for garnish

Remove any fat from steak. Cut meat into julienne strips about 2½ inches long by ⅓ inch by ⅓ inch.

Place half the butter in a frying pan and melt over low flame. Add onions and gently stir-fry until just limp. Do not let them brown. Add sliced mushrooms. Stir with onions for a minute to cook.

In another frying pan, melt remaining butter. Add steak and stir-fry just until rare inside. Add mushrooms and onions to steak pan. Blend in the sour cream and seasonings. Heat slightly, just until cream is hot. Serve at once. The idea is that the steak should remain rare in the delectable mushroom-onion sauce. Garnish with parsley. This will serve 2.

Note: Usually this is served with rice or egg noodles. Chilled champagne will add a happy Russian mood.

The California Cookbook

Mexican-Style Beef Stroganoff

2 pounds ground beef
1 cup finely chopped onion
2 cloves garlic, minced
2 tablespoons cooking oil
2 cups water
½ cup chili sauce
1 tablespoon paprika
1 tablespoon chili powder

2 teaspoons seasoned salt
1 teaspoon soy sauce
1 (8-ounce) carton sour cream
3 tablespoons all-purpose flour
1 (8-ounce) can sliced mushrooms,
  drained
Hot cooked noodles
Snipped chives (optional)

In 12-inch skillet, brown ground beef with onion and garlic in oil until meat is brown and onion is tender. Drain off fat. Add water, chili sauce, paprika, chili powder, seasoned salt and soy sauce. Cover; simmer 15 minutes. Stir together sour cream and flour; stir into meat mixture along with mushrooms. Cook and stir until bubbly. Cook 2 minutes more. Serve atop hot noodles. Sprinkle chives atop. Makes 8–10 servings.

Tasty Temptations

Lasagna in a Bun

8 sub or hoagie buns or round
  French bread
1 pound ground beef
1 large onion, chopped
1 cup spaghetti sauce
1 tablespoon garlic powder
1 tablespoon dried Italian
  seasoning

1 cup ricotta cheese
¼ cup grated Parmesan cheese
1 cup (4 ounces) shredded
  Cheddar, divided
1 cup (4 ounces) shredded
  mozzarella, divided

Cut thin layer off top of buns or bread. Hollow out centers, leaving ¼-inch-thick shells. Discard tops and centers. Brown ground beef and onion; drain. Add spaghetti sauce, garlic powder and Italian seasoning. Cook 4 or 5 minutes.

Combine ricotta, Parmesan, ½ Cheddar and ½ mozzarella cheese. Spoon meat mixture into buns. Top with cheese mixture. Place on baking sheet. Cover loosely with foil and bake at 350° for 25 minutes. Uncover; sprinkle with remaining cheeses. Bake 2 or 3 minutes more. Makes 8 servings.

New Covenant Kitchens

Easy Enchilada Pie

1 pound lean ground beef
1 small onion, chopped
1 (8-ounce) can tomato sauce
1 (1¼-ounce) package taco
   seasoning mix
1 (10¾-ounce) can condensed
   cream of chicken soup
½ cup milk (can use skim milk)
12 (6-inch) corn tortillas
8 ounces shredded Cheddar cheese
   (2 cups)

In a large skillet, brown ground beef and chopped onion. Drain off fat. Stir in tomato sauce and taco seasoning. Bring mixture to a boil. Reduce heat and simmer, uncovered, 5 minutes. Remove skillet from heat.

Stir together soup and milk. Spoon ½ soup mixture into a 9x13x2-inch baking dish. Cut tortillas in half. Use 12 halves to place over soup in dish. Spoon meat mixture over tortillas. Top with remaining tortillas and soup, then with cheese. Bake in a 350° oven for 30 minutes or until heated through. Serves 6–8.

Nuggets, Nibbles and Nostalgia

Better Than Steak

2 (10-ounce) packages frozen
   chopped spinach
1 cup sour cream
1 cup grated Cheddar cheese,
   divided
1 cup grated Jack cheese, divided
½ cup grated Parmesan cheese
¼ cup chopped green onion tops
1 teaspoon Italian herb seasoning
1 pound ground beef
¼ cup chopped green onion
Salt and pepper to taste
20–25 fresh mushrooms
Nutmeg

Thaw spinach and squeeze dry. Mix with sour cream, ½ cup Cheddar, ½ cup Jack, Parmesan cheese, onion tops and seasoning. Sauté ground beef with green onions, salt and pepper to taste and chopped mushroom stems. Place mushroom caps, cut-side-up, in center of a large shallow baking dish. Spoon spinach mixture around edges. Spoon meat mixture over mushrooms. Sprinkle top with remaining cheeses and nutmeg. Bake at 350° for 30 minutes or until hot and cheese is melted. Makes 4 servings.

Tried and True Recipes

Cabbage Rolls

Also known as Holiskes, Praakes, Galuptzi, or when raisins are added to sauce, Sarma.

1 large head cabbage
1 pound ground beef
1/2 cup cooked rice
1/2 large onion, grated
1 egg
1/2 teaspoon pepper
1 (8-ounce) can tomato sauce
1 (6-ounce) can tomato paste, divided

1 cup water
1/4 teaspoon sage
1/2 teaspoon ground bay leaves
1/4 cup packed brown sugar
2 or 3 tablespoons lemon juice (or vinegar)

Remove core from cabbage, place in pot, and cover with boiling water; let stand for 15 minutes. Mix ground beef and next five ingredients in a bowl. Stir in 2 tablespoons tomato paste. Drain cabbage and separate the leaves carefully. Place a heaping tablespoon of meat mixture (oval shaped) on each leaf. Tuck in the sides and carefully roll up cabbage leaves. You may have to use toothpicks to hold them together.

Consider every cabbage leaf a challenge to roll; those leaves that fail the test should be shredded and placed on the bottom of the pan. Gently place cabbage rolls on shredded cabbage. Combine remaining tomato paste and next 5 ingredients; pour over cabbage rolls. Cover and simmer over low heat, or place in 375° oven for 1 hour, then uncover pan, baste and put in oven again for 20–30 minutes to brown slightly. If any are left, they taste even better reheated. Serves 6.

Jewish Cooking from Here & Far

Alice's Stuffed Rolls

1 pound hamburger
1 onion, chopped
1/2 pound grated Cheddar cheese
1/4 cup chopped olives

1 (8-ounce) can Italian-style tomato sauce
Seasonings to taste
6 French rolls

Brown hamburger and onion. Mix in remaining ingredients, except rolls. Cook down a little. Hollow out rolls and fill with meat mixture. Wrap in aluminum foil and keep hot in oven at 300°. Can be frozen and reheated in the oven. Serves 6.

On the Road Again Cookbook

Tunnel of Spuds Meatloaf

The best diner food you ever had!

1 package instant mashed potatoes
1 1/2 pounds extra-lean (7% fat)
  ground beef
1 egg, slightly beaten
1/2 cup oatmeal
1/3 cup grated Parmesan cheese
1 teaspoon onion powder
1 teaspoon salt
1/2 teaspoon pepper
3/4 cup unsweetened applesauce
1/2 cup catsup
1/4 cup lemon juice
1/4 cup grape jelly

Preheat oven to 350°. Prepare 6 servings of instant mashed potatoes according to package directions and set aside.

Spray a medium-size baking dish with nonstick cooking spray. In a mixing bowl combine ground beef, egg, oatmeal, cheese, onion powder, salt, pepper, and applesauce. Mix well with your hands. Pat half of meat mixture into baking dish, shaping it into a rectangular loaf. Spread mashed potatoes over meat. Pat the rest of the meat over mashed potatoes.

In a small bowl, mix catsup, lemon juice, and grape jelly, and spread over top layer of meat. Bake for 1 hour. Yields 6–8 servings.

The 7 Day Cookbook

Hungry Boy Cheeseburgers

A cheeseburger with the works in a buttermilk biscuit.

1 pound extra-lean (7% fat)
   ground beef
1 teaspoon seasoned salt
¼ teaspoon garlic powder
⅛ teaspoon pepper
1 can (8) jumbo reduced-fat
   buttermilk biscuits

Mustard, catsup, pickle relish
4 thin slices sweet onion (optional)
4 slices reduced-fat Cheddar or
   American cheese

In bowl, mix ground beef, seasoned salt, garlic powder and pepper. Shape into 4 patties. In large nonstick skillet, brown patties over high heat. Remove from pan and drain on paper towel.

Preheat oven to 375°. On lightly floured board, roll each biscuit into 6-inch circle. Spread 4 circles with a little mustard and catsup. Place a beef patty on each of these circles. Place about a teaspoon of pickle relish and a slice of onion on each meat patty. Moisten edges of biscuits and top with remaining biscuit circles. Press edges together with fork and prick tops.

Bake on ungreased baking sheet 15–17 minutes. Place cheese slice on each biscuit, and continue baking just until cheese melts. Yields 4 large cheeseburgers.

The 7 Day Cookbook

Located deep in the heart of the magnificent redwood forests of California's scenic Santa Cruz Mountains, the colorful Roaring Camp and Big Trees Narrow-Gauge Railroad steam trains date back to the 1880s. From Santa Cruz Beach to Bear Mountain, passengers ride over the steepest railroad grades in North America. Not everything in California is the biggest: Roaring Camp Covered Bridge is the shortest in the U.S., only 36 feet long.

Mom's Tamale Pie

1 pound ground beef
1 cup finely chopped onion
1 (1-pound) can chopped tomatoes
1 (1-pound) can whole kernel
corn, drained
1 teaspoon chili powder (more
if you like it hot)
1 teaspoon salt
1/4 teaspoon freshly ground pepper
1 (15-ounce) can ripe medium
olives, drained
1 cup cold water
1/2 cup yellow cornmeal
1/2 cup grated sharp Cheddar cheese

Brown ground beef in skillet over medium heat, stirring occasionally. Pour off fat as it collects. When meat starts to brown, stir in onion. Cook until meat is well browned and onion softens, stirring occasionally. Slowly mix in tomatoes and corn. Blend in chili powder, salt and pepper. Cover skillet; simmer about 15 minutes. Stir in olives.

Heat oven to 350°. Have ready a buttered 9x13-inch baking pan, or coat it with a nonstick cooking spray. Whisk water with cornmeal in small saucepan. Cook over low heat until thickened, whisking constantly. Pour beef mixture into prepared pan. Spread cornmeal on top and bake 1 hour. Take pie out of oven and sprinkle top with cheese. Put back in oven and bake 5 minutes longer or until cheese melts. Yields 8 servings.

Jan Townsend Going Home

Picante Chili

1 large onion, chopped
2 tablespoons oil or butter
1 pound steak, cut into cubes
1 pound ground beef
1 (8-ounce) can tomato sauce
1 (28-ounce) can tomatoes
1 tablespoon chili powder
2 tablespoons chopped cilantro
or parsley
1 cup hot picante sauce, or to taste
1 clove garlic, minced
1/2 teaspoon salt
1/2 teaspoon oregano
1 ounce Mexican chocolate, grated
(or substitute baking chocolate
with 1 teaspoon sugar and
1/2 teaspoon cinnamon)
1–1 1/2 cups grated Cheddar or
Monterey Jack cheese (optional)

Brown onion in oil or butter in large skillet until soft. Transfer to crockpot. Brown cubed steak and ground beef, a little at a time, in same skillet. Transfer to crockpot.

Combine remaining ingredients and simmer until chocolate melts. Add to crockpot and mix well. Cook for 7–10 hours on LOW setting. Yields 6–8 servings. Serve with cornbread and a green or fruit salad.

Note: Transports well in the crockpot and will stay hot for several hours.

Only in California

Hot Lamb Satay with Mint and Garlic

16 (8-inch) bamboo skewers
1 pound boned leg of lamb,
  trimmed
½ cup hoisin sauce
¼ cup plum sauce
2 teaspoons orange zest

¼ cup dry sherry
2 tablespoons honey
1 tablespoon Asian chili sauce
⅓ cup chopped fresh mint
8 cloves garlic, minced

Soak bamboo skewers in hot water for 1–24 hours.

Cut lamb into ¼ x 4-inch strips. Combine hoisin sauce, plum sauce, orange peel, sherry, honey, chili sauce, mint and garlic in a small bowl. Thread lamb onto skewers and arrange in shallow baking dish. Pour in hoisin mixture. Marinate, covered, in refrigerator for 15 minutes to 2 hours.

Fire up grill. Brush oil over grill rack or coat with cooking spray. Place on grill. Arrange lamb on rack. Grill 2 minutes on a side or until meat is still slightly pink in center. Remove to serving plate. Yields 4 servings.

Hint: May also cook under broiler. Preheat oven to 550°. Place rack at highest position. Arrange lamb on baking sheet. Cover skewer ends with foil. Broil 2–4 minutes per side or until meat is still slightly pink in center.

Dining by Design

Lamb Loin with Pesto Mint Sauce

Lamb loin (1 loin serves 2 people)
Hot, sweet mustard
4 thin slices bacon or pancetta
Fresh mint or fresh rosemary,
  chopped (optional)
1 cup pesto, your own or jarred
  bought

2 tablespoons Cross & Blackwell's
  mint sauce
2 tablespoons chopped fresh mint
1 tablespoon chopped fresh
  rosemary, or 1 teaspoon dried
  rosemary

Spread lamb loin generously with mustard. Wrap with bacon or pancetta. Sprinkle with herbs. Preheat oven to 350°. Grill or pan-fry lamb on all sides. Place on cookie sheet or roasting pan and put in oven to finish cooking off. If you like your lamb rare, this should take about 5–10 minutes. Cook longer for more well-done lamb. Remove from oven and let meat rest 10 minutes before slicing.

To make sauce, combine pesto with mint sauce. Add fresh mint and rosemary. Combine well. Serve with sliced lamb. Serves 2.

Sounds Tasty!

Slow–Cooked Pork with Wine Sauce

2 pounds boneless pork (shoulder
  or butt)
½ tablespoon sugar
½ cup light soy sauce
¼ cup water

½ teaspoon black pepper
¼ cup dry sherry
½ teaspoon freshly grated ginger
2 green onions, chopped
2 cloves garlic, crushed

Mix all ingredients except pork. Place pork in ovenproof casserole dish (large enough to hold meat so it is covered by sauce). Pour sauce over pork; cover and bake at 275° for 6 hours.

San Ramon's Secret Recipes

Dito's Carnitas

1 (4- to 8-pound) pork roast
  (¾ pound per person)
3 cloves garlic per pound of roast
2 green bell peppers, sliced
1 red bell pepper, sliced

2–3 yellow onions, sliced
½ cup water
Garlic salt
Salt and pepper
2 cups salsa

Preheat oven to 300°. Trim away all excess fat from pork roast. Poke holes in roast and insert cleaned garlic clove slices. Lay sliced peppers and onions in bottom of pan. Place roast on top. Add ½ cup of water. Season liberally with garlic salt, salt and pepper. Top with your favorite salsa. Seal tightly with lid or aluminum foil. Cook 4–5 hours until falling apart. Drain excess liquid. Shred in pan and mix with cooked vegetables. Serve with hot corn tortillas, beans and rice. Save leftovers to be added to eggs as machaca for your next station brunch.

More Firehouse Favorites

Pork Roast
with Sausage & Spinach Stuffing

1 (10-ounce) package frozen chopped spinach, cooked and drained
¾ pound sweet Italian sausage links, removed from casing
½ cup bread crumbs
1 tablespoon fennel seeds
½ cup Parmesan cheese
1 onion, finely chopped

½ cup slivered almonds, toasted
2 eggs, slightly beaten
2 tablespoons chopped parsley
1 teaspoon thyme leaves, divided
1 teaspoon finely chopped garlic, divided
⅛ teaspoon pepper
1 (3-pound) boneless, center-cut pork loin roast

Preheat oven to 350°. In large bowl, combine and mix spinach, sausage, bread crumbs, fennel seeds, Parmesan cheese, onion, almonds, eggs, parsley, ½ teaspoon thyme, ½ teaspoon garlic and pepper; set aside. Butterfly roast* and spread spinach mixture evenly on cut side of roast. Roll, starting at long end, jelly-roll style; tie securely with string. Rub roast with oil. Then top with remaining garlic and thyme. Roast on rack seam-side-down for 1½ hours or until meat thermometer reaches 165°–170°.

*To butterfly roast: Place boneless roast fat-side-down. Starting at thickest edge, slice horizontally through meat, stopping 1 inch from opposite edge so that roast can open like a book. Lightly pound opened roast and remove any fat thicker than ¼ inch.

Centennial Cookbook

Pork Loin Roast with Date Glaze

1 boned and rolled pork loin   Salt and pepper to taste

Place pork loin in shallow roasting pan. Insert meat thermometer in center. Sprinkle with salt and pepper, and roast in uncovered 325° oven for 1½ hours.

DATE GLAZE:
1 (8-ounce) jar red currant jelly
1 cup chopped dates
2 tablespoons wine vinegar

1 teaspoon prepared mustard
½ teaspoon salt

Heat currant jelly over low flame until it liquefies. Add 4 remaining ingredients and cook 3–4 minutes, stirring constantly.

Remove meat from oven; baste generously with glaze. Return to oven and continue roasting for 30 minutes, or until thermometer reaches 180°. Baste occasionally with additional glaze. Serves 6–8.

Food Festivals of Southern California

Pork Mediterranean

Easy to fix, nice to serve.

1 pound boneless pork, cut into
  ¾-inch cubes
1 tablespoon vegetable oil
1 large onion, sliced and separated
  into rings
2 cloves garlic, minced
1 (16-ounce) can tomatoes, cut up
1 teaspoon instant chicken bouillon
  granules

1 teaspoon crushed thyme
⅛ teaspoon pepper
1 (3-ounce) can sliced mushrooms
¼ cup sliced ripe olives (optional)
2 tablespoons snipped parsley
1 tablespoon all-purpose flour

In a large skillet, brown ½ of the pork in hot oil. Brown remaining
pork with onion rings and garlic. Return all pork to skillet. Stir in
undrained tomatoes, bouillon granules, thyme and pepper. Bring
to boiling; reduce heat. Cover; simmer 45 minutes, or until tender.
Skim fat, if necessary.

Stir in mushrooms, olives, if desired, and parsley. Combine flour
and ¼ cup cold water; stir into pork mixture. Cook and stir until
thickened and bubbly. Cook and stir for 1 minute more. Serve over
hot, cooked noodles or steamed rice. Serves 4.

50th Anniversary Cookbook

Marinated Pork Tenderloin

MARINADE:
½ cup soy sauce
½ cup dry red wine
½ teaspoon ground ginger

½ teaspoon dry mustard
1 clove garlic, minced
1 tablespoon sugar

Mix Marinade ingredients. Pour over tenderloin. Marinate for 2–4
hours in refrigerator. Discard marinade.

1 (1½-pound) pork tenderloin   Sliced green onions for garnish

Roast tenderloin in a 325° oven approximately 30–40 minutes until
meat thermometer registers 160°. To serve, slice on platter and
garnish with sliced green onions. Yields 5–6 servings.

Variation: Marinate as above, omitting sugar from Marinade. Remove
meat from Marinade and pat dry. Coat with a mixture of ¼ cup honey
and 2 tablespoons brown sugar, then roll in white sesame seeds to cover.
Roast in greased pan.

Celebrating California

Pot–Roasted Pork Tenderloin Stuffed with Fruits

2 pork tenderloins
1 teaspoon sugar
Salt and freshly ground pepper
10 large prunes, soaked, halved, thinly sliced
2 cooked apples, sliced, cored, and and pitted

6 tablespoons butter, divided
5 tablespoons cold water
⅓ cup light cream
2 tablespoons flour
Pomegranate jelly (or currant jelly)

Split pork tenderloins lengthwise without separating the two halves, and pound the meat flat. Sprinkle each tenderloin with sugar, salt and pepper . Place prunes and apples over the tenderloins. Then roll each tenderloin up carefully, starting at one of the shorter ends. Tie the rolls securely with string.

In a heavy, flameproof casserole, brown tenderloins in 4 table-spoons butter, being careful not to loosen stuffing. Remove pork rolls from the pan. Add cold water to casserole, and, using a wooden spoon or spatula, scrape bottom of casserole clean. Pour in cream. Return rolls to casserole, cover, and simmer over low heat until meat is tender, about 30 minutes.

Lift rolls out of casserole; place on serving dish, and carefully remove string; keep meat warm.

In a saucepan, melt remaining 2 tablespoons butter and flour together, stirring constantly until flour is lightly cooked. Add a little more butter if necessary. Mix into the juices in the casserole, and stir until thickened. Adjust seasoning and flavor to taste with pome-granate or currant jelly. Pour some of the sauce on the pork rolls and serve the rest on the side. Serves 6.

Pea Soup Andersen's Cookbook

Orange–Garlic Pork Chops

The flavors of garlic, onion and ginger combined with the tang of fresh orange help to transform these pork chops into a truly exotic main course.

6 pork chops	¼ teaspoon powdered ginger
1 medium orange	Pepper to taste
4 cloves fresh garlic	1–2 tablespoons butter
½ small onion	Salt to taste

Remove fat from chops. Squeeze orange into small bowl, keeping as much pulp as possible. Press garlic into orange juice. Using garlic press, squeeze onion into orange-garlic mixture, being sure to remove onion skin. Add ginger and a pinch of pepper; stir well. Place chops in shallow baking dish, cover with marinade and let stand for at least 45 minutes.

Melt butter in skillet with lid. Remove chops from marinade, reserving marinade, and brown chops on both sides in butter. Cover with remaining marinade and cook, covered, for 10 minutes. Remove cover and cook until fork-tender. Add salt and more pepper to taste. Makes 6 servings.

The Complete Garlic Lovers' Cookbook

Charlotte's Mapled Pork Chops

6 (1-inch-thick) pork chops	½ teaspoon chili powder
¼ cup chopped onion	⅛ teaspoon pepper
1 tablespoon vinegar	¼ cup pure or maple-blended
1 tablespoon Worcestershire sauce	syrup
1½ teaspoons salt	¼ cup water

Lightly brown pork chops; place in flat baking dish. Mix together onion, vinegar, Worcestershire sauce, salt, chili powder, pepper, syrup and water; pour over pork chops. Cover; bake 45 minutes at 400°, basting occasionally. Uncover; bake 15 minutes more; place chops on platter. Thicken sauce with flour; pour over meat. Serves 4–6.

The Stirling City Hotel Favorite Recipes

Rosie's Terribly Spicy Ribs

Marinate for a full 24 hours to allow the aromatic flavors of garlic, fresh ginger and sesame to work their magic on these "terribly delicious" ribs!

1 rack (approximately 4 pounds) lean pork ribs, cut into double rib sections

MARINADE:

3 cloves fresh garlic, crushed
1 teaspoon minced fresh ginger root
1/2 cup soy sauce

1/2 cup honey
1/2 cup dry sherry
1/2 cup vermouth

In a glass or stainless steel bowl, combine Marinade ingredients. Add ribs and turn to coat. Cover with plastic wrap and marinate in refrigerator for 24 hours or longer, turning occasionally.

COATING:

5 tablespoons minced fresh garlic
3 tablespoons minced fresh ginger root
2 tablespoons Oriental sesame oil

1 cup sesame seeds, divided
1 cup finely chopped fresh cilantro, divided

Preheat oven to 325°. Remove ribs from Marinade and pat semi-dry. Combine coating mixture of garlic, ginger and sesame oil, and rub into meat. Combine 1/2 cup sesame seeds with 1/2 cup cilantro and roll ribs into this mixture. Bake for 20 minutes.

Turn ribs, sprinkle with half the remaining cilantro and sesame seeds, and bake another 20 minutes. Turn ribs again, sprinkle with remaining cilantro and sesame seeds, and bake for 15 minutes more or until tender. Makes 4 servings as a main dish, or 8 as an appetizer cut into single-rib pieces.

Garlic Lovers' Greatest Hits

Barbecued Spareribs

RIBS:

4 pounds pork spareribs	**2 teaspoons salt**
1 onion, quartered	**1/4 teaspoon pepper**

In a large kettle, place ribs, onion, salt, and pepper and cover with 3 quarts of water. Bring to a boil. Reduce heat, cover and simmer for 1 1/2 hours or until tender. Drain.

SAUCE:

1/2 cup cider vinegar	**1 tablespoon lemon juice**
1/2 cup ketchup	**1/2 cup light brown sugar**
1/4 cup chili sauce	**1/2 teaspoon dry mustard**
1/4 cup Worcestershire sauce	**1 clove garlic, crushed**
2 tablespoons chopped onion	**Dash cayenne pepper**

While ribs are cooking, in medium saucepan, combine all Sauce ingredients. Simmer uncovered for 1 hour, stirring occasionally.

Arrange spareribs on grill and brush with Sauce. Barbecue 10 minutes on each side, basting frequently. These can also be done under a broiler, 5 inches from the heat. Serves 4–6.

The Lafayette Collection

Tropic Sun Spareribs

3–4 pounds spareribs or	**1 (20-ounce) can crushed**
country-style ribs	**pineapple, undrained**
3 large cloves garlic, pressed	**1 (12-ounce) bottle chili sauce**
Salt and pepper	**1/2 cup brown sugar, packed**
1 large onion, sliced	**1 teaspoon ground ginger**
1/4 cup water	**1/2 teaspoon dry mustard**

Rub ribs with garlic. Sprinkle with salt and pepper. Arrange onion in large baking pan. Place ribs on top. Add 1/4 cup water to pan. Cover with foil. Bake in a 350° oven for 1 1/2 hours. Combine remaining ingredients. Spoon over ribs. Bake, uncovered, 1 hour longer. Serves 4.

...Fire Burn & Cauldron Bubble

Forgotten Short Ribs

3–4 pounds beef short ribs
Salt and pepper
1 (8-ounce) can tomato sauce
2 tablespoons vinegar

1 tablespoon instant minced onion
2 tablespoons molasses
1 teaspoon liquid smoke

Sprinkle salt and pepper on all sides of ribs and put into a Dutch oven or heavy 3-quart casserole. In a small pan, combine remaining ingredients. Bring to a boil and simmer for 5 minutes. Pour over ribs. Cover and bake at 275° for 3–4 hours or until tender. Makes 6–8 servings.

Can also be cooked in a crockpot on LOW for 8–10 hours. Leftovers make a wonderful stew with carrots and potatoes added. Also works very well with pot roast.

Tried and True Recipes

Poultry

Founded in 1776 by Franciscan Padres, Mission San Juan Capistrano is best known for its swallows, which return every year to their nests in the old stone church, the largest and most ornate of any of the missions.

Lime Grilled Chicken Breast with Cranberry Salsa

LIME GRILLED CHICKEN:

3 limes
6 boneless, skinless chicken breasts

½ cup butter
3 tablespoons honey

Squeeze limes for juice and marinate chicken for 1 hour only in the juice. (Lime juice will start cooking the chicken, so don't overdo it!) Grill chicken on BBQ grill for about 5 minutes each side. Melt together butter and honey; dip chicken in honey butter to serve with Cranberry Salsa. Makes 6 servings.

CRANBERRY SALSA:

1 can whole cranberry sauce
1 jalapeño pepper

Juice of 1 lime
Cilantro to taste

Combine all ingredients in food processor and blend together. This salsa should still be a little chunky. Freeze salsa and serve on side of Lime Grilled Chicken as a sorbet.

Dining Door to Door in Naglee Park

Chicken Opulent

4 chicken breasts
1 teaspoon salt
½ teaspoon pepper
1 teaspoon paprika
½ stick butter
1 (14-ounce) can artichoke hearts

½ pound mushrooms
1 pinch tarragon
3 tablespoons flour
⅓ cup sherry (or dry vermouth)
1½ cups chicken broth

Season chicken with salt, pepper, and paprika; sauté in butter. Place chicken in a casserole dish. Put artichoke hearts in skillet and sauté with mushrooms and tarragon for 5 minutes. Spoon artichoke heart mixture over chicken in casserole. Sprinkle flour over leftover juices in skillet; add sherry and chicken broth; stir and simmer for 5 minutes. Pour this sauce over casserole; cover and bake at 350°–375° for 45 minutes. This may be done ahead of time and reheated. Serves 4.

Mammoth Really Cooks Book II

Honey, This Is Chicken

1/3 cup chunky peanut butter
1/4 cup soy sauce
1/3 cup sherry
2 garlic cloves, minced
2 tablespoons grated fresh ginger
1/2 teaspoon freshly ground white pepper

2 tablespoons brown sugar, packed
3 tablespoons sesame oil
1/4 cup chopped green onion (white part only)
1 chicken, cut up
1/2 cup honey
1/2 cup Dijon mustard

Whisk the peanut butter with soy sauce, sherry, garlic, ginger, pepper, sugar, sesame oil, and onion. Pour over chicken pieces, and marinate overnight or up to 24 hours.

Heat oven to 450°. Have ready a buttered 9x13-inch baking pan, or coat it with nonstick cooking spray. Reserve marinade. Bake chicken in pan to sear meat on all sides. Lower heat to 350° and bake 1 1/2 hours, basting with reserved marinade first hour of baking; discard remaining marinade.

Put chicken on serving platter; cover with foil. Pour off excess fat from drippings. Stir honey with mustard. Heat and mix with chicken drippings. Cook over low heat until drippings are dissolved, then pour sauce over cooked chicken and serve. Yields about 6 servings.

Jan Townsend Going Home

Jamaican Chicken

2 (4-ounce) chicken breasts, skinned
1 teaspoon instant coffee, dissolved in 1 tablespoon hot water

1/2 cup low-fat vanilla yogurt
2 pineapple slices

Place chicken in a small baking dish. Stir dissolved coffee into yogurt. Pour yogurt over chicken and place pineapple on top. Bake in preheated 350° oven for 30–40 minutes. (May also be sautéed in a small skillet, adding yogurt and pineapple slices after chicken is cooked.) Yields 2 servings, 250 calories per serving.

Diversity is Delta's Main Dish

Dijon-Grilled Chicken Cutlets

3 tablespoons Dijon-style mustard
2 teaspoons fresh lime juice
1 teaspoon low-sodium teriyaki
   sauce
1 garlic clove, finely minced
Pinch ground red pepper
4 (4-ounce) skinless, boneless
   chicken breasts

In medium bowl with wire whisk, combine mustard, lime juice, teriyaki sauce, garlic, and ground red pepper. Dip chicken breasts into mixture, one at a time, coating both sides. Place on prepared pan. Spray an indoor ridged grill pan with nonstick cooking spray. Grill chicken, brushing with any remaining mustard mixture, 4 minutes on each side, until cooked through and juices run clear when pierced with a fork. Serves 4.

Centennial Cookbook

Forty-Clove Chicken Filice

1 frying chicken, cut in pieces
40 cloves fresh garlic
½ cup dry white wine
¼ cup dry vermouth
¼ cup olive oil
4 stalks celery, cut in 1-inch pieces
1 teaspoon oregano
2 teaspoons dry basil
6 sprigs minced parsley
Pinch crushed red pepper
1 lemon
Salt and pepper to taste

Place chicken pieces into shallow baking pan, skin-side-up. Sprinkle all ingredients except lemon, salt and pepper evenly over top of chicken. Squeeze juice from lemon and pour over top. Cut lemon rind into pieces and arrange throughout chicken. Cover with foil and bake at 375° for 40 minutes. Remove foil and bake an additional 15 minutes. Salt and pepper to taste. Serves 6.

Food Festivals of Northern California

 Lower Klamath National Wildlife Refuge has the largest concentration of wintering bald eagles in the lower 48 states.

Chicken Breast Dijonaise

1 tablespoon butter
1 tablespoon olive oil
Flour for dredging
2 boneless chicken breasts
Dried basil, thyme and oregano

1 clove garlic, minced
¼ cup Chardonnay wine
2 tablespoons Dijon mustard
¼ cup heavy whipping cream

Preheat oven to 400°. Heat butter and olive oil on stove top in an oven-proof skillet over medium heat until it sizzles.

Dredge chicken lightly in flour, shaking off excess. Add chicken to skillet, skin-side-down, and brown on both sides. Drain any remaining butter from pan and sprinkle chicken lightly with dried herbs and garlic. Add wine and mustard to skillet and stir to combine. Place skillet into oven for 20–30 minutes, until chicken feels firm to the touch. Remove skillet and place on stove top. Remove chicken to plates and keep warm. Add cream to skillet and cook over medium-high heat until sauce thickens and coats the back of a spoon. Pour over chicken and serve immediately. Serves 2. Serve with a Chardonnay.

Cooking with Wine

Sour Cream Chicken

This one is easy and will bring raves from guests.

1 large carton sour cream
¼ cup lemon juice
2 teaspoons Worcestershire
1 teaspoon salt
¼ teaspoon pepper
¼ teaspoon pepper
1 teaspoon celery salt

1 teaspoon paprika
1 clove crushed garlic
1 teaspoon garlic powder
12 skinned chicken breast halves
Ritz crackers and/or cheese
    crackers
2 tablespoons butter, melted

Mix sour cream, lemon juice, Worcestershire, and seasonings together and marinate chicken overnight. Roll in cracker crumbs, (½ cheese crackers and ½ Ritz crackers or all Ritz crackers.) Drizzle butter over chicken. Bake at 350° for 1 hour on a cookie sheet. Serves 6–8.

Cooking on the Fault Line—Corralitos Style

Sour Cream Chicken Enchiladas

2 cans cream of chicken soup	¾ pound grated Jack cheese
8–16 ounces sour cream	1 chicken, cooked and boned,
2 cans chopped green chiles,	cubed
drained	12–15 flour tortillas
1 small onion, chopped	½ cup grated Cheddar cheese

In a large bowl combine soup, sour cream, chiles, onion, and grated Jack cheese. Reserve ⅓ of this mixture. To other ⅔ add chicken pieces. Soften tortillas in microwave (1 minute). Fill tortillas, roll up and place in 9x13-inch pan. Spread remaining ⅓ mixture over top and sprinkle with Cheddar cheese. Bake at 350° until bubbly, 30–60 minutes. May be covered. Freezes well.

Cookin' with CASA

Chicken Quesadilla with Avocado and Cilantro Salsa

6 Roma tomatoes, divided	Tabasco to taste
2 avocados	Juice of 1 small lemon
4 tablespoons diced red onion	4 large flour tortillas
1 bunch cilantro leaves, chopped	2 Anaheim chiles
Minced garlic to taste	½ cup Monterey Jack cheese
Jalapeño pepper to taste, chopped	1 cup chicken white meat
1 tablespoon tomato juice	2 tablespoons corn oil
Cayenne pepper to taste	

Prepare salsa by peeling 3 tomatoes and dicing them with avocados. Add onion, cilantro, garlic, and jalapeño. Add tomato juice, cayenne, Tabasco and lemon juice. Set aside.

Cut flour tortillas in 3-inch circles. Blanch and peel 3 tomatoes, then slice. Charbroil chiles on open flame, then peel, remove seeds and slice. Charbroil or sauté chicken until well done and crisp, then slice. Between 2 tortilla circles, layer sliced tomato, chicken, pepper and grated cheese. Serve with salsa on side or top. Serves 4.

The Great California Cookbook
Recipe from Joachim Splichal, Patina

In the early 1700s Spanish Franciscan friars settled in Monterey and developed a method of converting an overabundance of milk to cheese. This soft, white, creamy cheese is known worldwide as Monterey Jack cheese. There are several theories of how the "Jack" got in the cheese, from the name of a vice used to apply pressure to the cheese, called a "housejack," to a Scottish entrepreneur by the name of David Jacks, who arrived in Monterey in the late 1800s and created a dairy industry with Swiss and Portuguese dairymen.

Unfried Mexican Chicken

6 boneless, skinless chicken breast
   halves (about 4 ounces each)
16 ounces bottled thick, chunky
   salsa (see Note)
5 cups fresh bread crumbs (use
   day-old Italian or French bread)
2 garlic cloves

1 teaspoon dried oregano
1/2 teaspoon salt
1 teaspoon ground chile, such as
   New Mexico Dixon
Olive oil or canola spray
2 tablespoons melted butter

Place the chicken breasts in a single layer in a glass baking dish. Pour the salsa over the chicken, turning to coat well on both sides. Let marinate for 1–2 hours.

Preheat oven to 375°. Combine the bread crumbs, garlic, oregano, salt and ground chile in a food processor; process to fine crumbs. Spread the crumb mixture on a long piece of wax paper. Remove the chicken from the salsa, keeping as many salsa chunks adhering to the chicken as possible. Place the breasts on top of the crumbs. Cover the breasts with more crumbs, pressing them on. Turn the chicken and press more crumbs on top. Spray a nonstick baking sheet with oil. Arrange the breasts on the baking sheet; drizzle with melted butter and spray with oil. Bake for 35 minutes. The chicken should be golden around the edges. Serves 6.

Note: For this recipe, bottled salsa is better than fresh, which can become watery.

The San Francisco Chronicle Cookbook

Chicken South of the Border

4 whole chicken breasts
12 corn tortillas
1 can cream of chicken soup
1 can cream of mushroom soup
1 soup can milk

1 minced onion
1 (4-ounce) can diced green chiles
1 pound sharp Cheddar cheese,
   shredded

Cut chicken into large pieces. Cut tortillas into 1-inch strips. Mix soups, milk, onion, and chiles. Add 3 tablespoons water to mixture. Place 1/2 of cut tortilla strips into bottom of a 9x13-inch greased baking dish, then layer 1/2 of chicken pieces, then 1/2 of soup mixture. Repeat. Top with cheese. Bake at 300° for 1 1/2 hours. Cool 15 minutes. Serves 8.

Treasured Recipes

Sonora Style Chicken

3 slices bacon, diced
1 large onion, coarsely chopped
3 cloves garlic, minced
1 (28-ounce) can tomatoes, drained
 and coarsely chopped

²/₃ cup picante sauce
¼ cup sliced green olives
1 (3-pound) fryer chicken, cut up,
 skinned and visible fat removed
¼ cup coarsely chopped cilantro

Cook bacon in 10-inch skillet until crisp. Remove with slotted spoon
to paper towel; reserve. Pour off all but 1 tablespoon of drippings.
Cook onion and garlic in drippings until tender, about 4 minutes.
Add tomatoes, picante sauce, and olives; bring to boil. Add chick-
en; spoon sauce over chicken. Reduce heat; cover and simmer until
chicken is tender, about 30 minutes. Remove chicken to serving
platter; cook sauce over high heat until thickened to desired consistency. Spoon sauce over chicken; sprinkle with bacon and
cilantro. Makes 4 servings.

Cookin' with CASA

Chip Shot Chicken

1 medium-size bag barbecued
 potato chips (crush enough to
 make 2 cups crumbs)

5–6 chicken thighs, skin removed
1 cup nonfat sour cream

Preheat oven to 350°. Tear a small hole in chip bag to let air out.
Crush chips in bag with a rolling pin. Dip chicken in sour cream
and roll in potato chip crumbs. Place on a baking sheet and bake
uncovered for 1 hour. Yields 4–6 servings.

The Golf Cookbook

Fabulous Chicken Cacciatore

1¾ ounces dried porcini
  mushrooms (no substitute)
1 cup water
3 whole chicken breasts, split in half
½ cup olive oil
3 beef bouillon cubes
1 medium onion, chopped
4–6 cloves garlic, crushed
2 teaspoons sweet basil (dried or
  fresh)

½ teaspoon salt
Pinch pepper
1 (6-ounce) can tomato paste
1 bay leaf
1 (16-ounce) can stewed
  tomatoes
1 cup rosé wine (no substitute)
2 green peppers, sliced

Preheat oven to 350°. Soak mushrooms in water for 15 minutes, reserving liquid. Brown chicken in olive oil; remove chicken, leaving oil in pan. Add bouillon cubes, onion, and garlic; sauté. Stir in basil, salt, pepper, and tomato paste. Then add mushroom liquid, bay leaf, stewed tomatoes, wine, and mushrooms. Place chicken in shallow baking dish. Cover with sauce. Bake covered for 30 minutes. Place pepper rings on top; continue baking another 40 minutes or until done. Serve with Polenta.

POLENTA:

1½ quarts water
2 teaspoons salt

1½ cups yellow polenta cornmeal
1 tablespoon Parmesan cheese

Bring water to a boil in 4-quart kettle. Add salt. Pour cornmeal into boiling water slowly, stirring constantly to keep from lumping. Reduce heat and cover. Cook over very low heat for another 20–30 minutes. You can now place mush in shallow baking dish and sprinkle with Parmesan cheese. Cut in squares and serve with cacciatore or any other Italian stew. Serves 6.

Cooking on the Fault Line—Corralitos Style

Del Monte, the first golf course west of the Mississippi, was opened in 1897, and by 1908 guests on a day's outing from the Hotel Del Monte would take a dirt road that wound 17 miles through the Del Monte Forest and along the coast, now known as the 17-Mile Drive.

Chicken Breasts with Lobster, Mushroom and Wine Sauce on Vermicelli

8 ounces vermicelli pasta
4 chicken breasts
6 tablespoons butter, divided
3/4 pound cooked lobster or crab meat, cut into cubes
2 large red bell peppers, sliced
1 cup sliced fresh mushrooms
2 tablespoons finely chopped fresh basil
Salt and pepper
1 cup Riesling wine, divided
1/2 cup grated fresh mozzarella cheese

Prepare vermicelli in boiling, salted water according to package instructions. Drain. Set aside and keep warm. Sauté chicken breasts in 2 tablespoons butter for 5–6 minutes on each side or until cooked through. Set aside and keep warm. In same pan, sauté lobster, bell peppers, mushrooms, and basil. Season with salt and pepper. Add 1/2 cup of the wine; heat. Then thicken with 2 tablespoons butter.

Place a chicken breast and a serving of vermicelli on each heated plate. Top with lobster/pepper mixture. Add remaining 1/2 cup wine and remaining 2 tablespoons butter to pan and deglaze. Cook rapidly to thicken and pour over chicken and pasta. Sprinkle with mozzarella cheese before serving. Serves 4. Serve with a Johannisberg Riesling.

Cooking with Wine

Lemon Chicken

6 skinless, boneless chicken breast halves
1/4 cup all-purpose flour
2 tablespoons vegetable oil
1/4 cup (1/2 stick) margarine
3 tablespoons lemon juice
2 tablespoons chopped parsley
1 (6.9-ounce) package Rice-A-Roni (chicken flavor)
1 1/2 cups broccoli flowerets
2 tablespoons grated Parmesan cheese

Dip chicken in flour. In large skillet, heat oil and margarine over medium-high heat. Add chicken; cook 5 minutes on each side. Remove chicken to ovenproof dish; set aside. In same skillet, stir lemon juice and parsley into oil-margarine mixture. Pour over chicken. Keep warm.

In skillet, prepare Rice-A-Roni mix as package directs, stirring in broccoli after rice has simmered 10 minutes. Top with chicken and parsley-lemon sauce; sprinkle with cheese.

Tahoe Parents Nursery School 40th Anniversary Alumni Cookbook

Coconut Orange Chicken in a Crock

Super easy, really good.

3 pounds chicken pieces, skin
  removed
2 teaspoons grated fresh ginger,
  or ½ teaspoon ground
1 teaspoon salt
⅛ teaspoon pepper
1 (6-ounce) can frozen orange juice
  concentrate

1 (11-ounce) can mandarin oranges
2 tablespoons cornstarch
1 tablespoon lite soy sauce
1 tablespoon brown sugar
½ cup shredded coconut
2 green onions, chopped (optional)

Spray inside of crockpot with nonstick cooking spray. Put chicken, ginger, salt, pepper, and frozen orange juice in crockpot and cook 6–8 hours on LOW.

Put meat on a beautiful serving platter and keep warm by covering with foil.

Drain oranges, reserving juice. Put juice from oranges and juice from chicken in a saucepan. Whisk in cornstarch, soy sauce and brown sugar. Bring to a boil. Stir until thickened.

Pour some sauce over chicken in serving dish. Arrange oranges around chicken. Sprinkle with coconut and green onions. Pass remaining sauce at table. Yields 4–6 servings.

The 7 Day Cookbook

Wild Rice and Chicken

Wild rice, which is not a rice at all but the grain of a tall, aquatic North American grass, is a true delicacy. It is prepared like ordinary rice, but takes a little longer to cook. It should maintain a bit of a chewy quality to be really good.

1 cup uncooked wild rice
2¼ cups chicken broth
8–10 cloves fresh garlic, minced
   or pressed
2 tablespoons soy sauce
2 teaspoons poultry seasoning
Coarsely ground black pepper

½ pound mushrooms, sliced
1 green bell pepper, chopped
6 stalks celery, chopped
6 chicken breast halves, boned and
   skinned
Chopped green onions for garnish

Rinse rice well at least 3 times. In casserole, place chicken broth, garlic, soy sauce, poultry seasoning, and black pepper. Stir. Then add rice, mushrooms, bell pepper, and celery. Mix well. "Bury" chicken in rice-vegetable mixture. Cover and bake at 350° for 1 hour. Remove from heat and let stand for 30 minutes with cover still on. Garnish with sliced green onions and serve. Makes 6 servings.

The Complete Garlic Lovers' Cookbook

Chicken & Tarragon Stuffed Artichokes

4–5 large artichokes
¼ cup butter
3 tablespoons flour
1 cup chicken broth
1 cup light cream

2 tablespoons sherry
½ teaspoon tarragon
2 cups diced chicken
Salt and pepper to taste

Preheat oven to 350°. Cook artichokes until tender. Drain and cool. Prepare artichokes for stuffing. Set in baking dish.

Melt butter and blend in flour. Slowly stir in chicken broth, light cream, and sherry, and cook until mixture thickens. Mix in tarragon, diced chicken and salt and pepper to taste. Stuff artichokes with chicken mixture and heat thoroughly, about 10–15 minutes.

The Artichoke Cookbook

Chicken Teriyaki

You can use bottled teriyaki sauce, but try making your own.

TERIYAKI SAUCE:

½ cup sake
½ cup soy sauce

½ cup mirin*
1 tablespoon sugar

In a medium saucepan, combine all ingredients. Bring to a boil, stirring to dissolve sugar. Reduce heat to low and simmer for 1 minute. Remove from heat. It is ready to use immediately, but will keep in refrigerator indefinitely. Makes about 1½ cups.

2 pounds skinless, boneless
chicken leg and thigh meat
2 cloves garlic, finely minced
¼-inch piece fresh ginger, peeled
and finely minced

½ cup Teriyaki Sauce
1 tablespoon corn oil
1 teaspoon ground sansho pepper*
1 teaspoon sesame seeds

Cut chicken meat into long strips, and pierce with a fork on both sides. In a bowl, combine chicken, garlic, ginger, and 2 tablespoons of teriyaki sauce. Mix well and let stand for 15 minutes.

In a large skillet, heat corn oil over medium-high heat. When it is hot, add chicken strips and brown evenly on all sides, 8–10 minutes; stir with a wooden spoon to prevent it from sticking or burning. Transfer chicken to a plate, but leave juices in skillet. Add remaining 6 tablespoons teriyaki sauce to skillet and bring to a boil. Stir well and reduce heat to low. Allow to reduce and thicken slightly for about 1 minute. Return chicken to skillet and heat until cooked through, about 5 minutes, stirring often to completely coat chicken with sauce. Remove from heat. Serve garnished with sansho and sesame seeds. Makes 4 servings.

*Mirin is a sweet Japanese rice wine used only for cooking. Sancho pepper is made from the berry of a prickly ash bush. Dried and ground, it is one of the most common spices used in Japan. Both are found in Asian markets.

Everybody's San Francisco Cookbook

 San Francisco's Chinatown, a 24-block area, is the largest Chinese quarter outside the Orient.

Hot Chicken Salad Casserole

2 cups cooked chicken meat
(1½ to 2 breasts)
1 cup chopped celery
1 tablespoon chopped onion
1 teaspoon lemon juice
1 can water chestnuts, drained and
sliced
1 can cream of chicken soup,
undiluted

3 hard-cooked eggs, chopped
1 cup cooked rice
¾ cup mayonnaise
1 teaspoon salt
1 cup buttered cornflakes or
bread crumbs
½ cup slivered almonds

Combine all ingredients except cornflakes and almonds and put into a greased casserole dish. Over the top sprinkle buttered cornflakes or bread crumbs and slivered almonds. Bake at 350° for 35–45 minutes or until brown. Can be made ahead, except for the topping, and frozen. Spoon topping on frozen casserole and bake for 1–1½ hours. Makes 8 servings.

Tried and True Recipes

Roast Chicken with Potatoes and Rosemary

1 chicken, cut up, or chicken thighs
6 large red potatoes, cut into wedges
1–2 yellow onions, cut into wedges
1–2 cloves garlic, cut in half
4 carrots, quartered lengthwise and
halved

1 red pepper, cored, seeded, cut
into strips
Seasoned salt and pepper to taste
Olive oil (as needed, up to ⅓ cup)
Fresh rosemary
Fresh lime slices

Place chicken, potatoes, onions, garlic, carrots, and red pepper in a large, greased baking dish. Season well with salt and pepper, then drizzle with olive oil. Place fresh rosemary sprigs on top and roast at 425° until well browned and tender, turning and basting as needed, approximately 40–45 minutes. Serve with fresh lime slices and fresh bread to soak up the juices. Yields 4 servings.

Only in California

 The first commercial film made in California was *The Count of Monte Cristo*, made in the Los Angeles area in 1907.

One Pot Italian Chicken

Great over noodles or rice.

2 (14.5-ounce) cans Italian stewed
  tomatoes
1 small onion, chopped
1 small or ½ large green pepper,
  chopped
1 (4-ounce) can sliced mushrooms
  (optional)

2 cloves garlic, chopped
4 chicken breasts, boned and
  skinned
2 tablespoons all-purpose flour

Mix tomatoes, onion, pepper, mushrooms, and garlic together. Coat chicken breasts with flour and arrange in 2-quart baking casserole dish. Pour tomato mixture over chicken. Cover and bake at 325° for 30–40 minutes or until chicken is cooked throughout. Yields 8 servings.

Nutritional Analysis Per Serving: Cal 180; Fat 3.2g; Chol 73 mg; Sod 325 mg.

Taste California

Chicken Curry Pot Pie

½ cup julienned carrots
½ cup corn kernels
¾ cup sliced crimini mushrooms
3 tablespoons butter, divided
½ cup peas
1 medium potato, cooked, diced
Pinch of salt and pepper
1½ cups cooked, diced chicken

½ cup chicken stock
2 tablespoons veloute* (heaping)
1 teaspoon curry powder
½ cup cream
2 teaspoons minced parsley
Pie crust for topping
Egg wash (mix 1 egg and
  1 tablespoon water)

Sauté carrots, corn, and mushrooms in 2 tablespoons butter for 3 minutes. Add peas and potatoes, cooking for 1 minute more. Season with salt and pepper. Add chicken and deglaze with stock. Whisk in veloute and let simmer. Add curry powder, cream, and parsley. Reduce by one-third. Finish with remaining 1 tablespoon butter.

Pour into a soufflé dish and top with your favorie pie crust. Egg-wash and bake in preheated 350° oven until golden, approximately 25 minutes. Serves 4.

*Veloute is a rich white sauce made from meat stock thickened with flour and butter.

San Francisco's Cooking Secrets

Chicken–Bread Pudding

6 slices white bread, crusts trimmed
2 cups chopped cooked chicken
4 tablespoons butter, divided
4 ounces sliced mushrooms
1 (8-ounce) can sliced water
   chestnuts, drained
¼ cup mayonnaise
1 cup shredded Cheddar cheese

1 cup milk
1 (10-ounce) can cream of celery
   soup
2 eggs, beaten
2 tablespoons chopped pimento
1 teaspoon salt
¼ teaspoon freshly ground pepper
½ cup bread crumbs

Line bottom of buttered 9x13-inch baking dish with bread slices, cutting to fit. Top with chicken. Melt 2 tablespoons butter in skillet. Sauté mushrooms in butter until browned; remove from heat. Stir in water chestnuts, and mayonnaise. Spoon over chicken layer. Sprinkle with cheese. Combine next 6 ingredients in bowl; mix well. Pour over cheese layer. Bake at 350° for 1 hour or until set. Sprinkle with bread crumbs; dot with remaining 2 tablespoons butter. Bake for 10 minutes longer or until crumbs are browned. Yields 8 servings.

California Gold

Broccoli and Chicken Casserole

4–6 chicken breasts
2 (10-ounce) packages frozen
   broccoli

1 cup Cheddar cheese
½ cup bread crumbs

CREAM SAUCE:
1 can cream of mushroom soup
1 can cream of chicken soup
1 cup mayonnaise

1 teaspoon lemon juice
¼ teaspoon curry powder
Salt and pepper to taste

Boil chicken until tender, about 45 minutes. Debone and remove skin and break into pieces. Pour boiling water over frozen broccoli. Drain. Line 9x13-inch greased baking dish with broccoli. Spread chunked chicken over broccoli, then cover with Cream Sauce. Sprinkle with grated Cheddar cheese and bread crumbs. Bake for 30 minutes at 325°.

Feeding the Flock

Broccoli–Turkey Casserole

2 cups cooked, cut-up turkey
1½ cups turkey gravy
1 carton sour cream (fat-free is okay)
1½ to 2 cups leftover dressing (or
 make some Stovetop)

2 packages frozen chopped
 broccoli, or chunks of cooked
 fresh broccoli
1 cup grated Cheddar cheese

Mix turkey, gravy, and sour cream together. Put dressing in bottom of casserole. Put turkey mixture on top of dressing. Put broccoli (if frozen, cook briefly and drain well) on top of turkey. Top with cheese. Bake about 1 hour. Serves 4–6.

Sharing Our Best

Scallopini

1 (1¾- to 2-pound) quarter-breast
 of turkey, skinned and boned,
 or 1 (2-pound) package turkey
 breast slices
¼ cup flour
1 teaspoon salt
1 teaspoon paprika
⅛ teaspoon white pepper
2 tablespoons butter or margarine,
 divided

2 tablespoons oil, divided
1½ cups small mushrooms, halved
¼ teaspoon pressed garlic
¾ cup dry white wine
1½ teaspoons lemon juice
¼ teaspoon Italian seasoning,
 crumbled
1 tablespoon minced parsley

Place turkey breast in freezer 45 minutes to 1 hour until surface of meat is thoroughly chilled and slightly firm. Cut meat crosswise in ¼-inch slices. Mix flour, salt, paprika, and white pepper together. Flour meat slices, shaking off excess. Heat 1 tablespoon each butter and oil in large skillet. Add layer of meat and brown lightly on both sides. As meat is browned, remove and keep warm. Brown remaining turkey, adding remaining butter and oil as needed. When all meat is browned, add mushrooms and garlic to skillet and sauté lightly. Return browned turkey meat to skillet. Combine wine, lemon juice, Italian seasoning, and parsley. Pour over all and simmer rapidly 5–10 minutes or until liquid is reduced and turkey is tender. Makes 6 servings.

Taste of Fillmore

Under-the-Skin Turkey

1 turkey breast (or 4 legs or thighs)
1 handful fresh parsley, finely
   minced
2 cloves garlic, finely minced
1–2 tablespoons olive oil

1 teaspoon herbs, Italian or
   Mexican seasonings, oregano or
   your favorite
1 orange, thinly sliced

Gently run your hand under turkey skin to loosen it from meat. Do not remove skin, simply loosen it. Mix parsley, garlic, olive oil, and herbs together. Dip orange slices in mixture to coat, and then gently push them under skin. Bake or barbecue in moderate heat (about 350°) 30 minutes or more, depending on size of turkey pieces. It's done when meat is firm to the touch and juices run clear—not pink—when pricked with a fork. Serves 6.

Variations: Use your favorite seasonings, or lemon instead of orange for a change. Also, chicken works in place of turkey.

The $5 Chef: How to Save Cash & Cook Fast

Brandied Cornish Hens

4 Cornish hens, split
Salt and pepper
Pecan-Spinach Stuffing

¼ cup butter or margarine, melted
½ cup fruit-flavored brandy

Sprinkle hens with salt and pepper. Stuff with Pecan-Spinach Stuffing, packing lightly. Combine melted butter with brandy and brush hens generously. May sprinkle additional salt and pepper on hens. Bake at 350° for 45–60 minutes uncovered; test with knife for doneness. Baste several times with brandy-butter mixture. Serves 4.

PECAN-SPINACH STUFFING:

2 tablespoons oil
4 cloves garlic, minced
1 cup chopped pecans
1 package frozen spinach
   (defrosted and well drained)

1 teaspoon dried thyme
½ teaspoon pepper
½ teaspoon salt
¼ teaspoon cinnamon
1 egg, well beaten

Heat oil in small skillet over low heat. Add garlic and pecans. Sauté about 3 minutes. In medium bowl, mix together spinach, thyme, pepper, salt, and cinnamon. To this mixture add egg and blend well.

Cooking with Booze

Apple-Walnut Stuffing

1 pound day-old loaf bread,
  cut into large croutons
3 large onions, chopped
4 tablespoons butter
5 stalks celery, chopped
2 cups sliced leeks
4 large Granny Smith apples, diced

2 cups toasted chopped walnuts
2 tablespoons celery seed
2 tablespoons chopped fresh sage
1 tablespoon poultry seasoning
2 eggs, beaten
4 cups dark turkey stock
Salt and black pepper to taste

Place croutons in a large bowl. In a saucepan sauté onions in butter until translucent. Add celery, leeks, and apples. Continue to cook a few minutes more. Pour mixture over croutons and cool to room temperature. Add walnuts, celery seed, sage, and poultry seasoning to cooled mixture; combine thoroughly. Mix in eggs and enough stock to moisten. Season with salt and pepper.

Transfer stuffing to lightly greased 9x13-inch baking dish. Cover with aluminum foil. Bake at 350° until stuffing is heated through, about 30 minutes. Uncover stuffing and bake until top is crisp, about 20 minutes. The dressing may also be stuffed into the turkey cavity. Serves 8.

An Apple a Day

Chicken Casserole Amandine

8 chicken thighs
1/2 cup honey
1/2 cup prepared mustard
1 tablespoon chopped onion

1 tablespoon lemon juice
1/2 teaspoon curry powder
1/2 cup slivered almonds

Place chicken thighs, single layer, in baking dish. Combine remaining ingredients (except almonds) and pour over meat. Cook, covered, 30 minutes at 300°. Remove cover, sprinkle slivered almonds over the top, and bake another 10 minutes, uncovered. Serves 4–6.

Durham's Favorite Recipes

Chicken Bundles

¾ cup chopped green onions	12 sheets phyllo
¾ cup mayonnaise	6 chicken breast halves, boned
3 tablespoons lemon juice	and skinned
3 cloves garlic, minced, divided	Salt and pepper to taste
¾ teaspoon dry tarragon	2 tablespoons grated Parmesan
⅔ cup margarine, melted	cheese

Mix togther onions, mayonnaise, lemon juice, 2 cloves garlic, and tarragon. Set aside. Combine remaining garlic and butter. For each bundle, place 2 sheets of phyllo on a board and brush with garlic butter. Spread one side of chicken breast with about 1½ tablespoons of mayonnaise mixture. Turn over onto corner of phyllo sheets and top with 1½ tablespoons more of mixture.

Wrap breast in phyllo as follows: Flip corner of phyllo over chicken. Roll once. Fold side over top and roll again. Fold opposite over, then roll up. Folds like an envelope. Place bundles slightly apart on an ungreased baking sheet. Brush with remaining garlic butter. Sprinkle with cheese. Bake at 375° for 20–25 minutes or until golden. Serves 6.

Note: May be frozen—but thaw completely, covered, before baking.

The Steinbeck House Cookbook

Seafood

San Francisco Bay is considered the world's largest landlocked harbor, and is host to several boating activities, including sailing and yacht racing.

Salmon with Basil Cream Sauce

1 (2-pound) salmon fillet, cut into
    6 (5⅓-ounce) fillets
1½ tablespoons unsalted butter
1 clove garlic, peeled and minced
3 shallots, peeled and minced
1½ cups chopped fresh basil
¼ cup chopped fresh parsley
¾ cup dry white wine
⅓ cup half-and-half
1 tablespoon lemon juice
¼ teaspoon white pepper
¼ teaspoon salt

Sear salmon in melted butter over medium-high heat on each side for 2 to 3 minutes. Remove and keep warm. Turn heat to low and sauté garlic with shallots for about 5 minutes. Add rest of ingredients to pan and cook on medium heat until sauce is reduced by half. Taste for seasoning, adding more pepper and salt as needed.

To serve, reheat fish gently in sauce until it flakes. The sauce is a nice green color. Spoon around fish on plates.

Note: The fish can be prepared up to 3 hours ahead, then reheated, uncovered, over low heat for 10 minutes. Serves 6.

Cooking with Herbs

Hazelnut Crusted Salmon
with Spicy Peach Sauce

1 cup ground, roasted hazelnuts
2 cups cracker crumbs
½ teaspoon thyme
½ teaspoon oregano
1 teaspoon cayenne pepper
1 tablespoon olive oil
4 salmon fillets (7–9 ounces each)
2 tablespoons butter
Spicy Peach Sauce

Preheat oven to 350°. Mix ground nuts, cracker crumbs, thyme, oregano and cayenne. Oil salmon and "bread" it with the nut-herb mixture. Brown salmon slightly in butter in an ovenproof frying pan.

Transfer frying pan to a 350° oven. Finish cooking for 8-10 minutes. Serve on Spicy Peach Sauce. Makes 4 servings.

SPICY PEACH SAUCE:
1 tablespoon olive oil
½ cup chopped sweet onion
4 peaches, peeled and cubed
½ cup light brown sugar
2 tablespoons raspberry vinegar
1 teaspoon chili powder
Salt and pepper

Heat oil in a pan, and sauté onion until soft, but not brown. Add peaches, sugar, vinegar and chili powder. Cook 10–15 minutes. Season to taste with salt and pepper. Serve with Chardonnay.

California Wine Country Herbs and Spices Cookbook

Fresh Salmon Cakes
with Spicy Lemon/Mustard Sauce

SALMON CAKES:

½ red bell pepper, finely diced
½ green bell pepper, finely diced
2 garlic cloves, chopped
1 tablespoon olive oil
2 tablespoons white wine or water
1 pound fresh salmon meat
½ cup fresh white bread crumbs

3 scallions, thinly sliced
3–4 tablespoons heavy cream
Salt and pepper to taste
Dash Tabasco sauce
1–2 dashes Worcestershire sauce
Olive oil, for frying

Sauté peppers and garlic in olive oil. Add white wine and cook until liquid evaporates. Remove from heat. Break up salmon meat, but do not chop. Mix salmon with bread crumbs. Mix in sautéed peppers, garlic, and raw scallions. Add cream until mixture binds, but is not mushy. Season to taste with salt, pepper, Tabasco, and Worcestershire. Cover and refrigerate for at least an hour.

SPICY LEMON/MUSTARD SAUCE:

4 garlic cloves, finely chopped
Juice of 1 lemon
2 tablespoons white wine or water
1 cup heavy cream

1 tablespoon Dijon mustard
Salt and pepper to taste
Tabasco to taste
Worcestershire sauce to taste

Fifteen minutes before you are ready to cook salmon, make sauce. Cook garlic, lemon juice, and wine over medium heat until very little liquid is left in saucepan. Add cream and bring to a boil. Reduce heat and simmer about 10 minutes until sauce is thickened. Stir in mustard, salt, pepper, dash of Tabasco, and dash of Worcestershire sauce. Set aside in a warm place. Shape salmon mixture into 3-ounce patties and fry in olive oil until golden brown. Drain on paper towels. Serve cakes with sauce while still warm. Makes 8 cakes; serves 4.

Carter House Cookbook

Californians tend to prefer the fresh local seafood caught in their region: Northern Californians favor salmon, crab, trout and sole, while Southern Californians opt for halibut, shark, swordfish and mahi mahi.

Swordfish
in Lemon–Ginger Marinade

Barbecuing over mesquite, with its special, smoky-sweet flavor, has become a trademark of California cooking. Swordfish steaks prepared in this manner assume an added tang when marinated in lemon and ginger for a special sweet-tart contrast.

MARINADE:

½ cup freshly squeezed lemon juice
2 medium cloves garlic, minced
1½ teaspoons minced fresh ginger
1 teaspoon minced lemon zest

1 tablespoon olive oil
2 tablespoons vegetable oil
¼ teaspoon salt
⅛ teaspoon finely ground pepper

Combine ingredients in a medium bowl. Whisk until blended.

6 swordfish steaks, ⅓ to ½ pound
each and no more than 1 inch thick.

In a large shallow non-aluminum dish, arrange fish steaks and pour Marinade over. Marinate fish for 2–4 hours in refrigerator. Prepare barbecue for medium-heat grilling. Remove fish from Marinade. Grill fish about 3 inches from heat for 5 minutes on each side. Heat remaining Marinade in a small saucepan over medium heat. Pour some of the remaining Marinade over and serve immediately. Serves 6.

Note: Freshly squeezed lime juice and minced zest may be substituted for lemon. Other firm-fleshed fish that may be used include shark, tuna and halibut. When barbecuing with mesquite charcoal or any other charcoal that burns at very high temperatures, cut the fish into pieces that are no more than 1 inch thick so the surface does not burn before the center is cooked.

The Cuisine of California

Rex Sole
in Saffron and Tomato Sauce

6 whole sole
Milk
Flour
1/3 stick butter
2 tomatoes, peeled, seeded and
   chopped

1 clove garlic, minced
1/4 cup dry white wine
Pinch saffron
Lemon juice
Salt and pepper

Make several diagonal slashes on either side of sole. Dip each fish in milk and then in flour. Heat butter in skillet over high heat and add fish. Turn fish over after about 3 minutes. Add tomatoes, garlic, wine, saffron, lemon juice, salt and pepper and lower heat to simmer until fish is opaque. Remove fish to platter and keep warm. Cook sauce until reduced, pour over fish and serve immediately. Serves 6.

A Slice of Santa Barbara

Mahi-Mahi
with Pineapple Chutney

4 (8- to 10-ounce) mahi mahi fillets,   1 tablespoon lime juice
   skinned

Sprinkle mahi mahi with lime juice and let marinate for 15 minutes. Grill the fillets about 7–8 inches from heat of grill for 1–1 1/2 minutes. Rotate fillets 45° to make a crosshatch pattern and cook 1 1/2 minutes more. The fish is done when it is almost firm.

PINEAPPLE CHUTNEY:

12 ounces pineapple chunks
8 ounces pineapple juice
3 ounces diced red pepper
3 ounces diced green pepper

1 ounce finely diced jalapeño
   pepper
1 tablespoon brown sugar
2 tablespoons rice wine vinegar

Combine and mix all chutney ingredients in a mixing bowl; set aside. Remove the fillets to plates, crosshatched side up. Stir chutney, spoon generously over fish and serve. Serves 4.

Little Dave's Seafood Cookbook

Trout with Almonds

1 stick butter, divided
1 cup white wine
Juice of 1 lemon plus grated rind
1/4 teaspoon paprika
1 tablespoon finely chopped
  parsley

1 teaspoon salt
1/4 teaspoon thyme
3 tablespoons olive oil
1 cup slivered almonds
1 pan-size trout or 6 fillets

Warm 1/2 butter to melt and combine all ingredients except trout, almonds, and other 1/2 butter. Melt reserved butter in a large lidded skillet, and arrange pan-size trout in pan and brown on one side. Turn trout and cover with first mixture and almonds. Cover and cook over medium heat until fin pulls away easily, or fillets flake. Serves 6.

From a Sourdough's Pot

Pan-Fried Fish Parmesana

Trader Vic's restaurant, a local tradition as well as a tourist favorite, suggested this tasty and unusual way to prepare fish.

1 tablespoon lemon juice
1 tablespoon Worcestershire sauce
2 pounds rock cod or red snapper
  fillets, cut into 6 pieces
Salt and freshly ground pepper
  to taste

1/2 cup flour
3 eggs, lightly beaten
1 cup grated fresh Parmesan
  cheese
3 tablespoons butter
2 tablespoons vegetable oil

Preheat oven to 400°. Combine lemon juice and Worcestershire sauce, and sprinkle on fish pieces. Salt and pepper fish, then dredge lightly in flour. Dip fish in eggs, then coat generously with grated cheese. In a heavy skillet, sauté fish in a mixture of butter and oil over medium heat 3–4 minutes to brown. Turn and brown other side. Place skillet in oven for 4–5 minutes to heat though. Serve immediately. Serves 6.

San Francisco à la Carte

Seared Tuna with Potatoes and Blackberry Sauce

Blackberries grow wild throughout much of California. You can tell the difference between native and introduced blackberries by their leaves; natives have three leaves, non-natives five. In this dish, blackberries and red wine are reduced to make an intensely flavored sauce. Good with pork, chicken, and grilled duck breast, too.

3 cups blackberries, divided
1 cup red wine, such as zinfandel, merlot, or sangiovese
¼ cup honey, warmed
2 tablespoons soy sauce
2 tablespoons raspberry vinegar, preferably low-acid black raspberry vinegar, divided
5 sprigs basil, divided

Kosher salt
Black pepper in a mill
1 pound fingerling or Yellow Finn potatoes, sliced thin and cooked until tender
2 tablespoons extra virgin olive oil
1 tablespoon minced basil
4 tuna steaks, preferably ahi, about 6–8 ounces each

Prepare a hot fire on an outdoor or stovetop grill. Purée 2 cups blackberries in food processor or blender, and pass purée through a fine sieve to strain out seeds. Bring puréed berries and wine to boil in small nonreactive saucepan over medium-high heat. Reduce heat slightly, and simmer until volume is reduced by half. Stir in the honey, soy sauce, and 1 tablespoon vinegar, add one basil sprig, and simmer, uncovered, for 10 minutes. Taste, and season with salt and pepper. Remove sauce from the heat, and set aside.

Put potatoes in medium bowl, add remaining vinegar, olive oil, and minced basil, and toss to combine. Taste, and season with salt and pepper. Season tuna steaks on both sides with salt and pepper. Grill steaks for 2–3 minutes on each side, until seared on the outside but rare on inside.

Divide the potatoes among 4 individual plates, and place tuna on top. Drizzle sauce over tuna and potatoes, and garnish with remaining blackberries and remaining basil sprigs. Serve immediately, with remaining sauce on the side. Serves 4.

California Home Cooking

Fish Marinade

¼ cup soy sauce
¼ cup frozen orange juice
  concentrate
2 tablespoons catsup

2 tablespoons salad oil
1 tablespoon fresh lemon juice
¼ teaspoon pepper
1 clove garlic, mashed

Mix all ingredients. Marinate 2 pounds fish fillets for 1½ hours.
Grill or broil.

More Firehouse Favorites

Fried Whole Trout with Shiitakes

3 strips bacon
2 tablespoons extra virgin olive oil
½ cup unsalted butter, divided
3 cups thinly sliced shiitake
  mushrooms
Salt and pepper to taste
1 cup flour
2 eggs

2 cups cracker meal
1 tablespoon Pisto's Sensational
  Seasoning (or blackening
  seasoning)
4 small trout, whole, cleaned
1 bunch watercress
3 lemons, quartered

In a large skillet, grill bacon well; then drain bacon and set aside
bacon grease.

Wipe skillet with paper towel. Add olive oil and 3 tablespoons
butter; sauté mushrooms for 3–4 minutes. Season lightly with salt
and pepper. Remove mushrooms and set aside.

Place 3 pie pans on counter top. Fill one pan with flour. Fill second pan with well-beaten eggs. Fill third pan with cracker meal seasoned with Sensational Seasoning, salt and pepper.

Coat trout with flour, then eggs, then cracker meal. Add bacon
grease and remaining butter to large skillet. Fry trout for 6–8 minutes on each side, or until done. To see if done, check thickest part
of fish just behind gills. Fish is done when meat is solid white and
still has a bit of spring to it. Remove trout and place each trout on
an individual serving plate. Place portion of sautéed mushrooms
around trout and sprinkle with crumbled bacon bits. Garnish with
watercress and lemon wedges. Serves 4.

Cooking with Mushrooms

Baked Red Snapper
in an Orange Citrus Sauce

¼ cup fresh orange juice
1 teaspoon grated orange rind
1 tablespoon soy sauce
1 tablespoon sesame oil

2 tablespoons minced green
   onion tops
Salt and pepper to taste
1 pound red snapper fillets

Combine all ingredients (except fish) in shallow baking dish, large enough to fit fish in one single layer. Stir with fork to blend ingredients. Add fish and cover with marinade. Cover and refrigerate at least 1 hour to absorb flavors.

Preheat oven to 400°. Place pan in oven, uncovered, and bake for 10 minutes or until fish is cooked (opaque throughout). Baste once with sauce while cooking. Be careful not to overcook. To serve, place fish with sauce on warmed plates. You might like to add a few orange slices for garnish. Serve 2.

Note: The fish may also be served chilled for hot weather dining.

The California Cookbook

Grilled Snapper
with Beurre Blanc Sauce

BEURRE BLANC SAUCE:

¼ cup dry white wine
Juice of ½ lemon
3 garlic cloves, crushed

1 cup sweet butter
Salt and pepper to taste

FISH:

Fresh snapper, 1 piece per person
Salt and pepper to taste

Fresh squeezed lemon juice
Minced garlic

Bring wine, lemon juice, and garlic to a boil over medium heat. Boil until liquid reduces down to 1½ tablespoons in volume. (This will happen very rapidly, approximately 3 minutes.) Reduce heat to very low. Whip in chunks of butter slowly. When all butter is mixed in and melted, salt and pepper to taste. Keep warm. Season Fish to taste with salt, pepper, lemon, and garlic. Grill until done. To serve, place Fish on a warmed plate, cover with sauce and serve.

Carter House Cookbook

Fisherman's Wharf Garlic Prawns

4 garlic cloves, crushed
1 teaspoon salt
2 teaspoons coarsely crushed
  black peppercorns
2 teaspoons lemon juice
1 tablespoon brandy

1 pound shrimp (prawns), 16–20
  count, peeled, deveined,
  butterflied
3 tablespoons olive oil
1/2 cup heavy whipping cream
Fresh chopped parsley

Combine crushed garlic with salt; add crushed peppercorns, lemon juice, and brandy. Mix well. Place prawns in saucepan or in heavy-duty cast-iron skillet. Add garlic mixture and olive oil. Cover and cook quickly until prawns change color. Stir in cream. Serve hot and sizzling in small bowls garnished with chopped parsley. Serves 2.

Little Dave's Seafood Cookbook

Shrimp with Orzo and Broccoli

2 1/2 cups chicken broth
1 (14-ounce) can tomatoes, drained,
  chopped
12 ounces broccoli, cut into small
  florets
1 cup uncooked orzo (tiny flat pasta)

12 ounces medium shrimp
1/2 teaspoon salt
1/4 teaspoon pepper
2 ounces feta cheese, crumbled
1/3 cup fresh chopped basil

In a large skillet, bring broth, tomatoes, and broccoli to boil over high heat. Add pasta and reduce heat. Cover and simmer 7–8 minutes, stirring occasionally.

Shell and devein shrimp. Add shrimp, salt and pepper to skillet. Return to simmer, cover and stir occasionally. Cook 3–4 minutes or until shrimp turn pink and broccoli and orzo (pasta) are tender. Remove from heat and stir in crumbled feta cheese and basil. Serves 4–6.

Delicious Recipes from the Nimitz Community

The city of Ventura derives its name from the Mission San Buenaventura, founded in 1782. The discovery of oil hastened the area's growth, and by 1925, the Ventura Avenue oil field was among the most productive in the nation.

Shrimp with Feta Cheese

This colorful, simple Greek dish can be served with a rice pilaf with pine nuts.

2 tablespoons butter
2 tablespoons olive oil
2 garlic cloves, crushed
1 tablespoon minced fresh rosemary
1 bunch green onions, thinly sliced, including green portions
¾ pound mushrooms, thickly sliced
¼ cup dry white wine
Juice of 1 lemon

1 lemon, thinly sliced
½ cup black olives, drained and pitted
3 Roma plum tomatoes, quartered
½ pound jumbo shrimp, shelled, deveined and butterflied
½ pound feta cheese, crumbled (about ½ cup)

In a large skillet, melt butter with oil over medium heat. Add garlic, rosemary, and green onions. Cook, stirring constantly for 2 minutes. Add mushrooms and cook until softened. Add wine, lemon juice, half of the lemon slices, olives, and tomatoes. Heat through over high heat. Add shrimp and cook, stirring constantly, until the shrimp turn pink. Remove from heat and quickly stir in feta cheese. Serve at once. Garnish with remaining lemon slices. Serves 2–3.

The Art Lover's Cookbook: A Feast for the Eye

Deviled Egg and Shrimp Casserole

8 eggs, hard-boiled, shelled and cooled
½ teaspoon salt
½ teaspoon dry mustard
¼ cup mayonnaise
1½ tablespoons light cream
½ teaspoon lemon juice
1 pound shrimp, peeled, deveined

Dash salt
1 bay leaf
2–3 slices of lemon
½ cup grated Cheddar or Swiss cheese
4 cups white sauce
1 cup bread crumbs
2 tablespoons butter

Cut eggs in half, lengthwise. Put yolks through sieve or give them a whirl in food processor. Season with salt. Add mustard, mayonnaise, cream, and lemon juice. Fill whites with mixture. Place in shallow baking dish. If using uncooked shrimp, cook for 10 minutes in boiling water with salt, bay leaf, and slices of lemon. Drain and devein. Add to baking dish, distributing evenly around eggs. Add cheese to white sauce and continue to cook until cheese melts. Pour over eggs and shrimp. Sauté bread crumbs in butter and sprinkle over top of casserole. Bake in 350° oven for 30–45 minutes, or until bubbly. Serves 6.

Sun, Sand and Sausage Pie

Garlic Shrimp

Here's one you can serve to company (plus it's quick and easy)!

8 cloves garlic, finely minced
1 tablespoon olive oil
1 cup dry white wine
4 whole cloves
2 fresh bay leaves
1 1/2 pounds shrimp, peeled, deveined

1 teaspoon Dijon mustard
Salt and pepper to taste
1/2 teaspoon Worcestershire sauce
2 cups cooked pasta
2 tablespoons chopped parsley

In a large skillet, brown garlic in oil. Add wine, cloves, and bay leaves. Cook slowly until wine reduces to 2/3 original volume. Add shrimp, mustard, salt, pepper, and Worcestershire sauce to garlic/wine mixture. Cook for 3–4 minutes or just until shrimp are tender.

Fork pasta onto 4 individual plates. Transfer shrimp onto pasta and pour remaining garlic/wine sauce over shrimp. Garnish with chopped parsley. Yields 4 (1-cup) servings.

Nutritional Analysis Per serving: Cal 354; Fat 10.3 mg; Chol 259 mg; Sod 376 mg.

Taste California

Easy Shrimp Creole

1/2 cup chopped onion
2 tablespoons chopped green pepper
1/4 cup chopped celery
1 clove minced garlic
1 1/4 cups canned tomatoes, cut up or crushed

1/4 cup butter
Salt and pepper to taste
3/4 teaspoon Worcestershire sauce
1/2 teaspoon marjoram
1 cup cooked shrimp or 1 (4.5-ounce) can

Sauté first 4 ingredients in butter until limp. Add remaining ingredients except shrimp and cover. Cook slowly 15 minutes. Add shrimp. Heat thoroughly. Serve over cooked rice. Serves 2.

Watsonville Community Hospital 40th Anniversary Edition

Shrimp and Scallop Linguine in Coriander Cream

3 tablespoons olive oil
½ cup finely chopped onion
3–5 garlic cloves, minced
2 tablespoons flour
1 teaspoon ground coriander seeds
¼ cup vermouth
1 cup heavy whipping cream or half-and-half

½ pound shrimp, uncooked, peeled and deveined
½ pound bay scallops
1 pound fresh linguine, cooked to package directions
Olive oil
¼ cup chopped parsley, divided

Heat oil in a heavy skillet over medium heat. Add onion and garlic. Sauté until lightly browned, 4–6 minutes. Stir in flour and coriander seeds and cook 1 minute more. Add vermouth and cream. Bring to a gentle boil, stirring constantly. Add seafood and cook about 5 minutes, until seafood turns opaque. Do not overcook. Set aside.

Toss drained pasta with a little olive oil and 2 tablespoons of the chopped parsley. Divide pasta among four plates and top with seafood sauce. Garnish with remaining parsley. Serve immediately. Serves 4.

California Sizzles

Some 20,000 gray whales pass California's shores every year on their journey to and from their feeding grounds in the Arctic and breeding lagoons in Baja. Other marine life seen on California shores include blue, fin, sperm, minke and killer whales as well as dolphins, sea lions, and seals.

Sizzling Garlic & Citrus Shrimp

The citrus juices add a wonderful flavor to this shrimp recipe.

24 jumbo shrimp, about 1½
  pounds, peeled (tails on) and
  deveined
⅓ cup fresh lime juice
⅓ cup fresh lemon juice
⅓ cup blood orange juice
4 ounces unsalted butter, melted
12 large cloves fresh garlic, peeled
  and finely chopped

Salt to taste
¼ cup chopped fresh cilantro
¼ teaspoon Pico de Gallo or
  cayenne pepper
1 large loaf French bread, thinly
  sliced
Citrus slices for garnish
Cilantro leaves for garnish

Arrange shrimp in a large, shallow non-reactive baking dish. To make sauce, mix remaining ingredients except bread; pour over shrimp. Cook shrimp and sauce under broiler, turning shrimp once or twice, until shrimp is opaque and just firm to the touch, about 8 minutes.

Immediately serve shrimp and sauce over thin slices of French bread. Garnish with citrus slices and sprigs of cilantro. Serve remaining bread on the side. Serves 8.

Variation: Substitute 1½ pounds scallops or calamari rings for shrimp; adjust cooking time as needed.

Garlic Lovers' Greatest Hits

Sea Scallops with Orange Tarragon Cream Sauce

Sliver of orange peel
¼ cup white wine
½ cup heavy cream
1 ounce orange juice

5 ounces fresh sea scallops
Fresh tarragon
Salt and pepper

Place one finely sliced orange peel in saucepan with wine, cream, and orange juice. Simmer over low heat until reduced by half. When it starts to thicken, toss in scallops for a mere 3 minutes on low heat. Add a big pinch of fresh tarragon, and salt and pepper to taste. Serves 1.

The Coastal Cook of West Marin

Classic Fresh Crab

Bay leaves, 1 for each crab
Fresh crabs
1 tablespoon salt

Drawn butter
Fresh lemon

In a large pot, bring water to a rolling boil. Add a bay leaf for each crab to be cooked and 1 tablespoon salt to boiling water. Place as many live crabs into boiling water as will easily fit into the kettle. Boil crabs for 25 minutes. Remove crabs from boiling water and rinse under cold water until they are cool. Remove backs, gills, and innards. Crack crabs and serve with drawn butter and lemon.

Carter House Cookbook

Cracked Crab

1 tablespoon whole black
  peppercorns
1 bay leaf, crumbled
1 cup dry white wine
2 cups water, or enough to almost
  cover the crabs
1 celery stalk, chopped

A few parsley stems (without
  leaves)
1 lemon, cut into wedges, plus
  extra lemon wedges for garnish
2 live Dungeness crabs
Clarified unsalted butter or melted
  butter, for dipping

Select a pan large enough to hold the crabs side by side. Heat the empty pan over low heat. Add the peppercorns and bay leaf and heat very briefly to release their flavor oils. Immediately add the remaining ingredients (except the crabs), squeezing the lemon in before adding it. Bring to a boil and add the crabs. Cover, lower the heat and simmer 10–12 minutes. Remove the crabs and let cool until you can handle them comfortably. Serve with butter for dipping.

The San Francisco Chronicle Cookbook

 Once a Chinese village, and later the home of Portuguese whalers, Cannery Row became the sardine capital of the world during the 1940s. John Steinbeck's novels *Cannery Row* and *Sweet Thursday* immortalized Cannery Row.

Crab Cakes

1 whole head of garlic, baked
1 cup mashed potatoes
3 cups crabmeat, shredded
Salt and pepper to taste

Juice of 1 lemon
2–3 tablespoons chopped chives
Bread crumbs
Olive oil for frying

Squeeze and mix garlic into mashed potatoes. In a bowl, gingerly mix together potatoes and crabmeat, salt, pepper, lemon juice, and chives to taste, just enough to bind. Pat into golf-ball-sized patties, then flatten around edges. Set in bread crumbs to coat each side. Fry in oil, until browned. Serve with tartar sauce, Asian peanut sauce or herb butter.

The Fork Ran Away with the Spoon

Santa Barbara Crab Enchiladas

6 corn tortillas
Vegetable oil
1½ cups crabmeat

6 tablespoons minced onion
Salsa with tomatillos
Shredded Monterey Jack cheese

Heat tortillas one at a time in hot oil until soft. Place ¼ cup crab-meat in center of each tortilla and sprinkle with 1 tablespoon onion. Spread with a little salsa with tomatillos, roll up and place seam-side-down in 8x11-inch baking dish. Cover with remaining salsa. Sprinkle with cheese. Bake at 400° for 10 minutes until hot and cheese is melted. Serve with Sour Cream Sauce. Serves 4–6.

SOUR CREAM SAUCE:
¼ teaspoon minced garlic
½ teaspoon salt
1 cup sour cream
2 tablespoons chopped onion

2 tablespoons chopped cilantro
2 tablespoons chopped green
    chiles

Mash garlic with salt; combine with other ingredients. Add more chiles if you prefer sauce to be hotter.

A Slice of Santa Barbara

Deviled Dungeness Crab

Very good first course, since it can all be prepared ahead and refrigerated. Elegant and easy.

6 tablespoons butter, divided	¾ pound fresh Dungeness crab or
2 tablespoons all-purpose flour	any locally available fresh crab
1 cup light cream	½ cup bread crumbs
½ teaspoon Worcestershire sauce	4 lemon slices
½ teaspoon grated onion	½ teaspoon paprika

Preheat oven to 425°. Melt 2 tablespoons butter in a saucepan until foamy. Add flour and cook 3 minutes. Slowly add light cream, Worcestershire sauce, and onion, stirring until thoroughly blended and thickened. Remove from heat and stir in crabmeat until well mixed. Spoon mixture into 4 scallop shells and refrigerate until well chilled.

Remove filled shells from refrigerator and top with bread crumbs, dots of remaining butter, lemon slices and paprika. Bake for 15 minutes or until bread crumbs are browned and crab mixture is bubbly. Serve immediately. Serves 4.

Editors Extra: If you don't have scallop shells, this works well in any shallow oven-proof dish.

San Francisco à la Carte

Crab Taco

1 corn tortilla	1 tablespoon cilantro
2 tablespoons finely shredded red	2 tablespoons shredded crabmeat
or green cabbage	1 tablespoon prepared mild salsa
1 tablespoon chopped green onion	1 tablespoon sour cream or
1 tablespoon chopped tomato	guacamole

Heat tortilla in a frying pan turning once or twice. Spread cabbage, onion, tomato, and cilantro across the center. Distribute crab on top. Top with salsa, sour cream or guacamole, and serve. Makes 1 taco.

Neptune's Table

Calamari Au Gratin

8 cleaned, blanched and sliced calamari	1 tablespoon fresh rosemary
	Salt and pepper to taste
½ cup sliced yellow onion	2 tablespoons melted butter
½ cup grated Swiss cheese	½ cup milk
½ cup chopped fresh parsley	1 tablespoon Dijon-style mustard

In an oven-proof dish, layer half the calamari, onion, cheese, parsley, and rosemary. Sprinkle on salt and freshly ground pepper. Repeat layering with remainder of first five ingredients. Pour on melted butter, then milk/mustard mixture. Cover with plastic wrap and microwave on high 12 minutes. Serve hot with a green vegetable and salad. Serves 2.

Neptune's Table

Calamari, Festival–Style

One of Gourmet Alley's greatest attractions is watching the preparation of calamari. Some argue that eating it is even better. Here is Head Chef Val Filice's recipe for calamari as it is served at the festival.

⅓ cup olive oil	1 teaspoon dry oregano
¼ cup white wine	or 1 tablespoon fresh oregano
¼ cup white sherry	¼ teaspoon dry crushed red
1 tablespoon crushed fresh garlic	pepper
½ lemon	3 pounds calamari (squid), cleaned
1 teaspoon dry basil	and cut
or 1 tablespoon fresh basil	

In large skillet heat olive oil at high heat. Add wine and sherry, then sauté crushed garlic. Squeeze juice of ½ lemon into pan and place lemon rind in pan. Sprinkle herbs over and add calamari. Sauté for approximately 4 minutes on high heat. Do not overcook.

RED SAUCE:

1 pound whole, peeled tomatoes, canned or fresh	1 stalk celery, chopped
	1 medium-size yellow onion,
1 tablespoon olive oil	chopped
½ green pepper, chopped	3 cloves fresh garlic, minced

Mash tomatoes with potato masher and set aside. In medium-size pan, heat oil, add remaining ingredients and sauté until onion is transparent. Add mashed tomatoes and simmer 30 minutes. Pour Red Sauce over calamari and heat 1 minute. Serves 8.

The Complete Garlic Lovers' Cookbook

Cold Avocado Seafood Quiche

QUICHE DRESSING:

½ cup mayonnaise
1 teaspoon white vinegar
1 teaspoon Dijon mustard

1 garlic clove, minced
Salt and pepper to taste

Combine ingredients and mix thoroughly.

PATÉ BRISEE (PIE SHELL):

1½ cups all-purpose flour
Pinch of salt
5½ tablespoons unsalted butter

3 tablespoons vegetable
   shortening
¼ cup ice water

Have all ingredients chilled. Sift flour and salt. In food processor, combine butter and shortening. Add water a little at a time to form a soft, pliable—though not sticky—dough. (If mixing by hand in a mixing bowl, cut in butter and shortening with sifted flour and salt, using 2 knives, until mixture resembles coarse meal. Mix in water with fork a little at a time and, with your hands, shape mixture into ball.) Flatten into circle and enfold in plastic wrap. Chill a few hours. On a lightly floured surface, roll pastry to ⅛-inch thickness. Place in an 8- or 10-inch quiche pan and trim off excess pastry. Prick bottom and sides with a fork. Line with aluminum foil. Weight with beans, rice or pie weights. Bake in preheated 400° oven for 15–20 minutes. When pastry begins to color around the edges, remove the weights and foil and continue to bake until pastry is golden in color and dry. Cover outer edges of the pastry with foil to keep from getting too brown. Cool. The Paté Brisee can be made ahead of time and frozen.

QUICHE:

1 medium ripe avocado, coarsely
   chopped
1 (7-ounce) can artichoke hearts,
   chopped
¼ pound fresh crabmeat, cooked
   and shredded
¼ pound ham, cooked and
   coarsely chopped

1 tablespoon capers, rinsed and
   drained
2 teaspoons tomato sauce
1 teaspoon lemon juice
4–6 medium shrimp, deveined,
   cooked and chopped
1½ cups Quiche Dressing
1 Paté Brisee (Pie Shell), baked

Mix first nine ingredients in a large bowl. Spoon into Paté Brisee. To decorate and designate individual servings, place thin slices of avocado and halves of shrimp, sliced lengthwise, around the Quiche as spokes of a wheel. A small sprig of dill can be added to avocado and shrimp. Serves 6–8.

Party Perfect and Pampered

Baja Fish Tacos

2 tablespoons olive oil or butter
1 onion, coarsely chopped
3 tomatoes, coarsely chopped
3 cloves, fresh garlic
1 pound cod or mahi-mahi, skinned
Sweet Hungarian paprika to taste
1 package of 12 tortillas, corn or
  flour

2 cups fresh salsa
1 pound Monterey Jack cheese,
  shredded
1 head lettuce, chopped
1 bunch cilantro, coarsely chopped
1 lemon, wedged

In a large sauté pan, combine olive oil, onion, tomatoes, and garlic. Cook for about 1 minute. Add fish and cook 5 minutes until soft. Add paprika. Grill each tortilla until soft. Top with flaked fish, salsa, cheese, lettuce, and cilantro. Serve with lemon wedges, ice cold beer, tortilla chips, and salsa. Serves 6.

Little Dave's Seafood Cookbook

Cakes

The U.S. Open Sandcastle Competition, the largest sandcastle-building contest in the country, is held annually at Imperial Beach. Professional master and amateur teams build spectacular sandcastles during the three-day festival.

PHOTO COURTESY CALIFORNIA TOURISM

Apple Cake

1 can apple pie filling	2 teaspoons cinnamon
½ cup oil	2 teaspoons baking soda
2 cups flour	1 teaspoon salt
2 eggs	1 cup chopped walnuts
2 cups sugar	

Preheat oven to 350°. Mix all ingredients and pour into greased and floured 9x13-inch pan. Bake 50–60 minutes. Cool. Frost.

FROSTING:

2 cups powdered sugar	1 stick margarine, softened
2 (3-ounce) packages cream cheese, softened	2 teaspoons vanilla

Mix all ingredients well. Frost cooled cake.

Cooking Treasures of the Central Coast

Fresh Apple Bundt Cake

CAKE:

3 cups flour	2 cups sugar
1 teaspoon salt	1 cup vegetable oil
1 teaspoon baking soda	2 eggs
3 cups diced, peeled apples	1 teaspoon vanilla
1 cup chopped nuts	

Sift together flour, salt, and baking soda. Add rest of ingredients and mix together until blended. Spread into a greased and floured tube pan. Bake 1 hour and 15 minutes at 350°.

TOPPING:

½ cup butter, melted	1 teaspoon vanilla
¼ cup sugar	Powdered sugar for sprinkling
1 tablespoon corn syrup	on top (optional)

Combine all ingredients except powdered sugar, and pour Topping down sides of hot cake while still in pan. Cool 30 minutes; remove from pan. Sprinkle top with powdered sugar, if desired.

Marilyn Thomas: The Homemaker Baker's Favorite Recipes

Delicious Red Raspberry Cake

1 package white cake mix
4 eggs
2/3 cup vegetable oil

1 package raspberry Jell-O
1 (12-ounce) package frozen
  raspberries, thawed

Combine first four ingredients; mix until well blended. Fold in raspberries. Pour into greased and floured 9x13-inch pan. Bake at 325° for 50 minutes. Serve with whipped cream or ice cream.

Cherished Recipes from the Valley

Cranberry Swirl Cake

2 cups flour
1/2 teaspoon salt
1 teaspoon baking powder
1 teaspoon baking soda
4 ounces margarine, softened
1 cup sugar
2 eggs

1 cup sour cream
1 teaspoon almond or vanilla
  extract
1 (7-ounce) can whole cranberry
  sauce
1/2 cup chopped nuts

Preheat oven to 350°. Sift together dry ingredients; set aside. In a large bowl, cream margarine; add sugar gradually. Add unbeaten eggs, one at a time, with mixer at medium speed. Reduce mixer speed and alternately add dry ingredients and sour cream, ending with dry ingredients. Add flavoring.

Grease an 8-inch tube pan. Put 1/3 of batter in bottom of pan; swirl 1/3 of the whole cranberry sauce into pan. Add another layer of batter and more cranberry sauce. Add remaining batter; swirl the remaining cranberry sauce on top. Sprinkle nuts on top. Bake for 55 minutes.

TOPPING:
3/4 cup powdered sugar
1 tablespoon warm water

1/2 teaspoon almond or vanilla
  extract

While cake bakes, mix together Topping ingredients in small bowl; set aside. Let cake cool in pan for 10 minutes. Remove carefully cake from pan and drizzle Topping over it. Serves 10.

California Kosher

Honey Cake
(Lekach)

4 eggs
1 cup sugar
1 cup honey
½ cup strong black coffee
  (1 teaspoon instant coffee in ½
  cup water)
2–3 tablespoons salad oil
3½ cups flour
1½ teaspoons baking powder

1 teaspoon baking soda
¼ teaspoon ground cloves
½ teaspoon allspice
½ teaspoon cinnamon
½ cup chopped nuts
½ cup raisins
½ cup finely cut citron or glazed
  mixed fruit
2 tablespoons cognac or brandy

Preheat oven to 300°. Spray 10x15x2½-inch baking pan or 10-inch tube pan with Pam or other nonstick vegetable spray. In a mixing bowl, beat eggs lightly. Add sugar gradually and continue beating until mixture is light and fluffy. Combine honey and coffee and stir into oil. Blend mixture into eggs and sugar. Sift dry ingredients: flour, baking powder, baking soda and spices together. Stir in nuts, raisins and glazed fruit; blend the mixture into the egg mixture. Stir in cognac or brandy and pour batter into prepared pan. Bake 1 hour. Cool on cake rack and slice. Serves 8–10.

Apples Etc. Cookbook

Easy Kahlúa Cake

1 package dark chocolate cake mix
1 small package chocolate instant
  pudding mix
4 eggs
¾ cup oil

½ cup Kahlúa
1 (16-ounce) container sour cream
1 (12-ounce) package semisweet
  chocolate chips
Powdered sugar (optional)

Preheat oven to 350°. Mix all ingredients together. Pour into a well-greased, floured (or sprayed) Bundt pan. Bake 65 minutes or until toothpick inserted near center comes out clean. Cool. Invert to remove. Sprinkle with powdered sugar, if desired.

Tahoe Parents Nursery School 40th Anniversary Alumni Cookbook

Almond Buttercream Cake

1 box Duncan Hines butter cake mix
1 stick margarine
3 eggs
2/3 cup water
1 large package vanilla pudding (not instant)
2 cups milk, divided

2 sticks unsalted butter, room temperature
1 (3¾-ounce) package sliced almonds
2 tablespoons butter
4 tablespoons sugar

Combine cake mix, margarine, eggs, and water until well blended. Bake in an angel cake tube pan according to directions on box. Let stand at least 4 hours.

Combine pudding mix and ⅓ cup milk. Mix until smooth. Bring remaining 1⅔ cups milk to a boil in a medium saucepan. Take off heat and combine with pudding mixture. Return to heat and bring to a full boil, stirring constantly. Cool 3–4 hours. Place a sheet of wax paper over top of pudding during cooling to prevent the formation of a skin.

To make buttercream, blend unsalted butter with electric mixer until creamy. Gradually add vanilla pudding to mixture by tablespoonful until all is used. (It is very important that pudding and butter are at room temperature or buttercream will curdle.)

To prepare toasted almonds, melt 2 tablespoons of butter over medium heat in a large frying pan. Stir in almonds and cook until they start to become golden. Add 4 tablespoons sugar and continue stirring until the sugar is melted and almonds are golden brown. Cool on wax paper.

To assemble cake: Cut into 3 layers using a sharp knife. Fill each layer with buttercream, reserving enough for top and sides. Reassemble and frost top and sides with buttercream. Cover completely with almonds. Serves 12.

Symphony of Flavors

Chuck Yeager first broke the sound barrier in an X-1 at Edwards Air Force Base in 1953. The San Diego Aerospace Museum features the International Aerospace Hall of Fame which highlights the extraordinary accomplishments achieved by the world's leading aviation pioneers, pilots, engineers and industrialists. Wilbur Wright, Amelia Earhart, Wally Schirra, and Chuck Yeager are among the many honorees.

Mocha Nut Torte

Make the topping first and let it cool while making the cake.

MOCHA TOPPING:

½ cup sugar	1 tablespoon butter
2 tablespoons cornstarch	2 teaspoons vanilla
1 cup strong cold coffee	1 cup whipping cream, whipped
1 ounce unsweetened chocolate	

In saucepan, mix sugar and cornstarch and gradually stir in coffee and chocolate. Cook, stirring constantly until mixture thickens and boils. Boil 1 minute. Blend in the butter and vanilla. When thoroughly cool, fold in the whipped cream. Refrigerate until ready to use.

TORTE:

6 egg yolks	6 egg whites
1 cup sugar, divided	1 cup finely ground walnuts
½ cup flour	½ cup fine dry bread crumbs
1 teaspoon baking powder	

Grease 2 (9-inch) pans. Line with greased wax paper.

Beat egg yolks with ¾ cup sugar until thick and pale. Add flour and baking powder and beat again until smooth. Beat egg whites until foamy; add remaining sugar and beat to soft peaks. Mix together the walnuts and crumbs. Add to yolk mixture. Stir to mix well. Fold egg whites into yolks and nut mixture. Spoon into prepared pans. Bake 30 minutes at 350° until slight imprint remains. Cool in pans 10 minutes. Invert onto rack, loosen, and peel off paper. Frost when cool. Refrigerate. Serves 10.

The Steinbeck House Cookbook

Easy Almond-Rum Cake

Makes a nice holiday gift.

1 package yellow cake mix (no pudding)
1/4 teaspoon nutmeg
1 1/2 cups eggnog (commercial)
2 eggs
1/4 cup butter, melted
2 tablespoons rum, or 1 teaspoon rum extract
2 tablespoons margarine, softened
1/2 cup sliced almonds, toasted

Beat the first 6 ingredients together for 4 minutes. Grease a spring-form or angel food cake pan with softened margarine, and pat toasted almonds against the side of pan, lining sides and also bottom. Put pan into refrigerator to help almonds stay in place.

Carefully pour or spoon the cake batter into pan and bake at 350° for 40 minutes, or until a toothpick comes out clean. Remove from pan carefully. Cake may be garnished with 5 red cherries and mint leaves, or holly leaves. Serves 8–10.

Cook Book

Five Flavor Pound Cake

This is different and so good!!!

3 sticks margarine
3 cups sugar
5 eggs, beaten
3 cups flour
1 teaspoon baking powder
1 cup milk
1 teaspoon each: vanilla, lemon, rum, coconut and butter flavorings

Cream margarine, and sugar. Add eggs, one at a time, beating after each addition. Combine dry ingredients and add alternately with milk. Add flavorings. Pour into a greased and floured 10-inch tube pan. Bake at 300° for 1 1/2 hours.

GLAZE:
1 cup sugar
1/2 cup water
1 teaspoon each: vanilla, lemon, rum, coconut and butter flavorings

Combine all ingredients in a saucepan. Bring to a boil and stir until sugar is dissolved completely. Pour while hot over hot cake in the pan. Let set until cake is cool. Makes lots of servings.

Tried and True Recipes

Buttermilk Spice Cake

CARAMEL PECAN FILLING:

1 cup toasted chopped pecans, divided **¼ cup caramel ice cream topping**

Mix together ½ cup pecans and ice cream topping.

BROWN SUGAR CARAMEL FROSTING:

1½ cups brown sugar **½ cup butter**
½ cup + 1 tablespoon heavy cream **3 cups powdered sugar**

Combine brown sugar, cream, and butter in saucepan. Bring to boil over moderate heat, stirring constantly. Boil for 2 minutes, stirring. Remove from heat; cool until comfortable to touch. Stir in sifted powdered sugar; beat well until frosting reaches spreading consistency.

CAKE:

2½ cups sifted all-purpose flour **¼ teaspoon ground ginger**
1 teaspoon baking soda **¾ cup margarine (room**
½ teaspoon salt **temperature)**
1 tablespoon ground cinnamon **1 cup granulated sugar**
1 teaspoon ground allspice **1 large egg**
1 teaspoon ground nutmeg **½ cup unsulfured molasses**
½ teaspoon ground cloves **1 cup buttermilk**

Grease two 9-inch round cake pans with shortening; dust with flour. Position rack on lower third of oven. Preheat oven to 350°. Sift together flour, baking soda, salt, and spices; set aside. In large bowl or electric mixer, cream together margarine and sugar until well blended. Beat in egg and molasses. Alternately add flour mixture and buttermilk, beating after each addition (beginning and ending with flour). Spread batter in prepared pans. Bake until cake tester comes out clean and top is lightly springy to touch. Cool cakes in pans on wire rack for 5 minutes.

Cut each cake layer in half. Top first layer with Brown Sugar Caramel Frosting. Top with second layer; spread Caramel Pecan Filling over second layer. Top with third layer; cover with Brown Sugar Caramel Frosting. Top with last layer; frost entire cake. Place ½ cup pecans on sides of cake. Garnish cake with remaining frosting.

Fair's Fare

Lemon Pudding Cake

1 ½ cups milk
4 tablespoons butter
3 eggs, separated
1 cup sugar
½ cup all-purpose flour

⅓ cup (5 tablespoons) fresh lemon juice
Grated zest of 1 lemon
⅛ teaspoon salt
1 cup whipping cream, whipped

Preheat oven to 350°. Butter a 1 ½-quart baking dish. Get out a slightly larger pan at least 2 inches deep, which will hold cake pan comfortably.

Put milk and butter into small saucepan and heat until hot and butter has melted. Remove from heat and set aside.

Put egg yolks into mixing bowl and whisk until blended. Add sugar, flour, lemon zest, salt and hot milk mixture. Stir until thoroughly blended.

Beat egg whites until stiff but still moist, then fold into batter. Spoon batter into baking dish. Set dish in larger pan and pour in enough hot water to come halfway up sides of the baking dish.

Bake for 35–45 minutes, or until cake springs back when touched lightly in center. Remove from oven and let cool. Don't refrigerate. Serve with softly whipped cream. Serves 6.

The San Francisco Chronicle Cookbook

Red Velvet Cake

2 (1-ounce) bottles red food coloring	1 cup buttermilk
3 tablespoons cocoa	2¼ cups flour
½ cup shortening	¼ teaspoon salt
1½ cups sugar	1 teaspoon vanilla
2 eggs	1 tablespoon vinegar
	1 teaspoon baking soda

Mix together food coloring and cocoa into paste and let stand. Cream shortening and sugar. Add eggs and coloring paste and mix well. Add buttermilk by hand. Add flour, salt, and vanilla. Beat well by hand. Add vinegar and baking soda. Bake at 350° for 30–35 minutes if using a 9x13-inch pan, or for 25 minutes in 3 (8-inch) cake pans.

FROSTING:

4 tablespoons flour	1 cup sugar
1 cup milk	Dash salt
½ cup butter	2 teaspoons vanilla
½ cup shortening	

Cook flour and milk until thick. Cool. Cream remaining ingredients, then add to milk mixture.

San Ramon's Secret Recipes

Brownie Sheet Cake

Will serve 70 or more. Always a hit.

5 cups sugar	5 eggs
5 cups flour	2½ teaspoons vanilla
½ cup plus ½ tablespoon cocoa	1¼ cups buttermilk
5 sticks margarine	2½ teaspoons baking soda
2½ cups water	1 teaspoon salt

Preheat oven to 400°. Grease large sheet (11x17-inch) cake pan. Mix sugar and flour in large bowl. Bring to a boil the cocoa, margarine, and water. Add to flour and sugar mix. Don't beat. Mix eggs, vanilla, buttermilk, baking soda, and salt together. Add to other ingredients. Pour into greased pan and bake 20 minutes.

New Covenant Kitchens

Drunken Chocolate Pecan Cake

12 ounces semisweet chocolate	½ cup bourbon
1 cup unsalted butter	1½ cups sugar, divided
8 eggs, separated	1½ cups whole pecans, ground

Preheat oven to 300°. Melt chocolate and butter in a saucepan, stirring to blend.

Combine egg yolks, bourbon, and ¾ cup sugar in top of double boiler. Cook over simmering water until creamy and light yellow, beating constantly with a wooden spoon.

Beat egg whites and remaining ¾ cup sugar in a large bowl until stiff peaks form. Fold in egg yolk mixture. Fold in melted chocolate and pecans. Spoon into a 10-inch springform pan. Bake for 1¾ hours. Let cool in pan. Remove pan side.

CHOCOLATE FROSTING:

1 pound semisweet chocolate	½ cup shelled pecan halves
¾ cup butter	Whipped cream

Melt chocolate and butter in top of double boiler over simmering water, stirring constantly until smooth. Let stand until thick enough to spread, stirring frequently. Level cake top, using a serrated knife. Frost cooled cake. Decorate with pecan halves. Serve topped with whipped cream. Yields 10–12 servings.

Dining by Design

Milky Way Cake

6 regular-size Milky Way bars	½ teaspoon baking soda
1 cup butter, divided	1¼ cups buttermilk
2 cups sugar	1 teaspoon vanilla
4 eggs	1 cup chopped nuts
2½ cups sifted flour	

Melt bars and ½ cup butter over low heat. Mix remaining butter and sugar until fluffy. Add eggs and beat well. Add flour and baking soda alternately with buttermilk. Stir in melted butter and candy, and beat well. Stir in vanilla and nuts. Pour into Bundt pan. (Do not grease and flour.) Bake at 350° for 1 hour and 20 minutes. Check near end of baking time; do not overbake.

Children's Hospital Oakland Cookbook

Banana Split Cake

CRUST:

5 tablespoons melted butter or margarine

2 cups graham cracker crumbs

Mix butter with crumbs and press into 9x13-inch pan.

CAKE:

3 egg whites*
2 cups sugar
1 stick butter or margarine
1 teaspoon vanilla
2 or 4 bananas

1 (15-ounce) can crushed pineapple, drained
8 ounces Cool Whip
1 cup chopped nuts
Maraschino cherries

Beat egg whites and sugar, softened butter, and vanilla for 10 minutes. Spread on top of graham cracker crust. Split bananas lengthwise and cover pan. Spread crushed pineapple over bananas. Spread Cool Whip over pineapple. Sprinkle with nuts and dot with cherries. Serves 6–8.

*See note page 75.

New Covenant Kitchens

Nut and Fruit Cake

This is quite different from other fruit cakes. I've given them as Christmas gifts to friends often. It's delicious!

4 cups shelled walnuts, as whole as possible
3½ cups shelled Brazil nuts, as whole as possible
1½ cups whole dates, pitted

8 eggs, separated
2 cups all-purpose flour
2 cups granulated white sugar
2 teaspoons salt
4 teaspoons vanilla

Place nuts and dates in large bowl. Break egg yolks over nuts and dates; mix until coated. Sift next 3 ingredients over mixture; mix as well as possible. Beat egg whites and fold in mixture with vanilla. Mix well; place in well-greased pans lined with wax paper. Makes 2 loaf pans or 5 small loaf pans, or it can be made in a cake pan and served in squares with whipped cream. Bake at 300° for an hour, or until toothpick inserted comes out clean.

50th Anniversary Cookbook

Fruit Cocktail Cake

Yummy! Especially good the next day.

2 cups flour
2 teaspoons baking soda
½ teaspoon salt
1½ cups sugar
2 eggs

1 (17-ounce) can fruit cocktail
   with juice
½ cup brown sugar
½ cup chopped nuts

Measure flour, baking soda, and salt into sifter. In large bowl mix sugar, eggs, and fruit cocktail. Sift in flour mixture. Mix well. Pour into a greased 9x13-inch pan and sprinkle brown sugar and nuts over top of batter. Bake at 350° for 30–45 minutes. (Some fruit cocktails have more juice, so be sure to test cake in the middle before removing from oven.)

ICING:

¾ cup sugar
1 stick margarine
1 (5-ounce) can evaporated milk

1 teaspoon vanilla
½ cup (or more) chopped walnuts

Boil the sugar, margarine, and milk for 2 minutes. Remove from heat and add vanilla and nuts. Pour over top while cake is still warm. Serves 15.

Grandma's House Restaurant & Family Recipes

Penguin Cake

1 (14-ounce) angel food cake
5–6 tablespoons light rum
12 ounces semisweet chocolate
  chips
3 eggs
1 tablespoon vanilla extract
Dash salt
1 1/2 pints whipping cream, divided
5 tablespoons powdered sugar,
  divided
1/4 cup toasted slivered almonds or
  chocolate shavings for garnish

Break cake into 2-inch pieces onto a cookie sheet. Sprinkle with rum. Set aside. Melt chocolate over simmering water in a double boiler, stirring constantly. Add eggs, 1 at a time. Add vanilla and salt and cook, stirring, for 1 minute. Remove from heat and cool slightly. Whip 1/2 pint of the whipping cream, gradually adding 2 tablespoons sugar until stiff peaks form. Fold into chocolate mixture.

In a buttered 9-inch springform pan, layer cake with chocolate mixture, beginning and ending with cake. (There should be 3 layers of cake and 2 of chocolate.) Refrigerate cake at least 6 hours.

After that time, run a sharp knife around sides of pan and then remove pan sides. Whip remaining pint of whipping cream with 3 tablespoons powdered sugar and generously frost top and sides of cake. Sprinkle with chopped nuts or shaved chocolate. Store in refrigerator, or cover and freeze. Serves 10–12.

California Sizzles

Very Easy Trifle

1 box Jiffy Vanilla Cake Mix
  (makes 1 layer)
2/3 cup cream sherry
1 can cherry pie filling
1 large package Jell-O Instant
  Vanilla Pudding
2 cups milk
1 cup half-and-half
1 medium container Cool Whip or
  whipped cream

Grease heat-safe trifle bowl or round cake pan. Follow package directions for cake. If using a round cake pan, cut cake to fit a non-heatproof trifle bowl. When cool, prick top with fork; pour sherry over it. Let stand for a few minutes. Pour cherry pie filling over cake.

Mix instant pudding according to directions, but note substitution of half-and-half for 1 cup milk. When just set, pour evenly over cherry filling, and refrigerate, preferably overnight. Top with whipped cream or Cool Whip and serve.

Note: Other pie fillings may be used, or fresh fruit in season.

Cooking Treasures of the Central Coast

Black Forest Cheese Cake

This recipe won a Grand Prize at a local contest. The judges' comment unanimously was, "You must try it to believe it!"

1 (20-ounce) package Oreo cookies	2 tablespoons lemon juice
1 pint small curd cottage cheese	1 teaspoon vanilla
2 (8-ounce) packages cream cheese	1/2 cup butter or margarine, melted
1 1/2 cups sugar	1 pint sour cream
4 eggs	1 (16-ounce) can cherry pie filling
1/3 cup cornstarch	

Process cookies (including filling) into fine crumbs. Butter sides and bottom of springform pan. Dust sides with cookie crumbs, then put 1 cup crumbs in bottom and spread for base.

Process cottage cheese and cream cheese until smooth. Mix sugar and eggs in large mixer bowl; add cheese mixture, blending well. With mixer on low, add rest of ingredients, mixing until smooth. Pour half the batter into prepared pan; sprinkle with 1 cup crumbs. Using a spoon, dip about half the cherries out of pie filling and carefully place at random on top of crumbs. Carefully pour rest of batter on top; sprinkle remaining crumbs over all. Bake at 325° for 70 minutes. Leave in turned-off oven to cool for 2 hours. Do not disturb! Before serving, decorate top with remaining cherry pie filling. Serves 12–15.

Didyaeverhavaday?

Italian Swirl Cheesecake

This cheesecake keeps well in refrigerator and also freezes well.

CHOCOLATE NUT CRUST:

**¾ cup chocolate wafer crumbs
(10 wafers)**
¾ cup finely chopped almonds

2 tablespoons sugar
3 tablespoons melted butter

Preheat oven to 350°. Mix chocolate wafer crumbs, nuts, and sugar together. Put in bottom of 9-inch springform pan. Pour melted butter over top and use a fork to blend mixture and press into bottom of pan. Cook 15–20 minutes until lightly browned. Remove and cool slightly. Reduce oven to 325°.

CHEESECAKE:

2 (8-ounce) packages cream cheese
1 cup sugar, divided
2 tablespoons flour
2 tablespoons vanilla

6 eggs, separated
1 cup sour cream
3 ounces semisweet chocolate
2 tablespoons amaretto

In food processor or with electric mixer, beat cream cheese until soft. Beat in ¾ cup of sugar, flour, and vanilla. Mix until well blended. Beat in egg yolks and sour cream. In a separate bowl, beat egg whites and ¼ cup sugar until soft peaks form. Fold egg whites into cream cheese mixture. Pour ⅔ of batter into baked crust. Melt chocolate with amaretto in top of double boiler. Add to remaining batter. Gently blend. Starting at outside edge, pour chocolate batter onto white batter in a swirl pattern, ending up in middle of pan.

Place in 325° oven for 50 minutes. Turn the oven off. Prop door open 2–3 inches and let cheesecake sit for 2 hours. Remove to rack to cool. Chill before serving. I usually serve this with chocolate sauce.

The Old Yacht Club Inn Cookbook

The first Academy Awards ceremony was held at the Hollywood Roosevelt Hotel in 1929. Today the Academy Awards event is held at the Los Angeles Shrine Auditorium.

Prize Winning Cheesecake

CRUST:

1 cup graham cracker crumbs
3 tablespoons sugar

3 tablespoons butter or margarine, melted

Heat oven to 325°. Combine crumbs, sugar, and butter in a 9-inch springform pan. Press into bottom. Bake 10 minutes. Remove from oven. Heat oven to 450°.

FILLING:

4 (8-ounce) packages cream cheese, softened
1 cup sugar
3 tablespoons flour

4 eggs
1 cup sour cream
1 tablespoon pure vanilla extract

In a medium bowl, mix together cream cheese, sugar, and flour until well blended. Add eggs, one at a time, mixing well after each. Blend in sour cream and vanilla. Pour batter over crust and bake 10 minutes. Reduce oven temperature to 250° and continue baking for 1 hour. Loosen cake from rim of pan. Cool completely before removing rim of pan. Chill in refrigerator for several hours before adding Topping.

TOPPING:

1 pint sour cream
3 tablespoons sugar

1 teaspoon vanilla extract

Mix together sour cream, sugar, and vanilla. Heat oven to 450°. Bake 5 minutes and remove from oven. After Topping cools, add fresh berries, cherry pie filling, blueberry pie filling, etc., if desired.

Friends of Cameron Airport Favorite Recipes

Fantasy Chocolate Cheesecake

CHOCOLATE CRUMB CRUST:

1⅓ cups Oreo cookie crumbs
1 tablespoon granulated sugar

4 tablespoons (½ stick) butter, at room temperature

Mix cookie crumbs with sugar, and butter. Pat in an even layer over bottom of a 9-inch springform pan.

CHEESECAKE:

¼ cup Kahlúa
1½ cups semisweet chocolate chips
2 tablespoons butter
2 eggs
⅓ cup granulated sugar

¼ teaspoon salt
1 cup (½ pint) sour cream
2 (8-ounce) packages cream cheese, room temperature
½ cup sour cream, for topping

Put Kahlúa, chocolate chips, and butter in small saucepan over low heat. Stir constantly until chocolate melts and mixture is smooth; set aside to cool slightly. Heat oven to 325°. Beat eggs in small bowl. Beat in sugar, salt, and sour cream. Drop small pieces of cream cheese into egg mixture, continuing to beat until smooth. Gradually beat in chocolate mixture. Pour into springform pan over crust. Bake until filling is just barely set in center, about 40 minutes.

Take pan out of oven and let stand at room temperature 1 hour. Spread on ½ cup sour cream; refrigerate cheesecake several hours.

KAHLÚA CHOCOLATE SAUCE:

1 cup semisweet chocolate chips
⅓ cup Kahlúa

⅓ cup light corn syrup

Heat chocolate chips with Kahlúa and corn syrup over low heat until chocolate melts and mixture is smooth.

Unhinge pan and cut cold cheesecake in small slices with thin, sharp knife dipped in cold water. Dip knife before each cut and wipe clean between cuts. Pour a bit of sauce over top of each slice. Yields 12 servings.

Jan Townsend Going Home

Creamy Cheesecake

CHEESECAKE:

12 ounces cream cheese
2 eggs beaten
¾ cup sugar

2 teaspoons vanilla
½ teaspoon lemon juice
1 prepared graham crust

Combine Cheesecake ingredients. Beat until light and frothy. Pour into graham crust and bake at 350° for 15 minutes. Remove and cool for 5 minutes

TOPPING:

1 cup sour cream
3½ tablespoons sugar

1 teaspoon vanilla

Combine Topping ingredients, then pour over pie and bake 10 minutes more. Serves 8.

California Kosher

Butterscotch Cheesecake

⅓ cup butter, melted
1½ cups graham cracker crumbs
⅓ cup firmly packed brown sugar
1 (14-ounce) can sweetened
 condensed milk (not evaporated)
¾ cup cold water
1 (3⅝-ounce) package butterscotch
 pudding and pie filling mix

3 (8-ounce) packages cream cheese,
 softened
3 eggs
1 teaspoon vanilla extract
Whipped cream
Crushed hard butterscotch candy

Preheat oven to 375°. Combine butter, crumbs, and sugar; press firmly on bottom of 9-inch springform pan. In medium saucepan, combine sweetened condensed milk and water; mix well. Stir in pudding mix. Over medium heat, cook and stir until thickened and bubbly. In a large mixing bowl, beat cream cheese until fluffy. Beat in eggs and vanilla, then pudding mixture. Pour into prepared pan. Bake 50 minutes or until golden brown around edge (center will be soft). Cool to room temperature. Chill thoroughly. Garnish with whipped cream and crushed candy. Refrigerate leftovers. Makes one 9-inch cheesecake.

The Stirling City Hotel Favorite Recipes

 The giant, fifty-foot-high "Hollywood" sign was constructed in 1923; the sign originally said, "Hollywoodland"—the "land" came off in 1941.

Hollywood Black Mint Cheesecake

This luscious cheesecake, laced with subtle chocolate mint flavor, is a real show-stopper at the end of an elegant dinner party.

CRUST:

8 ½ ounces chocolate wafers
⅓ cup unsalted butter, melted
and cooled

Generously butter a 9-inch springform pan. Break chocolate wafers into a food processor and pulse until fine crumbs form. Add melted butter and pulse until just blended. Press crumb mixture onto bottom and 2 inches up sides of the prepared pan. Refrigerate. (Can be prepared a day ahead.)

CHOCOLATE:

1 ½ cups mint chocolate chips,
divided

3 tablespoons water
1 tablespoon crème de menthe

Preheat oven to 325° and position oven rack in lower third of oven. Place 1 ¼ cups mint chocolate chips together with water in microwave-safe bowl; microwave on medium setting until melted, approximately 1 ½ minutes in 30-second increments. Blend in crème de menthe. Spoon chocolate mixture over bottom of crust, using back of a spoon to spread evenly. Set aside.

FILLING:

1 ½ pounds cream cheese, room
temperature
1 ¼ cups sugar

4 large eggs
2 teaspoons vanilla extract
2 cups sour cream

Place cream cheese in large bowl. Using a mixer, mix for 30 seconds until smooth and creamy. Add sugar in a steady stream, mixing for about 1 ½ minutes. Mixing on low speed, add eggs, vanilla, and sour cream, blending well. Pour the Filling over the chocolate, starting around the sides and then Filling in the middle. Bake for 50 minutes.

At end of 50 minutes, turn off oven and leave cake in oven for an additional hour without opening oven door. Remove from oven.

Chop remaining ¼ cup chocolate mint chips and sprinkle evenly on surface of warm cake. Cool on rack for 3 hours, then refrigerate for at least 24 hours before serving. To serve, run a thin knife around edge of pan and carefully remove the rim. Serve in wedges. Serves 10—12.

California Sizzles

Pumpkin Cheesecake
with Bourbon Sour Cream Topping

A beautiful presentation for your holiday table.

CRUMB CRUST:

¾ cup graham cracker crumbs
½ cup finely chopped pecans
¼ cup packed light brown sugar
¼ cup sugar
¼ cup butter, melted, cooled

Butter 9-inch springform pan. Combine crumbs, pecans, brown sugar, and sugar in bowl. Stir in melted butter. Press mixture over bottom and ½ inch up side of pan. Chill, covered, in the refrigerator for 1 hour.

PUMPKIN FILLING:

1 (15-ounce) can solid-pack pumpkin
3 eggs
2 teaspoons ground cinnamon
¾ teaspoon ground nutmeg
½ teaspoon ground ginger
½ teaspoon salt
½ cup packed light brown sugar
24 ounces cream cheese, softened
½ cup sugar
2 tablespoons whipping cream
1 tablespoon cornstarch
1 tablespoon vanilla extract
1 tablespoon bourbon

Preheat oven to 350°. Whisk pumpkin, eggs, cinnamon, nutmeg, ginger, salt, and brown sugar in a large bowl. Cut cream cheese into chunks and cream together with sugar in large bowl of an electric mixer. Beat in cream, cornstarch, vanilla, bourbon, and pumpkin mixture until smooth.

Pour into crust. Bake on the middle rack of oven for 50–55 minutes or until the center is set. Let cool in the pan on a wire rack for 5 minutes.

BOURBON SOUR CREAM TOPPING:

2 cups sour cream
2 tablespoons sugar
1 tablespoon bourbon
16 pecan halves

Whisk the sour cream, sugar, and bourbon in a bowl. Spread over the cheesecake. Bake for 5 minutes. Let cool in pan on wire rack. Chill, covered, for 12 hours. Remove sides; decorate with pecans. Yields 10–12 servings.

Dining by Design

White Chocolate Cheesecake with Raspberry Sauce

CRUST:

2 cups finely ground shortbread
   cookie crumbs
½ cup ground almonds, toasted

3 tablespoons sugar
¾ stick butter, melted

Preheat oven to 350°. Combine all crust ingredients. Press on bottom and sides of 10-inch springform pan. Bake 10 minutes. Reduce heat to 325°.

FILLING:

6 ounces white chocolate, finely
   chopped
4 (8-ounce) packages cream
   cheese, room temperature
¾ cup sugar, divided

1 teaspoon vanilla
½ teaspoon almond extract
5 large eggs
3 tablespoons flour

Melt chocolate in top of double boiler over hot, but not boiling water; cool. Beat cream cheese, ½ cup sugar, vanilla, and almond extract until smooth. Beat in eggs one at a time. Mix flour and remaining ¼ cup sugar, add to cheese mixture and beat until incorporated. Stir 1 cup of mixture into cooled chocolate. Mix in remaining Filling. Pour Filling over Crust. Bake for 45 minutes or until center of Filling moves slightly when side of pan is tapped. Cool and refrigerate.

TOPPING:

1 (14-ounce) package frozen
   raspberries, thawed and drained

⅓ cup light corn syrup

Purée raspberries in food processor; slowly add corn syrup. Press through sieve to remove seeds. Refrigerate until serving time. To serve, spoon a tablespoon of Topping over each slice. Serves 12.

A Slice of Santa Barbara

Creamy Baked Cheesecake

1 1/4 cups graham cracker crumbs
1/4 cup sugar
1/3 cup butter, melted
2 (8-ounce) packages cream
   cheese, softened
1 (14-ounce) can sweetened
   condensed milk

3 eggs
1/4 cup lemon juice
1 (8-ounce) container sour cream
Cherry or blueberry pie filling

Heat oven to 325°. Combine first 3 ingredients; press into 9-inch springform pan. In a large bowl, beat cheese until fluffy; beat in sweetened milk until smooth. Add eggs and lemon juice, beating until blended. Bake 50 minutes or until center is set. Top with sour cream; bake 5 more minutes. Cool. Chill and top with cherry or blueberry topping. Refrigerate leftovers.

Great Chefs of Butte Valley

Cookies & Candies

PHOTO CREDIT: ROBERT HOLMES/CALIFORNIA TOURISM

Sleeping Beauty's Castle is the focal point of Disneyland. It is said that one of the spires was not plated in gold, like the others, to serve as a reminder that the park would never be completed as long as there was imagination left in the world.

Almond Cookies

These cookies are very rich, so make small ones.

½ cup butter, melted
1 cup sugar
2 eggs
3 cups almonds, ground finely

1 teaspoon vanilla
1 teaspoon baking powder
¼ teaspoon salt
3 tablespoons wheat germ

Melt butter; combine with sugar and eggs. Add remaining ingredients and mix well. Chill for ½ hour. Drop by teaspoon on cookie sheet. Bake at 350° for 12 minutes or until lightly browned.

Cook Book

Almond Frosties

2¼ cups all-purpose flour
½ teaspoon salt
1 cup butter, softened

3 tablespoons granulated sugar
1 teaspoon almond extract

Preheat oven to 350°. Combine flour and salt in medium bowl. Beat butter, sugar, and almond extract in mixer bowl until light and fluffy. At low speed, beat in dry ingredients until blended. Shape dough into 1-inch balls. Place on ungreased cookie sheets. Flatten slightly to ¾ inch thick. Bake 15–17 minutes until golden. Cool on wire rack.

FROSTING:
1½ cups confectioners' sugar
2 tablespoons unsweetened cocoa
½ teaspoon vanilla extract

2–3 tablespoons hot water
½ cup slivered almonds, toasted

Combine confectioners' sugar, cocoa, and vanilla in bowl. Stir in water until spreadable. Frost cookies; top each with almonds. Makes 3 dozen.

Taste of Fillmore

Arrowroot Lemon Cookies

These thin dainty cookies, with just a hint of lemon, are lovely with a small dish of rich ice cream on a hot summer day or with a cup of herbal tea as a light snack.

1½ cups arrowroot powder (cornstarch)
⅓ cup all-purpose flour
1 teaspoon double-acting baking powder
¼ teaspoon salt

½ cup butter or margarine
⅓ cup granulated sugar
Grated rind of ½ lemon
Yolk of 1 large egg
Milk to mix (about ¼ cup)

In a medium bowl, sift together arrowroot, flour, baking powder, and salt. Cut the butter into small pieces and rub into flour mixture with fingertips. Add sugar, lemon rind, and egg yolk. Add milk needed to make a stiff dough. Knead to free from cracks, then chill. Roll out to ⅛-inch thickness, prick well and cut into shapes with a fancy cookie cutter. Bake at 350° for about 15 minutes or until light brown. Makes 30 cookies.

Each cookie contains about: 65 cal; 1g prot; 8g carbo; 0g fiber; 3g fat; 16mg chol; 61mg sod.

Roots: A Vegetarian Bounty

Oatmeal Nutmeg Cookies

3 cups rolled oats
2 cups white flour
1 cup whole-wheat flour
2 cups packed brown sugar
2 teaspoons ground nutmeg
1½ teaspoons salt
1½ teaspoons baking soda

1 cup butter or margarine, softened
1 cup buttermilk
1 cup raisins or assorted chopped dried fruits
½ cup chopped walnuts or almonds

In a large bowl, combine oats, flours, sugar, and spices. With a pastry cutter or fork, cut in butter until mixture is moist and crumbly. Stir in buttermilk. Add fruit and nuts.

Drop by heaping tablespoonfuls onto lightly greased baking sheets, 1 inch apart; lightly brush tops with buttermilk. Bake in 375° oven for about 12 minutes or until edges are lightly browned. Cool completely on racks. Store in airtight containers refrigerated or at room temperature. Cookies will stay moist up to 3 weeks. Makes approximately 4 dozen cookies.

Delicious Recipes from the Nimitz Community

Candy-Counter Cookies

1 cup all-purpose flour	½ teaspoon baking soda
1 cup regular oats	½ teaspoon baking powder
½ cup plain M&Ms	1 stick unsalted butter, softened
½ cup Reese's Pieces	½ cup light brown sugar, packed
½ cup chocolate-covered raisins	½ cup sugar
½ cup peanuts or peanut M&Ms	1 egg
½ teaspoon salt	

Preheat oven to 350°. Grease 2 baking sheets.

In a medium bowl stir together the flour, oats, M&Ms, Reese's Pieces, chocolate-covered raisins, peanuts or peanut M&Ms, salt, baking soda and baking powder.

In a large bowl cream the butter and sugars. Beat in the egg. Stir in the dry ingredients until just combined. By ¼ cupfuls, drop the batter onto the prepared sheets, spacing 2 inches apart. Flatten slightly. Bake, reversing the position of the sheets in the oven once, until the cookies are crisp and golden brown, about 11 minutes. Cool the cookies 5 minutes on the sheets, then transfer them to racks to cool completely. Makes about 16 cookies.

Symphony of Flavors

Forgotten Cookies

Put these in the oven and forget them until time to eat.

2 egg whites	**1 cup chopped nuts**
½ cup sugar	**1 cup chocolate chips**
1 teaspoon vanilla extract	

Preheat oven to 400°. Beat egg whites until stiff peaks form. Gradually add sugar and continue beating. Add vanilla. Stir in nuts and chocolate chips. Drop by teaspoons onto a foil-lined cookie sheet. Place in oven and turn it off. Forget for 1½–3 hours. Yields 3 dozen.

Variation: One cup chopped dates, coconut or maraschino cherries may be substituted for chocolate chips.

California Kosher

Cornflake Macaroons

2 eggs, well beaten
½ cup sugar
¼ cup brown sugar
1 teaspoon vanilla

2 cups cornflakes
1 cup angel flake coconut
½ cup chopped nuts

Beat eggs; add sugars and vanilla and beat until light lemon in color. Add remaining ingredients, drop onto parchment-lined cookie sheet, and bake at 350° for 10–12 minutes. It's important to line your cookie sheet with parchment paper, as these macaroons will stick. Don't remove cookies until cool. Makes approximately 2 dozen medium-size cookies.

Cooking Pure & Simple

Mt. Shasta Pecan Cookies

¾ cup flour
½ teaspoon salt
½ teaspoon cinnamon
¼ teaspoon baking soda
1 cup quick-cooking rolled oats, uncooked
⅓ cup sugar
⅓ cup brown sugar, firmly packed

½ cup soft butter
1 egg
1 teaspoon vanilla
1 cup pecans, cut into medium-sized pieces
½ cup raisins

Mix flour, salt, cinnamon, and baking soda in a small bowl. Mix oats into dry ingredients. Beat sugar, brown sugar, butter, egg, and vanilla in 1½-quart bowl until fluffy. Mix in dry ingredients. Stir in pecans and raisins. Drop by teaspoonfuls onto greased cookie sheet. Bake in center of 375° oven for 10–12 minutes. Makes about 3 dozen cookies.

California Country Cook Book

Tropical Fruit Cookies

An excellent healthy snack food for hiking. The dried tropical fruits are available at natural food markets.

1 cup butter, softened
1 cup firmly packed light brown sugar
1/2 cup granulated sugar
2 eggs
4 teaspoons anise seed, crushed
1 tablespoon cinnamon
2 cups flour
1 teaspoon baking soda
1/2 teaspoon salt
1/2 cup chopped macadamia nuts
1 cup dried California apricots
1 cup diced California Medjool dates
1 cup dried, diced, sweetened papaya
3 cups Instant Quaker Oatmeal

Cream butter and sugars. Add eggs, anise, and cinnamon. Beat well.

In a separate bowl, combine flour, baking soda and salt. Add to sugar mixture and mix well. Add nuts and fruits and mix. Add oatmeal and mix well. Form into small balls and place on greased baking sheets. Bake at 350° until just brown on the bottom for 10–12 minutes. Cookies should be soft. Makes 60 cookies.

Cooking with Herbs

Potato Chip Crisps

1 cup butter or margarine, softened
1/2 cup sugar
1/2 teaspoon vanilla
1/2 cup finely chopped nuts
1 1/2 cups unbleached flour
1/2 cup crushed potato chips

Cream butter or margarine and sugar; add vanilla. Add nuts, flour, and crushed potato chips. (If dough is sticky, refrigerate for about an hour.) Form into small balls and place on ungreased cookie sheet. Flatten with fork. Bake at 350° for 12–15 minutes until browned lightly. Makes about 2 dozen cookies.

Cooking Pure & Simple

The golden poppy is the state flower of California. The Antelope Valley California Poppy Reserve in Lancaster has 1,745 acres of poppies.

Praline Strips

24 whole graham crackers
1 cup butter (or margarine)
1 cup brown sugar

1 cup chopped nuts (black walnuts
lend a distinctive flavor)

Arrange crackers in ungreased 10x15-inch pan. Put butter and sugar in saucepan and heat to boiling point. Boil 2 minutes. Stir in nuts. Spread evenly over crackers. Bake at 350° for 10 minutes. Cut each cracker in half while warm. Makes 48 cookies.

Heavenly Creations

Cranberry Almond Biscotti

1 ¼ cups dried cranberries
2 eggs
¾ cup sugar, plus extra for topping
½ cup oil
2 tablespoons orange zest
1 teaspoon cinnamon
1 ¼ teaspoons baking powder

1 teaspoon vanilla
¾ teaspoon almond extract
¼ teaspoon salt
2 cups flour
1 cup slivered blanched almonds,
pounded

Preheat the oven to 350°. Place the dried cranberries in a bowl and cover with hot water. Let sit for 10 minutes.

In a large mixing bowl, combine the eggs, ¾ cup sugar, oil, zest, cinnamon, baking powder, vanilla, almond extract and salt. Whisk to blend. Drain the cranberries. Add the flour, cranberries and pounded almonds to the above mixture and stir to form dough. Place on heavily floured board and knead until smooth. Add more flour, if necessary. Knead only about 20 turns and divide the dough in half. Form each half into a log, 2 inches in diameter. Place logs on ungreased cookie sheets. Sprinkle tops with sugar. Bake for 25 minutes or until golden brown and firm to touch. Remove logs from oven, but leave oven on. Cut while warm with a large chopping knife. Cut slices diagonally ½ inch thick. Return slices with cut side down and bake 25 minutes or until cookie turns brown. Transfer to wire racks to cool. Makes 2 dozen.

Sounds Tasty!

Four–Star Rugelach

CREAM CHEESE DOUGH:

2½ cups unsifted all-purpose flour
½ teaspoon salt
1 cup (2 sticks) unsalted butter, chilled

8 ounces cream cheese, chilled
¼ cup sour cream, chilled

FILLING:

½ cup sugar
1 teaspoon ground cinnamon
4 tablespoons strained apricot jam

1 cup finely chopped walnuts
½ cup dried currants

Process flour and salt in food processor just to combine. Cut butter and cream cheese into cubes and scatter over flour mixture, along with sour cream. Process with on/off pulses just until mixture comes together into a cohesive ball. Divide dough into quarters; shape each quarter into a flat disc. Wrap each in plastic and refrigerate until firm, or freeze, well wrapped, up to 1 month.

When ready to assemble and bake, position rack in the lower third of the oven. Preheat oven to 350°. Line baking sheet with aluminum foil. Combine the sugar and cinnamon in a small bowl.

Remove 1 dough package from the refrigerator 10 minutes before rolling it. Keep the remaining dough chilled. Roll out dough on lightly floured work surface into a 10- to 11-inch diameter circle about ⅛ inch thick. Using small metal spatula, spread 1 tablespoon of the jam very thinly over the dough. Sprinkle with 2 tablespoons of the cinnamon-sugar, then ¼ cup of the nuts and 2 tablespoons of the currants. Using the rolling pin, lightly roll to press the filling ingredients into the dough. Cut the circle into 16 pie-shaped wedges. Beginning at the wide end, roll up each wedge toward the point. Place the rolls 1 inch apart on the foil-lined baking sheet.

Bake for 15–20 minutes, or until golden brown. Cool 5 minutes, then transfer the cookies to a wire rack to cool completely. Repeat shaping and baking with remaining dough and filling. Yields 64 Rugelach.

The San Francisco Chronicle Cookbook

Coconut Lime Bars

A superb alternative to lemon bars.

1 cup butter or margarine, softened	**1 tablespoon grated lime peel**
¼ teaspoon salt	**5 tablespoons fresh lime juice**
½ cup confectioners' sugar	**2 cups sugar**
2¼ cups flour, divided	**1 cup flaked coconut**
4 eggs, slightly beaten	

Preheat the oven to 350°. Combine the butter, salt, confectioners' sugar, and 2 cups of the flour in a bowl, mixing to make a soft dough. Press evenly into an ungreased 9x13-inch baking pan. Bake for 15–20 minutes or until golden.

Combine eggs, lime peel, lime juice, sugar and the remaining ¼ cup flour in a bowl; blend until smooth. Spoon over the crust. Sprinkle the coconut over the lime mixture. Reduce the oven temperature to 325°. Bake for 25 minutes or until firm. Cool. Cut into bars. Yields 3 dozen bars.

Dining by Design

 The celebrity footprint/handprint tradition at Grauman's Chinese Theatre began in 1927 when silent screen star, Norma Talmadge, accidentally stepped in a sidewalk of wet cement.

Caramel–Cream Cheese Apple Bars

PASTRY:

3 cups flour
1/4 cup sugar
1 1/4 teaspoons salt
1 stick plus 2 tablespoons butter

1/4 cup cooking oil
1 egg
1/4 cup water

Combine flour, sugar, and salt. Cut in butter and mix well. In separate bowl blend together oil, egg, and water. Blend both mixtures together and form into a square. Place on 17x11-inch piece of foil that has been sprayed with Pam. Roll Pastry to fit foil and place on cookie sheet. Flute edges of crust.

APPLE FILLING:

5 cups sliced, peeled apples
1/4 cup flour

3 tablespoons lemon juice
1 cup sugar

Place all ingredients in mixing bowl and blend well. Spread Apple Filling evenly over Pastry.

CREAM CHEESE TOPPING:

1 (8-ounce) package cream cheese, softened
1/4 cup sugar

1 egg
3/4 cup chopped walnuts

Blend all ingredients together except walnuts and whip until smooth. Set aside.

CARAMEL TOPPING:

1/2 pound caramels

1/4 cup cream or canned milk

Combine milk and caramels in double boiler. Heat until caramels melt and are blended with milk. Spread a portion of Cream Cheese Topping in a 1 1/2-inch wide strip the length of the Pastry. Spread a portion of the caramel in the same manner next to the cream cheese. Continue this alternating pattern until the entire top of the Apple Filling is covered. Sprinkle with chopped walnuts. Bake at 375° for 35 minutes. Let cool and cut into squares to serve. Makes about 16 squares.

Marilyn Thomas: The Homemaker Baker's Favorite Recipes

Break Your Diet Bars

1 package butter recipe cake mix
⅓ cup oil
2 eggs
1 (12-ounce) package chocolate
   chips
1 cup white chocolate chips

3 (1.4-ounce) chocolate-covered
   toffee bars, cut into pieces
½ cup butter or margarine
32 caramels, unwrapped
1 (14-ounce) can sweetened
   condensed milk

Preheat oven to 350°. Grease a 9x13-inch baking pan and set aside. In a large bowl, combine cake mix, oil, and eggs and blend well. Stir in chocolate chips, white chocolate chips, and candy bar pieces. (Mixture will be very thick.) Press half of mixture into bottom of pan. Bake for 10 minutes. Meanwhile, in a medium saucepan, combine butter, caramels, and sweetened condensed milk. Cook over medium-low heat until caramels are melted and mixture is smooth, stirring occasionally. Slowly pour caramel mixture evenly over partially baked crust. Drop remaining cake mix mixture over caramels by teaspoons and press softly into caramel mixture. Bake an additional 25–35 minutes or until top is set and edges are deep golden brown. Cool 20 minutes. Run knife around sides of pan to loosen bars. Cool 40 minutes, then refrigerate 1 hour. Cut into bars. Store in refrigerator. Makes about 24 bars.

Symphony of Flavors

Toffee Butter Bars

These are extremely easy to make yet earn rave reviews everywhere!

1 cup butter, softened
1 cup sugar
1 egg
1 teaspoon vanilla extract
2 cups flour

1½ to 2 (7-ounce) bars Hershey Special Dark Chocolate, broken into squares
½ cup finely chopped walnuts or pecans

Preheat oven to 350°. Grease a 9x13-inch baking pan. Cream butter and sugar until fluffy. Beat in egg and vanilla. Add flour gradually, mixing well. Spread mixture in prepared pan. Bake for 20 minutes (cookie bottom may not appear done, but is fully baked). Place chocolate squares on top of cookie bottom immediately after removing from oven. When chocolate is melted, spread evenly with spatula. Sprinkle on nuts. Cut into bars immediately. Makes 24 bars.

California Sizzles

Lemon Glazed Persimmon Bars

1 cup persimmon pulp with 1½ teaspoons lemon juice
1 teaspoon baking soda
1 egg
1 cup sugar
½ cup salad oil

8 ounces pitted dates, chopped
1¾ cups flour
1 teaspoon cinnamon
1 teaspoon nutmeg
¼ teaspoon cloves
1 cup chopped pecans (or walnuts)

Mix pulp with baking soda. Lightly beat egg. Stir in sugar, oil, and dates. Combine flour with cinnamon, nutmeg, and cloves. Add to date mixture alternately with the persimmon pulp just until well blended. Stir in nuts. Spread evenly in a greased and floured jellyroll pan (10x15-inches). Bake in a 350° oven until lightly browned, about 25 minutes. Cool for 5 minutes, then spread with Lemon Glaze. Cool thoroughly, then cut into bars, about 3x1½-inches. Keep well wrapped. Makes about 30 bars.

LEMON GLAZE
1 cup unsifted powdered sugar

2 tablespoons lemon juice

Blend until smooth.

Durham's Favorite Recipes

Fresno Apricot Bars

⅔ cup dried apricots	1 cup brown sugar
½ cup butter (4 ounces) at room temperature	2 eggs, well beaten
¼ cup white sugar	½ teaspoon baking powder
1⅓ cups all-purpose flour, sifted, divided	¼ teaspoon salt
	½ teaspoon vanilla or rum
	½ cup chopped walnuts

Cover dried apricots with water in a saucepan and simmer uncovered for 10 minutes. Drain and cool.

Mix butter with white sugar and 1 cup flour. Blend with your hands or a fork until mixture is crumbly. Lightly grease an 8-inch cake pan. Press crumbled mixture into bottom of pan. Bake at 350° for 25 minutes. While this is baking, in a large mixing bowl, add brown sugar to beaten eggs and beat together until well blended. In a separate bowl, sift remaining ⅓ cup of flour together with baking powder and salt. Chop apricots coarsely and add to egg mixture, along with flavoring, nuts and flour mixture.

When bottom "crust" has baked, remove from oven and spread apricot mixture over it. Return pan to oven and bake at same temperature an additional 25 minutes. Cool pan on a rack. Cut into squares or bars. Makes 32 (2-inch) squares.

The California Cookbook

Mincemeat Bars

2 cups flour	½ cup oil
1 cup sugar	¼ cup milk
½ teaspoon baking soda	2 cups mincemeat
½ teaspoon salt	1 cup chopped walnuts

Combine flour, sugar, baking soda, and salt in large bowl; mix well. Add oil and milk, stirring until moistened and crumbly. Reserve 1 cup mixture for topping. Press remaining mixture into 9x13-inch baking pan coated with nonstick cooking spray. Spread with mincemeat near, but not to, edge. Sprinkle with walnuts and reserved crumb mixture. Bake at 400° for 20 minutes or until golden brown. Loosen edge of warm layer with knife. Cool. Cut into bars. Store, loosely covered, at room temperature. May use green tomato mincemeat, if desired. Yields 24 servings.

California Gold

Lemon Cheesecake Bars

5 tablespoons butter or margarine,
  softened
½ cup brown sugar
½ cup chopped nuts
1 cup flour
½ cup sugar

1 (8-ounce) package cream cheese
1 egg
2 tablespoons milk
1 tablespoon lemon juice
¼ teaspoon vanilla

Preheat oven to 350°. Spray 8-inch square pan or 9x13-inch pan with nonstick cooking spray. Cream butter and brown sugar. Add nuts and flour and mix thoroughly. Set aside 1 cup of mixture for topping. Press remainder in pan. Bake 12–15 minutes or until golden brown.

Blend sugar and cream cheese until smooth. Add egg, milk, lemon juice and vanilla. Beat well. Spread over baked crust. Sprinkle with topping. Return to oven and bake an additional 10–15 minutes. Depending on cut size, makes 30–48 squares.

A Slice of Santa Barbara

Raspberry–Fudge Brownies

4 ounces unsweetened chocolate
½ cup butter
3 eggs
1½ cups sugar
1 teaspoon vanilla
½ teaspoon salt
¾ cup flour
¾ cup nuts (optional)

1 (6-ounce) package chocolate
  chips
1½ teaspoons vegetable
  shortening (not butter or
  margarine)
8 ounces seedless red raspberry
  jam

Melt unsweetened chocolate and butter in top of double boiler or in microwave oven. Beat eggs until foamy. Add sugar and beat only a few seconds. Add vanilla, salt, and chocolate mixture, being careful not to overbeat. Mix in flour; add nuts. Turn into greased and floured 9-inch square pan. Bake at 350° for 30 minutes. (Toothpick should be barely clean when inserted in center of cake; cake will be moist.)

While brownies cool, melt chocolate chips with vegetable shortening. Spread raspberry jam over brownies in pan, then melted chocolate chips over the jam. Cool in refrigerator before cutting into pieces. Yields 18 (1½ x 3-inch) brownies.

Only in California

Raspberry Cheesecake Brownies

BROWNIE LAYER:

4 ounces fine-quality bittersweet chocolate, chopped
2 ounces unsweetened chocolate, chopped
1 stick unsalted butter
1¼ cups sugar
3 large eggs
1½ teaspoons vanilla
¾ teaspoon salt
¾ cup all-purpose flour

Preheat oven to 350°. Butter and flour a 9x13-inch baking pan and set aside. In a metal bowl set over a pan of barely simmering water, melt chocolates with butter, stirring, then cool. Whisk in sugar and eggs, 1 at a time, then whisk in vanilla and salt. Fold in flour until just combined, and spread batter evenly in prepared pan.

CHEESECAKE LAYER:

8 ounces cream cheese, softened
⅔ cup sugar
2 teaspoons fresh lemon juice
1 large egg
½ teaspoon vanilla
¼ teaspoon salt
2 tablespoons all-purpose flour
1½ cups raspberries
1 tablespoon sugar
Confectioners' sugar for sprinkling brownies (optional)

In a bowl with an electric mixer, cream together cream cheese and ⅔ cup sugar until light and fluffy. Beat in lemon juice, egg, vanilla, and salt. Beat in flour and spread evenly over brownie layer. Scatter raspberries over top and sprinkle with 1 tablespoon sugar. Bake brownies in the middle of oven 35–40 minutes, or until top is puffed and pale golden and a tester comes out clean with crumbs adhering to it. Cool brownies completely in pan on a rack and chill, covered, at least 6 hours or overnight.

Cut brownies into bars and sprinkle with confectioners' sugar. Serve cold or at room temperature. Makes 24 brownies.

Symphony of Flavors

Fudge Squares

3 eggs
2 cups brown sugar
1 cup flour
¼ teaspoon each baking soda,
    baking powder and salt

1 cup chopped walnuts
1 teaspoon vanilla

Beat eggs. Add sugar, then flour, baking soda, baking powder, and salt mixture. Add chopped walnuts and vanilla. Put into greased loaf pan. Bake ½ hour at 350°. Remove from oven and cut in squares.

Our Favorite Recipes

Rocky Road Bars

1 (6-ounce) package semisweet
    chocolate chips, divided
2 tablespoons margarine or butter
2 cups Bisquick baking mix
1 cup sugar

½ teaspoon vanilla
2 eggs
1 cup miniature marshmallows
¼ cup chopped nuts

Heat oven to 350°. Grease bottom of a 9x13x2-inch pan. Heat ½ cup of the chocolate chips and the margarine in heavy 1-quart saucepan over low heat, stirring occasionally, until melted. Mix baking mix, sugar, vanilla, and eggs. Stir in chocolate mixture; spread in pan. Bake 15 minutes. Sprinkle with marshmallows, nuts, and remaining chocolate chips. Bake 10–15 minutes or until marshmallows are light brown. Cool completely; cut into 2-inch squares. Makes 30 bars.

Sharing Our Best

Hawaiian Caramac Brownie Wedges

CRUST:

2 cups ground Oreo cookies
2 tablespoons melted butter
½ cup semisweet chocolate chips

½ cup chopped macadamia nuts
20 caramels
2 tablespoons heavy cream

Preheat oven to 350°. Spray a 9-inch springform pan with nonstick spray. Combine cookie crumbs and butter. Press into bottom of pan. Bake for 15 minutes. Remove from oven and sprinkle with chocolate chips and nuts. Combine caramels with cream in a microwave-safe bowl. Microwave on high 1 minute. Drizzle over nuts and refrigerate while preparing Brownie.

BROWNIE:

¾ cup unsalted butter
4 ounces unsweetened chocolate, chopped
3 tablespoons macadamia nut liqueur, or 2 tablespoons crème de cacao

3 large eggs
2 cups sugar
1 cup flour
¼ teaspoon salt
¾ cup chopped semisweet chocolate

Melt butter and unsweetened chocolate in large saucepan, stirring until smooth. Remove from heat. Whisk in liqueur, eggs, and sugar. Stir in flour, salt, and semisweet chocolate. Pour over crust. Bake until wooden pick inserted in center comes out with moist crumbs, 60–65 minutes. Cool on rack. Refrigerate until firm. Remove from pan; cut into wedges. Brownies will be thick and fudgy, not like cake.

GANACHE:

½ pint heavy whipping cream
10 ounces high-quality semisweet chocolate, chopped

Heat whipping cream in medium saucepan until hot. Add chocolate and stir until completely blended. Pour Ganache over top and sides of each wedge, covering completely. Refrigerate until set. Decorate with chocolate hibiscus leaves, macadamia nuts, and caramel drizzle, if desired.

Fair's Fare

White Chocolate Peanut Brittle

1 pound white chocolate
1 cup crushed pretzel sticks

1 cup Spanish peanuts
2 tablespoons peanut butter

Melt chocolate slowly in microwave or in top of double boiler. Add remaining ingredients and stir well. Spread as thinly as possible on wax paper on a cookie sheet. When cool, break into bite-size pieces.

Heavenly Creations

Almond Roca

2 cups butter
4 cups superfine sugar
2 cups whole almonds

4 cups semisweet chocolate chips, divided
2 cups finely ground walnuts

Melt butter in heavy saucepan over medium heat. Add sugar, stirring vigorously. Cook until caramel in color (or to 270° on candy thermometer), stirring constantly. Add almonds. Cook until medium brown in color (or to 290° on candy thermometer), stirring constantly. Pour onto buttered baking sheet. Top with 2 cups chocolate chips, spreading evenly. Sprinkle half the walnuts on top. Chill until set. Turn candy over. Melt 2 cups chocolate chips; spread over candy. Sprinkle with remaining walnuts. Let stand until set. Break into pieces. Yields 32 pieces.

California Gold

Peanut Butter Cups

1 pound butter, softened
2 cups peanut butter
3 teaspoons vanilla

2½ to 3 pounds powdered sugar
1 pound dipping chocolate*

Cream butter and peanut butter. Add vanilla. Add enough sugar to form balls the size of marbles. Pour a little bit of chocolate in the bottom of paper candy cup. Drop ball in while chocolate is soft. Pour more chocolate on top to rim of cup. These balls can also be dipped in chocolate using a toothpick for dipping fork. Candy freezes well—if it lasts that long. Makes 125 pieces.

*Melt dark or milk chocolate pieces over hot water or in microwave.

We're Cookin' in Cucamonga

Creamy Nuts

½ cup brown sugar
¼ cup white sugar
¼ cup sour cream

½ teaspoon vanilla
1½ cup nuts

Combine sugars and sour cream over low heat, stirring constantly. Continue to cook until it forms a soft ball when dropped into cold water. Remove from heat; add vanilla and nuts. Stir until light sugar coating begins to form on nuts. Turn onto wax paper.

Feeding the Flock

Peanut Brittle

Every bit as good as what you can buy and it's easy, too.

1 cup sugar
½ cup light corn syrup
1 cup roasted, salted peanuts

1 teaspoon butter or margarine
1 teaspoon vanilla
1 teaspoon baking soda

In a 1½-quart casserole, stir together sugar and corn syrup. Microwave at HIGH for 4 minutes. Stir in peanuts. Microwave at HIGH for 4–5 minutes, or until light brown. Add butter and vanilla, blending well. Microwave at HIGH 1–2 minutes more. Peanuts will be lightly browned and syrup very hot. Add baking soda and gently stir until light and foamy. Pour mixture onto a lightly greased cookie sheet, or nonstick coated cookie sheet. Let cool ½–1 hour. When cool, break into small pieces and store in an airtight container. Makes about 1 pound.

Tried and True Recipes

Peanut Butter Balls

These are easy enough to have the kids do at the cooking table.

½ cup peanut butter
2 tablespoons raisins
¼ cup coconut
2½ tablespoons nonfat dry milk

2 tablespoons honey
Graham cracker crumbs, coconut,
   sesame seeds (optional)

Mix first 5 ingredients and form into balls. Roll in graham cracker crumbs, coconut, sesame seeds or whatever sounds good. Enjoy!

Tahoe Parents Nursery School 40th Anniversary Alumni Cookbook

Fleur de Ly's Chocolate Truffles

1¾ cups cream
¼ cup honey
1 pound bittersweet chocolate, cut
   into ¼-inch pieces

7 tablespoons butter, at room
   temperature
2 tablespoons dark (or light) rum
½ cup unsweetened cocoa powder

Place the cream and honey in a saucepan and bring to a boil, stirring occasionally. Remove from heat and stir in chocolate. Cover, and let mixture stand for 5 minutes. Whisk in butter, 1 tablespoon at a time, until smooth. Transfer mixture to a small mixing bowl and stir in rum. Let cool for 30 minutes, then refrigerate for 1½ hours. Using small ice cream scoop or large melon baller, scoop out 1-inch balls and place on a baking sheet lined with parchment paper or aluminum foil. Refrigerate 15 minutes.

Place cocoa in a shallow dish and roll chocolate balls, one at a time, in cocoa, until completely covered. Don't worry if the truffles are irregular in shape and size—they will only look more authentic. Serve truffles in fluted paper candy cups, allowing 3 or 4 per person. Yields about 3 dozen.

Chef Hubert Keller's Notes: Allow about 2½ hours to prepare. You can roll the truffles in a variety of coatings. For example, chopped pistachios, toasted hazelnuts, toasted almonds, macadamia nuts, shredded coconut, or melted and tempered bittersweet chocolate. (Use a good-quality chocolate, such as Valhrona or Callebaut.) Feel free to substitute Grand Marnier, cognac, eau de vie, or your favorite liqueur for the rum in the recipe.

I recommend serving coffee or espresso instead of wine with these truffles.

The Cuisine of Hubert Keller

Pies & Other Desserts

PHOTO CREDIT: ROBERT HOLMES/CALIFORNIA TOURISM

The Tehachapi Pass is one of the world's largest producers of wind-generated energy. More than 5,000 wind turbines collectively generate more than 1.4 billion kilowatt-hours of electricity per year—with no environmental hazards.

My Best Apple Pie

8 cups tart apple, cored, peeled,
sliced
1 cup sugar
1/3 cup flour
1/3 cup pineapple juice
Pinch salt
1 egg
4 tablespoons butter

1 teaspoon cinnamon
1/2 teaspoon nutmeg
1/4 teaspoon ginger
1 teaspoon vanilla
Pastry for 10-inch double-crust pie
3 tablespoons canned milk
1 tablespoon brown sugar

In large bowl, combine sugar, flour, juice, salt, egg, butter, cinnamon, nutmeg, ginger, and vanilla. Beat to blend. Pour over apple slices and toss to blend. Pour into pastry-lined 10-inch pie pan; brush top with milk and brown sugar combination. Bake at 400° for 45–55 minutes or until golden. Serves 6–8.

Didyaeverhavaday?

Apple Custard Pie

1 cup sugar
1 1/2 tablespoons flour
1 teaspoon apple pie spice or
cinnamon

1 stick butter, melted
2 eggs, slightly beaten
1 unbaked pie crust
2 cups chopped apples

Mix dry ingredients. Mix with melted butter. Add 2 eggs. Pour into unbaked pie shell and add chopped apples. Bake at 375° for 30–45 minutes. Serves 6–8.

An Apple a Day

Sue's Apple Pie

This is perhaps the best apple pie recipe ever! I have been using it for nearly 27 years. The recipe is over 100 years old.

**12 or 13 Jonathan, Winesap or
  McIntosh apples
1 cup (or more) sugar
1 teaspoon (or more) ground
  cinnamon
¼ teaspoon ground nutmeg**

**¼ teaspoon salt
Pie Pastry
5 teaspoons (or more) lemon juice
3 tablespoons butter, chopped,
  divided
Cinnamon-sugar to taste**

Peel, core, and thinly slice apples. Mix sugar, 1 teaspoon cinnamon, nutmeg, and salt together. Fit one of the pastry rounds into a 10-inch pie plate. Sprinkle with a generous layer of sugar mixture. Alternate layers of the apples and sugar mixture until all ingredients are used. Drizzle lemon juice over top. Dot with 2 tablespoons of butter. Top with remaining pie pastry, sprinkle lightly with cinnamon-sugar and dot with remaining butter. Seal edge and cut vents. Line bottom of oven with heavy-duty foil, as pie is sure to run over. Place pie in preheated 450° oven. Bake for 12 minutes. Reduce temperature to 350°. Bake for 1 hour longer or until juices run over and the whole place smells heavenly. Turn oven off and let pie cool in oven. Serve with vanilla ice cream or a sharp Cheddar cheese. Yields 8 servings.

PIE PASTRY:
**1½ cups sifted flour
½ teaspoon salt**

**8–10 tablespoons shortening
5 tablespoons ice water**

Mix flour and salt in a bowl. Cut in shortening with a pastry blender until crumbly. Add ice water and toss with a fork until dough clings together. Divide into 2 portions and roll into rounds on a lightly floured surface.

La Jolla Cooks Again

During the mid-1800s, gold drew miners to eastern San Diego County. Today it is apples, where 260 tons are turned into pies each year by the Julian Pie Company.

Etna's Apple Cobbler

A heritage of Corralitos cooking.

6–8 medium apples	1 cup flour
¼ cup butter	1 teaspoon baking powder
2 cups sugar, divided	Pinch salt
2 teaspoons cinnamon	1 egg

Peel and thinly slice apples into 9x13-inch baking dish and dot with butter. Mix 1 cup sugar with cinnamon; sprinkle over apples. Sift together flour, 1 cup sugar, baking powder, and salt. Stir egg in with fork. Sprinkle over apples. Bake at 350° for 45 minutes. Other fruits can be used. Serves 8.

Cooking on the Fault Line—Corralitos Style

Walnut Apple Crisp

5 cups tart apples, sliced	1 teaspoon nutmeg
2 tablespoons lemon juice	Dash salt
¼ cup water	½ cup butter or margarine,
½ cup flour	softened
½ cup rolled oats	1 cup walnuts, coarsely chopped
1 cup packed brown sugar	

Toss apples with lemon juice and water in a shallow 2-quart baking dish. In large bowl, combine flour, oats, sugar, nutmeg, and salt. Mix to blend thoroughly. With a pastry blender, cut in butter until mixture resembles coarse crumbs. Mix in walnuts. Crumble over apples to cover completely. Do not pack down.

Bake in 350° oven for 40–45 minutes or until top is lightly browned. Serve warm or at room temperature. Accompany with ice cream or pour cream over, if you wish. If top turns dark too fast, cover baking pan loosely with foil. Serves 6–8.

Cook Book

Grandma's House Walnut Pie

3 eggs, beaten
2 cups sugar
1 cup white Karo
1 teaspoon salt

2 teaspoons vanilla
¼ cup melted margarine
2 cups walnuts or pecans
2 unbaked (9-inch) pie shells

Mix eggs, sugar, Karo, salt, and vanilla. Stir in melted margarine and nuts. Pour into unbaked pie shells. Bake at 350° for 45 minutes to 1 hour or until filling is firm. Each one serves 6–8.

Grandma's House Restaurant & Family Recipes

Walnut Orange Tart

CRUST:
1 cup flour
½ cup butter, chilled and diced
  small

1 teaspoon vanilla
1–2 teaspoons ice water, if needed

Quickly combine flour, butter,, and vanilla until dough resembles coarse oatmeal. If too dry, add drops of ice water. Gather into a ball, cover with plastic and chill for at least 30 minutes. Roll out dough to fit a 9-inch loose-bottom tart pan. Prick dough well and bake for 6–7 minutes in a preheated 350° oven until Crust is set and very lightly browned. Cool.

FILLING:
¾ cup sugar
¾ cup cream
1 tablespoon zest from one
  medium orange
½ teaspoon vanilla

Big pinch of salt
2 tablespoons Grand Marnier or
  other orange brandy
1½ cups whole walnuts

Heat sugar and cream in a saucepan until it just simmers and mixture becomes translucent. Stir in zest, vanilla, salt, and brandy. Fill shell with an even layer of walnuts and pour cream mixture over. Place tart on a baking sheet and bake 30–35 minutes at 350°. Tart should be lightly browned on top. It will bubble as it bakes. Cool and serve warm or at room temperature. Do not refrigerate. Garnish with fresh berries and a little crème anglaise or lightly sweetened whipped cream. Serves 8.

Sonoma County...its bounty
Recipe by Chef Jeffery Madura, John Ash and Company

Mocha Polka Walnut Torte

1 package brownie mix (or your
  own recipe)
2 eggs
¼ cup water
¾ cup coarsely chopped nuts

2 cups whipping cream
½ cup firmly packed brown sugar
2 tablespoons instant coffee
Walnut halves

Follow cake-like method for preparing brownie mix, adding eggs and water as directed; add nuts. Spoon into 2 greased 9-inch cake pans. Bake at 350° for 20 minutes. Turn onto racks to cool. Whip cream until it begins to thicken. Gradually add brown sugar and instant coffee. Continue beating until of spreading consistency. Spread between layers of torte and swirl over top and sides. Polka-dot with walnut halves. Chill overnight. This is very rich, so one torte serves 10–12.

Mammoth Really Cooks Book II

Cranberry Walnut Pie

2 cups fresh or frozen
  cranberries
1/2 cup chopped walnuts
1 1/2 cups sugar, divided

1 stick butter
1 cup flour
1 teaspoon almond extract
2 eggs, beaten

Grease 10-inch pie pan with oil. Cover bottom with cranberries and nuts. Sprinkle with 1/2 cup sugar. Melt butter, add flour, almond extract, sugar, and eggs. Mix, pour over cranberries and nuts. Bake at 350° for 35–40 minutes or until knife inserted in center comes out clean. Raisins may also be added. Serves 6–8.

The Stirling City Hotel Favorite Recipes

Ruth's Yam Peach Pie

POLENTA CRUST:
1/2 cup water
1 1/2 cups apple juice

1/2 cup white or yellow cornmeal
1 teaspoon cinnamon

Bring water and apple juice to a boil, and slowly stir in the cornmeal and cinnamon. Continue stirring until liquid is absorbed and polenta becomes quite thick (about 20 minutes). Remove from heat. Spoon polenta into a glass pie plate. Let cool until it can be pressed into a crust. For crisper crust, bake at 425° for 10–15 minutes. Poke a fork into the bottom of crust if it bubbles up.

FILLING:
2 cups baked yams (approximately
  1 large yam)
1 tablespoon peach juice (or apple,
  orange, etc.)

1 teaspoon cinnamon
2 cups diced fresh peaches
  (approximately 2 peaches)

Remove the skin from the cooked yams, and purée in a food processor with fruit juice and cinnamon. Put peaches into a large bowl. Add yam purée and stir well.

Preheat oven to 350°. Pour Filling into Polenta Crust, and smooth over top with a spoon. Bake for 20 minutes. Allow to cool completely before slicing.

Variations: In place of peaches, try 2 cups sliced bananas or 2 cups pumpkin, puréed with yams. Serves 8.

Per serving: Cal 110; Prot 1.5gm; Fat 4gm; Linoleic Acid 2gm; Fiber 2.8gm; Cal 18mg; Sod 7.4mg; Iron 9mg; B-Carotene 558ug; Vit C 8mg; Vit E 1.6mg; Selenium .001mg; Zinc 3mg.

The Health Promoting Cookbook

Spiced Pear & Razzleberry Crisp

When this is on the menu, it sells almost as fast as our Bread Pudding.

TOPPING:

1½ cups all-purpose flour
1⅓ cups brown sugar (packed)
⅔ cup sliced or slivered almonds
1 tablespoon grated lemon peel

2 teaspoons ground cardamom
12 tablespoons butter, slivered
(let sit 10 minutes at room
temperature)

Combine all Topping ingredients, and using a pastry blender, cut through until crumbly. Set aside.

FILLING:

1 cup sugar
4 tablespoons all-purpose flour
2 teaspoons ground cardamom
1 teaspoon ground nutmeg
½ teaspoon salt

5 pounds ripe pears, any type,
peeled, cored, coarsely chopped
2 cups frozen raspberries, thawed
2 cups frozen blackberries, thawed
2 tablespoons lemon juice

Preheat oven to 350°. Mix sugar, flour, spices, and salt in large bowl. Add pears; toss to coat. Add berries and lemon juice; toss gently, coating all. Transfer to a buttered 10x15–inch glass baking dish. Sprinkle topping over filling. Bake until liquid thickens and topping is golden, about 55 minutes. Serve with freshly beaten whipped cream.

Incredible Edibles

Apricot Crisp

Rich in vitamin A; easy because the fruit needs no peeling.

4 cups fresh apricots, cut in thin
slices and chunks
¾ cup firmly packed brown sugar
½ cup whole-wheat flour

¾ cup rolled oats
¾ teaspoon ground cinnamon
¾ teaspoon ground nutmeg
⅓ cup margarine

Preheat oven to 375°. Place cut fruit in 8-inch square baking pan. Blend remaining ingredients with pastry knife. Spread mixture over fruit evenly. Bake about 30 minutes or until knife cuts fruit easily. Serve warm. Yields 6 (½ -cup) servings.

Nutritional Analysis Per Serving: Cal 283; Fat 11.4gm; Chol 0mg; Sod 127mg.

Taste California

Lemon Pie Deluxe

PIE PASTRY:

1 cup whole-wheat pastry flour ¼ cup oil
¼ teaspoon salt 3 tablespoons water

Place flour and salt in 9-inch pie pan. Combine oil and water. Beat with fork until oil is emulsified. Pour over flour, stirring with fork to distribute moisture as evenly as possible. Mix until well blended. Press into pie pan with fingers and prick with fork. Bake at 375° for 20 minutes.

WHIPPED SOY TOPPING:

⅔ cup fortified soy milk powder 1 tablespoon grated lemon rind
1 cup water Speck of salt
2 tablespoons oil 1 tablespoon lemon juice

Combine soy milk powder and water in blender until well mixed. Add oil, lemon rind, salt, and just enough lemon juice to thicken. Put in covered container. Chill.

FILLING:

¼ cup sugar (may be brown) 1 tablespoon margarine
⅓ cup cornstarch Few drops natural yellow food
1½ cups unsweetened pineapple   coloring
    juice, divided 1 Pie Pastry
¼ cup lemon juice 1 cup Whipped Soy Topping, chilled
2 tablespoons grated lemon rind

Mix sugar and cornstarch and moisten with ¼ cup of pineapple juice. Put rest of pineapple juice into saucepan and bring to a boil. Stir in cornstarch and sugar mixture and stir until thickened and clear. Reduce heat. Add lemon juice, rind, margarine, and coloring. Stir until blended. Let cook slowly an additional 10 minutes.

Chill. Spoon half of filling into baked Pie Pastry. Chill other half of filling. Add chilled Whipped Soy Topping to remaining Filling and mix just enough to give a marbleized effect. Spoon lightly on top of pie. Serves 6–8.

The Oats, Peas, Beans & Barley Cookbook

Lemons are grown 12 months a year in California, and grapefruits are grown 11 months; strawberries 10 months. Artichokes, avocados, broccoli, cabbage, carrots, cauliflower, celery, lettuce, mushrooms, squash, spinach are all grown year round.

Lemon Cream

A good keeper. Excellent served over strawberries.

⅓ cup sugar	1 egg, beaten
1 tablespoon flour	1 cup marshmallows, halved,
1 teaspoon grated lemon peel	or 1 cup miniature marshmallows
¼ cup lemon juice	1 cup dairy sour cream

In saucepan, combine sugar and flour. Stir in the peel, juice and egg and mix until smooth. Add marshmallows and stir over low heat until mixture thickens and marshmallows melt (10–15 minutes). Cool slightly, then stir in the sour cream. May be refrigerated for 2–3 weeks. Serves 12.

The Steinbeck House Cookbook

Lemon–Blueberry Cream Pie

1 cup sugar	¼ cup lemon juice
3 tablespoons cornstarch	1 (8-ounce) carton sour cream
1 cup milk	2 cups fresh blueberries
3 egg yolks, beaten	1 (9-inch) baked pastry shell
¼ cup butter	Sweetened whipped cream
1 tablespoon finely shredded	(optional)
lemon peel	Lemon slices (optional)

In a saucepan, combine sugar and cornstarch. Add milk, egg yolks, butter, and lemon peel. Cook, stirring, over medium heat until thickened and bubbly; cook, stirring, for 2 minutes more. Remove from heat; stir in lemon juice. Transfer to a bowl; cover surface with plastic wrap and refrigerate until cool.

When cool, stir sour cream and blueberries into mixture; pour into pastry shell. Cover and chill at least 4 hours. If desired, stir a little lemon peel into sweetened whipped cream and pipe or spoon on top of pie. Garnish with lemon slices. Makes 8 servings.

Delicious Recipes from the Nimitz Community

Raspberry Sherry Trifle

A winner at family get-togethers, Thanksgiving and Christmas. A traditional English dessert.

Angel food or yellow cake	2 ounces sherry
Raspberry jam	½ pint half-and-half or milk
1 (8-ounce) package frozen raspberries (defrosted)	3 egg yolks
3 to 4 ounces pecans	1 teaspoon cornstarch
1 (3-ounce) package raspberry Jell-O	1 ounce (⅛ cup) sugar
	½ pint heavy whipping cream

Slice cake and spread raspberry jam on each piece. Then line a glass trifle bowl with them about ⅓ of the way, with jam face up. Drain raspberries. Keep juice to the side. Spread raspberries and half of the pecans over cake. Make Jell-O (per box instructions) with juice of raspberries and water. Pour over cake when luke-warm, just enough to soak. Sprinkle sherry on top (optional). Refrigerate.

To make custard, heat half-and-half (or full milk) in pan. Blend egg yolks, cornstarch, and sugar together. When milk is hot, slow-ly pour over egg mixture, while constantly stirring. Return mixture to pan and stir until thick, over low heat. Pour over cake and refrig-erate until cool.

When ready to serve, whip cream and pipe or spread over top. Decorate with remaining pecans, chocolate shavings or some extra raspberries. Serves 6–8.

Dining Door to Door in Naglee Park

An architectural marvel, the Winchester Mystery House has 160 rooms, more than 10,000 windows, three working elevators and 47 fireplaces, including staircases leading to nowhere, doors that open onto blank walls, upside-down posts, and a window built into the floor, all part of the bizarre phenom-ena that gave the mansion its name. Sarah Winchester, heiress to the rifle fortune, was convinced by a medium that continuous building of her Victorian mansion would appease the evil spirits of those killed by the famous "Gun That Won the West" and help her attain eternal life...so the hammers pounded 24 hours a day for 38 years!

Easy Layered Dessert

1 cup flour
2 tablespoons sugar
1/2 cup margarine
1 cup chopped pecans, divided
1 (8-ounce) package cream cheese, softened

1 cup powdered sugar
1 (8-ounce) carton Cool Whip, divided
1 (5 1/2-ounce) package instant pudding of your choice
2 1/2 cups cold milk

Mix flour, sugar, margarine, and 1/2 cup chopped pecans. Press into a 9x13-inch pan. Bake 15 minutes in 350° oven. Cool. Blend cream cheese with powdered sugar. Mix in 1 cup Cool Whip. Spread on cooled crust. Mix pudding with cold milk until well blended. Pour over cream cheese mixture. Refrigerate until firm. Now spoon on remaining Cool Whip topping and spread lightly with spatula. Sprinkle with remaining 1/2 cup chopped pecans. Refrigerate until ready to serve. Makes 12–16 servings.

Calvary's Cuisine

Cinnamon Plum Tart

CINNAMON PASTRY:
1 1/2 cups flour
1 stick margarine or butter, softened

1/3 cup sugar
1/4 teaspoon ground cinnamon

Combine flour, margarine, sugar, and cinnamon. Mix just until blended with fingertips. Press dough on bottom and up sides of 9-inch tart pan with removable bottom. Preheat oven to 375°.

FILLING:
1 1/2 pounds plums (about 10–12)
1/2 cup sugar
2 tablespoons flour
1/2 teaspoon ground cinnamon

1/4 teaspoon almond extract
1/4 cup chopped almonds or walnuts

Cut each plum in half and remove pit; slice plums. Toss plums, sugar, flour, cinnamon, and almond extract. Arrange plum slices, closely overlapping, to form concentric circles in tart shell. Sprinkle chopped nuts over plum slices. Bake 45 minutes or until pastry is golden and plums are tender. Cool tart in pan on wire rack. Carefully remove side from tart pan and transfer to serving plate. Whipped cream or vanilla ice cream is delicious on top. Enjoy!

The Potluck Cookbook

Winter Fruit Crumble

Good served with yogurt.

CRUMBLE TOPPING:

1 cup whole-wheat pastry flour	1 tablespoon cinnamon
1 cup Sucanat*	1 teaspoon cardamom
1 stick (¹/₂ cup) cold butter	1 cup chopped walnuts or pecans

Combine all ingredients and work with a pastry cutter or with your fingers until mixture looks crumbly. Makes 3¹/₂ cups.

2 bananas, sliced	1 half pint homemade jam
5 kiwis, peeled and chopped	1 cup Crumble Topping
2 cups apple sauce or pear sauce	

Preheat oven to 350°. Butter baking dish. Add bananas, kiwis, apple or pear sauce, and jam. Sprinkle Crumble Topping over top. Put crumble on middle shelf in oven and bake for 45 minutes. Serve hot from oven or let cool to warm. Makes 6 servings.

*Sucanat is a natural sweetener found in natural food stores.

The Organic Gourmet

Fresh Fruit Tart

PASTRY:

2 cups flour
2 tablespoons chopped crystallized
    ginger
1 cup brown sugar

1 teaspoon vanilla
1/2 teaspoon salt
1 cup unsalted butter, cut in pieces

Preheat oven to 350°. Mix flour, ginger, brown sugar, vanilla, and salt in food processor. Add pieces of butter one at a time, while processing, until ball of dough sets. Roll out on floured surface and place in 9- or 10-inch pie pan (or 11-inch tart pan). Bake about 12 minutes or till lightly browned.

FILLING:

Fresh sliced peaches, nectarines,
    apples or cherries, etc.
1/2 cup whipping cream or
    half-and-half
6 ounces cream cheese
1 cup sugar

4 eggs
1/2 teaspoon cinnamon
Pinch allspice
Pinch nutmeg
1/2 teaspoon rum extract
Whipped cream

Arrange sliced fruit or cherries decoratively in cooled shell. Blend cream, cream cheese, and sugar in food processor. Add eggs one at a time. Add cinnamon, allspice, nutmeg, and rum extract. Pour over fruit and bake 30 minutes or until knife inserted in center comes out clean. Serve warm or cold with softly whipped cream. Serves 8–10.

Sausalito: Cooking with a View

Fried Cream

Fried cream is a dessert with a long tradition in San Francisco. It is delicious, spectacular, and up to the final frying stage it can—in fact must—all be done in advance. It is worth the last-minute effort for the impressive results.

3 egg yolks
¼ cup sugar
1 tablespoon plus ¼ cup dark rum
Pinch of salt
5 tablespoons cornstarch
3 tablespoons milk
2 cups heavy cream, scalded and cooled

1 (½-inch) cinnamon stick
1 cup ground almonds
1 egg, beaten
1 cup zwieback crumbs
Oil for deep frying

Beat together egg yolks, sugar, 1 tablespoon rum, and salt until lightly thickened. Mix cornstarch and milk into smooth paste and add to egg yolk mixture. Stirring constantly, gradually add cream and cinnamon stick. Cook in the top of a double boiler over boiling water, stirring constantly, until thick and smooth. Remove cinnamon stick and pour cream mixture into a buttered shallow 9x13-inch pan to a depth of ¾ inch. Chill thoroughly.

Cut cream into diamond shapes and roll in ground almonds. Dip pieces in beaten egg, then roll in zwieback crumbs. Chill once more. Heat oil to a deep-fry stage and fry cream until lightly browned, then drain on paper towels and arrange on a heated serving platter. Heat ¼ cup rum in a small saucepan, ignite, and pour over cream. Serve immediately. Serves 6–8.

San Francisco à la Carte

The name of the road linking the early Spanish missions, presidios, and pueblos from San Diego to Santa Clara is known as El Camino Real (the Royal Road). Along "The King's Highway," twenty-one famous California Missions were established, starting in 1770. The oldest California building still in use is The Chapel—Mission San Juan Capistrano. Mission San Luis Rey, known as "King of the Missions," is the largest.

Italian Frangelico Pie

PIE CRUST:

**1½ packages Pepperidge Farm
hazelnut cookies**

½ stick soft, sweet butter

Crush cookies in a blender or by hand. Mix in butter with hands until mixture is uniform in texture. Press into 12-inch pie plate with spoon.

FILLING:

**16 ounces white chocolate chips
(dark will do nicely, but
changes the color)
2 (15-ounce) packages ricotta
cheese**

**4 ounces Frangelico liqueur
(hazelnut flavored)
Chopped nuts for garnish
Chocolate curls for garnish**

Melt white chocolate chips in double boiler. Put ricotta cheese and liqueur in blender. Blend, adding melted chocolate to cheese mixture as it is blending. Pour into pie shell. Chill. Top with chopped nuts and shaved chocolate curls.

The Coastal Cook of West Marin

Espresso Pecan Fudge Pie

**3 ounces coarsely chopped
chocolate (unsweetened or
semisweet)
3 tablespoons butter
1 teaspoon instant espresso
powder (or French roast)
1 cup sugar**

**1 cup light corn syrup
3 tablespoons coffee-flavored
liqueur
1 teaspoon vanilla
3 eggs, lightly beaten
1½ cups pecans
Partially baked pie shell**

Preheat oven to 350°. Combine chocolate and butter over low heat until butter melts. Remove from heat; whisk chocolate mixture until smooth. Mix in espresso powder until dissolved. Whisk in sugar, corn syrup, coffee liqueur, vanilla, and eggs until smooth. Stir in pecans. Pour into partially baked pie crust. Bake 45 minutes or until set. Cool. Serve with whipped cream. Serves 6–8.

Delicious Recipes from the Nimitz Community

Ghirardelli Gay Nineties Silk Pie

The Ghirardelli family of San Francisco established one of the world's finest chocolate companies in 1852. Today a Ghirardelli confectionery shop still stands in San Francisco's historic Ghirardelli Square. Silk Pie is a recipe from their culinary collection.

CRUST:

4 ounces (4 squares) bittersweet chocolate
1 cup coarsely chopped pecans

½ cup packed brown sugar
1 tablespoon butter, cut up

Break chocolate into small pieces and combine with remaining ingredients in a blender or food processor; process for 20 seconds, or until crumbly. (If a blender is used, blend chocolate first, then add remaining ingredients.) Press crumbs into a 9-inch pie plate. Chill while preparing Filling.

FILLING:

1 cup butter, softened
1½ cups sifted powdered sugar
3 eggs, well beaten*

2 tablespoons bourbon whiskey
8 ounces bittersweet chocolate
¼ cup heavy cream

Cream butter with sugar until fluffy. Beat in eggs and bourbon. Break chocolate into small pieces. In a heavy saucepan, melt broken chocolate with cream, stirring constantly. Mix chocolate into creamed mixture. Spread into prepared Crust. Freeze for 1 hour, or until slightly frozen. Spread with White Laced Whipped Cream to serve. Makes 8 servings.

WHITE LACED WHIPPED CREAM:

¾ cup heavy cream
1 tablespoon powdered sugar

1 teaspoon bourbon whiskey
¼ cup chopped pecans

Combine all ingredients except pecans and beat until stiff. Spread all over pie. Sprinkle top with pecans.

*See note page 75.

A Little San Francisco Cookbook

In 1869, wire-rope manufacturer Andrew Hallidie watched horrified as a horse-drawn streetcar slid backwards down a steep wet cobblestone street, dragging the five horses to their deaths. He and his partners decided to do something about it. The first Clay Street cable line started public service in 1873 and cable cars have been running up and down the hills of San Francisco ever since.

Hershey's® Kiss Pie

Try serving in parfait glasses.

1 (12- to 13-ounce) package
  Hershey's candy kisses
2 ounces milk

1 (8-ounce) package cream cheese
1 (12-ounce) carton Cool Whip
1 chocolate ready-made pie crust

Melt kisses over medium heat in the milk. When melted, add cream cheese and stir until completely melted. Rapidly stir in Cool Whip with the heat off. (Be careful it doesn't burn.) Pour into crust. Refrigerate until set. Serves 6–8.

More Firehouse Favorites

Warm Chocolate–Brownie Cups

These individual cakes with an oozing, velvety chocolate center will delight the child in everyone. They can be made ahead of time and refrigerated until the next day, or frozen.

6 ounces bittersweet chocolate,
  chopped
¾ cup (1½ sticks) unsalted
  butter
3 eggs, at room temperature
3 egg yolks, at room temperature
6 tablespoons sugar

1 tablespoon pure vanilla extract
½ teaspoon salt
5 tablespoons flour
¼ cup ground pecans (optional)
Crème fraîche, fresh
  raspberries, and fresh mint sprigs
  for garnish

Preheat oven to 375°. Butter and flour 6 (6-ounce) custard cups or ramekins. Set aside. In a medium saucepan, melt chocolate with butter over low heat. Let cool slightly. In a medium bowl, combine eggs, egg yolks, and sugar. Beat until mixture is pale and a slowly dissolving ribbon forms on the surface when beaters are lifted, about 10 minutes. Mix in vanilla and salt. Beat in flour and optional pecans. Add chocolate mixture and beat until thick and glossy, about 5 minutes. Pour batter equally into the cups or ramekins. (At this point, the cups or ramekins can be covered with plastic wrap and refrigerated or frozen until future use.)

Remove cups or ramekins from refrigerator or freezer and place immediately in preheated oven. Bake until each cake is set around the edges, but moves slightly in center, about 10 minutes, or 15 minutes if frozen; do not overbake. Let cool slightly. Run a knife around edges and invert onto dessert plates. Garnish each with a dollop of crème fraîche, fresh raspberries, and a mint sprig. Serves 6.

San Francisco Flavors

Chocolate Peppermint Torte

CRUST:

1 cup crushed chocolate wafers   2 tablespoons butter, melted

Stir together wafer crumbs with melted butter and press into a 9-inch springform pan. Bake at 350° for 10 minutes.

FILLING:

1 cup butter, softened	2 teaspoons vanilla
1½ cups sugar	1½ teaspoons peppermint flavoring
6 ounces unsweetened chocolate, melted	6 eggs*
	1 cup whipping cream

Beat butter until creamy; add sugar and beat until light and fluffy. Beat in chocolate, vanilla, and peppermint flavoring. Add eggs, one at a time, beating 3 minutes after each addition.

Whip cream until stiff but not dry, and fold into chocolate-egg mixture. Spoon onto cooled crust. Cover lightly and chill 4 hours. May be garnished with chocolate curls before serving. Can be prepared one day in advance. Yields 8–10 servings.

*See note page 75.

Only in California

Fudge Pudding

Makes its own sauce.

1 cup flour	½ cup milk
2 teaspoons baking powder	2 tablespoons shortening, melted
¼ teaspoon salt	1 cup coarsely chopped walnuts
¾ cup sugar	1 cup firmly packed brown sugar
5½ tablespoons cocoa powder, divided	1¾ cups hot water

Sift flour; measure. Sift again with baking powder, salt, sugar, and 1½ tablespoons cocoa. Add milk, shortening, and nuts; mix well. Spread into well-greased 8x8x2-inch cake pan. Combine remaining cocoa and brown sugar; sprinkle over top. Pour hot water into tablespoon allowing to overflow into mixture. Bake at 350° for 45 minutes. Serves 8.

Tasty Temptations

Tiramisu

3 egg yolks*
1 cup mascarpone cheese
¼ cup sugar
½ cup cream, whipped

7 cups espresso or strong coffee
½ cup dark rum
About 50 lady fingers
Ground chocolate for garnish

In a mixer, beat egg yolks, mascarpone, and sugar until fluffy and creamy. Fold into whipped cream. Set aside.

Combine coffee and rum. Dip each lady finger in coffee-rum mixture, sugar-side-down, for 1 second (lady fingers get soggy very quickly). Layer lady fingers in a 3-inch deep rectangular pan. Cover with mascarpone mixture. Repeat procedure until all mascarpone and lady fingers are used. Chill for 2 hours.

CRÈME ANGLAISE:
7 egg yolks
½ cup sugar

2 cups milk
2 tablespoons vanilla extract

In a mixing bowl, whisk together egg yolks and sugar for about 2 minutes. Set aside.

In a double boiler, over medium heat, bring milk and vanilla to a boil. Add egg mixture to milk and whisk quickly so eggs don't curdle. Cook until 145° is reached. Cool before serving.

*See note page 75.

Monterey's Cooking Secrets

Bread Pudding with Chocolate Chips

Even better the next morning, cold, for breakfast, if you have any left!

8 cups stale, cubed bread
1 cup chocolate chips
4 cups scalded milk
1 cup sugar

4 eggs, slightly beaten
½ teaspoon salt
1 teaspoon cinnamon

Place cubed bread in a 9x13-inch baking dish. (You can try and dress it up with sourdough, etc., but the most inexpensive white bread, left on the counter to get stale, works the best.) Mix in chocolate chips. In a separate bowl, blend milk, sugar, eggs, salt, and cinnamon.

Pour over bread. Place baking dish in a larger pan of hot water (1 inch) and bake at 350° for 40–45 minutes, until browned and knife inserted into middle comes out clean. Serve hot in a bowl with a little milk poured over the top, if desired (half our family likes it with milk, half just plain).

Taste of Fillmore

Grand Marnier Bread Pudding

8 cups cubed French bread
4 cups whipping cream, divided
1 cup granulated sugar
½ cup light brown sugar
4 egg yolks, beaten
1 cup raisins
1 cup chopped pecans

1 cup shredded coconut
3 teaspoons vanilla
2 teaspoons honey
1 stick unsalted butter, melted
Cinnamon
Brown sugar

Place bread in bowl and pour 2 cups whipping cream over it. Let stand 20 minutes. Combine 2 cups whipping cream, sugars, egg yolks, raisins, pecans, coconut, vanilla, honey, and butter. Set aside.

PASTRY CREAM:

4 cups whipping cream
¼ cup powdered sugar

4 egg yolks, beaten
2½ tablespoons Grand Marnier

In saucepan reduce 4 cups whipping cream to 3 cups, simmering over medium heat. Turn heat to low and add powdered sugar and beaten egg yolks. When mixture simmers, add Grand Marnier.

In oiled 9x13x4-inch baking dish, place ⅓ bread in layer on bottom. Spread ½ raisin mixture on top. Top with ¼ Pastry Cream. Add another layer of bread, raisin mixture and ¼ Pastry Cream. Top with last layer of bread. Sprinkle with cinnamon and brown sugar, cover with foil and bake at 350° for 40 minutes. Remove cover and bake additional 10 minutes. Serve warm on pool of pastry cream with a little drizzled over top. Serves 12–14.

Puddings from A–Z

Grandma's Bread Pudding

At long last, our Bread Pudding and Brandy Sauce recipe! For all of you who call in on Sunday mornings to see if we have it, here you go—now you can treat yourself every day!

6 cups sourdough bread (ends are okay) cut in ½-inch cubes
1 Granny Smith apple, peeled, cored and diced
¼ cup raisins
4 large eggs
1 cup granulated sugar
¼ cup brown sugar
½ teaspoon nutmeg
1½ teaspoons ground cinnamon
1 teaspoon vanilla extract
2 cups whole or 2% milk
Whipped cream and cinnamon for garnish

Preheat oven to 400°. Prepare 9x13-inch pan by spraying with Pam or buttering. Place bread cubes in large bowl and add diced apples and raisins. Beat eggs in medium-size bowl until frothy. Add sugars, spices, and vanilla. Mix well. Blend in milk. Pour mixture over bread and toss to coat. Pile into prepared pan, and press down lightly, spreading evenly in pan. Cover tightly with foil. Place pan in slightly larger pan. Place in oven. Pour boiling water into larger pan, (be careful not to pour too much water into pan). Bake for 1 hour. Take foil off last 10 minutes until lightly brown. Serve with Gram's Brandy Sauce and top with whipped cream and a touch of cinnamon.

GRAM'S BRANDY SAUCE:
½ cup butter or margarine
1 cup sugar
1 large egg
¼ cup brandy

Melt butter or margarine in small heavy saucepan, being careful not to burn. In a medium bowl, mix sugar and egg with wire whisk, until well blended. Gradually pour in melted butter and blend well. Return mixture to saucepan. Stir with whisk over low heat for 60 seconds or until sugar is dissolved (do not boil). Add brandy and blend. Remove from heat immediately after blending or egg will set and turn brown. Serve over Bread Pudding or your favorite crisp. Serves 10–12.

Incredible Edibles

Fluffy Frozen Peanut Butter Pie

GRAHAM CRACKER CRUST:

12 graham crackers, crushed	**¼ cup butter, melted**
2 tablespoons sugar	

Blend all ingredients together and press into a 9-inch pie plate. Bake in a 325° oven for 12–15 minutes.

FILLING:

8 ounces cream cheese	**½ cup milk**
1⅓ cups powdered sugar	**1½–2 cups defrosted Cool Whip**
Scant ½ cup peanut butter	**¼ cup finely chopped peanuts**

Whip cream cheese at low speed until soft and fluffy. Beat in sugar and peanut butter. Slowly add milk. Fold in Cool Whip. Pour in shell and sprinkle with peanuts. Freeze. (Can easily be sliced while frozen.) Serves 6–8.

Children's Hospital Oakland Cookbook

Great Putt Peanut Butter Pie

1 cup crunchy peanut butter	**1 (8-ounce) tub low-fat frozen**
1 cup sugar	**whipped topping, thawed**
1 (8-ounce) package reduced-fat	**1 (9-inch) ready-to-use chocolate**
cream cheese	**crumb pie crust**
1 teaspoon vanilla	**Shaved chocolate or peanuts**
2 teaspoons melted butter	**(optional)**

Beat peanut butter, sugar, cream cheese, vanilla, and butter thoroughly until creamy. Fold in whipped topping. Pour into pie crust and refrigerate overnight or freeze for several hours. Garnish with shaved chocolate or peanuts. Serves 6–8.

The Golf Cookbook

 The population growth of California between 1940 and 1970 averaged 500,000 per year.

Ten-Dollar Banana Split

CHOCOLATE SAUCE:

**8 ounces semisweet chocolate
(preferably Guittard's French
Vanilla)
1/2 cup unsalted butter**

**2 tablespoons brandy or cognac
1 tablespoon triple sec
3/4 cup light corn syrup
3/4 cup heavy cream**

Cut chocolate and butter into small pieces and place with brandy, triple sec, and corn syrup in double boiler and allow to soften. Butter will melt, but chocolate chunks will hold their shape until pressed. Remove from heat and whisk together. When mixture is smooth, stir in cream.

PINEAPPLE SAUCE:

**1/2 fresh pineapple, peeled
and cored**

Sugar to taste

Purée pineapple in a processor or blender and add enough sugar to sweeten sauce.

STRAWBERRY SAUCE:

**1 pint strawberries, hulled,
divided
1/3 cup sugar**

**Juice of 1/2 lemon
2 tablespoons Kirsch or triple sec**

Place half strawberries, sugar, and lemon juice in a blender or processor, and purée. Strain into serving bowl. Slice remaining strawberries, and mix with purée, together with Kirsch or triple sec.

JAMAICAN HOT BUTTERED RUM SAUCE:

**1/2 cup sugar
1/4 cup water
1/4 cup light corn syrup
3 tablespoons Myer's dark rum**

**1/3 cup heavy cream
1/4 teaspoon grated nutmeg
1 tablespoon unsalted butter**

Combine sugar, water, and syrup in a saucepan and bring to boil. Reduce heat and simmer until a caramel forms. Remove pan from heat and slowly add remaining ingredients, being careful not to burn yourself on the steam and liquid boiling up in the pan. Stir well to incorporate, return to heat, and cook until the mixture is completely melted and smooth, about 3 minutes.

**4 bananas, peeled and split in half
lengthwise
12 large scoops vanilla ice cream
1/2–3/4 cup Chocolate Sauce
1/2–3/4 cup Pineapple Sauce**

**1/2–3/4 cup Strawberry Sauce or
Jamaican Hot Buttered Rum Sauce
1/2 cup heavy cream, whipped
4 maraschino cherries**

(continued)

(continued)

Preferably using banana split dishes, lay banana halves lengthwise on dishes. Arrange 3 scoops ice cream over bananas, one on each end, and one in middle. Top each scoop with 2 tablespoons of each of three sauces. Top middle scoop with dollop of whipped cream and maraschino cherry. Serves 4.

Fog City Diner Cookbook

Papaya-Coffee Ice Cream Flambée

For each guest, remove seeds from half a papaya and fill with coffee ice cream. Pour a small amount of Cointreau over the ice cream and put a dollop of whipped cream on top. Soak sugar cubes in lemon extract and place one cube on the top of each mound of whipped cream. Ignite just before serving.

Party Perfect and Pampered

Danish Cherry Wine Sundae

1 part Cointreau liqueur
4 parts Andersen's Danish cherry
   wine

2 parts simple syrup*
8 parts Andersen's cherry
   preserves

Mix all ingredients together and refrigerate overnight. Serve over French vanilla ice cream.

*Simple syrup: Dissolve 1 cup sugar in $1/2$ cup boiling water. Allow to cook 3 minutes.

Pea Soup Andersen's Cookbook

Apricot or Cherry Noodle Pudding

Pareve kugel recipes are hard to find; this one is delicious.

4 ounces unsalted margarine,
  melted
16 ounces wide noodles, cooked
4 eggs, beaten
½ cup sugar

1 teaspoon vanilla extract
1 (20-ounce) can pineapple,
  crushed and drained
10 ounces apricot jam or 1
  (20-ounce) can cherry pie filling

Melt margarine; pour into noodles. Add eggs, sugar, vanilla, and pineapple; mix together. Pour ½ noodle mixture into greased 3-quart pan. Spread with filling, then cover with rest of noodle mixture.

TOPPING:
1 cup cornflakes
1 tablespoon sugar

1 teaspoon cinnamon

Mix together cornflakes, sugar, and cinnamon; sprinkle over top. Dot with margarine. Bake at 350° for 40 minutes. Serves 10–12.

California Kosher

Wine Cranberry Mousse

1 cup red wine
1 (3-ounce) package raspberry
  gelatin (or grape or strawberry)

1 (16-ounce) can whole berry
  cranberry sauce
1 cup nondairy whipped topping

In medium-size saucepan, heat wine to just before boiling point. Dissolve raspberry gelatin in heated wine and pour into low bowl or square Pyrex dish. Add whole berry cranberry sauce to gelatin and stir and blend. Place the combined mixture in the refrigerator to chill for 2 hours. After 2 hours fold in non-dairy whipped topping. Return to refrigerator for at least 2 more hours, chilling mixture to a desired firmness. Serves 4–6.

Cooking with Booze

At 1,645 feet in depth, Lake Tahoe is the deepest and largest alpine lake in North America. Its waters could cover the entire state of California to a depth of about one foot. Shasta Dam is the largest man-made waterfall in the world, three times higher than Niagara Falls.

Fresno Pudding

1 cup flour
⅔ cup sugar
1½ teaspoons baking powder
¼ teaspoon salt
1 cup seedless raisins

½ cup milk
2 cups water
1 cup brown sugar
2 tablespoons butter

Sift dry ingredients together. Mix in raisins and milk. Spread in buttered baking dish. Heat water, brown sugar, and butter until sugar is dissolved. Pour syrup over batter and bake at 350° 30–40 minutes. Serve warm with cream. Serves 6–8.

Puddings from A–Z

Fresh Peach Sauce

Serve warm on pound cake or chill sauce to make up parfaits to place in freezer for future use.

2 cups crushed fresh peaches
  (about 4)
½ cup sugar
½ cup orange juice

2 teaspoons lemon juice
1 teaspoon vanilla (or use half
  almond extract)

In 1½-quart saucepan, mix crushed peaches, sugar, and orange juice. Place over high heat and stir until boiling. Reduce heat to low and let simmer for 15 minutes or until thick, without covering. Remove from heat; stir in lemon juice and extract. Makes 2 cups.

Cherished Recipes from the Valley

Toasted Walnut Tart with Wild Blackberry Sauce and Crème Fraîche

Sour cream makes a ready substitute for Crème Fraîche.

TART SHELL:

1 egg yolk	**⅛ teaspoon salt**
3 tablespoons water	**2 tablespoons sugar**
1¼ cups flour	**¼ cup sweet butter**

Preheat oven to 400°. Mix egg yolk with water. Blend well. Set aside. Place the remaining ingredients into a large bowl and work with hands until you have a lumpy yellow mixture. Add yolk and water mixture and mix rapidly with fingers until all ingredients are well blended and cohere into a ball. Take care not to overmix. Roll dough on lightly floured board to about ¼-inch thickness. Place a 9- or 10-inch flan ring about 1-inch high onto a cookie sheet. Roll pastry dough onto rolling pin and transfer onto flan ring. Ease pastry down inside ring, taking care not to break it. Press along sides and bottom. With a knife, cut off excess dough, following along contour of ring. Line dough with wax paper and fill it up with rice or dried beans to weigh it down. Bake for 20 minutes. Remove wax paper and filler. Place shell back in oven for another 8-10 minutes, until inside is slightly browned. Remove from oven and let cool at room temperature.

FILLING:

4 eggs	**2 tablespoons brown sugar**
1 cup heavy cream	**1½ cups coarsely chopped**
¼ cup clear honey	**toasted walnuts**

Preheat oven to 425°. In a bowl, beat together all ingredients except walnuts. Use a wire whisk, being careful not to overwork. Add walnuts, tossing until nuts are coated. Distribute Filling evenly inside Tart Shell. Bake 15–20 minutes.

WILD BLACKBERRY SAUCE:

2 cups fresh wild blackberries	**Juice of 1 fresh lemon**
¼ cup sugar, or to taste	

Put all sauce ingredients into food processor and purée until smooth. Strain to remove seeds and set aside.

CRÈME FRAÎCHE:

1 cup heavy cream	**2 tablespoons buttermilk**

(continued)

(continued)

Bring cream and buttermilk to room temperature. Combine in a warmed glass jar. Cover the jar securely, and set in a warm place (approximately 75°). Allow mixture to thicken for 8 hours or more. Refrigerate after Crème Fraîche thickens appropriately. Crème Fraîche will keep in the refrigerator for 10 days. Yields 1 cup.

To serve, put Wild Blackberry Sauce on individual serving plate. Position a slice of tart on plate. Sift powdered sugar heavily over tart. Top with Crème Fraîche.

Carter House Cookbook

Rebecca Sauce

1½ cups sour cream
¼ cup firmly packed brown sugar
1 tablespoon white rum

1 tablespoon whiskey
¼ cup raisins

Combine ingredients except raisins in medium bowl and whisk until smooth. Blend in raisins. Cover with plastic wrap and refrigerate at least 2 hours. Serve over fresh fruit. Serves 6–8.

Heavenly Creations

Grand Marnier Sauce

Wonderful with fresh fruit.

4 egg yolks
1 teaspoon cornstarch
½ cup sugar
1 cup warm milk
2 tablespoons Triple Sec liqueur

¼ cup Grand Marnier liqueur
1 teaspoon vanilla
1 teaspoon grated orange rind
1 cup whipping cream, whipped

In top of double boiler, beat egg yolks, cornstarch, and sugar until pale yellow. Add warm milk and blend. Set over simmering water. Stir constantly with the wire whisk until mixture thickens and coats a spoon heavily. Remove from heat.

Stir in liqueurs, vanilla and orange rind. Let cool, then refrigerate for 2–3 hours. Just before serving, fold whipped cream into sauce. Another tablespoon of Triple Sec may be added, if desired. Sprinkle more Triple Sec over fresh fruits, if desired. Makes about 3 cups.

Sausalito: Cooking with a View

Sautéed Bananas

Sautéed fruit makes a quick and easy dessert. I've used bananas here, but peaches, nectarines, pears, or thinly sliced apples also work well.

1 tablespoon butter	Zest and juice of 1 orange
2–3 tablespoons sugar, or to taste	4 bananas, peeled and sliced
¼ cup rum, Cointreau or fruit juice	lengthwise

In an nonstick pan, heat butter, sugar, and liquids until sugar dissolves. Add bananas and cook on low to medium heat until barely soft. Serve warm, garnished with zest, alone or with whipped cream or ice cream. Serves 4.

The $5 Chef: How to Save Cash & Cook Fast

Avocado Sorbet

1 cup sugar	2 tablespoons lemon juice
1 cup light corn syrup	1 tablespoon lime juice
2 cups water	Fresh raspberries
1 teaspoon grated lime peel	Crisp cookies
3 avocados, seeded, peeled and mashed	

Bring sugar, corn syrup, and water to boil in large saucepan. Remove from heat and stir in grated lime peel. Cool 1 hour. Blend avocados and lemon and lime juices in blender or food processor until smooth. Add cooked sugar mixture and blend until thoroughly combined. Pour into 9x13x2-inch pan. Freeze 1 hour. Remove sorbet from freezer and beat 2–3 minutes until light and creamy. Pour back into pan, cover with plastic wrap, and freeze until firm, about 4 hours. Makes 1 quart. Serve with fresh raspberries and crisp cookies. Serves 6.

Food Festivals of Southern California

Contributing Cookbooks

One of many coastal California beaches, Stinson Beach is located on historic Highway One. Three and one-half miles of sand allow plenty of access to swimmers, surfers, and sunbathers.

Catalog of Contributing Cookbooks

All recipes in this book have been selected from the cookbooks shown on the following pages. Individuals who wish to obtain a copy of any particular book may do so by sending a check or money order to the address listed by each cookbook. Please note the postage and handling charges that are required. State residents add tax only when requested. Prices and addresses are subject to change, and the books may sell out and become unavailable. Retailers are invited to call or write to same address for discount information.

AN APPLE A DAY

by Rea Douglas   Fax 619-281-8325
6402 Seaman Street   619-583-9410
San Diego, CA 92120   rearelief@aol.com

This cookbook is made up entirely of recipes using apples in one form or another. The collection was gathered over the years from friends and family and includes some very old recipes from the 1800s along with a very funny sampling of Victorian personal grooming hints. The book contains 92 pages and has about 120 recipes.

   $9.75 Retail price
    $.75 Tax for California residents
   $2.00 Postage and handling

Make check payable to Rea Douglas

APPLES ETC. COOKBOOK

Santa Cruz, CA Chapter of Hadassah
213 Wixon Avenue
Aptos, CA 95003   831-688-8085

The many good cooks and bakers of Santa Cruz Hadassah are pleased to present *Apples Etc.*, an attractive, spiral-bound 124-page cookbook containing 265 great recipes. A new section about Traditional Jewish Sabbath and Holiday Recipes will teach you how to make delicious kugel, latkes, matzo balls and more. Enjoy!

   $10.00 Retail price
    $2.50 Postage and handling

Make check payable to Santa Cruz Hadassah

THE ART LOVER'S COOKBOOK: A FEAST FOR THE EYE

Fine Arts Museums of San Francisco   Fax 415-750-7692
De Young Museum, Golden Gate Park   415-750-3606
San Francisco, CA 94118   publications@famsf.org

Varied recipes from the many nationalities and traditions represented on the West Coast of this country. Images from the museums' collections (still lifes, genre scenes, cartoons, photos, and decorative arts) illustrate the amusing and complicated relationships we have with food, our sustenance and our delight.

   $24.95 Retail price   Visa/MC accepted
    $2.12 Tax for California residents
    $5.00 Postage and handling

Make check payable to COFAM   ISBN 0-88401-096-1

THE ARTICHOKE COOKBOOK

by Patricia Rain
Celestial Arts
P. O. Box 7126
Berkeley, CA 94707

A celebration of the artichoke from the central California coast. Anthropologist Patricia Rain has provided a colorful history of the artichoke's illustrious story, along with know-how on preparing and dining on this elegant, edible thistle. Over 150 recipes using this succulent—and nutritious—California classic.

$11.95 Retail price

Make check payable to Patricia Rain   ISBN 0-89087-415-8

BOUTIQUE BEAN POT

by Kathleen Mayes and Sandra Gottfried
Woodbridge Press   Fax 805-963-0540
P. O. Box 209   800-237-6053
Santa Barbara, CA 93102   woodpress@aol.com

More than 70 bean varieties, exotic and familiar, with color illustrations. Where to buy interesting beans, how to cook and use them in a wide variety of flavorful dishes that will satisfy the family and intrigue the epicure. Useful tables and figures. New, scrumptious recipes for a 'beyond the bean' taste.

$12.95 Retail price   Visa/MC accepted
  $1.03 Tax for California residents
  $2.00 Postage and handling
Make check payable to Woodbridge Press   ISBN 0-88007-196-6

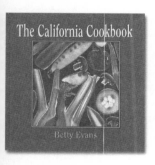

THE CALIFORNIA COOKBOOK

by Betty Evans
Gulf Publishing Company   Fax 713-520-4438
P. O. Box 2608   800-231-6275 ext. 300
Houston, TX 77252-2608   ezorder@gpcbooks.com

Renowned California cook and author Betty Evans has gathered more than 250 recipes adapted from Alice Waters, M.F.K. Fisher, Julia Child, Luther Burbank and Robert Louis Stevenson. Bursting with California's fresh flavors, these recipes reflect the people, history, and natural resources of the Golden State.

$21.95 Retail price
  $3.95 Postage and handling ($1.00 each additional)
Make check payable to Gulf Publishing Co.   ISBN 088415-197-2

CALIFORNIA COUNTRY COOK BOOK

Golden West Publishers   Fax 602-279-6901
4113 N. Longview Avenue   800-658-5330
Phoenix, AZ 85014-4949   goldwest@goodnet.com

Bring the farm fresh goodness of California home to your family! Enjoy delectable delights made with mouth-watering fruits, wholesome vegetables, savory meats, tasty nuts and golden citrus. Experience the harvest of California's bounty at your table.

  $5.95 Retail price   Visa/MC accepted
  $3.00 Postage and handling
Make check payable to Golden West Publishers
ISBN 1-885590-17-2

CONTRIBUTING COOKBOOKS

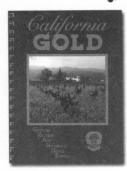

CALIFORNIA GOLD
California State Grange
2101 Stockton Boulevard   Fax 916-739-8189
Sacramento, CA 95817   916-454-5805

California Gold is a compilation of 400 favorite recipes of Grange members, covering 200 pages. Many of these dishes are thoroughly enjoyed at potlucks around the state (and nation) and the cookbooks are popular items for gifts and especially for collectors.

$12.00 Retail price
Make check payable to California State Grange
ISBN 0-87197-355-3

CALIFORNIA HOME COOKING
by Michele Anna Jordan
The Harvard Common Press   Fax 617-695-9794
535 Albany Street   888-657-3755
Boston, MA 02118   adwinell@harvardcommonpress.com

Now everyone can enjoy the warmth and vibrancy of California in their kitchen, with these 400 recipes! California cooking has defined the way Americans eat today, with a focus on fresh, flavorful, healthy, and easy-to-prepare meals. The award-winning author's acclaimed masterpiece!

$16.95 Retail price (paperback) $29.95 (hardcover)
  $3.00 Postage and handling
Make check payable to The Harvard Common Press
ISBN 1-55832-119-5

CALIFORNIA KOSHER
Women's League of Adat Ari El
12020 Burbank Boulevard   Fax 818-505-9223
North Hollywood, CA 91607   800-786-9426

You don't have to be Jewish to enjoy this collection of contemporary and traditional recipes which combine fresh foods available year round in California with observation of traditional Jewish dietary laws. Includes menu suggestions for American and Jewish holidays. A contemporary classic in its sixth printing.

$19.95 Retail price   Visa/MC accepted
  $1.65 Tax for California residents
  $4.00 Postage and handling
Make check payable to *California Kosher*   ISBN 0-9630953-0-7

CALIFORNIA SIZZLES
The Junior League of Pasadena, Inc.
149 South Madison Avenue   Fax 626-796-5764
Pasadena, CA 91101   626-796-0162

Whether for a picnic basket or an elegant dinner party, these recipes are as fresh as the region they represent, reflecting the distinctive flavors of trend-setting Southern California. The ease of preparation and simple, yet imaginative dishes enhance an active healthy lifestyle.

$21.95 Retail price   Visa/MC accepted
  $1.81 Tax for California residents
  $5.00 Postage and handling
Make check payable to Junior League of Pasadena, Inc.
ISBN 0-9632089-1-8

CONTRIBUTING COOKBOOKS

CALIFORNIA WINE COUNTRY COOKING SECRETS
by Kathleen DeVanna Fish
Bon Vivant Press   Fax 831-373-3567
P. O. Box 1994   800-524-6826
Monterey, CA 93940   contact@millpub.com

Napa and Sonoma are the very heart of the American wine industry. Come with us—savor the bounty, sample the secret recipes of notable chefs, and learn the secret hideaways, romantic and adventurous inns and wonders decidedly off the beaten track.

$14.95 Retail price   Visa/MC accepted
$1.08 Tax for California residents
$4.50 Postage and handling

Make check payable to Millennium Publishing Grp.
ISBN 1-883214-08-4

CALIFORNIA WINE COUNTRY HERBS AND SPICES
by Virginia and Robert Hoffman
The Hoffman Press   Fax 707-538-7371
P. O. Box 2996   800-852-4890
Santa Rosa, CA 95405   hoffpress@worldnet.att.net

This collection of 212 recipes by the best chefs of the California Wine Country features herbs and spices. Some have made this region world renowned. Includes a glossary of herbs and spices, recipes for spice mixes, and how to make herbed and spiced oils and vinegars.

$14.95 Retail price   Visa/MC/AmEx accepted
$1.12 Tax for California residents
$3.00 Postage and handling

Make check payable to The Hoffman Press   ISBN 0-9629927-5-5

CALVARY'S CUISINE
Calvary Lutheran Church
10 Concordia Lane   Fax 530-533-5203
Oroville, CA 95966   530-533-5017

This book was compiled by members of our church representing the best of their tried-and-tested recipes. All recipes are easy to understand and easy to make. 249 pages. 600 recipes.

$5.00 Retail price
$.36 Tax for California residents
$3.39 Postage and handling

Make check payable to Calvary Lutheran Church

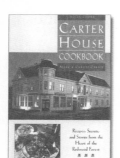

CARTER HOUSE COOKBOOK
by Mark and Christi Carter
Ten Speed Press   Fax 707-444-8067
301 L. Street   707-444-8062
Eureka, CA 95501   carter52@carterhouse.com

Enjoy the incredible garden-to-table cuisine of the Carter House Victorians and Restaurant without ever leaving home. This collection of over 75 recipes ranges from the simple elegance of Zinfandel Poached Pears to such classic favorites as Filet Mignon with Cognac Cream.

$8.95 Retail price   Visa/MC/AmEx
$.65 Tax for California residents
$3.00 Postage and handling

Make check payable to The Carter House Victorians
ISBN 0-89815-773-0

CELEBRATING CALIFORNIA

Children's Home Society of California
3200 Telegraph Avenue   Fax 510-655-9139
Oakland, CA 94609   510-655-7406

Brie and Mango Quesadillas, Fettuccine with Walnuts and Avocado, Crab Pizza...capture the spirit and lifestyle that make California unique. Prize-winning recipes from 17 California food festivals. Easily prepared kitchen-tested recipes. Full-color, 6x9, laminated hardcover. Opens flat for convenience.

$17.95   Retail price   Visa/MC accepted
  $1.48   Tax for California residents
  $3.00   Postage and handling

Make check payable to Children's Home Society of California
ISBN 0-9622898-1-7

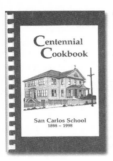

CENTENNIAL COOKBOOK

San Carlos School
450 Church Street   Fax 831-375-9736
Monterey, CA 93940   831-375-1324

San Carlos School Centennial Cookbook was put together by alumni and current student families. Recipes reflect our varied ethnic student body. The book includes many tasty recipes for everyday cooking. 164 pages of 385 family favorites plus an interesting section of this and that. Spiral bound.

$10.00   Retail price
  $3.00   Postage and handling

Make check payable to San Carlos School

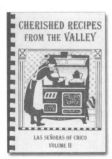

CHERISHED RECIPES FROM THE VALLEY

Las Senoras of Chico
c/o Lorraine Seale-Hibdon
701 E. Lassen Avenue #248
Chico, CA 95973   530-343-9222

Most of the recipes contain products grown in Northern California. Funds are used to perpetuate Bidwell Mansion upkeep and docent-training. We are currently restoring the kitchen to 1908, which was the original, planned by Annie Bidwell. 104 pages and over 200 recipes.

  $7.50   Retail price
   $.54   Tax for California residents
  $1.50   Postage and handling

Make check payable to Las Senoras of Chico

CHILDREN'S HOSPITAL OAKLAND COOKBOOK

Chestnut Branch
c/o Marge Trindell   Fax 510-886-9552
5370 Camino Alta Mira   510-581-8296
Castro Valley, CA 94546   mctrindell@aol.com

Children's Hospital Oakland has joined forces with the cookbook industry by collecting family favorite recipes that have been handed down over the years, and eliminating countless hours spent in the kitchen. The cookbook, as a fundraiser, is just one product that helps provide our kids with a happier and healthier future.

$15.00   Retail price
  $1.50   Postage and handling

Make check payable to Children's Hospital Oakland

THE COASTAL COOK OF WEST MARIN

by Laura Riley
Riley and Company   Fax 415-868-1337
P. O. Box 925   415-868-9526
Bolinas, CA 94924   mowry@earthlink.net

Over 100 original recipes accompanied by profiles of their extraordinary contributors from a dozen small towns along the rural coast of western Marin County. Author Laura Riley's column, "The Coastal Cook," which appears in the Pulitzer Prize-winning newspaper *The Point Reyes Light*, supplies her with stories and recipes. 230 pages.

$12.95 Retail price

Make check payable to Riley and Company   ISBN 0-9628426-0-5

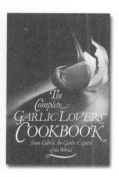

THE COMPLETE GARLIC LOVERS' COOKBOOK

Gilroy Garlic Festival Association, Inc.
P. O. Box 2311   408-842-1625
Gilroy, CA 95021-2311   clove@gilroygarlicfestival.com

This hardcover book combines recipes from *The Garlic Lovers' Volumes I & II*. Many come from long-time Gilroyans and are accompanied by recipes from the festival's own 'gourmet alley' and from around the world. Also includes a garlic glossary, and tips on selection and storage. 349 pages; 400+ recipes.

$24.95 Retail price   Visa/MC accepted
 $2.06 Tax for California residents
 $3.50 Postage and handling

Make check payable to Gilroy Garlic Festival   ISBN 089087-503-0

COOK BOOK

Mary Martha Society of Redeemer Lutheran Church
1355 Hawthorne Avenue
Chico, CA 95926   530-342-6007

Our recipes were gathered from congregation members to compile this cookbook. We believe we are blessed with great cooks. The recipes submitted tend to reflect the agriculture of our area. Many varieties of fruits and nuts are grown locally. Rice is also a major crop. 166 pages; spiral bound; 500 recipes.

$10.00 Retail price

Make check payable to Mary Martha Society

COOKIN' WITH CASA

CASA Choices for Children
P. O. Box 206   Fax 530-842-1409
Yreka, CA 96097   530-842-7091

Recipes submitted by volunteers who support CASA, Court Appointed Special Advocate Program, in Yreka. There are favorites that will delight children as well as adults.

$6.00 Retail price
 $1.25 Postage and handling

Make check payable to CASA

COOKING ON THE FAULT LINE—CORRALITOS STYLE

Corralitos Valley Research and Educational Association
378 Corralitos Road
Corralitos, CA 95076   831-722-3913

A 352-page collection of recipes from a diverse ethnic group within the Corralitos Valley. Recipes feature many of the fruits and vegetables grown in the Monterey Bay area.

$15.50   Retail price
 $2.50   Postage and handling
Make check payable to C.V.R.E.A.

COOKING PURE & SIMPLE

by June K. Hunter
Kincaid House Publishing   Fax 714-751-8140
3905 Marcus Avenue   949-646-6306
Newport Beach, CA 92663-3237   hunterpj@pacbell.net

A natural starting place for eating more nutritiously—good basic cooking with emphasis on low sugar, fresh produce, whole grains and high fiber. Breakfast and brunch, appetizers to desserts! 194 recipes with hints, equivalents and conversions, and glossary. 216 pages, indexed.

$13.95   Retail price
 $1.08   Tax for California residents
 $2.50   Postage and handling
Make check payable to Kincaid House Publishing
ISBN 0-9443793-53-X

COOKING TREASURES OF THE CENTRAL COAST

International Quota Club of Morro Bay
2550 Rodman Drive   805-528-3628
Los Osos, CA 93402   Lildean98@aol.com

This artist-illustrated, 450-recipe cookbook, offers a collection of easy, tested recipes from California's central coast. Designed as a fund raiser for the International Quota Club of Morro Bay who aid the hearing impaired as well as disadvantaged women and children.

$10.75   Retail price
 $.75   Tax for California residents
 $2.00   Postage and handling
Make check payable to International Quota Club of Morro Bay

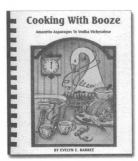

COOKING WITH BOOZE

by Evelyn Barbee
5440 E. Swift Avenue   559-292-2639
Fresno, CA 93727   eebarbee@aol.com

Alcoholic beverages used in cooking vegetables, fish, meat or desserts enhance flavors to delight the palate. Be an adventurous host and substitute with the beverages you have on hand as you try the 200 recipes within 100 pages. Your guests always go home sober because the alcohol cooks out while retaining the delicious flavors. *Cooking with Booze* is user friendly.

$14.95   Retail price
Make check payable to Pleasure Foods   ISBN 0-9647146-0-4

CONTRIBUTING COOKBOOKS

COOKING WITH HERBS

Quail Botanical Gardens Docent Society
P. O. Box 230005   Fax 760-436-0917
Encinitas, CA 92023-0005   760-436-9236

Cooking with Herbs salutes herbs grown in Quail Botanical Gardens
with over 100 recipes. Our Docent Society shared favorite recipes,
some simple, others more inventive; some adapted, others treasured
family originals. We tested and evaluated every recipe, then selected
this collection. Total price benefits Quail Botanical Gardens.

$12.00 Retail price   Visa/MC accepted

Make check payable to Quail Botanical Gardens Cookbook
ISBN 0-9656332-2-5

COOKING WITH MUSHROOMS

by John Pisto
Pisto's Kitchen   Fax 831-373-4227
786 Wave Street   800-45 PISTO
Monterey, CA 93940   Jpisto@redshift.com

International television chef John Pisto has produced this cookbook as
an introduction to the West Coast's most abundant and flavorful mushrooms, showcasing over 75 mushroom recipes. Many are from his
successful television show, *Monterey's Cookin' Pisto Style*. Chef Pisto
shares mushroom-hunting experiences, as well as important information about wild mushrooms.

$12.95 Retail price

Make check payable to Pisto's Kitchen   ISBN 0-9640828-0-2

COOKING WITH WINE

by Virginia and Robert Hoffman
The Hoffman Press   Fax 707-538-7371
P. O. Box 2996   800-852-4890
Santa Rosa, CA 95405   hoffpress@worldnet.att.net

The largest collection of cooking with wine recipes ever published,
with the most complete index of wine with food pairing ever assem-
bled. Three years of research and testing went into the production of
this book. Eighty-six chefs share 172 of their favorite recipes for cooking with wine and pairing wine with food.

$14.95 Retail price   Visa/MC/AmEx accepted
  $1.12 Tax for California residents
  $3.00 Postage and handling

Make check payable to Hoffman Press   ISBN 0-9629927-3-9

THE CUISINE OF CALIFORNIA

by Diane Rossen Worthington
Chronicle Books
85 Second Street   Fax 800-858-7787
San Francisco, CA 94105   800-722-6657

Widely acknowledged as the bible of a culinary phenomenon, this is
the book savvy cooks across the country turn to again and again.
Now in a new edition, this cookbook lets you prepare incredible meals
in the style made famous by Alice Waters, Wolfgang Puck, and other
world-class California chefs.

$14.95 Retail price
  $1.27 Tax for California residents
  $3.50 Postage and handling

Make check payable to Chronicle Books   ISBN 0-8118-1651-6

THE CUISINE OF HUBERT KELLER

by Hubert Keller with John Harrisson
Ten Speed Press   Fax 510-559-1629
P. O. Box 7123   800-841-2665
Berkeley, CA 94707   order@tenspeed.com

A truly original cuisine has emerged from Hubert Keller's varied career: he observes classic French principles and maintains a California-style commitment to healthfulness.

$35.00 Retail price   Visa/MC/AmEx accepted
  $4.50 Postage and handling ($1.00 each additional)
Make check payable to Ten Speed Press   ISBN 0-89815-807-9

DELICIOUS RECIPES FROM THE NIMITZ COMMUNITY

Nimitz PTA
545 Cheyenne Drive   408-245-6413
Sunnyvale, CA 94087   joemonica@worldnet.att.net

Wonderful recipes from around the world are scattered throughout this 172-page cookbook. A special feature is the Kid's Favorites; you're sure to enjoy these selections.

$10.00 Retail price
  $.82 Tax for California residents
  $4.18 Postage and handling
Make check payable to Nimitz PTA

DIDYAEVERHAVADAY?

by Pamela Weis
Raspberry Patch Press
P. O. Box 36   530-283-1086
Quincy, CA 95971   noelr@jps.net

This cookbook has 483 pages and includes more than 1200 recipes along with stories that take a comical look at rural living. The recipes were collected from the author, her mother, grandmother, and mother-in-law. Also included are recipes that date back before 1900 found in an old ranch house.

$18.88 Retail price
  $1.36 Tax for California residents
  $2.50 Postage and handling
Make check payable to Pamela Weis   ISBN 0-9621841-0-1

DINING BY DESIGN

The Junior League of Pasadena, Inc.
149 South Madison Avenue   Fax 626-796-5764
Pasadena, CA 91101   626-796-0162

Dining by Design features recipes that are easy to prepare and gourmet in taste, perfect for mid-week family meals or weekend get-togethers with friends. Also look for helpful hints and tips, a special section for families so everyone can join in the kitchen, menu ideas for special occasions and more.

$24.95 Retail price   Visa/MC accepted
  $2.06 Tax for California residents
  $5.00 Postage and handling
Make check payable to Junior League of Pasadena, Inc.
ISBN 9-780963-208934

DINING DOOR TO DOOR IN NAGLEE PARK

The Campus Community Association Fax 408-297-2995
305 South 11th Street 408-282-1500
San Jose, CA 95112 marianne@salasobrien.com

A collection of favorite recipes from Downtown San Jose's Historic Campus Community neighborhood. Exquisitely illustrated with Victorian and Craftsmen homes in renowned Naglee Park. Contains heart-warming personal anecdotes. Some well-known public figures contributed. 262 recipes, 244 pages.

$20.00 includes postage and handling

Make check payable to CCA Cookbooks

DIVERSITY IS DELTA'S MAIN DISH

Delta Sigma Theta Sorority, Inc.
P. O. Box 91623
Long Beach, CA 90806

This cookbook was compiled by the members of Delta Sigma Theta Sorority, Inc., Long Beach Alumnae Chapter. It is 96 pages of 249 recipes highlighting the cultural diversity of our community. Proceeds to support our community service projects.

$10.00 Retail price

Make check payable to Delta Sigma Theta Sorority, Inc.

DURHAM'S FAVORITE RECIPES

Durham Woman's Club
P. O. Box 283
Durham, CA 95938

Durham's Favorite Recipes includes 743 recipes, many using locally grown products from our farming community. All are treasured recipes from local residents both past and present. We hope you enjoy these favorites within the 221 pages.

$10.00 Retail price
 $3.00 Postage and handling

Make check payable to Durham Woman's Club

EVERYBODY'S SAN FRANCISCO COOKBOOK

by Charles Lemos
Good Life Publications/Great West Books
P. O. Box 1028
Lafayette, CA 94549 925-283-3184

An exciting celebration of San Francisco's vibrant ethnic cuisine, revealing the secrets of cooking the city's global dishes—Italy, India, China, Southeast Asia, Latin America, and much more. De-mystifies ethnic cooking, featuring recipes, menus, and a glossary of ingredients making it easy to get started.

$16.95 Retail price
 $1.40 Tax for California residents
 $2.50 Postage and handling

Make check payable to Great West Books ISBN 1-886776-01-6

THE EXPANDING LIGHT COOKBOOK
by Blanche Agassy McCord
Crystal Clarity Publishers   Fax 530-478-7610
14618 Tyler Foote Road   800-424-1055
Nevada City, CA 95959   clarity@crystalclarity.com

Softcover, 199 pages, 140 recipes. Tasty, low-fat vegetarian recipes
that are the tried-and-true "guests favorites" from a large yoga retreat.
Easy to prepare, easy to find ingredients, easy to digest and applaud-
ed by both lifelong vegetarians and non-vegetarians.

$12.95 Retail price   Visa/MC accepted
  $.95 Tax for California residents
 $4.00 Postage and handling

Make check payable to Crystal Clarity Publishers
ISBN 156589-128-7

FABULOUS FAVORITES
Los Altos United Methodist Women
655 Magdalena
Los Altos, CA 94024

Over 400 of the favorite recipes of the women of Los Altos United
Methodist Church contained in 170+ pages. Also included are a number of kitchen charts including metric conversions, substitutions, meat
cuts, can sizes, etc., as well as a section containing over 400 very
handy household hints.

$4.00 Retail price
 $.32 Tax for California residents
$3.50 Postage and handling

Make check payable to United Methodist Women

FAIR'S FARE
Del Mar Fair
2260 Jimmy Durante Boulevard
Del Mar, CA 92014

Fair's Fare is a collection of prize-winning recipes from the Del Mar
Fair. Included are first place winners from pre-fair competition (items
entered and judged before the fair opens) and first through fifth place
winners of contests held during the fair. We publish a new edition each
year.

$10.00 Retail price
  $2.00 Postage and handling

Make check payable to Del Mar Fair

FEEDING THE FLOCK
Church of the Nazarene   Fax 707-994-4042
P. O. Box 1085   707-994-4008
Clearlake, CA 95422   rebean@jps.net

This book is put together by all the ladies of the church. This fund-rais-
ing project raised enough money for equipment needed in our church.
Recipes old and new submitted by the good cooks of the Church of the
Nazarene.

$10.00 Retail price

Make check payable to Church of the Nazarene

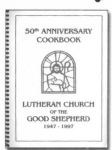

50TH ANNIVERSARY COOKBOOK

Lutheran Church of the Good Shepherd
50th Anniversary Cookbook Committee
12854 Jade Drive
Salinas, CA 93906   831-449-8283

Lutherans have always shown our caring and sharing through food. You are always invited. There will always be enough. These recipes are the dishes we share most often. Our cookbook has 170 pages with 345 recipes. One section includes recipes from around the world.

$8.00 Retail price
  $.57 Tax for California residents
$2.50 Postage and handling

Make check payable to *50th Anniversary Cookbook*

"...FIRE BURN & CAULDRON BUBBLE"

by Julie Lugo Cerra
Cerra Enterprises   Fax 310-559-7310
4022 Lincoln Avenue   310-558-3818
Culver City, CA 90232   jlugocerra@aol.com

A 224-page melting pot of well-used recipes, family traditions, photos, and local history. Specially designed format yields cooking ease for every day or entertaining, and time for the chef to socialize. True California, from Albondigas Soup to Pasta to Zucchini Bread.

$16.00 Retail price
  $1.32 Tax for California residents
  $1.50 Postage and handling

Make check payable to Cerra Enterprises   ISBN 1-879415-27-5

THE $5 CHEF FAMILY COOKBOOK

by Marcie Rothman
Five-Spot Press   Fax 619-226-1966
P. O. Box 6789   888-243-3535
San Diego, CA 92166-0789   marcier@home.com

With more than 200 recipes, this book shows you how to shop for great-tasting, inexpensive, wholesome food to prepare quickly at home. Shopping tips feature fresh seasonal ingredients and cooking tips to make fast and easy meals that taste great.

$12.00 Retail price
  $.93 Tax for California residents
$3.50 Postage and handling

Make check payable to Five-Spot Press   ISBN 0-7615-0653-5

THE $5 CHEF: HOW TO SAVE CASH & COOK FAST

by Marcie Rothman
Five-Spot Press   Fax 619-226-1966
P. O. Box 6789   888-243-3535
San Diego, CA 92166-0789   marcier@home.com

This 130-page book is packed with money-saving shopping tips and delicious fast recipes. Learn to add dash to foods with herbs and spices, and cook more than 100 fast and tasty dishes organized alphabetically by main ingredients. It's a companion to the new "No-Brainers or Quick & Easy Cooking" video.

$5.00 Retail price
  $.38 Tax for California residents
$3.50 Postage and handling

Make check payable to Five-Spot Press   ISBN 09630542-0-1

CONTRIBUTING COOKBOOKS

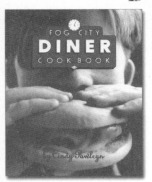

FOG CITY DINER COOKBOOK

by Cindy Pawlcyn
Ten Speed Press
P. O. Box 7123
Berkeley, CA 94707

Fax 510-559-1629
800-841-2665
order@tenspeed.com

This wonderful cookbook from the world-famous Fog City Diner has been a home-cooking favorite for years, with modern comfort food that evokes the diner's contemporary take on good food and good times. Paperback.

$21.95 Retail price   Visa/MC/AmEx accepted
  $4.50 Postage and handling ($1.00 each additional)

Make check payable to Ten Speed Press   ISBN 0-89815-999-7

FOOD FESTIVALS OF NORTHERN CALIFORNIA
FOOD FESTIVALS OF SOUTHERN CALIFORNIA

by Bob Carter
Falcon Publishing, Inc.
P. O. Box 1718
Helena, MT 59624

800-582-2665

Award-winning travel writer Bob Carter presents the best annual food festivals of Southern and Northern California. He guides you through festival events and offers festival recipes that help recreate the experience at home. Feastings from small-town finger foods to metropolitan restaurant entrées.

$14.95 Retail price each   Visa/MC/AmEx Accepted
  $4.00 Postage and handling

Make check payable to Falcon Publishing, Inc
ISBN 1-56044-527-0 (Northern) 1-56044-528-9 (Southern)

THE FORK RAN AWAY WITH THE SPOON

by Laura Riley
Riley and Company
P. O. Box 925
Bolinas, CA 94924

Fax 415-868-1337
415-868-9526
mowry@earthlink.net

This collection of kitchen conversations and recipes is the sequel to *The Coastal Cook of West Marin* with 320 pages of prized recipes from each family or individual who appeared in author Laura Riley's weekly column. Gleaned from folks with fascinating tales to tell.

$16.95 Retail price

Make check payable to Riley and Company   ISBN 0-9628426-1-3

FRIENDS OF CAMERON AIRPORT FAVORITE RECIPES

Friends of Cameron Airport
c/o Ethel Manthey
3115 Boeing Road
Cameron Park, CA 95682

530-677-8157
jereth@directcon.net

Our cookbook provides 114 pages of wonderful tried-and-true recipes, favorites of our small airpark community. Many of the recipes were used in dishes for our potluck functions held about four times a year. The cookbook has been a "bestseller" in our community!

$7.50 Retail price
 $.54 Tax for California residents
$1.00 Postage and handling

Make check payable to Friends of Cameron Airport

CONTRIBUTING COOKBOOKS

FROM A SOURDOUGH'S POT
by Tom Visel
P. O. Box 1186   Fax 909-659-2826
Idyllwild, CA 92549   909-659-5625

Collected and developed by a "Sunset Chef of the West," *From a Sourdough's Pot* includes a mind-boggling collection of readable and easy-to-follow recipes based on cuisine found in Southern California. Information included is not limited to how, but also why, and bits of history.

$8.00 Retail price
$.72 Tax for California residents
$1.28 Postage and handling
Make check payable to Tom Visel

GARLIC LOVERS' GREATEST HITS
Gilroy Garlic Festival Association, Inc.
P. O. Box 2311   408-842-1625
Gilroy, CA 95021-2311   clove@gilroygarlicfestival.com

This book, all original recipes, is a special reflection of the success of the Gilroy Garlic Festival and the widespread devotion of hundreds of thousands of people to the bountiful bulb of garlic. 162 pages; 196 recipes.

$16.95 Retail price   Visa/MC accepted
$1.40 Tax for California residents
$3.50 Postage and handling
Make check payable to Gilroy Garlic Festival
ISBN 0-89087-877-3

THE GOLF COOKBOOK
by Sharon Gerardi and Nadine Nemechek
Redbank Ranch
10683 E. Bullard Avenue
Clovis, CA 93611

Spend less time at the kitchen range, more time on the driving range, and still put a delicious dinner on the table. Each of the 128 recipes has golf tips, trivia, quotes, etc. to help you talk a good game while impressing your partners and family with tasty delights.

$10.95 Retail price
$.86 Tax for California residents
$2.00 Postage and handling
Make check payable to Redbank Ranch   ISBN 0-9657500-1-9

GRANDMA'S HOUSE RESTAURANT & FAMILY RECIPES
by Flo Barnes
Grandma's House Restaurant   Fax 530-842-2060
123 Center Street   530-842-5300
Yreka, CA 96097   tomnflo@inreach.com

This collection of recipes from Grandma's House Restaurant in Yreka was published in honor of Grandma Doyne's 85th birthday. It includes favorites from the restaurant, as well as family and friends. Humor and food-for-thought are sprinkled throughout.

$11.95 Retail price   Visa/MC/AmEx/Disc accepted
$.87 Tax for California residents
$3.00 Postage and handling (3 or more no shipping charge)
Make check payable to Grandma's House

THE GREAT CALIFORNIA COOKBOOK
by Kathleen DeVanna Fish
Bon Vivant Press   Fax 831-373-3567
P. O. Box 1944   800-524-6826
Monterey, CA 93940   contact@millpub.com

A Publishers Marketing Association Ben Franklin Award-winning book, this is the company's all-time bestseller! It's filled with diverse and healthy cuisines. Includes a culinary tour through origins of California cuisine and includes sights and attractions of favorite cities in the state.

$15.95 Retail price
  $1.16 Tax for California residents
  $4.50 Postage and handling

Make check payable to Millennium Publishing Grp.
ISBN 1-883214-22-X

GREAT CHEFS OF BUTTE VALLEY
Butte Valley Chamber of Commerce
P. O. Box 541
Dorris, CA 96023   530-397-2601

Our cookbook, *Great Chefs of Butte Valley,* contains recipes from the diverse residents of this unique high plateau valley of Northern California. A number of the recipes have roots tied to the first settlers in the 1860s, along with more recent entries in the more than 80 pages.

$8.50 Retail price
  $2.50 Postage and handling

Make check payable to Butte Valley Chamber of Commerce

THE GREAT VEGETARIAN COOKBOOK
by Kathleen DeVanna Fish
Bon Vivant Press   Fax 831-373-3567
P. O. Box 1994   800-524-6826
Monterey, CA 93940   contact@millpub.com

This gold medal award-winning book offers an unbeatable combination: four-star chefs and food that's healthful and delicious. Forty-three of America's finest chefs contributed 180 kitchen-tested, simplified recipes. Prepare a meal from this book for those who scoff at vegetarian dishes—they'll change their tune!

$15.95 Retail price   Visa/MC accepted
  $1.16 Tax for California residents
  $4.50 Postage and handling

Make check payable to Millennium Publishing Grp.
ISBN 1-883214-24-6

THE HEALTH PROMOTING COOKBOOK
by Dr. Alan Goldhamer
Book Publishing Company
HPC 6010 Commerce Boulevard #152   707-586-5555
Rohnert Park, CA 94928   dracg@worldnet.att.net

Recipes in *The Health Promoting Cookbook* have been used successfully by over 4,000 residential health care patients who have learned to eat and live healthfully. By following the easy-to-prepare recipes, anyone (including those on restrictive diets) can create tasty, satisfying, uncomplicated meals. 192 pages, 7x8, paper, lay-flat binding.

$15.00 includes tax and shipping

Make check payable to The Health Promoting Clinic
ISBN 1-57067-024-2

CONTRIBUTING COOKBOOKS

HEAVENLY CREATIONS
Community Church of the Monterey Peninsula Fellowship Committee
3850 Rio Road #76
Carmel, CA 93923-8622 831-626-8861

This cookbook answers the questions of many of our church members—"Can you give me the recipe for that tasty dish you brought to the luncheon?" As a result, 70 pages ranging from appetizers to desserts and even this-and-that are included in *Heavenly Creations*.

$6.95 Retail price
$3.00 Postage and handling

Make check payable to Margaret Lenck

HOT WOK
by Hugh Carpenter and Teri Sandison
Ten Speed Press Fax 510-559-1629
P. O. Box 7123 800-841-2665
Berkeley, CA 94707 order@tenspeed.com

With 50 tempting recipes and more than 50 gorgeous photographs, *Hot Wok* shows you how to make gastronomic triumphs. *Hot Wok* meets our fast-paced, health-oriented society's need for quick-to-prepare, highly flavorful food.

$17.95 Retail price Visa/MC/AmEx accepted
$4.50 Postage and handling ($1.00 each additional)

Make check payable to Ten Speed Press ISBN 0-89815-678-5

INCREDIBLE EDIBLES
by Jai Baker Fax 530-268-1172
160 Sacramento Street 530-888-9857
Auburn, CA 95603 bakerlop@aol

Incredible Edibles provides 148 recipes of the culinary magic that has made Awful Annie's Restaurant a favorite in Northern California for over 20 years. From the gourmet breakfast and lunch specialties to the awfully good desserts, these delicious delights will tantalize your taste buds and are a welcomed addition to any kitchen.

$21.95 Retail price Visa/MC/AmEx accepted
$1.59 Tax for California residents
$3.00 Postage and handling

Make check payable to Awful Annie's Restaurant

INTERNATIONAL GARLIC FESTIVAL® COOKBOOK
by Caryl Simpson
Gourmet Gold Press Fax 408-842-7087
P. O. Box 1145 888-GARLICFEST
Gilroy, CA 95021-1145 www.garlicfestival.com

THE book for lovers of "the stinking rose." A collection of 148 pages of garlicky fare from Gilroy, the "Garlic Captial of the World." Garlicky recipes from festivals, restaurants, chefs, and fellow garlic lovers all over the world. You can create a garlic extravaganza to rival even the famous Gilroy Garlic Festival.

$9.95 Retail price
$.83 Tax for California residents
$3.00 Postage and handling

Make check payable to Garlic Festival

CONTRIBUTING COOKBOOKS

JAN TOWNSEND GOING HOME

by Jan Townsend
11637 Lakeshore South
Auburn, CA 95602-8241

530-268-2709
townsend@foothill.net

A 196-page treasury of 286 real recipes for real cooks with no fancy ingredients or complicated techniques. From an award-winning food writer, the book also offers tales of a close-knit family and humorous anecdotes about the newspaper and food industries.

$22.00 Retail price
  $1.60 Tax for California residents
  $3.00 Postage and handling

Make check payable to Jan Townsend   ISBN 0-9654919-0-0

JEWISH COOKING FROM HERE & FAR

Congregation Beth Israel
5716 Carmel Valley Road
Carmel, CA 93923

Fax 831-624-4786
831-624-8272

This book reflects traditions and memories from our mothers' kitchens with 250 easy-to-follow recipes include family favorites, healthy updated recipes and a special holiday section, all enhanced with photos and family stories. Winner of the 1995 regional McIlhenny Community Cookbook Award. 180 pages.

$13.95 Retail price   Visa/MC accepted
  $1.01 Tax for California residents
  $3.00 Postage and handling

Make check payable to Congregation Beth Israel   ISBN 0-9642644-0-4

THE LAFAYETTE COLLECTION

Lafayette Arts and Science Foundation
P. O. Box 923
Lafayette, CA 94549

925-943-6559
lasfhq@aol.com

Conceived as a fund raiser benefitting the public schools of Lafayette, the second printing of The Lafayette Collection was built from over 1500 recipes tested by 177 families. The final result is a 198-page collection of 154 eclectic recipes.

$15.00 Retail price   Visa/MC accepted
  $2.00 Postage and handling

Make check payable to Lafayette Arts and Science Foundation

LA JOLLA COOKS AGAIN

La Jolla Country Day School
9490 Genesee Avenue
La Jolla, CA 92037

Fax 858-792-6030
858-453-3440
sap@sd.znet.com

A collection of 350 favorite recipes from The La Jolla Country Day School Community. The high-quality dishes, handed down from generation to generation, transcend trendy food fashion. Includes celebrity endorsement from acclaimed cookbook author Jeanne Jones. Nutritional profile for every recipe.

$19.95 Retail price
  $1.45 Tax for California residents
  $5.00 Postage and handling

Make check payable to LJCDS–Parents Association
ISBN 0-9614176-1-7

THE LAZY GOURMET

by Valerie Bates
14023 Sunset Drive   Fax 562-693-0460
Whittier, CA 90602   562-698-5585

For the person who doesn't have hours to spend in the kitchen; this book is for you! The 212-page collection of delicious, quick, and easy recipes have a gourmet touch that makes them special. *The Lazy Gourmet* is a must for today's busy cook!

$9.95 Retail price
 $.82 Tax for California residents
$2.00 Postage and handling

Make check payable to Valerie Bates

A LITTLE CALIFORNIA COOKBOOK

by John P. Carroll
Chronicle Books   Fax 800-858-7787
85 Second Street, Sixth Floor   800-722-6657
San Francisco, CA 94105   www.chronbooks.com

California cooking is a style steeped in ethnic diversity, modern innovations, and one that taps the region's impressive bounty. John P. Carroll compiled thirty, simple quintessentially California recipes for home cooking. Hardbound, 4x5¾ inches, full color, 60 pages.

$6.95 Retail price
 $.59 Tax for California residents
$3.50 Postage and handling

Make check payable to Chronicle Books   ISBN 0-8118-0097-0

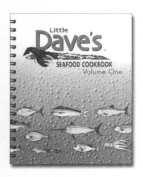

LITTLE DAVE'S SEAFOOD COOKBOOK, VOLUME ONE

by David J. Harvey
Playa Vista Publishing
7741 Airport Boulevard   310-216-7197
Los Angeles, CA 90045   djharvey2002@hotmail.com

Despite the country's love for seafood, fish is fraught with anxiety. Serving seafood for dinner or for entertaining guests can be intimidating. This book contains 63 recipes from raw to baked that will show you how easy it can be to clean, prepare and serve seafood.

$13.95 Retail price
 $1.14 Tax for California residents
 $2.90 Postage and handling

Make check payable to David J. Harvey

A LITTLE SAN FRANCISCO COOKBOOK

by Charlotte Walker
Chronicle Books   Fax 800-858-7787
85 Second Street, Sixth Floor   800-722-6657
San Francisco, CA 94105   www.chronbooks.com

A Little San Francisco Cookbook lets both residents and visitors take a bit of the city's splendid cuisine home with them. Like its colorful history, the richness of San Francisco's cultural diversity has contributed to the variety of foods associated with the city. Hardbound, 4x5, full color, 60 pages.

$5.95 Retail price
 $.51 Tax for California residents
$3.50 Postage and handling

Make check payable to Chronicle Books   ISBN 0-87701-619-4

CONTRIBUTING COOKBOOKS

MAMMOTH REALLY COOKS BOOK II

Mammoth Hospital Auxiliary
P. O. Box 1399
Mammoth Lakes, CA 93546

The excellent cooks of Mammoth Lakes put together 400 newly tried recipes for Book II after Book I sold out. Being a small community nestled in the High Sierras at 8500 feet, recipes were adjusted where needed. Many wonderful "outdoorsman" recipes included. Proceeds go towards equipment for our 15 bed hospital.

$8.41   Retail price
 $.59   Tax for California residents
$2.00   Postage and handling

Make check payable to Mammoth Hospital Auxiliary

MARILYN THOMAS: THE HOMEMAKER BAKER'S FAVORITE RECIPES

by Marilyn Thomas
P. O. Box 892
Camino, CA 95709   530-644-1119

Most of these 130 recipes have been demonstrated on the NBC affiliate station in Sacramento (KCRA-TV, Channel 3). Marilyn spent 25 years baking in her unique bake shop in Apple Hill. The book contains specialties of fresh fruit pies and desserts, all easy but from scratch.

$7.95   Retail price
 $.55   Tax for California residents
$2.00   Postage and handling

Make check payable to Marilyn Thomas

MENDOCINO MORNINGS

by Jim and Arlene Moorehead
Joshua Grindle Inn
P. O. Box 647   800-GRINDLE / 707-937-4143
Mendocino, CA 95460   stay@joshgrin.com

Our book came to be by the constant urging from our guests so that they could enjoy our breakfasts at home. With their help and our great staff we were able to put together this 143-page cookbook, also filled with interesting stories and events in our area. We hope you enjoy it.

$16.95 Retail price   Visa/MC accepted
 $1.25 Tax for California residents
 $3.00 Postage and handling

Make check payable to Joshua Grindle Inn   ISBN 0-9655474-0-X

MONTEREY'S COOKIN' PISTO STYLE

by John Pisto
Pisto's Kitchen   Fax 831-373-4227
786 Wave Street   800-45 PISTO
Monterey, CA 93940   Jpisto@redshift.com

Chef John Pisto is the owner of four award-winning restaurants and hosts his own television cooking show. Within the pages of this cookbook he will introduce you to his unique California/Italian cooking techniques and philosophy by sharing his personal experiences along with historical photographs of Monterey's Italian heritage.

$12.95 Retail price

Make check payable to Pisto's Kitchen   ISBN 0-9640828-0-2

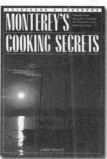

MONTEREY'S COOKING SECRETS

by Kathleen DeVanna Fish
Bon Vivant Press   Fax 831-373-3567
P. O. Box 1994   800-524-6826
Monterey, CA 93940   contact@millpub.com

Falling in love with the Monterey Peninsula is easy to do, especially if you know its secret hideaways. We include recommendations for unforgettable places to stay. The bulk of this book is about exquisite food—kitchen-tested, simplified recipes from the most noteworthy chefs who ply their profession in paradise.

$13.95 Retail price   Visa/MC accepted
  $1.01 Tax for California residents
  $4.50 Postage and handling

Make check payable to Millennium Publishing Grp.   ISBN 0-962047-26-0

MORE FIREHOUSE FAVORITES

San Diego Fireman's Relief Association   Fax 619-281-8325
10509 San Diego Mission Road, Ste. F   619-281-0354
San Diego, CA 92108   rearelief@aol.com

To celebrate our 90th anniversary, we received over 230 recipes from firefighters who have a reputation for their great cooking ability. Included are their favorite breads, soups, salads, main dishes, desserts and miscellaneous marinades, dips and appetizers. Proceeds from the book benefit our widows, orphans and distressed firefighters fund.

$8.00 Retail price
$2.00 Postage and handling

Make check payable to San Diego Fireman's Relief Assn.

MUFFIN MAGIC . . . AND MORE

by Kathleen Mayes
Woodbridge Press   Fax 805-963-0540
P. O. Box 209   800-237-6053
Santa Barbara, CA 93102   woodpress@aol.com

Contemporary, elegant styling in wholesome muffins and quick breads—real down home comfort foods with flair! A special section on "Ultralite Muffins,"a new baking concept—low-fat, low cholesterol, high-quality baking. A wealth of how-to pointers for baking success.

$12.95 Retail price   Visa/MC accepted
  $1.03 Tax for California residents
  $2.00 Postage and handling

Make check payable to Woodbridge Press   ISBN 0-88007-201-6

NEPTUNE'S TABLE: COOKING THE SEAFOOD EXOTICS

by Don Hubbard
Sea Eagle Publications
P. O. Box 180550   800-804-0438
Coronado, CA 92178   eaglepubs@aol.com

Neptune's Table, the supreme shellfish cookbook, includes 200+ mouth-watering recipes in 177 pages. Chapters on clams, crab, lobster, mussels, oysters, and shrimp, as well as recipes dealing with calamari, octopus, abalone, sea snails, limpets and sea urchin.

$17.95 Retail price
  $1.39 Tax for California residents
  $3.75 Postage and handling

Make check payable to Sea Eagle Publications ISBN 0943665-06-X

NEW COVENANT KITCHENS
by Jill Neff
11135 Cooper Drive
Grass Valley, CA 95945   530-273-5218

New Covenant Kitchens fulfills a life-long dream—to produce a cookbook with great tried-and-true recipes. Some have been handed down through several generations, others are newly-found favorites. Enjoy.

   $7.25   Retail price
   $2.00   Postage and handling
Make check payable to Jill Neff

NUGGETS, NIBBLES AND NOSTALGIA
Kern County Museum Foundation   Fax 661-322-6415
3801 Chester Avenue   661-852-5000
Bakersfield, CA 93301   shmartindale@kern.org

Many of the recipes included in this cookbook are from the archives of the Kern County Museum or have been passed from generation to generation. Interspersed throughout the 180 pages are photographs and advertisements from the past. We believe this cookbook demonstrates the importance and fun of preserving our past.

 $10.00   Retail price   Visa/MC accepted
    $.73   Tax for California residents
  $3.00   Postage and handling
Make check payable to Kern County Museum Foundation

THE OATS, PEAS, BEANS & BARLEY COOKBOOK
by Edyth Young Cottrell
Woodbridge Press   Fax 805-963-0540
P. O. Box 209   800-237-6053
Santa Barbara, CA 93102   woodpress@aol.com

Balanced nutrients from simple, inexpensive food sources. Over 450 recipes, 100 main dishes, breads as a protein food—high-protein waffles with as much protein as an 8-ounce steak. "Meat-and-dairy-like" products from soybeans. Desserts without sugar, vegetables, food preservation, nutritional guidance.

 $12.95   Retail price   Visa/MC accepted
   $1.03   Tax for California residents
  $2.00   Postage and handling
Make check payable to Woodbridge Press   ISBN 0-912800-85-2

THE OLD YACHT CLUB INN COOKBOOK
by Nancy Donaldson   Fax 805-745-1805
431 Corona Del Mar Drive   805-684-2805
Santa Barbara, CA 93103   ndoyci1@aol.com

Almost four years in the making, this 120-page cookbook started from requests for dishes served at the Inn. Includes simple recipes as well as more exotic recipes and sample menus.

  $8.00   Retail price
    $.62   Tax for California residents
  $1.00   Postage and handling
Make check payable to Nancy Donaldson

ONLY IN CALIFORNIA

Children's Home Society of California
3200 Telegraph Avenue   Fax 510-655-9239
Oakland, CA 94609   510-655-7406

Savory Picante Chili, refreshing Strawberry Spinach Salad, decadent Raspberry Fudge Brownies...a mix of traditional, ethnic and nouvelle cuisine. Elegant dishes. Easily prepared, home kitchen-tested recipes. Full color, 6x9 laminated hardcover. Opens flat for convenience.

$17.95 Retail price   Visa/MC accepted
 $1.48 Tax for California residents
 $3.00 Postage and handling

Make check payable to Children's Home Society of California
ISBN 0-9622898-0-9

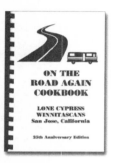

ON THE ROAD AGAIN COOKBOOK

Lone Cypress Winnitascans   Fax 408-270-0584
3420 Lake Lesina Drive   408-270-6031
San Jose, CA 95135   hopesy1@aol.com

Almost 200 pages, over 400 recipes, easy-to-make dishes perfect for campers, RVers, students and any others who don't want to spend a lot of time in the kitchen. Some are treasured family keepsakes, and some are new. All are delicious.

$8.00 Retail price
$3.00 Postage and handling

Make check payable to LCW

THE ORGANIC GOURMET

by Barbara Kahn
Frog, Ltd.   Fax 510-547-3948
P. O. Box 12327   800-337-2665
Berkeley, CA 94712   orders@northatlanticbooks.com

A healthy and delicious alternative to today's increasingly toxic corporate food machine. This informative yet fun book contains resources on organic certification organizations and organic food suppliers. Meat-eaters and vegetarians alike will delight in these delicious recipes.

$16.95 Retail price   Visa/MC accepted
 $1.40 Tax for California residents
 $5.00 Postage and handling

Make check payable to North Atlantic Books
ISBN 1-883317-32-3

OUR FAVORITE RECIPES

Placer Nevada Cattlewomen
c/o Maxine Turner
2452 Coefield Road
Auburn, CA 95603   530-885-6361

A cookbook composed of tried recipes from members of Placer Nevada Cattlewomen. All are good cooks, having cooked for trail rides and cattle drives. Recipes are simple and tasty for small groups as well as large.

$7.50 Retail price
$1.50 Postage and handling

Make check payable to Placer Nevada Cattlewomen

CONTRIBUTING COOKBOOKS

PARTY PERFECT AND PAMPERED

by Sally Holbrook
Sabill Press   Fax 626-792-7110
1440 Vista Lane   626-792-4497
Pasadena, CA 91103   wsholbrook@msn.com

Includes all of the many facets of successful parties presented in detail
with examples, suggestions, sources. With proven, creative concepts
for themes, decorations, invitations and favors. Food presentations
and 67 recipes for the novice and experienced. 215 pages.

$24.95 Retail price
  $2.06 Tax for California residents
  $1.58 Postage and handling
Make check payable to Sabill Press   ISBN 0-9631225-1-7

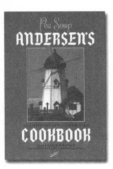

PEA SOUP ANDERSEN'S SCANDINAVIAN–AMERICAN COOKBOOK

by Chef Ulrich Riedner
c/o Patricia Rain
P. O. Box 3206
Santa Cruz, CA 95063

A delightful journey down memory lane, Pea Soup Andersen's remains
a California icon from the days when Hearst Castle was a destination
point for the rich and famous. A true California landmark, readers will
enjoy the story of its humble beginning and the recipes that made it
famous. Currently out of print.

THE POTLUCK COOKBOOK

Bodega Land Trust
P. O. Box 254   707-876-3422
Bodega, CA 94922   marysand@sonic.net

Bodega is famed for its food and its potlucks. Fishing, dairying, sheep
and cattle ranching characterize this area, with potatoes a traditional
crop and apples nearby. Ninety local cooks share their best potluck
recipes. A beautifully designed book about real food.

$13.50 Retail price
  $1.01 Tax for California residents
  $2.50 Postage and handling
Make check payable to Bodega Land Trust   ISBN 1-889451-02-9

PUDDINGS FROM A–Z

by Fred Brengelman and Russ Levenworth
Poppy Lane Publishing Company
P. O. Box 5163   559-299-4639
Fresno, CA 93755   bette1234@aol.com

Puddings from A–Z is designed to stand up for ease in following the
recipes. There are wonderful bread pudding recipes and Chocolate
Bread Pudding is a must. Also included are main course puddings.
One of a trilogy: *Salads from A–Z* and *Soups from A–Z.*

$14.95 Retail price
  $1.20 Tax for California residents
  $3.20 Postage and handling
Make check payable to Poppy Lane Publishing Company
ISBN 0-938911-09-0

RÖCKENWAGNER

by Hans Röckenwagner with Brigit Binns
Ten Speed Press   Fax 510-559-1629
P. O. Box 7123   800-841-2665
Berkley, CA 94707   order@tenspeed.com

One of the country's most talented new chefs combines his old-world training and L.A. style to create 150 exciting, accessible recipes for decadent brunches, delightful lunches and exceptional dinners. (hardcover)

$29.95 Retail price   Visa/MC/AmEx accepted
 $4.50 Postage and handling ($1.00 each additional)
Make check payable to Ten Speed Press   ISBN 0-89815-875-3

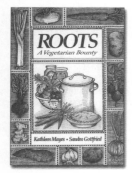

ROOTS: A VEGETARIAN BOUNTY

by Kathleen Mayes and Sandra Gottfried
Woodbridge Press   Fax 805-963-0540
P. O. Box 209   800-237-6053
Santa Barbara, CA 93102   woodpress@aol.com

Root vegetables are fresh, crisp and juicy when raw; succulent and tender when cooked, and they are very healthful—high in fiber, beta carotene, vitamins and minerals, yet low in fat, calories and cholesterol. Here are 120 vegetarian recipes for the full menu, using 31 different root vegetables.

$14.95 Retail price   Visa/MC accepted
 $1.16 Tax for California residents
 $2.00 Postage and handling
Make check payable to Woodbridge Press   ISBN 0-88007-206-7

SALADS FROM A–Z

by Frances Levine
Poppy Lane Publishing Company
P. O. Box 5136   559-299-4639
Fresno, CA 93755   bette1234@aol.com

Salads from A–Z is the second of the trilogy and is a stand-up cookbook designed for ease and convenience. There are old favorites, variations—some main courses, some follow a course and some for picnic or barbecue. One of a trilogy: *Puddings from A–Z* and *Soups from A–Z.*

$14.95 Retail price
 $1.20 Tax for California residents
 $3.20 Postage and handling
Make check payable to Poppy Lane Publishing Company
ISBN 0-938911-20-4

SAN FRANCISCO À LA CARTE

The Junior League of San Francisco   Fax 415-775-4599
2226A Filmore Street   415-775-4100
San Francisco, CA 94115   hq@jlsf.org

A collection of recipes from The Junior League of San Francisco that reflects the culinary bounty of the Bay Area. From soups to desserts, something for everyone.

$10.00 Retail price   Visa/MC/AmEx accepted
 $3.50 Postage and handling
Make check payable to The Junior League of San Francisco

THE SAN FRANCISCO CHRONICLE COOKBOOK

Edited by Michael Bauer and Fran Irwin
Chronicle Books   Fax 800-858-7787
85 Second Street, Sixth Floor   800-722-6657
San Francisco, CA 94105   www.chronbooks.com

This definitive collection truly represents the best of California cuisine—simple and stylish, with an appreciation for ethnic flavors and a commitment to fresh ingredients. Echoing the melting-pot nature of San Francisco, *The San Francisco Chronicle Cookbook* features many ethnic dishes. Paperback, 424 pages.

$18.95 Retail price
  $1.61 Tax for California residents
  $3.50 Postage and handling
Make check payable to Chronicle Books   ISBN 0-8118-1445-9

SAN FRANCISCO FLAVORS

The Junior League of San Francisco   Fax 415-775-4599
2226A Filmore Street   415-775-4100
San Francisco, CA 94115   hq@jlsf.org

The Junior League of San Francisco brings you an all new collection of sophisticated, contemporary recipes inspired by the cultures and cuisines of the city by the bay. Whether you're planning an intimate dinner for two or a festive brunch buffet, these recipes will delight family and friends.

$27.50 Retail price   Visa/MC/AmEx accepted
  $2.34 Tax for California residents
  $4.50 Postage and handling
Make check payable to The Junior League of San Francisco
ISBN 0-8118-2342-3

SAN FRANCISCO'S COOKING SECRETS

by Kathleen DeVanna Fish
Bon Vivant Press   Fax 831-373-3567
P. O. Box 1994   800-524-6826
Monterey, CA 93940   contact@millpub.com

San Francisco is rich in scenery, history, amusements, world-renowned food and accommodations, so it's easy to overlook secret hideaways that make you fall in love with America's favorite city. Includes 15 unforgettable places to stay, and incomparable San Francisco food.

$13.95 Retail price   Visa/MC accepted
  $1.01 Tax for California residents
  $4.50 Postage and handling
Make check payable to Millennium Publishing Grp.   ISBN 1-883214-00-9

SAN RAMON'S SECRET RECIPES

San Ramon Library Foundation
100 Montgomery
San Ramon, CA 94583   usaaddict@aol.com

The over 300 recipes in our cookbook are as diverse as our community. You may find that lost favorite, as many of our "secret" recipes come from various parts of the country and the world. Collected to benefit the San Ramon Library, you're sure to find a favorite new one.

$10.00 Retail price
  $3.00 Postage and handling
Make check payable to San Ramon Library Foundation

CONTRIBUTING COOKBOOKS

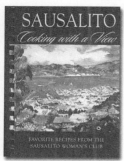

SAUSALITO: COOKING WITH A VIEW

Sausalito Woman's Club
P. O. Box 733   Fax 415-332-3724
Sausalito, CA 94966

A charming and eclectic collection of favorite recipes from one of America's most sophisticated yet funky home towns. Featuring a range of practical to panacheful dishes chosen for their ease in preparation and freshness, well flavored with anecdotes of local color reflection of historical schmoozing sure to ease a smile and please the palate.

$20.00 Retail price
  $1.50 Tax for California residents
  $3.00 Postage and handling
Make check payable to SWC Cookbook Fund

SEASONS: FOOD FOR THOUGHT AND CELEBRATION

Christ Episcopal Church
1040 Border Road   Fax 650-948-1193
Los Altos, CA 94022   650-948-6032

Seasons was created by the members of Christ Church. The theme was established around our glorious windows which tell the story of the seasons of life, the seasons of the liturgy and the biblical references. The recipes are good, standard American fare developed by families through tradition and affection. 192 pages, over 300 recipes.

$15.00 Retail price
  $1.25 Postage and handling
Make check payable to Christ Church cookbook

THE 7 DAY COOKBOOK

by Nadine Nemechek and Sharon Nemechek Gerardi, D.O.
Redbank Ranch
10683 E. Bullard Avenue
Clovis, CA 93611

The dreaded question: "What's for dinner?" With the help of over 200 easy low-fat recipes, menu planner, and shopping lists you will know what's for dinner and have all the ingredients on hand to create delicious, nutritious meals for the most important event of the day—the family dinner.

$13.95 Retail price
  $1.10 Tax for California residents
  $3.00 Postage and handling
Make check payable to Redbank Ranch   ISBN 0-9657500-0-0

SHARING OUR BEST

Sycamore Glen Retirement Community
1199 Diablo Avenue   Fax 530-894-0386
Chico, CA 95973   530-894-0384

This cookbook is a combination of recipes from the residents who live at Sycamore Glen Active Retirement Community. The residents range in age from 65 to 100 years old and many of the recipes are from their families. 98 pages, 204 recipes.

  $7.00 Retail price
  $3.00 Postage and handling
Make check payable to Sycamore Glen Retirement Community

SIMPLY VEGETARIAN!

Dawn Publications   Fax 530-478-0112
P. O. Box 2010   800-545-7475
Nevada City, CA 95959   nature@dawnpub.com

For this age of greater awareness about the need for more balance in our diet, *Simply Vegetarian!* offers a complete variety in all categories. Easy-to-find ingredients and reasonable preparation times accommodate the schedules of the busiest cooks.

$11.95 Retail price   Visa/MC accepted
  $.88 Tax for California residents
$4.50 Postage and handling
Make check payable to Dawn Publications   ISBN 0-916124-53-3

A SLICE OF SANTA BARBARA

Santa Barbara Junior League
229 East Victoria Street   Fax 805-568-0901
Santa Barbara, CA 93101   805-963-2704

A Slice of Santa Barbara—California Riviera Cuisine, is a unique collection of recipes that reflect the richly diverse culture of California and Santa Barbara. Recipes were triple-tested and are presented in a simple easy-to-read format.

$15.95 Retail price
 $1.75 Tax for California residents
 $2.00 Postage and handling
Make check payable to Junior League of Santa Barbara
ISBN 0-89951-084-1

SONOMA COUNTY . . . ITS BOUNTY

Editor Ellen Moorehead
64 Jessie Lane
Petaluma, CA 94952   707-778-8852

A special cookbook from a Northern California county famous for its food production, wineries, and chefs/restaurants—all chosen by a culinary committee of highly reputed chefs, critics, etc. The book has 244 pages, over 200 recipes, and sketches by a well-known artist. Excellent reviews and quite popular.

$19.95 Retail price
 $1.50 Tax for California residents
 $3.00 Postage and handling
Make check payable to Clover Stornetta Farm   ISBN 0-9658701-0-3

SOUNDS TASTY!

KAZU-FM
P. O. Box KAZU
Pacific Grove, CA 93950   831-375-7275

KAZU-FM serves the Monterey Bay region with diverse, non-commercial radio programming. *Sounds Tasty!* celebrates diversity with a tempting collection of over 500 recipes, all contributed by supporters of KAZU-FM. This collection not only includes recipes from world-famous chefs who live and work in our area, but also includes family secrets which have finally been shared.

$15.00 Retail price   Visa/MC accepted
 $1.08 Tax for California residents
Make check payable to KAZU-FM

SOUPS FROM A–Z

by Frances Levine
Poppy Lane Publishing Company
P. O. Box 5136   559-299-4639
Fresno, CA 93755   bette1234@aol.com

A unique cookbook designed to stand up for ease in viewing. Each page serves as a recipe card for convenience in preparing your favorite soup. The favorites are Hangover Soup and U.S. Senate Soup. One of a trilogy: *Salads from A–Z* and *Puddings from A–Z*.

$14.95 Retail price
  $1.20 Tax for California residents
  $3.20 Postage and handling

Make check payable to Poppy Lane Publishing   ISBN 0-938911-08-2

THE STEINBECK HOUSE COOKBOOK

The Valley Guild
The Best Cellar
132 Central Ave.
Salinas, CA 93901   831-757-5806

One hundred pages of tried-and-true recipes currently being served to guests at the Steinbeck House, a popular restaurant for 25 years in the birth home of John Steinbeck.

$12.00 Retail price   Visa/MC accepted
  $.87 Tax for California residents
  $2.50 Postage and handling ($4.00 postage for 3 books)

Make check payable to The Best Cellar

STERLING PERFORMANCES

The Guilds of the Orange County Performing Arts Center
c/o Brenda Arthur
22802 Via Orvieto   949-499-0963
Monarch Beach, CA 92629   BAJA714@aol.com

Sterling Performances is a gourmet cookbook with easy-to-follow recipes which promises a "sterling performance" for your dining pleasure. The perfect cookbook for the hostess who wants elegant, yet easy entertaining.

$19.95 Retail price
  $3.00 Postage and handling

Make check payable to *Sterling Performances*
ISBN 0-9638430-0-1

STIRLING CITY HOTEL AFTERNOON TEA

by Charlotte Ann Hilgeman/Illustrated by Linda Hilgeman
C/L Productions
P. O. Box 130
Stirling City, CA 95978-0130   530-873-0858

Afternoon Tea should be a colorful experience, so each book contains your own box of crayons. Color each teapot as you choose. With twenty perfect recipes, savor delights as enjoyed in the refinement of olden times. Return to the elegance and romance of yesteryear.

$8.95 Retail price
  $.65 Tax for California residents
  $2.50 Postage and handling

Make check payable to Stirling City Hotel

CONTRIBUTING COOKBOOKS

THE STIRLING CITY HOTEL FAVORITE RECIPES

by Charlotte Ann Hilgeman/Illustrated by Linda Hilgeman
C/L Productions
P. O. Box 130
Stirling City, CA 95978-0130   530-873-0858

More than a cookbook, each of the twenty recipes has a full-color design suitable for framing. Truly a beautiful book that will pleasure all the senses. Comes with its own protective envelope and bookmark. These are recipes that will become your own favorites.

$16.95 Retail price
  $1.23 Tax for California residents
  $2.50 Postage and handling

Make check payable to Stirling City Hotel

SUN, SAND AND SAUSAGE PIE . . .

by Sally Holbrook
Sabill Press   Fax 626-792-7110
1440 Vista Lane   626-792-4497
Pasadena, CA 91103   wsholbrook@msn.com

A charming, fun-to-read cookbook. Childhood memories of weekends/vacations at the family beach house are blended with 100 easy-to-follow, proven recipes and culinary tips from three generations of experienced cooks. Old fashioned, family ambience. 112 pages.

$19.95 Retail price
  $1.65 Tax for California residents
  $1.58 Postage and handling

Make check payable to Sabill Press   ISBN 0-9631225-0-9

SYMPHONY OF FLAVORS

Associates of the Redlands Bowl
P. O. Box 492
Redlands, CA 92373   909-794-4058

The Associates of the Redlands Bowl proudly present *Symphony of Flavors*, a cookbook created to honor the Redlands Bowl's Diamond Jubilee. Easy-to-read format features a collection of over 250 treasured recipes for the beginner to the gourmet cook and includes complete menus for every occasion.

$16.70 Retail price
  $1.29 Tax for California residents
  $4.00 Postage and handling

Make check payable to Associates of the Redlands Bowl

TAHOE PARENTS NURSERY SCHOOL
40TH ANNIVERSARY ALUMNI COOKBOOK

Tahoe Parents Nursery School
2339 Wasabe Drive
Tahoe Paradise, CA 96150   530-577-5339

A collection of 264 recipes compiled by the alumni and current membership to commemorate the 40th anniversary of the co-op nursery school. There are 102 pages of easy and delicious family favorites.

  $8.00 Retail price
  $3.00 Postage and handling

Make check payable to Tahoe Parents Nursery School (TPNS)

TASTE CALIFORNIA

California Dietetic Association
7740 Manchester Avenue #102
Playa del Rey, CA 90293-8499

Fax 310-823-0264
310-822-0177
cdaep@aol.com

One hundred and seventy recipes that incorporate California's cornucopia of fresh and delicious foods. These easy-to-prepare recipes were
created, contributed, tested and edited by California dietitians with
backgrounds as diverse as the state where they reside.

$11.95 Retail price   Visa/MC accepted
  $.99 Tax for California residents
 $3.00 Postage and handling

Make check payable to California Dietetic Association
ISBN 0-9638619-0-5

TASTE OF FILLMORE

Fillmore Christian Academy
461 Central Avenue
Fillmore, CA 93015

Fax 805-524-1139
805-524-1572

Enjoy tasty recipes from Fillmore, a beautiful town nestled in the orange
and avocado groves of Santa Clara Valley. Favorite recipes from
Fillmore's historic dinner train, to original Mexican dishes like Papas
con Chorizo and Tinga, to scrumptuous Orange Cake; this cookbook
receives rave reviews.

$10.00 Retail price
 $2.50 Postage and handling

Make check payable to FCA or Fillmore Christian Academy

TASTY TEMPTATIONS

The Ladies of the Knights of Columbus
5202 Curtis Street
Fremont, CA 94538   510-656-0730

Tasty Temptations has over 200 wonderful recipes that have been well
received at many "pot luck" dinners. Ease of preparation with basic
ingredients you usually have in your pantry makes this cookbook very
tempting. Full-color divider pages and cover.

$10.00 Retail price
  $.83 Tax for California residents
 $2.00 Postage and handling

Make check payable to Ladies of the Knights of Columbus

TREASURED RECIPES

St. Joseph of Cupertino Parish and School
10120 N. De Anza Boulevard
Cupertino, CA 95014

Fax 408-252-9771
408-252-6441

More than 200 pages of favorite family recipes, gathered from several generations of school families. Contains more than 700 recipes,
many reflecting light, healthful dishes. A diverse collection of easily
prepared recipes—representing the broad diversity of California.

$10.00 Retail price
  $.83 Tax for California residents
 $1.75 Postage and handling

Make check payable to St. Joseph of Cupertino School

TRIED AND TRUE RECIPES
by Dixie Rien
Walter's Publishing   Fax 707-445-9455
925 Dowler Drive   707-443-7954
Eureka, C 95501   howdix@earthlink.net

This 110-page book, containing 170 recipes, was originally compiled at the request of my son. After being encouraged by many people, I decided to have it published with all profits going to our local Hospice and Sr. Citizen Foundation. I am a senior and a Hospice survivor.

$10.00 Retail price
  $2.00 Postage and handling
Make check payable to Dixie Rien

WATSONVILLE COMMUNITY HOSPITAL SERVICE LEAGUE FAVORITE RECIPES 40TH ANNIVERSARY EDITION

Watsonville Community Hospital Service League
75 Nielson Street
Watsonville, CA 95076   billsbetty@aol.com

This is an easy-to-use book of simple recipes from the kitchens of home-town wives and moms. Lots of family favorites and over 300 time-tested recipes. Spiral binding and plastic cover let pages lie flat for convenient viewing.

$10.00 Retail price
  $3.00 Postage and handling
Make check payable to WCH Service League

WE'RE COOKIN' IN CUCAMONGA
by Betsy Neil
9857 Candlewood
Rancho Cucamonga, CA 91730   909-987-5710

A collection of tasty recipes of family and friends, easy-to-make recipes, easy-to- find ingredients, and lots of helpful hints for the beginner. 241 pages.

$12.00 Retail price
  $.95 Tax for California residents
  $2.05 Postage and handling
Make check payable to Betsy Neil

Index

The average yearly rainfall in Death Valley is less than 2 inches. The lowest point in the Western Hemisphere, it is one of the hottest places on earth—134 degrees was recorded in 1913, second only to 136 degrees in Libya in 1936.

INDEX

INDEX

INDEX

INDEX

INDEX

INDEX

INDEX

INDEX

INDEX

INDEX

Special Discount Offers!

The Best of the Month Club

Experience the taste of our nation, one state at a time!

Individuals may purchase BEST OF THE BEST STATE COOKBOOKS on a monthly (or bi-monthly) basis by joining the **Best of the Month Club**. Best of the Month Club members enjoy a 20% discount off the list price of each book. Individuals who already own certain state cookbooks may specify which new states they wish to receive. No minimum purchase is required; individuals may cancel at any time. For more information on this purchasing option, call 1-800-343-1583.

Special Discount

The entire 41-volume BEST OF THE BEST STATE COOKBOOK SERIES can be purchased for $521.21, a 25% discount off the total individual price of $694.95.

Individual BEST cookbooks can be purchased for $16.95 per copy plus $4.00 shipping for any number of cookbooks ordered. See order form on next page.

Join today! 1-800-343-1583

Speak directly to one of our friendly customer service representatives, or visit our website at **www.quailridge.com** to order online.

Recipe Hall of Fame Collection

The extensive recipe database of Quail Ridge Press' acclaimed BEST OF THE BEST STATE COOKBOOK SERIES is the inspiration behind the RECIPE HALL OF FAME COLLECTION. These HALL OF FAME recipes have achieved extra distinction for consistently producing superb dishes. *The Recipe Hall of Fame Cookbook* features over 400 choice dishes for a variety of meals. The *Recipe Hall of Fame Dessert Cookbook* consists entirely of extraordinary desserts. The *Recipe Hall of Fame Quick & Easy Cookbook* contains over 500 recipes that require minimum effort but produce maximum enjoyment. *The Recipe Hall of Fame Cookbook II* brings you more of the family favorites you've come to expect with over 400 all-new, easy-to-follow recipes. Appetizers to desserts, quick dishes to masterpiece presentations, the RECIPE HALL OF FAME COLLECTION has it all.

All books: Paperbound • 7x10 • Illustrations • Index
The Recipe Hall of Fame Cookbook • 304 pages • $19.95
Recipe Hall of Fame Dessert Cookbook • 240 pages • $16.95
Recipe Hall of Fame Quick & Easy Cookbook • 304 pages • $19.95
The Recipe Hall of Fame Cookbook II • 304 pages • $19.95

NOTE: The four HALL OF FAME cookbooks can be ordered individually at the price noted above or can be purchased as a four-cookbook set for **$40.00**, almost a 50% discount off the total list price of $76.80. Over 1,600 incredible HALL OF FAME recipes for about three cents each—an amazing value!

Best of the Best State Cookbook Series

Best of the Best from
ALABAMA
288 pages, $16.95

Best of the Best from
HAWAI'I
288 pages, $16.95

Best of the Best from
MINNESOTA
288 pages, $16.95

Best of the Best from
OREGON
288 pages, $16.95

Best of the Best from
ALASKA
288 pages, $16.95

Best of the Best from
IDAHO
288 pages, $16.95

Best of the Best from
MISSISSIPPI
288 pages, $16.95

Best of the Best from
PENNSYLVANIA
320 pages, $16.95

Best of the Best from
ARIZONA
288 pages, $16.95

Best of the Best from
ILLINOIS
288 pages, $16.95

Best of the Best from
MISSOURI
304 pages, $16.95

Best of the Best from
SO. CAROLINA
288 pages, $16.95

Best of the Best from
ARKANSAS
288 pages, $16.95

Best of the Best from
INDIANA
288 pages, $16.95

Best of the Best from
NEVADA
288 pages, $16.95

Best of the Best from
TENNESSEE
288 pages, $16.95

Best of the Best from
BIG SKY
Montana and Wyoming
288 pages, $16.95

Best of the Best from
IOWA
288 pages, $16.95

Best of the Best from
NEW ENGLAND
*Rhode Island, Connecticut,
Massachusetts, Vermont,
New Hampshire, and Maine*
368 pages, $16.95

Best of the Best from
TEXAS
352 pages, $16.95

Best of the Best from
CALIFORNIA
384 pages, $16.95

Best of the Best from
KENTUCKY
288 pages, $16.95

Best of the Best from
TEXAS II
352 pages, $16.95

Best of the Best from
COLORADO
288 pages, $16.95

Best of the Best from
LOUISIANA
288 pages, $16.95

Best of the Best from
NEW MEXICO
288 pages, $16.95

Best of the Best from
UTAH
288 pages, $16.95

Best of the Best from
FLORIDA
288 pages, $16.95

Best of the Best from
LOUISIANA II
288 pages, $16.95

Best of the Best from
NEW YORK
288 pages, $16.95

Best of the Best from
VIRGINIA
320 pages, $16.95

Best of the Best from
GEORGIA
336 pages, $16.95

Best of the Best from
MICHIGAN
288 pages, $16.95

Best of the Best from
NO. CAROLINA
288 pages, $16.95

Best of the Best from
WASHINGTON
288 pages, $16.95

Best of the Best from the
GREAT PLAINS
*North and South Dakota,
Nebraska, and Kansas*
288 pages, $16.95

Best of the Best from the
MID-ATLANTIC
*Maryland, Delaware, New
Jersey, and Washington, D.C.*
288 pages, $16.95

Best of the Best from
OHIO
352 pages, $16.95

Best of the Best from
OKLAHOMA
288 pages, $16.95

Best of the Best from
WEST VIRGINIA
288 pages, $16.95

Best of the Best from
WISCONSIN
288 pages, $16.95

All cookbooks are 6x9 inches, ringbound, contain photographs, illustrations and index.

Special discount offers available! *(See previous page for details.)*

To order by credit card, call toll-free **1-800-343-1583** or visit our website at **www.quailridge.com**
Use the form below to send check or money order.

Call 1-800-343-1583 or email **info@quailridge.com** *to request a free catalog of all of our publications*

- -

Order form

Use this form for sending check or money order to:
QUAIL RIDGE PRESS • P. O. Box 123 • Brandon, MS 39043

❏ Check enclosed

Charge to: ❏ Visa ❏ MC ❏ AmEx ❏ Disc

Card # _____

Expiration Date _____

Signature _____

Name _____

Address _____

City/State/Zip _____

Phone # _____

Email Address _____

Qty.	Title of Book (State) or Set	Total

Subtotal _____

7% Tax for MS residents _____

Postage ($4.00 any number of books) **+   4.00**

Total _____